Reading Old Friends

Also by John Matthias

Poetry:

Bucyrus 1970
Turns 1975
Crossing 1979
Bathory & Lermontov 1980
Northern Summer 1985
A Gathering of Ways 1991

Translations:

Contemporary Swedish Poetry 1980
(with Göran Printz-Påhlson)

Jan Östergren: Rainmaker 1983
(with Göran Printz-Påhlson)

The Battle of Kosovo 1987
(with Vladeta Vučković)

Editions:

23 Modern British Poets 1971
Introducing David Jones 1980
David Jones: Man and Poet 1989

John Matthias

Reading Old Friends

Essays, Reviews,
and Poems on Poetics 1975–1990

State University of New York Press

Published by
State University of New York Press, Albany

© 1992 State University of New York

All rights reserved

Printed in the United States of America

For information, address State University of New York
Press, State University Plaza, Albany, N.Y., 12246

Production by E. Moore
Marketing by Dana E. Yanulavich

Library of Congress Cataloging-in-Publication Data

Matthias, John, 1941–
    Reading old friends : essays, reviews, and poems on poetics,
1975–1990 / John Matthias.
        p.   cm. — (SUNY series, the margins of literature)
    ISBN 0–7914–0879–5 (alk. paper). — ISBN 0–7914–0880–9 (pbk. :
alk. paper)
    1. Poetics—Poetry.   2. English poetry—History and criticism.
3. American poetry—History and criticism.   I. Title.   II. Series:
SUNY series, margins of literature.
PS3563.A858R44   1992
801'.951—dc20   90–28980
                                                                                        CIP

10 9 8 7 6 5 4 3 2 1

Contents

v

Preface

    This book is a selection of a poet's essays, mostly on the subject of contemporary poetry, from the past fifteen years. Consistent with the experimental nature of the "Margins of Literature" series, it also contains three poems on poetics. These metapoetical texts engage, in their way, theoretical issues foregrounded in some of the essays but, in most of them, left implicit rather than made explicit and explored. The essays are mostly examples of that species of literary journalism which responds to specific editorial assignments or seeks to make better known certain works of particular value to the author. A few are scholarly and rather specialized; but all are available to the general reader. This sort of book has, for generations, been put together by poets once they find they have written enough essays on a range of sufficiently related subjects for a selection of them to assume a shape of sorts.

    A shape *of sorts.* I certainly did not have a book in mind when I began accepting invitations to write reviews or contribute prose for this occasion or that. What I did have in mind was that I would focus on what seemed most neglected in discussions of modern poetry in this country, namely modern British poetry. In part, because I have lived a lot in England, I have read and admired more British poetry than have many of my contemporaries. I would make—I do in fact make—large claims for the best modern British poets. What I also had in mind when I began writing reviews—in fact it was an express condition of my reviewing at all—was that I would insist on being allowed to quote enough to illustrate or support what I wanted to say, and that I would insist on being allowed to say enough to say *something.* We have seen not only the number of poetry reviews shrink disastrously over the last couple of decades, but also the space given to those reviews that continue to be published.

Often the reviewer has no more than a couple of paragraphs in which to assess a book. At any rate, I have twice been given forums in which to write the sort of reviews that seem to me worth writing—in *Poetry* magazine during the 1970s and in *Another Chicago Magazine* during the 1980s. This book is organized, more or less, in reverse chronological order. The section called "After Auden" comprises most of the *Poetry* reviews (two of them—one about David Jones and the other about Geoffrey Hill—appear in Part II), and the section called "Not For Sale in USA" contains the *ACM* pieces from the column of the same title published during the 1980s. Although the *Poetry* reviews include a few Americans, the *ACM* pieces are exclusively about the British and the Irish. I initially intended my *ACM* title to cover just about as much ground as possible. I meant that much of the British poetry discussed literally could not be obtained in this country—or at least couldn't be at the time of writing—but also that no poetry is "for sale" in the USA in the way that used cars, compact discs, postmodern theory, or David Lynch movies are for sale. Taken together, the two series of reviews constitute a running commentary on English, Irish, Scottish, and Welsh poetry by one reader over a decade and a half. This type of involvement with contemporary poetry differs radically from what a retrospective approach to the same body of work might look like as it sought to demonstrate a thesis years or decades after the work was written. There is no thesis. Instead, there is an extended record of interested engagement.

The longer pieces in parts I and II of this book come from a similar impulse but expand the focus of attention to genres other than poetry, writing other than British, and authors from periods other than the present. Two of these essays deal with painting and music as well as poetry, and others attempt to establish or reestablish, meaningful trans-Atlantic connections—between Wendel Berry and Jeremy Hooker, for example; or between Robert Duncan and David Jones. But there is also a more subjective focus here. "Reading Old Friends" is about exactly that, and the longest essay of all, "Places and Poems: A Self-Reading and a Reading of the Self in the Romantic Context from Wordsworth to Parkman," is just what the subtitle indicates. This is the one piece that was given initially as a lecture, and it retains, I hope, something of its original informality in spite of the many footnotes which I have added.

I have rewritten little, and I have allowed all references or allusions to the original occasions of the essays to stand. For they are all occasional. The reader will even have to endure, now and then, reading the same paragraph more than once. Having begun to substitute a new paragraph in "Poetry of Place" for the one cannibalized in "Places and Poems," I realized the futility of this sort of thing and decided to let everything stand. It would be a mistake to tidy things up or to make the book look more composed than it really is. The reader, after all, will know what he's reading. So there is no need to explain that my discussion of Wyatt's *Against Capitulation* was written before the events of 1989 in Eastern Europe, or that "Places and Poems" was not only written after but also, in part, *about* "Poetry of Place," or that Desmond Clarke no longer directs sales at Faber and Faber, or that I have changed my mind about some things between 1975 and the present. I have read reviews of miscellanies such as the present one that go something like this: "The book reads as if the author had simply dumped everything out of his bottom drawer and published it." But that is exactly what I *have* done. Moreover, this book is intended for people who *like* reading the contents of a poet's bottom drawer, not for people who don't. With such a range of new and old material in the book, and with such a range of occasions, the tone of the essays, not surprisingly, varies quite considerably. It runs the full range, in fact, from making me sound something like an enfant terrible to making me sound something like a curmudgeon. To have come so far in fifteen years! At any rate, it is important, for a variety of reasons, for the reader to observe the date at the conclusion of each essay. The poems are not dated, but they all come from *Turns,* my book published in 1975. Having finished there with the metapoetics, I was able later to get on with poems of an entirely different kind.

Acknowledgments

All of the essays and reviews in this book have been published previously, sometimes under different titles. Grateful acknowledgment is made to the following.

To *The Southern Review* for "Reading Old Friends," "Poetry of Place: From the Kentucky River to the Solent Shore," and "W. H. Auden and Benjamin Britten";

To Rutgers University Press for "A Self-Reading and a Reading of the Self in the Romantic Context from Wordsworth to Parkman," from *The Romantics and Us*, edited by Gene W. Ruoff;

To *Ironwood* for "Robert Duncan and David Jones: Some Affinities";

To *PN Review* for "Dai Greatcoat";

To *The New Review* for "Poet-Critics of Two Generations";

To *Tärningskastet* for "Some Notes on the English Poetry of Göran Printz-Påhlson," which appeared in a Swedish translation by Lars-Håkan Svensson;

To *Another Chicago Magazine* for "Anthologies of Contemporary British Poetry," "Poet-Translators and Translator-Poets," "Of Publishers, Readings, and Festivals, Circa 1986," "Anglo-Welsh Poetry," Hugh MacDiarmid and Scottish Poetry," "Scottish Poetry after MacDiarmid," "Inside History and Outside History: Seamus Heaney, Eavan Boland, and Contemporary Irish Poetry";

To *Poetry* for "Michael Hamburger," "R. S. Thomas and Edwin Morgan," "Elizabeth Daryush and Barbara Guest," "Jon Stallworthy," "Paris Leary," "Anne Stevenson," "David Steingass," "William Hunt and William Everson," "John Fuller," "Elizabeth Jennings and

Peter Porter," "John Cotton and D. M. Thomas," "The Later Poetry of David Jones," and "Such a Kingdom: The Poetry of Geoffrey Hill 1952–1971";

To Swallow Press for "Turns: Toward a Provisional Aesthetic and a Discipline," "Double Derivation, Association and Cliché: From the Great Tournament Roll of Westminster," and "Clarifications for Robert Jacoby: "Double Derivation . . . ," part iv, 11. 1–10, part vii, 11. 1–15, 22–28 (from *Turns*, by John Matthias).

Part I

Old Friends and Old Selves

Reading Old Friends

Robert Hass, *Twentieth Century Pleasures: Prose on Poetry*, Ecco Press; Jiri Wyatt, *Against Capitulation*, Quartet Books; Michael Anania, *The Red Menace*, Thunder's Mouth Press.

I

Robert Hass begins one of the pieces in *Twentieth Century Pleasures* by saying that he has been "worrying the bone of this essay for days" because he wants to say some things against the poems he has agreed to discuss in a special issue of a journal celebrating the work of James Wright. I have been worrying the bone of this essay for days as well, but not because I want to say anything against the work I intend to discuss. I have decided to write in an autobiographical way beginning in this issue of the *Southern Review* devoted to autobiography and continuing in the issue for Winter 1987 about three books—a volume of essays, a novel, and a historical meditation—which are themselves autobiographical in different respects and which are, as it happens, all by old friends. I thought at first that it would be a very simple business to give a strictly personal and subjective account of these books. There would be no need to feign anything like a critical disinterest; it was specifically agreed that I should write about the work of friends from the perspective of a friend. But this is not an easy task. The chief reason why it isn't is that years ago all these books began for me as conversations or as an exchange of stories growing out of conversations—long talks with Hass first at Stanford and then later in the pubs and coffee shops of Cambridge about the art of poetry, stories traded back and forth with Anania driving in Chicago traffic jams, accounts exchanged

3

with Wyatt in the London of the later 1960s as we struggled for a language to articulate a politics and describe our primal childhood memories—and not as something printed on a page. Reading these conversations back into the texts, which is something that I find I cannot keep myself from doing, I am acutely aware that other readers are *not* doing this, although some are doubtless reading different, even contradictory, conversations back into the texts. Should my account include the conversations or restrict itself to the texts? If I am to be the autobiographer of my reading, as Robert Hass often is of his in *Twentieth Century Pleasures*, I must risk talking about a book that no one else can read. For example, there is a point in Hass's essay on Robert Lowell's "Quaker Graveyard in Nantucket" where he deprecates "the slough of poetry" engendered by *Life Studies* beginning typically "Father, you. . . ." I remember his making that point in a coffee shop across from Trinity College, and I remember saying: "Yes, but your father is still alive." Then he said—but it doesn't really matter *what* he said; he went on to qualify or modify the remark by saying something else. What began in conversation and was open to the natural processes of conversation becomes a telling point, decisively made, in an essay where I still hear the resonance and backwash of an exchange which occurred ten years ago. This conditions my reading and my response and, while both can be communicated, the second probably cannot be fully shared. It also suggests that it may be more difficult to talk about work by someone you know than by someone you don't.

Then there is the question of voice, or, as the theorists like to say, the question of presence. The related questions of voice, conversation, and presence are taken up by Denis Donoghue in his recent book on current theory and ideology called *Ferocious Alphabets*. This has suddenly become a very useful book to me precisely because the form of language which Donoghue wishes to privilege, which in fact he thinks *is* privileged, is conversation. Arguing that conversation is so radically different from the notion of communication proposed by such early twentieth-century theorists as Jacobsen and Richards that we should regard it as communion rather than communication, Donoghue writes that conversation is made memorable "by the desire of each person to share experience with the other, giving and receiving."

All that can be shared, strictly speaking, is the desire: it is impossible to reach the experience. But desire is enough to cause the reverberations to take place which we value in conversation. . . . The resonating force in a genuine conversation is not admiration, but desire. In conversation . . . the words enact desire . . . the "I" and "you" are constantly changing places; not only to maintain the desire of communion but to keep it mobile. The two voices are making a music of desire, varying its cadences, tones, intensities.

When you separate these two communing and fully embodied voices in such a way that one becomes a writer and the other a reader, certain kinds of compensation must occur. The writer's compensation for the lack of conversation's true communion is style. The reader in his turn "makes up for the tokens of absence which he finds in written words. . . . He is not willing to leave words as [he] finds them on a page [but] wants to restore words to a source, a human situation involving speech, character, personality. . . . We read to meet the other. The encounter is personal, the experience is satisfying in the degree of presence rather than knowledge."

If this kind of reading, which Donoghue has an ugly word for—he calls it *epireading*—commits one not only to the *epos* of speech but to the logocentrism attacked by the kind of reader engaged in an activity for which he has an even uglier word—*graphireading*—the objections of the graphireaders might be summarized in the most severely reductionist terms by a bit of graffiti appearing in a recent *Times Literary Supplement* that looks to have been written by a deranged graduate student:

> D'ya wanna know the creed 'a
> Jacques Derrida?
> Dere ain't no reada
> Dere ain't no wrider
> Eider.

I don't know if I can be an "epireader" in general, but I think I am unavoidably and inescapably an "epireader" of my friends. I hear their voices and I feel the pleasure of their presence in their words. At the end of *Ferocious Alphabets,* Donoghue says that he detests the "current ideology which refers, gloatingly, to the death of the author, the obsolescence of the self, the end of man, and so forth. . . . To be sure that I exist, all I have to do is catch a cold or stumble on the pavement. Pleasure achieves the same effect more agreeably. . . . Knowledge is debatable, pleasure is not." Robert Hass calls his book *Twentieth Century Pleasures* and, I think, shares most of Donoghue's basic assumptions about the nature of literature and language. Still, he writes in his essay on Robert Creeley that underneath some of the typical pleasures of our time are uncomfortable things "which the mind must, slowly, in love and fear, perform to locate itself again, previous to any other discourse." And in his best known poem he writes:

> Longing, we say, because desire is full
> of endless distances.

In reading the work of friends, something of desire's communion in the pleasure of familiar voices is very present and very real; but so, of course, is the longing, and so are the distances. We fall asleep in the middle of a conversation and awake with a page of prose in our hands.

II

I am surprised that Helen Vendler in a review of *Twentieth Century Pleasures* and some other books about contemporary poetry feels that Hass fails to engage some of the questions and assumptions touched on or alluded to above. Taking the part of the theorists in the 7 November 1985 issue of the *New York Review of Books*, she argues that all practical criticism "assumes positions silently taken" about basic premises and says that she would like to see Hass and the others consider first principles or at any rate make the reader confident that "the theoretical questions had been silently put, and satisfactorily answered, before the writing was undertaken." Vendler is also worried about the autobiographical element in Hass's writing—its familiar tone, its "determined effort toward the colloquial," its attempt through what she calls "interpolated narratives" to communicate the idea that the texts under discussion have some connection with his own sensual life and the life of the times, that the books have literally been lived with for a while and not just read and rapidly reviewed to meet a deadline. Actually, Hass engages the fundamental premises of the theorists and implies his own in any number of his essays. The piece on Creeley, for example, deals in Lacanian and Derridian terms with a poetics "which addresses the tension between speaking and being spoken through language," but also makes clear through some "interpolated narratives" why such an "austere and demanding" poet as Creeley could communicate with a large and often uninstructed audience during the 1960s. The "interpolated narratives" imply a "premise" as fundamental as anything in Lacan and Derrida—namely, that art unfolds both in individual lives and our collective history, and that factors which only narrative can reveal condition our response to it. But of course there is no systematic statement of principles, no prolegomenon to any further study of contemporary poetry, in a book like this. It achieves its unity and authority from the manner in which art is shown to intersect with life. It *is* an autobiography of sorts.

Epireader of this text that I must be, the first thing I am conscious of in *Twentieth Century Pleasures* is a voice. It is a familiar voice, and it sounds like this:

> I've been trying to think about form in poetry and my mind keeps returning to a time in the country in New York when I was puzzled that my son Leif was getting up a little earlier every morning. I had to get up with him, so it exasperated me. I wondered about it until I slept in his bed one night. His window faced east. At six-thirty I woke to brilliant sunlight. The sun had risen.

> Wonder and repetition. Another morning I was walking Kristin to her bus stop—a light blanket of snow after thaw, the air thick with the rusty croaking of blackbirds so that I remembered, in the interminable winter, the windy feel of June on that hill. Kristin, standing on a snowbank in the cold air, her eyes alert, her face rosy with cold and with some purity of expectation, was looking down the road. It was eight-fifteen. Her bus always arrived at eight-fifteen. She looked down the road and it was coming.

Helen Vendler objects to what she feels marks a difficulty in controlling tone in a passage similar to this one taken from the final and most fully autobiographical essay in this book, which I am going to quote a little later on. It is an intentionally vulnerable passage and functions, along with others like it, to make clear exactly what elements, insofar as Hass is conscious of them, combine to condition his reading and his response, to make it *his* reading and *his* response rather than mine or Helen Vendler's or someone else's. It tells us some of what we need to know in order to understand his perceptions, his reactions, and his judgments. And it is especially in passages like it, and like the one quoted above, that I hear the familiar, amused, vigorous, disarming voice often touched with a Chekhovian irony and sadness that I know. I sense the presence of a friend and not a difficulty in controlling tone. One function of the passage about Hass's children is, of course, to get an essay about form begun in a relaxed and graceful way. No academic categories introduced, no pedagogical solemnities. But we are also persuaded by this kind of writing that his coincident experiences of "trying to think about form" and remembering the power of repetition in the lives of his young children yield the surprised perception out of which the essay grows, that "though *predictable* is an ugly little word in daily life, in our first experience of it we are clued to the hope of a shapeliness in things. . . . Probably, that is the psychological basis for the power and the necessity of artistic form." But let me take an example from the first essay in the book to demonstrate more fully the usefulness of narrative and autobiography.

On these terms, Lowell's prayer moved me.

What are "these terms," and what conditions them? The prayer which Hass is moved by occurs in Part V of "The Quaker Graveyard in Nantucket"—"Hide / our steel, Jonas Messias, in Thy side"—and the terms of his being moved are conditioned by the way in which his own inherited Catholicism has been modified or transmuted by a range of experiences and some important reading by the time it meets the intense but unorthodox Catholicism of a convert's poem.

At the beginning of his essay, Hass says that it's difficult to conduct an argument about the value of music in favorite poems once it's gotten into the blood: "It becomes autobiography there." But so does the meaning of favorite poems become a kind of auto-biogrpahy—so conditioned is it by the times and places and the circumstances of initial or repeated readings—and only narrative can really show us how this happens. After explaining the "enormously liberating perception" found in Robert Duncan's prose that "the mistake of Christianity was to think that the soul's salvation was the only human adventure" and, Christ seen therefore on an equal footing with the other gods, Pound's idea that they all were "forms of consciousness which men through learning, art and contemplation could inhabit," Hass writes this paragraph:

> I got my Catholicism from my mother's side, Foleys from Cork by way of Vermont who drank and taught school and practiced

law on the frontiers of respectability until they landed in San Francisco at the turn of the century. My father's side was Protestant and every once in a while, weary probably with the catechisms of his children, he would try to teach us one of his childhood prayers. But he could never get past the first line: "In my father's house there are many mansions. . . ." He would frown, squint, shake his head, but that was as far as he ever got and we children who were willing to believe Protestants capable of any stupidity including the idea that you could fit a lot of mansions into a house, would return to memorizing the four marks of the true church. (It was one, holy, catholic, and apostolic.) But that phrase came back to me as a way through the door of polytheism and into myth. If Pound could resurrect the goddesses, there was a place for a temple of Christ, god of sorrows, desire of savior, resting place of violence. I could have the memory of incense and the flickering candles and the battered figure on the cross with the infinitely sad and gentle face and have Aphrodite as well, "the fauns chiding Proteus / in the smell of hay under olive trees" and the intoning of Latin with which we began the mass: *Introibo ad altare Dei*. On these terms, Lowell's prayer moved me: "Hide our steel, Jonas Messias, in thy side."

The essay on Lowell is important for a lot of reasons. It is the generative essay of the volume, written in England in the cold winter of 1977 when Hass and his family were living in the Cambridgeshire village of Little Shelford in a huge house owned by the master of St. John's College, which I had lived in two years before. The essay may be as personal, as autobiographical, as it is in part out of compensation for not being able to write, there in Little Shelford, the poems he had hoped to write in the course of the year away from his familiar turf in Berkeley and San Francisco. Actually, I feel vaguely guilty about this. I persuaded Hass to go to Cambridge for the year rather than to York where his Bicentennial Fellowship was really supposed to take him, thinking that it would be good to spend the year near one another—I was once again to be in the area—and that the big house in the little village would be as productive a place for him to live and work in as it had been for me two years before. Once the weather turned, all the poems were frozen out of his system—the house "has central heating," but the system is in a permanent state of disrepair—and he wrote very little poetry until the San Francisco sun had warmed his blood and spirit again eight or nine months later. He did, however, write a lot of prose, and he wrote this first essay of the present book which, I think, led to his wanting to write the others and established their characteristic tone and point of view. It begins and ends with recent and more distant memories of voices—that of a mild-looking schoolteacher in the Shelford pub who, when the subject of favorite poems came up one night, treated the locals to a recitation of Kipling's "Gunga Din," and the surprise of Robert Lowell's when Hass finally got to hear it at a reading, which sounded "bizarrely like an imitation of Lionel Barrymore" or "like a disenchanted English actor reading an Elizabethan sonnet on American television." So much, perhaps, for the possibility of being an epireader of poets whom we haven't heard give readings or of those we don't or cannot know. Hass's own poems returned to him again once he was back in the world where he and his brother, as he remembered in the pub, had also, like the Shelford teacher, loved as children reading Kipling aloud "on summer nights . . . in our upstairs room that looked out on a dusty fig orchard and grapevines spilling over the wooden fence." I suppose it would have been even colder in York than it was in Cambridgeshire. Anyway, the one piece in *Twentieth Century Pleasures* actually called a memoir returns Hass to "the San Francisco Bay Area as a culture region." It is a rich and evocative autobiographical essay, and it connects with the important reading of Milosz that comes just before and the remarkable "Images" which comes afterward.

In his Bay Area memoir, Hass is dealing in the most delicate and often amusing and ironic way with the fundamental mysteries of our common world as they were given a local habitation and a name in the area where he grew up. The memoir glosses his desire, in the Lowell essay, to have "the battered figure on the cross . . . and Aphrodite as well," and provides a context both for the way in which he deals with the Gnostic side of Milosz and his celebration of the image in the final essay of the book. It begins, in fact, by recalling Hass's attempt to write another essay—for one Sister Reginald to enter on his behalf in a competition sponsored by the National League for Decency in Motion Pictures about how fine a film could be made from a book called *Stranded on an Atoll*. In his comical account of the revisions and reversals of attitude while working on this junior high school project, Hass's memory connects Sister Reginald's austere Dominican habit first with the order itself, "founded in the twelfth century as a kind of Papal CIA to root out the Gnostic heresy of the Cathars," and then, to his surprise, with the modest dress of the Cathar women who had been burned alive at Monségur and elegized, as he had found years later, by both Pound and Robert Duncan. Hass's essay, revised at school but recopied at home before his favorite radio show came on—*I Love a Mystery*, heard ritually each night against the family rules but with his father's visible acquiescence—won a ten-dollar money order from a local bookshop where he bought, dizzy and confused by all the possibilities, *A Comprehensive Anthology of American Poetry*. Unable to understand any of the poems, he stumbles onto Stevens' "Domination of Black" with its cry of the peacocks. Although the young Hass does not at first remember the cry of the peacocks from the front yard of his Portuguese babysitter, the reader does at once, having read about them "trailing their tails in the dust" under a palm tree in the first paragraph of the memoir. Stevens' peacocks seem to announce the existence of another world. Hass read the poem again and again. "I read it exactly the way I lined up for a roller-coaster ride with a dime tight in my fist at Playland across the bay." It made him, he says, "swoon"—and it made him "understand what the word *swoon* meant" a year before he found himself actually riding the Playland roller coaster beside a girl in his ninth-grade class whom he thought to be "the most beautiful being I had ever come close to in my life, which may also account for some of the previous year's swooning."

Mysteries, then. The young boy's fascination with the Sister's habit and her "long beautiful hands which she waved in the air like doves when she conducted us at Mass in the singing of the *Tantum Ergo* and *Pange Lingua*," the Cathars at Montségur, the theosophical and Gnostic writings standing behind the poetry of Robert Duncan later given association with these early memories, the hypnotized amazement at the sound of peacocks crying in what seemed to be an incomprehensible poem read over and over again like a mantra nevertheless, the similarity hypnotized amazement at the existence—at the otherness—of a beautiful girl, a radio program called *I Love a Mystery* mysteriously allowed to be heard even though it violated family rules, and the sound of peacocks crying in a babysitter's yard unconnected with the ones that cried in the poem, even unnoticed.

In the same year he won the essay prize, Hass and his friends were playing baseball on teams sponsored by businessmen's clubs and insurance companies with hilarious names, especially when seen stitched on players' uniforms in competition, like *Optimists* and *California Casualty*. Playing center field, he heard the "irritated, prenocturnal cries of the peacocks" in the yard of the Portuguese babysitter. And the grown man writes:

> I never once associated them with the Wallace Stevens poem. Art hardly ever does seem to come to us at first as something connected to our own world; it always seems, in fact, to announce the existence of another, different one, which is what it shares with Gnostic insight. That is why, I suppose, the next thing artists have to learn is that this world is the other world.

Beside the baseball field ran a creek called "Papermill." By the time Hass reads a poem by Kenneth Rexroth, who published "the first readable book of poems by a resident" of San Francisco in 1941, he is a little older. But reading that "Under the second moon the / Salmon come, up Tomales / Bay, up Papermill Creek, up / The narrow gorges to their spawning beds in Devil's Gulch" moves him deeply, and in a way very different from that in which he had been moved by "The Domination of Black" before. It is the presence of Papermill Creek in the poem that provides the final jolt and makes it "seem possible that the peacocks in Wallace Stevens and the scraggly birds under the palm tree could inhabit the same world."

These are some of the factors that condition the mind—the being-in-the-world—of the man who will read Milosz for us (and Rilke and Wright and Transtromer and Brodsky) and tell us about the nature of images, the music of poetry, and a poetic form which is "one body." We learn to trust his voice because he does not seek to mute its characteristic tones and intonations in the idiom of critic-talk or theoreze, and because, as they used to say in the 1960s, we know—we are specifically told—where he's coming from. One of the places he is coming from *is* the 1960s, and Helen Vendler is right to point this out in her review. But she is wrong to stress the notion that Hass's aim is to rehabilitate the familiar essay. The familiar essay may be rehabilitated along the way in some of these pieces—and very winningly so at that—but the *aim* of the autobiography and "interpolated narratives" is to dramatize as vividly as possible the inevitable historical conditioning of both the texts to be read and the perceptions of the reader who intends to talk about them. Hass does not attempt to clear his mind of everything that's in it before turning to the poem on the page; instead, he gives us an account of what is in his mind when he begins to read and how it comes to be there. He does not stop living while he struggles with intractable profundities in Milosz or in Rilke; he shows us daily life as an illumination of the struggle. Even poems that do announce the existence of another world must be perceived in this one, and the history—both personal and social or political—which shapes the circumstances of their being read by this particular reader in this particular time in this particular place becomes, in Hass's writing, essential to the work at hand. The premises for which Helen Vendler is looking are found, essentially, in the narrative and autobiographical passages of the book. And not only premises, but a whole implied poetics. There is a moment—and Vendler doesn't like it; it is the passage she objects to in terms of what she regards to be a descent into bathos and a failure of tone—when Hass the particular reader becomes for a brief moment the perfectly average American of his time and place, which is one aspect of his existence as person and poet and reader of poems which he knows he must acknowledge.

> I am a man approaching middle age in the American century, which means I've had it easy, and I have three children, somewhere near the average, and I've just come home from summer vacation in an unreliable car. This is the *selva oscura*.

That is the passage which Vendler quotes. But it goes on: "Not that it isn't true, but that it is not the particular truth. It is the average, which is different from the common; arbitrary, the enemy of form." And Hass is the friend of form.

In the Milosz essay, the Berkeley native, conditioned by a life that makes him in some ways a hostage to what he calls "the seemingly eternal Saturday afternoons of *l'homme moyen sensuel*" and in others a gifted and utterly displaced member of the diaspora of poets and readers of poems still half listening for the peacock's cry that announces the existence of another world, must deal with the fiercely isolated and visionary Berkeley immigrant from Lithuania who refuses "in the privacy of his vocation as a poet to become an accomplice of time and matter." This last, says Hass, is a difficult step for the American imagination to take.

Hass's imagination as a poet does not take that step, but his imagination as a critic follows with deep sympathy and understanding the voyage of Milosz as *he* takes it. The essay on images which ends the book probably comes closer than anything else to being Hass's *Ars Poetica*. The essay on Milosz, to use a word borrowed I think from Robert Duncan in these essays, gives "permission" for its affirmation of the world—of time and matter—by testing the most typical manifestations of the American poetic imagination against Milosz's "leap into dualism or gnosticism" seen against the full history of the poet's life and thought and, again, the factors conditioning the critic's reading. "It might be useful," he says, "to begin by invoking a time when one might turn to the work of Czeslaw Milosz."

The time turns out to be the later 1960s, and the first scene recalled is a protest march to the napalm plant in Redwood City which I remember very well participating in. Bearing our pathetically inadequate signs and listening to the hopelessly inane or merely rhetorical speeches, we did indeed "feel sheepish between gusts of affection for this ragtag army of an aroused middle class." In three pages of narrative and description as good as anything in *Armies of the Night*, Hass evokes the atmosphere of guilt, commitment, generosity, illusion, disillusion, cynicism, and craziness culminating in what he calls "a disease that was on me." He remembers the World War II veteran who shaved his head, smeared himself with red dye, and began attending Quaker meetings carrying an American flag; the careerist professor who returned from a European antiwar demonstration "to wear jeans, T-shirt and a Mao cap to teach his course in Victorian bibliography"; a friend arrested with dynamite in his trunk driving off to blow up a local air base. On his way home from the Redwood City demonstration, he even catches a glimpse of his loathed double twenty years before its time, a version of "the man approaching middle age in the American century" from the essay on images in the form of a vacationing paterfamilias driving his wife and somewhere-near-the-average-number-of-children off to enjoy dinner "on a deck from which you can admire green pines, grey granite, blue sky . . . thousands of miles away [from] fear, violence, brothels, villages going up in an agony of flames." He thinks about myth and decides that "myth is about eating each other . . . man's first tool for sanctifying the food chain. . . . The world was a pig-out; or the matter-universe was a pig-out. As if there were some other universe to distinguish this one from."

The disease that was on him had various names—philosophy, theology, eschatology—and the one thing he felt he knew about them "was that they were the enemies of poetry." But they were the enemies of a poetry inherited from Williams and Pound, an American modernism which sought to render things rather than ideas, to build a poetry out of natural objects or pictographs "as if no one had ever thought before and nothing needed to be thought that was not shot through with the energy of immediate observation." The problem was that the things and objects and pictographs of an imagist or imagist-derived poetics threw "the weight of meaning back on the innocence and discovery of the observer, and something in the dramatic ambivalence of that gesture rhymed with the permanent unconscious of the man with the boat," the vacationing paterfamilias noticed while returning from Redwood City. Hass felt "vaguely ashamed" when he saw this in the poems he was reading. "I wanted to read a poetry by people who did not assume that the great drama in their work was that everything in the world was happening to them for the first time." He finds such a poetry in the work of Milosz, but also a poetry willing to postulate a universe different from this one, different from the pig-out matter-universe of Hass's eschatological disease which the medicine of American poetry didn't seem to cure.

Hass discusses or alludes to twenty-nine books by Milosz in his long and loving consideration of the full career, and I haven't space enough to outline the entire argument. For my own purposes, I want to focus on the end of the piece, the pages where Hass's poetic imagination sidles up most closely to Milosz's own, but where—because Milosz really does locate the disease Hass was suffering from in the matter-universe itself, and not in a particular subjective aberration caused by a particular objective moment in a nation's history—the two imaginations also must part company.

Hass argues that Simone Weil's lesson to Milosz that "contradiction is the lever of transcendence" gave the poet, who had also taken Eros as one of his teachers, permission to dwell in contradiction: "and once that happened, Eros—in the form of dream, memory, landscape—comes flooding back into his work" after the years in Paris during the 1950s. But since erotic poetry "is usually intense because it is narrow and specific, mute and focused," when the focus of Milosz's work "widens through a terrible and uncompromising love of his own vanished experience, the poetry, refusing to sacrifice the least sharpness of individual detail to that wider vision, makes a visceral leap into dualism or gnosticism." Hass writes three closely argued pages explaining exactly how this happens, concluding thus:

> If you do not want one grain of sand lost, one moment lost, if you do not admit to the inexorable logic of the death or suffering of a single living creature, then you might, by a leap of intuition, say that it is *all* evil, because then nothing could be judged. Because it all dwelt in limitation or contradiction or, as

Blake said, in Ulro. But the universe could be saved if you posited a totally independent but parallel universe of good in
which each thing also had an existence. Thus, when the
matter-universe fell away, the good universe survived.

Again, if you like, the cry of peacocks. But for Hass himself the other
world announced must be this very world he's living in—the other
universe, the only universe we know.

   In the final essay in the book—and I am passing over a brilliant reading of Rilke which falls between the Milosz essay and the
essay celebrating images, not to mention half a dozen others of
enormous interest—Hass becomes "an accomplice of time and matter." To praise things is not necessarily, as it comes to be in Milosz,
"to praise the history of suffering; or to collude with torture and
mutilation and decay." The American will out (with a little help
from the Japanese), his illness purged perhaps by contemplating all
the implications of the *gnosis* vouchsafed to the Lithuanian. But the
most extraordinary thing about this essay is that it requires from life
a vision as remarkable as any given to a Catholic mystic or a Gnostic
prophet, and that life cooperates with all the urgency that literature
could possibly require of it.

   It's difficult to know even what to call the essay on images.
Like other essays in the book—but maybe here more fully
achieved—it may invent a new nongeneric form of writing in its
combination of vivid anecdote, personal reminiscence, literary history and analysis, meditation on life and death and imagery found
in poetry, fiction, painting, sculpture, mythology, and ordinary quotidian experience. Hass begins by gathering some images from his
recent domestic life and running them through his mind along with
others found in Chekhov, Buson, and Issa to demonstrate their
power and the extent to which we may be haunted by them. He
examines the nature of "the moment, different for different memories, when the image, the set of relationships that seems actually to
reveal something about life, forms." Then he picks out such a moment: a woman camping with him and his family in a canyon about
to tell a story of early sorrow: a frying pan in one hand, a scouring
pad in the other, a Stellar's jay perched in the tree above her, Hass's
son playing card tricks, a long granite moraine behind them, a
meadow in the distance. Then Issa, then Buson, then Tu Fu who
said of the power of images: "It's like being alive twice." Neither
idea, nor myth, nor always metaphor, images do not explain or sym-
bolize: "they do not say this is that, they say this is."

Hass walks through the rooms of his house feeling his life to be in part "a long slow hurdle through the forms of things." It is a sensation he resists because it implies a kind of passivity, but he would doubt the absence of the sensation because he knows his life is lived among the forms and facts and objects of the natural world. "The terror of facts is the purity of their arbitrariness. I live in this place, rather than that. Have this life, rather than that. It is August not September." Then comes the sentence about being a man approaching middle age in the American century having come home from a summer vacation. The true haiku of his recent domestic life would have to go, he says, something like this: "Bill and Leif want to climb Mount Allac and Karen and I are taking the Volkswagen to go fishing, so can you and Mom walk to the beach now and pick up Luke at Peter's later in Grandma's car?" Collecting images, beginning his essay, these distracting twentieth-century pleasures had begun to eat him up. He felt "a means to a means to a means" and longed for a little solitude in which to think about poems as arresting as Basho's haiku written just before his death: "Sick on a journey, / my dream hovers / over the withered fields."

At this point, Hass breaks off writing. The second part of his essay begins by unexpectedly incorporating an experience which has just occurred. "Because it is summer," he says, "I have been in the mountains again and am now back at the typewriter." The experience in the mountains has been shattering. Walking a path in Desolation Wilderness, Hass began to feel the prickly sensation and notice the rash of an allergic reaction which he sometimes gets. He ignored it and kept walking until the inside of his mouth began to swell, the sign of a generalized reaction which can end in one's throat closing up. He took two antihistamines, but the reaction intensified nevertheless, and he began to feel dizzy and frightened. He thought of the worst that might happen: that his son would have to punch a hole in his trachea with a knife; no, that he would die. The images and attendant memories that he had been collecting passed through his mind, including Basho's dream that "hovers over the withered fields." Then his legs gave way and he was on his back looking at the hillside and the sky. "Everything green in the landscape turned white, and the scene flared and shuddered as if it were on fire." Later, after the antihistamines had taken hold and he had recovered, he felt as if he had been granted a vision of death. "White trees, white grass, white leaves; the snow patches and flowering currant suddenly dark beside them; and everything there, rock, tree, cloud, sky, shuddering and blazing. It was a sense, past speaking, past these words, that everything, all of the earth and time itself, was alive and burning."

This is an amazing passage to encounter in the middle of a literary discussion, and it ought finally to make clear that phrases such as "interpolated narratives" or categories like "familiar essay" don't begin to say enough about how Hass's writing works on us. After the death vision—and it *is* a vision of death, not resurrection, not the vision of Czeslaw Milosz where "the demiurge's workshop will be stilled . . . / And the form of every single grain will be restored in glory"—Hass returns gratefully to time and things and human beings to celebrate the world of the peacocks in the babysitter's yard, the other world which is this world, and the sensation which great art and image-making give us of marrying that world, of living in the grain at the permission of eros and "in the light of primary acts of imagination." He doesn't give up the idea from the Milosz essay that many things bear thinking about that are not "shot through with the energy of immediate observation," but he does, here, affirm that energy as one of the supreme values in poetry. In spite of this, or maybe even because of it, the essay is death-haunted to the end, and this is one of the things that makes it so exceptionally memorable. "The earth turns, and we live in the grain of nature, turning with it. . . . When the spirit becomes anguished or sickened by this cycle, by the irreversibility of time and the mutilation of choice, another impulse appears: the monotheist rage for unity. . . ." One sometimes finds this rage in Hass's work both as poet and critic, but not very often; not, at any rate, unless it appears as the "fuel" which he says can power "the natural polytheism of the life of art." Remember the essay on Lowell's monotheistic rage in "The Quaker Graveyard" and the terms according to which Hass was able to be moved by the prayer at the end of its fifth part. For the rest, the essay delicately builds a collage of images from the haiku masters, from Pound and Williams and H.D., from Whitman and Chekhov and Cézanne, and comments on them, bringing life's experiences—his own and those of the artists whose work he loves—to bear upon that commentary. If we are lucky, he says, the images in terms of which we live our lives "are invisibly transformed into the next needful thing." (The danger is in clinging just to one, to the exclusion of yet others which should naturally compose themselves.) Although there is something of Basho's spirituality and a lot of Issa's humanity in the prose of *Twentieth Century Pleasures*, I associate the author of these essays most of all with the spirit of Buson whose "apparent interest in everything that passed before his eyes and the feeling in his work of an artist's delight in making" provide a sense of "something steadying and nourishing" for Hass. I am similarly steadied and nourished by his own work here, and by the sound of a voice that I think I know. Concluding his book by quoting a final Buson haiku about whale-watching, Hass remembers his own participation in a West Coast version of that ritual and says: "We go to glimpse being." And of the poet himself, whose whale-watchers in the haiku find no whales: "Buson is not surprised by the fullness and the emptiness of things."

III

Jiri Wyatt's *Against Capitualation* deals directly with many of the issues which Hass takes up in his essay on Milosz and indirectly with those taken up in "Images." More obviously autobiographical in its intention than *Twentieth Century Pleasures*, the book nonetheless is difficult to classify generically. It, too, is very much the prose work of a poet. Falling into two uneven parts—a twenty-five page essay published before the rest of the book was even conceived, and a sequence of twenty-three often oddly titled chapters ranging from childhood reminiscence through political analysis and travelogue to something like dream-vision and prose-poetry—the book deals with Wyatt's childhood in Fascist Slovakia; his later life in South America, the United States, Canada, and England; his trip back to Slovakia in 1978; and his attempts to clarify his thoughts about the Holocaust, revolution, socialism, Stalininsm, the 1960s, and his identity as a Jew, a son, a father, a Slovak, a New Yorker, a writer, and a radical. The sweep of the book is ambitious enough to require all of its unusual means. And it is good enough to take an honorable place beside the work of those more recently exiled Czechoslovak writers, Milan Kundera, Josef Skvorecky, and Jiri Gruša.

Once again, as in *Twentieth Century Pleasures*, I find myself listening to a familiar voice telling both familiar and unfamiliar stories, advancing arguments I've heard in conversation many times and some that are entirely new. Jiri Wyatt, however, is not a familiar name; it is a pseudonym made necessary for the same reason that other people's names and identities have been disguised in the book—to protect the men and women who, in the Holocaust of 1939–1945, saved the author's life. There is a certain irony in the fact that this is necessary. *Against Capitulation* begins with a scene set in a small bedroom with a single window looking over a bleak Manhattan

landscape. Here the author's parents came "one surprising evening and announced matter-of-factly that they planned to change
our family name." He was sixteen at the time. His parents said,
"We're doing this for you. You don't know what it means to be Jewish." The book, then, has to do in part with "Jiri Wyatt" learning what it means to be "Jiri Weinwurm," learning, not perhaps
until the visit to Slovakia in 1978, what it means to have been born
"a Jew in the town of M—." But it also has to do with two forms
of hubris—that of parents and that of children—and the literary
means of discovering the nature of these while simultaneously engaged in attempting to regain the past without sacrificing the felt
life of the present and learning, as Hass says of Milosz, "to dwell
in contradiction."

In the same spring of 1966 that Hass participated in the demonstration at the Redwood City napalm plant and began to sense
"the disease that was on [him]," Wyatt—and perhaps Hass, too; I
wasn't there myself this time—occupied the office of J. Wallace Sterling, the president of Stanford University, with a group of war pro-
testors. The first part of *Against Capitulation*—the essay that was
published separately—concludes with a description of the occupa-
tion and an evocation of the period when "events invited a millennialist vision to which we felt egotistically equal." In the second
part—the long account of the visit to Slovakia and its background—
Wyatt writes of another millennialist vision, that of the Holocaust
survivors who project onto their children a "raging, primal need to
see themselves reproduced. . . . The parents are possessed by a vision of their fulfillment so intense, so millennial, that they are
wholly unaware that they are possessed. They, the parents, embody
the message, and now the children will speak it." Because Wyatt
finds "the experience of survival equivocal," he cannot accept Elie
Wiesel's position that religious witness must be paid to those who
"set eyes on 'an event that weighs on man's destiny.' " Wyatt's own
experience of survival made Wiesel's notion that "persecution be-
stows upon the victims moral stature" less than self-evident.

> I lived what amounted to a life without moral example, em-
> broiled in survival but lacking the dignity of an asserted self-
> respect or of a proud history. My parents retrieved from the
> Holocaust a determination that they would not be caught out
> again: out of the disorder forced upon them they would secure,
> less for them than for me, a permanent inviolable stability. This
> turned out to be an emphasis in their lives with few affirma-

tives: the chief rules were don'ts, and the sum of these don'ts was a deadly practicality aimed against belief in any of its delusory and dangerous forms—against belief in anything but the worst.

Both Wyatt and his parents could not, he saw, have what they wanted—"They a vicarious triumph through me, and I my own life." Insisting on denying his parents their vicarious triumph by becoming himself, Wyatt attempted in high school to annihilate his past by taking hold of fate in a Sartrian manner and, free to choose his identity, trying to make "the authentic daily assertion of individual freedom." Insisting on belief—on belief in nothing but the best against his parents' fear of belief in anything but the worst—he became the politically committed radical sitting in the president's office at Stanford where "events invited a millennialist vision." But nightmares of his childhood in hiding mocked Sartre's *Being and Nothingness* with images of a past which he could no more escape than he could choose his dreams; and a sense emerged, after the fact, that there was something hubristic in "the pleasure of absolute certainty" sitting there in the Stanford president's office confident that the future would prove one absolutely right.

At about the time his daughter was born in 1970, Wyatt and his parents began to share "the suppressed history" of their lives between 1941 and 1945, and slowly his determination formed to visit Slovakia. Much of the long second part of *Against Capitulation* has to do with images—how they are manifested in dreams and nightmares, arise unexpectedly before the traveler, compose and recompose themselves and then dissolve, draw one to the past or lead one to the future or hold one in the present moment—images of justice, tyranny, life, death, pain, pleasure, and joy. The danger with images, as Hass points out, is to cling to one alone as if it embodied the entire truth. For example, the image of "a raving inarticulate parent, replete with impossible demands, posturing like an Old Testament prophet." Or of oneself as Stanford's Bob Dylan telling Wallace Sterling how he doesn't know what's happening, does he Mr. Jones. Images, says Hass, "either . . . dry up [and] are shed, or . . . are invisibly transformed . . . or we act on them in a way that exposes both them and us." "What do you want to go there for?" Wyatt's mother asked him when he told her that he planned to visit Slovakia. One reason was to trace to their source his primal memories that appeared to him "not as sequences of actions but as images accompanied by specific and powerful emotions. . . . My lost childhood, my forgotten sensuous past, this darkness rank with smell, taste, and terror—that was what I wanted." Another reason, he discovered, was to act on certain images which had begun to petrify in such a way as to expose, in Hass's terms, both himself and them— to form thereby another image, for example, of the figure making impossible demands and posturing like an Old Testament prophet. "One of my reasons for going," he says, "was to love my parents."

The journey itself begins in America with a visit to several surviving relations who might possibly give Wyatt information which will allow him better to connect those images which the word *past* conjures in his mind with the people and places he needs to see in order, at last, to ground them in a fully personal, historical, and geographical context. *Past* had conjured an almost contextless vision of interiors in sequence: "a ground-floor room . . . with windows at one end . . . my mother is ironing . . . outside the world is snow . . . soldiers on skis are working their way up the hill"; or another room, a mountain bunker with wooden boards to sleep on, a stool on which a child stands to suck his mother's breasts; or the house in M— where the child will not leave the window looking out into the darkness of the village as he waits impatiently for his parents to return. But sometimes *past* had conjured other images—images which were not constricting or frightening, but which seemed to open into a world of peace accompanied by emotions "which approached euphoria." He remembered "being pulled by [his] father out of the mountains on a sledge . . . after the Russians had swept through [their] sector of the White Carpathians," and before that "crossing a brook or small stream under a stunning night sky" heading for a second bunker which his father had built higher in the mountains feeling "wonder and peace as we crossed that stream, exactly as if the forest and the overwhelming clear arc of the night sky and the stream were themselves a little in awe." In Boston, Wyatt's uncle Pepo asks him "Who can you go visit . . . ? There's no one left." And in Atlanta his Aunt Sharon opens on her lap a box stuffed "with every scrap of paper—every railroad ticket, letter, note, telegram—from the years 1939–1945" which she has saved from a life of hiding, flight, and exile. She has kept all this to document their family's history and pass it on to their daughter, Wyatt's cousin Valery, who isn't interested. Valery's parents, like Wyatt's, had come to America "with the Holocaust raging behind them. They were, they knew, survivors; their lives had been threatened and spared, and they aimed to recoup what in truth they could not regain through the life they would give their children." Valery, in a style utterly different from the young Wyatt's, had abandoned her Jewish and Slovakian identity to survive the lives of her survivor parents. Wyatt tries to explain to his aunt. "Can you ask us to live for you? We didn't want to make your dreams come true, we just wanted to be ourselves." But his own situation in regard both to survival and identity is now more complicated than his cousin's, and he leaves for Bratislava with the names of "a few good people," an improved sense of geography, a year's tutoring in Czechoslovak under his belt, and a headful of images—including the box of papers open on his aunt's lap in Atlanta.

After being met in Bratislava by his cousin Miro, Wyatt almost immediately inquires after the quality of the cuisine in a restaurant in Hviezdoslav Square. He had come to Slovakia not only to look and see and listen and talk, but to touch and smell—and eat. He wanted "the food of memory"—chicken paprika, *gnochky*, and *palachinky*. At the first opportunity, he goes to the restaurant on the square for lunch and sits at the table "with a virtually ritual antici- pation, like a child," only to be profoundly disappointed when the food arrives and he finds that "he could have done a lot better had he cooked the meal himself." Or could he have? Perhaps the food of his childhood, the one "constant" of his childhood, was misremem- bered or "just wasn't to be had," lost, somehow, like so much else he was seeking. This initial disappointment predicts the comically qualified sense of success at the end of the book when Slovakian cooking becomes the metaphor for Wyatt's ability to give his daugh- ter the experience of his journey by writing and dedicating to her *Against Capitulation*. He struggles for several weeks after his return home to bake proper cheese *buchty* for dessert, experimenting again and again with the dough and a variety of cheeses. In the end, he serves it up. "The *buchty* looked good—just the right depth of brown, risen to a nice thickness . . . and they weren't bad— 'yummy!' my daughter said. Not bad, but not quite right."

What Wyatt learns, of course, is that what was once available to him in Slovakia exists only as memory, as a past which can be given voice to and remembered more precisely as his early images and their attendant sensations are clarified and given back their de- fining contexts, but that past really does mean *past* if he should be asked (as he is by the Kafkaesque inquisitor he posits at the end of the book) to say who he is. He can no longer give "the perfectly simple answer: I am a Slovak Jew from the town of M—." He must journey among identities, understanding that "the place of begin- nings" which had been "a blank of darkness rank with sensuous power but entirely without definition" may be given definition in the course of the journey only to an extent which will be at best "Not bad, but not quite right." Although Wyatt does revisit the house in M—, it still lives chiefly in his mind's eye, in his memory. By being made more vivid the past becomes more vividly the past.

But the desire to embrace the past, or, rather, to embrace those images and icons of its absence which are present to him in Slovakia, is intense. After spending some time with his aunt and uncle, Monika and Joseph, in Bratislava, he travels by train to the town of M— where his cousin Honza shows him the house where he lived briefly after the war which, like other houses in the village, soon will disappear to make way for prefab high rises with hot running water. Calling himself for the first time "an autobiographer" or "at best the historian of an idea he cannot name," he wants nothing to change here, wants "the old streets to remain as a living model," though "he does not know of *what*." He begins to feel that he "had come on a foolish errand: to repossess what I could never have again . . . that house and gate across the road, so familiar, so alien." Beyond the town of M— is the tiny village of Kamen, and beyond that the series of bunkers in the hills. Honza and Oliver, the Partisan who hid with Wyatt and his family in the bunkers, travel on with him to the home of Franzi Holub in Kamen with its "one street without any sidewalks" where the houses are "unpainted cement squares and triangles" and the look of the place recalls, Wyatt thinks, the set for *Shane*. The Holub's front room, where the Wyatts first had hidden, was the source of one of the primal, ungrounded images presented early in the book which, as it were, had brought him here. The image composes itself, decomposes, recomposes. His mother was ironing at the window and the German soldiers passed on skis. But what could his mother have been ironing? He had remembered bright, white linen—sheets. But they had brought nothing with them, not even clothing. And "what sort of iron would it have been?" Perhaps she was doing something else. And yet "I see her clearly at the ironing board at the back of the room, the steam swirling, whiteness the colour of snow fall." Because it is too late in the year and the woods are wet and flooded, Wyatt never manages to get to the bunkers in the hills, the source of the other and more powerful images of pristine earliness, those which were accompanied by emotions "that approached a kind of euphoria." Later, when Franzi's slivovitz and sausages have run through his system, he goes into the field behind the house to defecate. "What I had come [to Slovakia] for," he says, "was lying in the mist of the hills behind me." The sources of his most powerful early memories and most vividly haunting mental images remain inaccessible, subject still to "longing"—a term that Wyatt earlier invokes perhaps because, as Hass says in his poem, desire must remain "full of endless distances."

In a later chapter, Wyatt considers another reason why the boy that he was could never fully come to life in him again, and why he could not repossess the house he lived in or even spontaneously and innocently grasp for the intense sensations, the "memories made palpable," which he sought. He no longer belonged in M— not only because "no amount of Slovak food could force from my identity the decades I had spent away . . . but also because grown up I had become an observer, a perennial third party, the one who writes." When his cousins went to bed at night, he wrote in his notebook. Old images and their defining contexts were not only actively to be sought, but they were to be given a verbal shape and submitted, along with the perceptions of the seeker, to analysis. The same was true of new images and their defining contexts. "If I do not belong in M—," Wyatt wonders, "do I belong anywhere else?" The act of self-conscious observation and analysis itself alienates, deracinates such a "perennial third party." When the Kafkaesque inquisitor at the end of the book asks Wyatt "Who, truly, are you," he desperately runs through a mental list of possibilities—"Fresser, Jew, Slovak, New Yorker, Radical, Writer (??), U.S. Citizen c. 1956, Socialist"—and jumps to his feet crying out "Jew." We understand that any of these answers would be wrong in Wyatt's journey among identities, but if I were forced to choose one for him from the list, it would be "Writer."

As a writer, then—but also as a Jew, a Slovak, a New Yorker, and a Radical—Wyatt seeks out or stumbles onto new images as well as old remembered ones, images and their defining contexts which establish a potent tension between the present and the past. It was inevitable, for example, that he should wish to visit Terezin Fortress and the medieval Jewish cemetery in Prague. One of the three epigraphs to *Against Capitulation* is a line from Geoffrey Hill's austere and shattering poem "September Song," with its note "born 19.6.32—deported 24.9.42." Hill's elegy for the child who died in one of the camps ends abruptly, as if he had intended to write much more and suddenly stops in disgust over having written anything at all, with the line Wyatt quotes: "This is plenty. This is more than enough." (One of Hill's constant preoccupations is the danger of committing what he calls "the tongue's atrocities." "Artistic men prod dead men from their stone," he writes in a poem on Auschwitz.)

Wyatt is not sickened by his own desire to meditate both on Terezin and in Terezin, consciously to collect images, or to write of what he sees and feels. He does not deny that "the unspeakable renders you blessedly speechless, since only silence is equal to your impossibly contradictory, besmirched emotion, and your awe," but he goes on to recognize that "silence is also incommunicable and opaque," which is why those writers on the Holocaust who "perceive its unique adequacy wind up composing sentences nevertheless." Not sickened, therefore, by collecting and presenting images like the two white roses and the red one on a wooden table in the dormitory vaults "faded, pale, but brilliant and piercing the blankness and the utter silence of the cells" beside the faded note "in memory of R.F. who was a prisoner in this cell," he *is* sickened upon emerging from Terezin "to see people pursuing their innocently ordinary lives," and this involves him in some contradictions that he must learn to live with and write from. Upon leaving Terezin, Wyatt sees complicity written into the most common human activities—"the unexamined routine of the ordinary person appears vile. It appears to bear in its malleable commonsense the seed of all cruelty." The image at Terezin of human cruelty having become "stone, brick, and mortar," having become "that quintessential human creation: a building," makes him feel so "violated, soiled, and corrupted" that he cannot see a simple act in the present moment—"the ability to go shopping, say"—as not utterly tainted by corruption.

Images, as Hass points out, often say *this is*. But they also say, like Terezin, *this was*, or, like any *memento mori* (such as the brilliantly described stones in the medieval cemetery beside the Pinkas Synagogue) *this will be*. If the danger of clinging to the second or third kind of image is that one grows increasingly unable to live in the present, the danger of grasping at the first is that one grows increasingly unable to see the present responsibly as a product of the past with a future that depends on human will, or even other competing presents which cry out *these are* against *this is* because they're made invisible by the brilliance of an isolated moment. Wyatt, in fact, cultivates and presents such brilliant moments now and then, most notably in the image of a young woman on the Charles Bridge in Prague "tossing bits of bread to the gulls."

The birds swirled round her. No sooner would she toss a piece of bread into the air than a gull would swoop to catch it. Each time this happened the woman's face opened into the purest delight, and she'd give out an enraptured little cheer. Over and over she threw her bread into the air and beamed with pleasure as a gull snapped it in his beak.

Wyatt calls this "a salvaged moment, beyond necessity and outside power." He has been walking the streets of Prague with a dissident and discussing Charter '77. Had the woman on the bridge heard of it? Was she here in 1968 when the Russian tanks rolled in? Would she have stood there throwing bread to gulls in 1943? Would she have known what went on in Terezin? Is she guilty of complicity in the repressions of the present regime, or gifted with the grace to live in the present moment, or both? Some of these questions are mine rather than Wyatt's, but they are all implicit in the little scene and its defining context. Looking over his shoulder for the police, he mentions his surprise that such things as feeding bread to gulls go on in the Prague of 1978, and his dissident friend says: "What do you expect, that life will stop?" Wyatt doesn't by any means. And although much of this book is obsessed with the past, the exhilaration of reading it, one realizes, comes from the vivid sense which it communicates of what it feels like to live the present moment to its fullest.

There is nothing for Wyatt to do but embrace the contradictions of his experience, and write as clearly and as honestly as he can out of his divided identity and multiple allegiances. It is a difficult balancing act—one achieved necessarily in the present, but with one eye on the future and one eye on the past. There is a marvelous moment just before the three-part conclusion—the Kafkaesque self-interrogation, an analysis of broken covenants, and the *buchty* episode—when Wyatt is on the train from Mikulas to Bratislava. Although the train would not stop at M—, Honza and his family had insisted on waiting for it to pass under the large sign with the town's name written on it in order to wave and shout goodbye, and Wyatt wanted a last nostalgic look and to wave himself. As the train speeds past M— into the future, he frantically dives across the compartment to catch a final glimpse of his cousin and the sign with the word that more than any other stands for his past. "After a moment I became conscious that the wind was cold and that, the train careening at a fast clip, I was hanging dangerously halfway out of the window. In a fright I pulled myself back in. The thought flashed through my mind: I don't want to die. I love my life." Yes, and in a world where one *does* throw bread to gulls and say *this is* to the cacophonous *these are, this was,* and *this will be.*

Wyatt's account of his trip to Slovakia extends and in some ways responds to and interrogates the original short essay printed as the title chapter of *Against Capitulation.* That essay concludes with some firm judgments and what sounds like the making of a personal covenant, an affirmation "of the long Jewish resistance to oppression, or resistance to Fascism, and of the revolutionary Socialism which gave (and continues to give) that resistance shape and fire." By the end of the book, Wyatt writes about the breaking of covenants—between God and the Jewish nation, and between a purposeful History and mankind whose free and just millennium was to have been assured at the end of the dialectical spiral—in a world where old certainties, religious and political, no longer hold. The conclusion is full of questions and doubts rather than certainties and doctrines: "You set out on a journey to the place of origin with vague hopes, excitement, and more contradictory feelings than you can be aware of. You return enlivened and puzzled. Your puzzlement is your fate." The questioning at the end even extends to the questioners, to the Czech dissidents and our own image of them in the West—the fact that, because these men and women have opted for clear consciences, we can deceive ourselves into believing "that the old certainties hold." Also, by the end of the book, Wyatt is thinking as much about his daughter as of his parents (a daughter whose birth I remember being announced on a card with a Vietcong guerrilla on one side and an inspirational poem by Chairman Mao on the other—whose message was *she* supposed to speak in 1970?), and wondering what it is he has to offer her. Instead of offering something like an affirmation of "the long Jewish resistance to oppression . . . and revolutionary Socialism," he offers her "what I have set down in these pages"—a sequence of images generating a narrative and ending in puzzlement. The aim throughout this book is to understand (by puzzling over) the events experienced and the history recovered rather than to judge them. For this reason, images are truly sought, retrieved, shed, transformed, exposed, and discovered; the act of doctrinal judgment would simply have frozen some of them. I don't mean to imply an absence of political commitment at the end of the book; Wyatt is clearly still "against capitulation," and still a radical—even more so than before if a radical approach to our experience does mean getting at its roots. Ironically, he also, in the end, speaks the message which his parents and their generation embodied, bears them a kind of witness, and gives them, if not a vicarious victory, then perhaps a sort of vicarious strategic retreat or flanking action. Although it wasn't exactly what they had in mind, I wonder if they wouldn't have understood—and maybe even approved, had they been able to follow this journey to its end.

IV

"Images," says Hass, "are powers: it seems to me quite possible that the arsenal of nuclear weapons exists, as Armageddon has always existed, to intensify life." Michael Anania's *The Red Menace*— "a fiction," he calls it; I call it an oral autobiography which he has dictated to himself—begins with the image of an atomic test on a television screen seen over the cereal bowls and milk bottles of countless American homes in the 1950s. I remember these tests well. The images certainly provided a bizarre focus for our scarcely conscious minds as, groggy and irritable, we stared uncomprehendingly at the black-and-white flickerings of those primitive TVs. For Anania, the images became a fundamental element in what he thinks of as "the snarl of things we call awareness." This is what we all were looking at and what it is that Anania's characters (his friends and/or antagonists) go off to school talking about.

> The screen was instantly blank, not bright, just blank; then slowly from its edges, as though seeping back, the gray of the sky circled in around a light at the center, which in turn began to grow outward against the recovered sky. The circle of light grew to the size of a baseball, darkening at the edges, rising on a column of smoke that ridged and fluted itself as it supported the ball, the ball itself grown smoky, flattening as it moved upward. The horizon was plain again, and to the right of the burgeoning cloud there were three thin streamers of smoke that rippled as they extended off the top of the screen. The wooden shed was gone. The screen belonged to the cloud, which stood still, or seemed still except for the constant enfolding of smoke shadows at the top and sides, and the constant pumping of smoke into the crown from the column below. The announcer droned on about height, times, size, and the picture changed.

"Jee-zus," one of the boys says, while the others rise "as though responding to a benediction." "Shee-it" . . . "Fuckin' A" . . . "Damn Straight" the rest incant in their turn, reacting to various outrageous claims—"you know you could carry one of them things in a suitcase?"—made by one or another of them about the bomb. The jive, too, is part of the snarl of things which Anania says we call awareness and which, in his own case, we might just as well call memory. Anania is a great rememberer. My own method of dealing with the particular madness of the 1950s was simple—the cultivation of total amnesia. I hated and feared both the strange intensities and stultifying inertias of the decade, from its music, cars, movies, heroes, and politics to its style of sexual swagger or sexual innocence. As soon as it was possible to forget—at about the time, I suppose, of Kennedy's inauguration—I forgot. But Anania forces memory upon me. To some extent, his experiences were also mine— which was not the case, of course, with what Jiri Wyatt remembers from his childhood in Slovakia. But 1950s America is another country, too, and many of its characteristic or defining images are as simultaneously familiar and alien, once held up in their own authentically garish light, as a half-remembered room in an eastern European village is to a returning exile.

The snarl of things . . . awareness and the memory of awareness and the awareness of memory. Anania grew up in Omaha, Nebraska, and lived in a housing project named for Logan Fontenelle, the last chief of the Omahas. German on his mother's side, he got his "bits and pieces" of a Bremen pastoral mainly from his grandmother, who returned to Germany as an old woman after the war. His mother's immigrant experiences "foreclosed all but a few images of an earlier, green life in another world." Anania's father, whose southern Italian background made him something of a *don* both in his own mind and in the Calabrian community, died young after a life in which tuberculosis made steady work impossible. He shined shoes, sold papers, dealt cards, helped build a water wall for WPA, and ended up on welfare living "not so much by his wits as his sense of style." Outside Omaha was the Macy reservation where some of Anania's friends, none of whom seems actually to live there, visit older relatives on weekends. Russell, the Omaha in Anania's high school who has a plan to steal the bomb, has the classic profile of the figure on a buffalo nickel and drives a Pontiac with its Indian hood ornament "jutting into the traffic." (Anania, importantly enough at the end of the book, drives a Plymouth with the *Mayflower* on its hood.) High school friends and acquaintances include a range of ghetto blacks, ethnic working-class whites, inaccessible upper-middle-class girls ("Cottonwood fluff"), and some truly violent delinquents for whom high school provided a kind of pastoral interlude "before the weight of lower-middle American life settled in" on them. All the boys brooded on the bomb—made it their own "by right of attentive devotion"—while brooding with an analogous intensity on particular girls "attended to, watched carefully, offered the role of leading lady in the movies in our heads," and particular cars which were "nosed" and "decked" with "an almost Bauhaus purity" to the point that they resembled bombs or bullets. The music accompanying all of this was either black rhythm and blues (aggressively defiant and kept off the radio and out of downtown record stores) or early white rock 'n' roll. Movies in the mind were based on movies in the movie theaters, dangerously suggestive films like *Blackboard Jungle* on one hand, and studies in the conflict between masculine honor and domesticity like *Shane, High Noon,* and *Rebel without a Cause* on the other. South of town was Offutt Air Force Base which, as headquarters of the Strategic Air Command, would make Omaha a certain target for a Soviet nuclear attack. Lewis and Clark stopped on their journey west to hunt on the river bluffs into which the SAC administrative building, a kind of inverted skyscraper, was sunk down to its lowest subterranean level where Curtis LeMay sat before the NORAD communications system dreaming of *grands prix* and his Ferrari like a high school student before a blackboard dreaming of the dragstrip and his Olds or Merc.

Anania early on establishes a connection between the bomb and sex, and between both of these and the souped-up cars that looked like bombs in which sexual desire could be relieved in the backseat or, more often, compensated for by tearing down a country road at ninety miles an hour. The "Red Menace" of the title is simultaneously the threat of the bomb in enemy hands; a name given to Russell, the Omaha, by one of his classmates; the swollen phallus of the sexually famished but frightened teenage male; and any of several bright, fast, dangerous, and desirable cars. While Anania's book begins with an atomic test assuring us again of the actual possibility of the much imagined cataclysm of nuclear holocaust, it ends, after episodes in which the dilemma of sexual power, like that of political power, is seen to be powerlessness and defeat, with an emblem for the cataclysm in what he calls an "autoclysm"—an orgasmic crash, described in nearly pornographic detail, in which the car is "totalled" and everyone is killed.

If the autoclysm is the most memorable emblem in *The Red Menace,* it may be that "The Real McCoy" is the most important. Readers of Anania's poetry will remember the real McCoy, a re-volver which Anania's father kept in a green steel box wrapped in a handkerchief, from an early poem in *The Color of Dust* called "The Temper." There as here, it represents someing solid, authentic, and durable in the threatened and unstable atmosphere of Anania's world. This is the passage from "The Temper":

It is something to covet—
what my father said of the real McCoy,
the gesture and all of
holding the revolver in his hand,
tapping the butt on the table,
saying, that is solid,
more than this table, solid,
tempered blue sheen thunk
reflected on the table top,
snubnosed, hammerless real McCoy.

In *The Red Menace*, the real McCoy surfaces in the third chapter, in which Anania's father successfully organizes a funeral for a woman who suddenly dies in the housing project, and then breaks up a neighborhood fight that develops in an afternoon of drinking when the group of pallbearers returns home. Anania's memories of his father constitute remarkable "islands of clarity," as he calls them, retrievable moments and images very like those presented in the early pages of *Against Capitulation*. Remembering his father's pleasure in breaking up the fight, Anania also remembers the day he sat him down at the kitchen table and showed him the gun which the young boy thought he might also have shown to the men in the fight in order to stop it. The gun "was a lesson in the weight and hardness of real things." Anania's father traces the crosshatch of the grip, turns it in the light to show off the bluing on the trigger guard and muzzle, and then, as in the poem, "holding it just above the table, he let the butt fall, thunk, and the whole kitchen seemed to shake." Anania thinks his father was obsessed by "the spectacular reality presented by the surfaces of finely accomplished things— his gold watch, the case work on our Zenith radio, the leather box he kept loose tobacco in." He hankered, Anania thinks, "after a hard lustre in things, the deep burnish of the real in metal, the weight of leather, the flex in a hat brim of Italian felt." Well, the father's aesthetic, one feels certain, is also the son's, and the distance from the real McCoy to the cars customized with a Bauhaus purity to the textures of Anania's verse and prose is not very great. Anania admires energy, even deadly energy, held in elegant control, and the powerful sports car which he covets today is only the child of James Dean's customized 1949 Mercury in *Rebel without a Cause*.

Even when the energy is not held in control, elegantly or otherwise, Anania draws aesthetic implications and establishes implicit analogies. In the concluding "Autoclysms" chapter, it is as if the real McCoy were no longer simply admired for its workmanship, but fired point-blank into somebody's face. Along with the final and appalling car crash in which four of his high school classmates are killed, Anania describes several others—including two close shaves of his own—and also the "corpse of a Studebaker Golden Hawk" that had been "front-ended," resting in a towing company garage. The Studebaker's windshield is fractured in such a way that the passenger's headprint is discernible and a cigarette, with a faint trace of lipstick on the filter tip, is embedded in the rubbery film of safety glass to which a few strands of blond hair are still attached. "The mangled front end, impacted bumper and grillwork, fenders closed like concertinas, all of it radiates from that collision in the glass, as though the whole wreckage were a crystal whose center was perfect and which grew amorphous only at its most extreme edges." He says that it verges on the sublime, and calls it "a geode . . . revealing in its deadly amethyst the impeccable record of the moment of impact." "Verges?" he asks. "It's hard to imagine anything more awesome, more eloquent in its obedience to natural law." And when he describes an accident in which he himself is involved as three cars and a boat being towed behind one of them "angled off into various ditches like billiard balls in a trick shot," he talks about "another kind of time" when "all the clocks changed," something that had to do "with the sudden perception of cause . . . as well as with increased adrenaline and focused attention, an instantaneous etiology that alters the perception of time." These are essentially aesthetic responses: that of the connoisseur (to the geode of the smashed Golden Hawk), and that of the artist himself tangled in the processes which he has unleashed but over which he loses control. Does aesthetic experience at its most intense require violence or danger? Must the real McCoy resonate with either suicidal or homicidal implications? Does the arsenal of nuclear weapons exist, as Hass says Armageddon has always existed, "to intensify life?"

Another kind of violence entirely results in what one might call the book's alternate ending—violence done to Anania's system and perceptions by an experiment in sacred mushroom eating at the Macy reservation. After Whisky-Nose Louie—about whom more will be said in a moment—Russell, who is in fact the great-grandson of Logan Fontenelle, is my favorite among Anania's acquaintances in the book. Russell doesn't say very much, but he represents a great deal. And he is the one who is responsible for Anania's hallucinatory or visionary experience. Russell is contrasted early on with a mixed Otto, Ponca, and Pawnee named John who wants to become a nuclear physicist and, as it were, acquire the bomb, which really means becoming a kind of Indian Oppenheimer who would build someone else's bomb and be someone else's scientist. Russell, who would steal the bomb rather than build it, "had never given up the essential secrets of himself as an Indian. Tough as he was, his real strength was in mystery. Remembering that early, his deep antagonisms to the society were crucial to that bomb-stealing vision of his." When Russell claimed that the Indians had taken the bomb off the testing tower in the desert and hidden it in a mountain cave at the end of an Apache trail that no one but an Apache could follow, what he understood . . .

> was what all the rhetoricians of apocalypse have always understood—that the signal points of our real fears are lying all about us and that turning them to any purpose is a poetic act of cultural alignments, a fine tuning, conducted through language, of what is already in scrambled view. Finally, the bomb is no more real than the stereotypical movie Apache, the painted desert no more tangible than the hulking Russian agent. There is no measured ontology to the stuff of this culture; there are only levels of energy. In one way or another everything in America is an icon.

When Russell and his cousin and uncle out at the Macy reservation share their hallucinatory mushroom with Anania so that they might "all dream together," Anania, thinking he's been poisoned, jumps in his Plymouth, and heads for home. On his way, he notices "a second highway brightly lit that veered to the right and upward, as though following the face of a steep hill that was not there." He tries to blink away the vision, but it persists; the car seems to be pulled by some kind of force toward this second road which "lifted and furled, banking as it turned westward, a finely worked contrail spiraling against the pure lapis of the summer sky." If this is the road not taken by the culture—and it clearly is—it's a road no longer takeable as well. Anania's car jolts to a halt in loose earth of the first road's shoulder, "weed crowns splitting across the bowsprit of the *Mayflower* at the point of the Plymouth's hood." After falling asleep in his car, he wakes to a final, fleeting vision: Russell and his cousin lifting the remains of the firebird which the cousin had earlier described to him, and placing it on its tail where "it looked more like a mushroom than a bird." In the form of a firebird, Russell and his cousin have the bomb. The visionary writing in these paragraphs of *The Red Menace* is exceptionally beautiful, and a good contrast to something like Hugh Brody's very plain account of the trail to heaven in *Maps and Dreams*. But the road Anania sees cannot be taken in his Plymouth. "We have come back to the Indian now for his secrets and his blessing," he says. "If he is smart, he will give us neither."

For the rest, there is a great deal of *talk* in this book—*talk* as when one says colloquially "*just* talk," the voluble bluster of verbal bravado—and much of it is hilariously funny. The best of the talkers is Whisky-Nose Louie, an alcoholic dishwasher at the grease joint where Anania works whose nonstop monologues make the jive of even the most advanced talkers at Tech High School sound amateurish by comparison. "He could go on . . . for eight hours, rasping out sexual advice, insult, salvation, and could curse longer without repeating himself than anyone I ever knew." One of his favorite subjects is the Communists and communism, and one set piece in a scene taking place in the grease joint is worth the price of the book. "You ever see the women that go around with Communists?" Louie asks. "Ugly and fat, every damned one of them, big fat arms, legs like pool tables. That's cause they hate good lookin' women, just hate 'em." "Louie," someone says, "that doesn't make any sense."

> Course it doesn't. If they make any sense, they wouldn't be Communists. You meet a Communist, you ask 'em what he thinks about good-looking' women, then look out, cause you're gonna get a two-hour speech about capitalism and jewelry and widows with nine kids hitched up to plows and bankers and how a poor woman suffers for every jewel a fancy woman wears. All the while, he's got some quarter section a beef in a brown dress sittin' in the corner bitin' her fingernails. Never trust a man who's got a smart reason for havin' somethin' he don't want. . . . I was in Portland one night, in a freightyard, not botherin' nobody, drinkin' Seattle wine with this here gandy-dancer. And up come this Communist. Spends half-a-minute talkin' 'bout the weather, then gets goin' on the capitalists and how they put us all outa work, and I says to him "Where's your fat girlfriend?" And he says he ain't got a fat girlfriend, and I tells him that the Communists fucked him

straight cause he's entitled to a fat girlfriend. Then me and that gandy-dancer bust a gut laughin'. And he asks what's so funny, and I says, "They're s'posed to give you a fat girlfriend. It goes with bein' a Communist." And he says he ain't no Communist, he's a socialist worker. And I says, long as you're gonna be somethin' dumb, might as well be a Communist, cause a fat, ugly woman is better than no woman at all.

All this, needless to say, is *talk*, not conversation à la Denis Donoghue, and the book is electric with it in a variety of idioms. In the end, however, it is sad rather than funny. For *The Red Menace* ends with talk exactly like the talk that began it—the simultaneously aggressive and self-protective teenage jive which has an analogue in the gossip of adults. After the final autoclysm that kills Linda, Arnie, and Meatball and decapitates Darlene on a telephone pole guidewire, the talk echoes off into silence. "No shit, you could see 'em flying off in every direction. . . . Arms and legs out, towels, bathing suits, everything in the car." Anania has written a poem called "Esthétique du Râle" which is as intimately related to the conclusion of *The Red Menace* as "The Temper" is to the episode at the housing project when his father takes out the real McCoy. It has to do in part with the degenerative history of modern art—from imagism and cubism to the work of minimalists and conceptualists and the "body art" of someone like Jack Broden—and with the deaths of modern artists, whether a James Dean, a Jackson Pollock, or an Albert Camus, in the autoclysms of the 1950s. "Something is ending," Anania writes; and, "Perhaps it was too much / to ask them to resolve our difficulties." If artisitic style, as Denis Donoghue maintains, is a compensation for the loss of conversation's true communion, then gossip, *talk*, a voyeuristic (and indeed a journalistic) focusing of attention on an artist's life and death, is certainly our compensation, and a very poor one too, for the loss of art. "We know / how the day went, the guest list / of the party down the road, the Cadillac's fish tail and impact . . ." Anania writes in his poem. And in the final lines of it a field of flowers as inauspicious as the jive about Darlene and Meatball waits, as talk, to receive the wreckage of one Red Menace among others:

> It is only in isolate flecks, swift
> and mutable, light finds its shape,
> all that the form fails to excude,

the almost unbearable clamor, every
gesture ambled among traffic; this day
or any other, talk settling in with the
portioned words, meant, I think, to be

a flower, a field of flowers, where
the wreckage seems oddly comfortable,
a seaside morning dew over bent metal
and blue Quaker ladies, *le dernier cri.*

At the outset of this essay, I said that the three books here considered all began for me as converstions, and that is true. The distinction between conversation and what I have called *talk*, however, is
about as great in one direction as the distance between conversation
and Denis Donoghue's notion of literary style in the other. It may be
the business of one kind of criticism to turn literature back in the
direction of conversation by engaging it somewhat more intimately
than is usual from a slightly privileged point of view. The danger is
that such criticism may simply degenerate into *talk*, Whisky-Nose
Louie's version of Anania rather than Anania's version of Whisky-
Nose Louie. Perhaps fearing that, I realize that I have slowly grown
less intimate in my discussion of the books by Wyatt and Anania
than I was in my discussion of Hass's, and that I have pretty much
ceased to claim the privilege of a friend's point of view. What began
as "epireading" has tended in the direction of "graphireading" in
the act of writing, and some kind of moral may hang on that. As for
The Red Menace—whether fiction or autobiogrpahy, memoir or essay,
and whether narrated by Michael Anania or "Michael Anania" (and
I have for convenience claimed the author and narrator to be one, as
I think mostly they are)—it is as remarkable an act of recovery as Jiri
Wyatt's *Against Capitulation*. Like *Twentieth Century Pleasures*, it is also
often a meditation on the forms in which the imagination manifests
itself in our time. And like both these other books, it is an excellent
example of the real McCoy.

From *The Southern Review*, 1986

Places and Poems:
A Self-Reading and a Reading of the
Self in the Romantic Context from
Wordsworth to Parkman

My title is awkward and long, but it is intended to suggest as accurately as possible what I intend to talk about this afternoon. I was invited to discuss my own work in the context of romanticism, and, although that initially seemed perhaps a rash and certainly an immodest thing to do—egotistical, but not sublime—the temptation to accept, proceed, and see what happened simply, in the end, overcame good sense. For what does my work have to do with romanticism? I have never admitted it had anything to do with it. Furthermore, I must confess that I have read the romantics systematically only once, and that one time was under the stern eye of Yvor Winters at Stanford University in the middle 1960s. Yvor Winters—the great *anti*-romantic of twentieth century criticism. I can still hear him growling in his mockery, adding a line to the Immortality Ode.

> The Rainbow comes and goes,
> And lovely is the Rose,
> The baby's playing with his toes.

And I can hear him pause in a lecture on Whitman to tell us that a student seemed to have written "Good descriptive elements!" in the margin of the text he was considering. "Ladies and gentlemen," he said, "these are *bad* descriptive elements."

Well, that was graduate school, and one reason for my being here at all is that I went to England to write poetry in 1966 rather

than finishing graduate school. But although I never again systematically read the romantics in an academic and responsible way, I
have since read certain romantic texts for more pressing personal
reasons which will be seen to have something to do with the self-
reading threatened in my title and the issue of place which provides, I hope, a legitimate connection between my own work and
that of Wordsworth, Francis Parkman, and, incidentally, some of the
artists whose paintings surround us today in the Historical Society.

However, as I have said, I am by no means an expert on romanticism and I am therefore anxious to defer to some critics who
are experts in order to provide a context for my remarks. All other
things being equal, I want to cite the work of people making a direct
contribution to this conference, whether in person or through their
essays appearing in Kenneth R. Johnston's and Gene W. Ruoff's *The
Age of William Wordsworth* or in the catalogue for "William Wordsworth and the Age of English Romanticism."

I was interested to find Morris Dickstein writing in the
Johnston-Ruoff volume that "perhaps the crisis of feeling described
by so many writers in the nineteenth century is something we no
longer experience in any significant way," but going on to argue
that, nonetheless, "a crisis of feeling is a consistent, unrecognized
symptom of contemporary criticism itself. As our critical vocabular-
ies have flourished on the analytic side, they have atrophied on the
affective side. We have no accepted language in which to examine
what really moves us in a writer."[1] Dickstein is remembering and
commending the language of Matthew Arnold and John Stuart Mill.
Arnold, he reminds us, "paid tribute to Wordsworth's 'healing
power' that revived the wounded capacity for feeling in his contemporaries," while Mill, as everyone knows, turned to Wordsworth
"for medicine for [his] state of Mind" having become, as a result of
his rigorous analytical and utilitarian training, a kind of stock or
stone in which, he felt, all feeling might be dead.[2] Wordsworth himself, of course, had feared much the same thing. Writing in book 10
of the 1805 *Prelude*, he speaks of the period when his own early
habit of analysis in the categories of Godwinian rationalism, together with his agonized support of the Revolution, brought him to
the state of mind which these famous lines describe.

> Thus I fared,
> Dragging all passions, notions, shapes of faith,
> Like culprits to the bar, suspiciously

Calling the mind to establish in plain day
Her titles and her honours, now believing,
Now disbelieving, endlessly perplexed
With impulse, motive, right and wrong, the ground
Of moral obligation—what the rule,
And what the sanction—till, demanding proof,
And seeking it in every thing, I lost
All feeling of conviction, and, in fine,
Sick, wearied out with contrarieties,
Yielded up moral questions in despair. . . .

Wordsworth, like Mill, had sought to be a reformer of the world, and, like Mill, had cultivated a "habit of analysis" which had "a tendency to wear away the feelings" and "strengthen the associations between causes and effects [and] means and ends."[3] Although I do not have a vocabulary at my disposal adequate to reanimate for contemporary discourse the affective side of a critical language which, as Dickstein correctly notes, has atrophied— certainly not anything better than Arnold's language or Mill's—I need to record the fact that, at a particular point in the 1960s, I went as intentionally to Wordsworth as one might reach for the right medicine in the medicine chest, and I went to him remembering what he had done for Mill and how his own distorted and traumatized emotional life was reoriented and restored to proper health through memory and the disciplined play of an imagination interacting with nature in a particular place.

It is a bit shy-making to acknowledge that one needed and actively sought the Wordsworthian therapy for a state of mind that seems in retrospect almost a parody of the one he describes, but so in fact I did. I was not, I suppose, untypical of my generation in the 1960s by becoming sufficiently caught up in the machinery of protest and the language of neo-Marxist analysis to feel in the end both confused and inauthentic, "dragging passions, notions, shapes of faith / Like culprits to the bar," and subjecting everything, including the pleasures I took in a new marriage, in the birth of my first child, in solitude, and in the arts to a rigorous inquistion with respect to means and ends considered in the context of political activism. I remember telling a friend in late 1968 that I felt oddly off balance, that I was trying to regain that balance by reading Wordsworth. I also remember his response: "In a year like this one's been," he said, "I'm prepared to believe anything."[4] The 1960s, like the 1790s and the first decades of the twentieth century, briefly held out millennial expectations leading one to find, with Wordsworth, that it was bliss to be alive and very heaven to be young. But if Robespierre and Stalin led the dialectics of two revolutions to gag on their own contradictions, 1960s activism simply exhausted the emotional energy of its partisans without producing much more than the temporary radicalization and political self-consciousness of an outraged fraction of the middle class. "A dull, dishonest decade," as W. H. Auden called the 1930s? Well, it certainly wasn't dull.

It's not that I exactly abandoned "present objects, and the busy dance / Of things that pass away" for "a temperate show / Of Objects that endure " by turning to Wordsworth at this time, and eventually he led me neither to a Natural Supernaturalism, nor a Via Naturalitar Negativa, nor a Burkian Second Nature, nor an Established Church,[5] but simply to a place—and not *his* place either, but a place of my own. Or, to be absolutely accurate, he led me to *realize* that I had been led to a place of my own. Perhaps I misread him; or at any rate misread him at a crucial points (the Spots of Time, the Prospectus, crossing the Alps, Mount Snowdon), for, as many critics have made clear to me, Wordsworth is not always the sort of poet of place that I thought he was.[6] In any case, two years before turning in my postactivist consternation first tentatively to standard anthology pieces and then in earnest to "Home at Grasmere" and *The Prelude* for whatever therapy they could provide, I had begun to spend my summers at my wife's home in the tiny village of Hacheston, in Suffolk. Arriving one year by ship—a Russian ship named for the romantic poet Lermontov, in fact—I bade my farewell to the 1960s radical in a parodic idiom that was Byronic rather than Wordsworthian. Although written in the middle 1970s, it casts off a persona from the late 1960s which had begun to vanish from my actual life the more I travelled to Suffolk and the longer I lived there. It also casts off anything that might have been left of my superficially assimilated Marxism except for its epistemology (which I still found useful in spite of the parenthetical joke), leaving me "with children and a wife" and "middle class for life."

> Said Marx (correctly)
> men will make their history, all right,
> but not exactly
> as they think or choose.
> (Even he had everything to lose
> with that excuse.)[7]

It was my wife, of course, who introduced me to Hacheston, the Aldeburgh coast, Orford, Framlingham, the rivers Stour and Alde and Orwell and Deben, and other places the names of which are utterly resonant for me now but which, at first, meant nothing. I had spent most of 1966 and 1967 in London, only rarely venturing into the countryside and writing my first published poems under the influence of an eclectic range of American modern and postmodern poets. My sense of "the country" was as generic as my sense of trees and flowers and crops—which is to say totally generic. And I didn't, indeed, "make history," my private history, exactly (or anything like) what I might have thought or initially chosen. In the end, I chose what I had been given, but at the beginning I didn't even see that I had been given something. Utterly urban to the age of twenty-five, I had grown up in an uninteresting city—Columbus, Ohio—which had given me only a negative sense of place, a sense only of a place I wanted to be away from. California was melodramatically impressive, but clearly wasn't mine—and I remember, too, that I arrived there just in time for the success of Philip Roth's first book, *Goodbye, Columbus,* which an ex-student of Roth's liked to taunt me with, then singing out for good measure: "Oh me Oh My Oh / Why did I ever leave Ohio?"

It took several years of summer visits—roughly form 1967 to 1970—for Suffolk to begin to do its work on me, and it took Wordsworth in *The Prelude,* "Home at Grasmere," "Poems on the Naming of Places, " and related works of the period 1798–1814 to make me consciously aware of what I had begun unconsciously to feel— namely, that whatever I was and whatever I was going to write that might have any merit was bound up, for the present at least, with a place I had come to love, and that I was gong to have to learn, somehow, to write *from* that place as well as *about* it. It doesn't matter that Wordsworth's place was the Lake District and that mine turned out to be Suffolk—for surely Karl Kroeber is right when he says of Wordsworth and Constable that "their art makes us feel not that we would enjoy Cumberland or East Anglia but that we are at home on the earth. "[8] Predictably, once I found that I could feel "at home on the earth" in Suffolk, I also found that I could write with a good deal of sympathy about Ohio. But only in Suffolk! And it's fair to say that Constable *had* made me feel that I would enjoy East Anglia.

I love the way Kroeber in *Romantic Landscape Vision* talks about Wordsworth taking possession of his place in "Home at Grasmere" like a predator or a preagricultural Indian in contrast to Constable, whose relationship to place in a painting like *The Leaping Horse* is compared to farming, which is, as Kroeber says, "a shaping of the natural world." "A farmer who does not understand nature," Kroeber notes, "will plant crops in poor soil, pasture sheep in the wrong field, generally will not get the most out of the land, animals, and plants. But to make nature work to his advantage, the farmer must be aggressive, must rearrange natural patterns. Constable, analogously, is true to nature in order to reshape it."[9] Kroeber finds the various versions of *The Leaping Horse* to be showing Constable as "maneuvering the phenomeana which are his subject to realize some mental scheme, not a chance falling out of events. Yet he is not arbitrary. His originality lies in rejecting conventional artistic schemes (the sublime, the picturesque, and so on) while refusing merely to copy natural appearances. His psychic patterns and nature's physical patterns, 'in here' and 'out there,' must be made to *fit*."[10] This description reminds me very much of what a contemporary farmer-poet, Wendell Berry, has said of his own work in a book called *Standing by Words*. Berry begins a long essay on "Poetry and Place" by asking if the connections he once saw and wrote about between his work on the Kentucky hill farm where he lives and his work as a poet has anything to it. What he wrote was that "the place has become the form of my work, its discipline, in the same way the sonnet has been the form and discipline of the work of other poets: if it doesn't fit it's not true."[11] At the end of his essay, Berry concludes that, in its essentials, his initial observation was sound. The farm is not, of course, a literary form, "but it is *like* a literary form, and it cannot properly be ignored or its influence safely excluded by any literary form that is made within it. Like any other form, it requires us to do some things, and forbids us to do others. Some acts are fitting and becoming, and some acts are not. If we fail to do what is required and if we do what is forbidden, we exclude ourselves from the mercy of Nature; we destroy our place, or we are exiled from it."[12]

But Wordsworth's personal and poetic relationship to Grasmere Vale is not like that of the figurative painter-farmer or the literal farmer-poet. Kroeber stresses the fact that, in "Home at Grasmere" (and one can add as well books 1 and 13 of *The Prelude*), Wordsworth and his sister "are newcomers to the vale" and that Grasmere is a place they *choose* to live in which provides "a territory in which to roam." What Wordsworth does in Grasmere is "to fit himself to nature, and fit nature to himself, not in the fashion of a farmer, a pastoral poet, or a modern exurbanite, but, strange as it sounds, in the fashion of a predator such as a wolf."[13] This is a wonderful analogy, I think, and, although Kroeber does not press it, he says he "knows no better way to define the poet's preferred relationship to nature, because it excludes conventional attitudes toward possession and property in its emphasis upon territorial familiarity."[14] Dropping the lycanthropic comparison, Kroeber ultimately settles on an analogy between Wordsworth's attitude to place and "that found in pre-agricultural societies, whose concepts of 'land possession' are to us almost incomprehensible . . ." but who seem "to feel that they belong to their territory as fully as it belongs to them."[15] Perhaps Bruce Chatwin's recent book about the "songlines" of the Australian aborigines provides an extension of this analogy which is usefully far-fetched. One might see Wordsworth on a kind of aboriginal walkabout singing, as Chatwin writes of the aborigine following the labyrinth of invisible pathways which constitute the songlines, "the name of everything that crosses [his] path and so singing the world into existence." Chatwin tells us that there is "hardly a rock or a creek or a stand of eucalyptus that isn't an 'event' on one or other of the songlines. In other words, the whole of Australia can be read as a musical score."[16] So, in its domestic and circumscribed terms, can the world of Grasmere Vale in Wordsworth's poetry.

If farming provides an analogy for the form of a Constable painting and a poem by Wendell Berry, clearly Wordsworth's relationship to the prospect before him in Grasmere is analogous to the prospect before him in his writing. In all three cases, the work at hand is like the artist's chosen relationship to his place. The self in Wordsworth, having been spiritually displaced during the period of his revolutionary sympathies, takes up residence in a place which is like a poem and a poem which is like a place. Kroeber reminds us that he treats the mind, too, as a territory, as a "haunt" and a "region" in the conclusion to "Home at Grasmere" which became the "Prospectus" for *The Recluse;* and that he defines the self as an entity "created through deliberate fitting of one's individuality to the external world and of the external world to one's mind." [17] In the enclosed and self-contained world of his place, he is, Kroeber feels, suggesting a third analogy to accompany those of the predator and the preagricultural Indian, like a child "in the microcosmic environment of a garden, a farm, or a country place."[18] Futhermore, because he appears to do no work, his life seems indolent. Raisley Calvert's legacy has freed him for his poetry. He is in a position, as Whitman said, to "loaf and invite the soul."

I wonder how many people know, let alone enjoy, "Home at Grasmere." It causes critics like Goeffrey Hartman a good deal of embarrassment,[19] and it gives us Wordsworth at his most Whitmanic, writing ecstatically, allowing the words to tumble over themselves all but out of control. This is not a poetry of emotion recollected in tranquility: it reads in places like an attempt to write a poetry of lovemaking while actually enjoying sex. It is important for an understanding of the kind of influence I am trying to acknowledge to point out that this poem is not the sort of thing I approved of intellectually or held as a conscious model or recommended to anyone else—which is why, in fact, I was reading it, as it were, in secret. It seemed, and it still seems, something very strange; and it is something I read seriously only once.

The opening of *The Prelude* is similar, but more restrained and more controlled. It too is concerned with the business of getting started with the right poem in the right place. The place, again, sponsors the poem. Wordsworth contemplates "Long months and undisturbed delight / . . . in prospect" in his "known Vale." This time he "spares to tell of what ensued, the life / In common things"—having done just that in "Home at Grasmere"—but instead grapples with a range of possible subjects, suffers indeed a kind of temporary writer's block brought on by the very freedom and the range of possibilities he contemplates, and then, remembering the Derwent, surrenders to memory, evokes the earliest "spots of time, " and at last realizes that the poem that he must write will tell "the story of [his] life." Thousands of lines later, the poem returns to its beginning and the poet returns to Grasmere, the place, as it were, containing the present memories of the poet's far-flung past as the binding of the book contains the pages of its telling. And in books 12 to 14, where Grasmere is reintroduced and the spots of time return, the writing, under the influence of Dorothy's ministrations, begins, now and then, to echo that of "Home at Grasmere."

But it's now past time to say that my own initial relationship to place in Suffolk and then later in East Anglia more generally, a relationship brought to full consciousness in part by a reading of Wordsworth's relationship to *his* place, was neither like that of a farmer nor that of a predator or an Indian; it was, oddly and literally, that of a spouse. When I married my wife, I also married East Anglia, Suffolk, the Aldeburgh and Orford coasts, the river Deben, the town of Woodbridge and the village of Hacheston. My initial response to English village life was pretty condescending. This was the place where farmers got on with whatever it was that farmers did and where my wife's parents lived in retirement in a rambling house which had been pieced together by joining three Elizabethan cottages made of local mud and horse hair. But the house itself became, in a couple of years, as numinous for me as Howards End is for Margaret Schlegel; and my mother-in-law, a repository of all the local legends and a fine amateur historian, proved to be, especially after the death of her husband, as mysterious a presence as Mrs. Ramsey herself and as nurturing an influence on my family as all the Wordsworth women put together. Accepting, as one does and must in a marriage with children, a life which made me a father and a son-in-law as well as my wife's lover and friend, I slowly opened myself to the full geological, topographical, natural, historical, and social context of the region where I came, able during these summers to loaf and invite the soul, to write.

In a paragraph which is more general than Wendell Berry's describing the manner in which a poem can be like a farm or Karl Kroeber's on the way a poem can resemble the territory of a predator, Jeremy Hooker writes in an afterword to his new book of poems that, consciously returning to his own original home in the south of England, he was "thinking of a poem that is like a place."

> Entering a place that is new to us, or seeing a familiar place anew, we move from part to part, simultaneously perceiving individual persons and things and discovering their relationships, so that, with time, place reveals itself as particular identities belonging to a network, which continually extends with our perception, and beyond it. And by this process we find ourselves not as observers only, but as inhabitants, citizens, neighbours, and locate ourselves in a space dense with meanings.[20]

If this is essentially what Wordsworth did, first with such abandon in Grasmere and in "Home at Grasmere," and then more soberly throughout the vale and in the poems it later sponsored, it is also what I sought to do in Suffolk, both in the place itself and in those poems I wrote which tried to take the measure of the place and find my proper station in it. But my initial explorations were necessarily tentative, as "Epilogue from a New Home," my first sustained poem written there, makes clear.

There's a plague pit
  just to the edge of the village.
Above it, now mostly covered with grass,
  a runway for B-17s: (American
Pilots back from industrial targets). Tribes
  gathered under my window;
They'd sack an imperial town: I'll wave
  to my wife at the end of the Roman road.
At night I said
  (the odd smell of the house recalling home)
"My father sits up in his grave.
  I'm too unstrung to love you now. Look:
Children play in the garden with bones."

Enclosed within a boundary of stones
  they died in isolation. All of us have
Colds; we visit the parish church and read: "Names.
  The numbers of persons who died of bubonic plague."
Grey-stone cottages across the road,
  a stream at the end of the church-yard,
Giant harvesters working the mechanized farms. . . .

Yesterday I walked to see the black,
  malignant huts that held the bombs.
After the war, nobody tore them down. Some
  are full of hay. Mechanics counted, standing
There, the number of planes that returned. I don't
  understand the work men did in the fields, or do.
I don't know the names of the crops. I don't
  know the uses of gears.
A church has grown on every hill like a tree.

Green on green: texture, shade, & shadows:
  opening out, folding in, surrounding.
Before the planes, someone counted ships: counted
  once that ancient one across the Deben
Where, from Woodbridge, you can almost see the site
  where his retainers set about to bury it,
A cenotaph, a King's.

Cynouai says: "I don't like my name. I won't have
  a name and I'll just be a girl."
Laura, three and deferential, understands. I open
  a bottle of wine.[21]

These lines from 1972 register something of the post-Vietnam state of consciousness parodied in the poem written on board the Lermontov and quoted earlier. But here, as the elements constituting the place begin coming together—the Roman road, the ruined air base, the farm, the cottages, the Sutton Hoo ship burial, Woodbridge, the Deben, the church with its memorials to those who died of plague (perception of which is conditioned partly by the shock of my father's recent death and partly by the first full realization that I was now myself a father)—the healing process, I think, can be seen to begin. But it's important to stress that, from the beginning, the place for me was inseparable from what I was reading about it, and the following stanzas are distinctly bookish. This husband and father aimed also to be a historian of sorts, and the poems do not draw much, as Wordsworth does, on oral sources and traditional lore, but on books.

> A whir of looms where wool was wealth:
> (*nidings voerk, nidings voerk*) the baths long
> Drained, the polyglot army long before withdrawn.
> If the Trinovantian coins & the legionary oaths,
> If the pentatonic lyre in the Royal Ship
> prefigure here a merchant—*upon his head*
> *A Flaundrish bever hat*—,
>   is that more odd
> than that my children's rhyme recalls
> The plague, the unattended fields & the dissipation
> of the feudal claims, or that the final
> Metamorphosis of Anna's luck should find its
> imagery—like Christ's—in bas-reliefs
> Depicting animals domesticated by domesticating
> Saxon heirs?
>
> We picnic by these graves, these strata of
> the dead: Celtic, Roman, Viking, English—
> All of them killers, all of them dead, they'd moralize
> on one another's end. Christian to pagan, power
> To power, and I am also implicated here: the woodwose
> in the spandrels of a door lifts up his club,
> A voice begins to speak of Fifteen Signs.[22]

These last three stanzas sound to me a bit more confident and rooted than the initial stanzas do. Fearing, perhaps, the dangers of the picturesque, what Wordsworth in *The Prelude* calls a "strong infection of [his] age—giving way / To a comparison of scene with scene, / Bent overmuch on superficial things, / . . . with meager novelties / Of colour and proportion," I turned early on to books and documents and histories to discipline my seeing. Now this is, strictly speaking, anti-Wordsworthian. James Chandler has shown clearly Wordsworth's aversion to documentary history together with his feeling that it posed a threat to his oral and traditionary material—"a plague on your industrious antiquarianism, " he wrote to Scott who had offered to send him some documents about the Norton Uprising for "the White Doe of Rylstone."[23] Karl Kroeber argues that the form and subject of *The Prelude* are largely explained by Wordsworth's "effort to escape the limiting condition of history" and work only with "what has been transformed by tradition or imaginative enthusiasm into legend."[24] For myself, however, any fitting of the mind to the external world very soon required learning from the books in my mother-in-law's library, the documentary contents of which seemed as much a part of the soil as the flints I turned up with the toe of my shoe. I met with few Michaels or Pedlars or leech gatherers in Suffolk, but 1969 was the year that Ronald Blyth—that Wordsworth with a tape recorder—published *Akenfield*, and shortly after that I carried on my walks the books on Suffolk and The Iknield Way by those Wordsworthian wanderers Julian Tennyson and Edward Thomas.[25] And there were also specialized and scholarly books—whole bibliographies of such—which I read with plesure for materials they provided for the structures I began to build. The poem from which I have been quoting ends: "I'm but half oriented here. I'm digging down." The facts I learned from books were what I dug with.

> *The child is father of the man*
> but not the child the poet meant.
> The child of flesh and blood
> and not the ghost of former selves
> is father of the man. . . .[26]

So begins the conclusion of a poem for my daughter written late in the series of East Anglian poems from the first decade of summer visits there. In the end, much of what I wrote was a result of watching my children play in their grandmother's garden. It has always surprised me that Wordsworth, who wrote so much about himself as a child, wrote so little about his children. If my own route to the responsibilities of being an adult was through my children, it was also through my children that I found the route to childhood. And one thing that I wanted to learn on my way to childhood and back again had something to do with the meaning of play. In "Double Derivation . . . ,"a poem glossed by another addressed to Robert Jacoby, my older cousin, I drew on Johan Huizinga:[27]

> In proper costume, Homo Ludens wears
> Imagination on his sleeve, . . .

. . . and went on to speak of "a field in Suffolk / So like the one we used to play in, in Ohio, / When we were boys." Feeling increasingly rooted in East Anglia, I had begun—East Anglia had made it possible for me—to remember Ohio without condescending to what was an authentic richness in my own early experience. And so I ask my cousin if *he* remembers:

> all those games
> we used to play: the costumes,
> All the sticks & staves, the whole complicated
> paraphernalia accumulated to suggest
> Authentic weaponry and precise historical dates,
> not to mention exact geographical places. . . .

all of which constituted:

> a world of imagination,
> Lovely and legitimate, uncovering, summer after
> summer, a place that we no longer go,
> A field we do not enter now, a world one tries
> to speak of, one way or another,
> In a poem. . . .

But remembering Robert and remembering the games through which we tried to fit our minds to the external world and the external world to our minds, I remembered also another cousin, James. This one valued *work* instead of play. With his "bicycles / and paper routes and baseballs" he was a "miniature / Adult" who "looked askance at our elaborate rituals. He laughed outright, / Derisively. No mere chronicler, he was reality itself." The *news* was, as I go on to tell my cousin:

that he, not you and I, made
Without our knowledge, without our wigs and
epaulets, with bricks he had a right
To throw, binding rules for our splendid games.[28]

In an article I'm truly grateful for, Jeremy Hooker has said about this aspect of the poem that "the poet at his creative play makes poems that are themselves worlds, but makes them out of the stuff of reality, which exists independently of him, makes its own claims, questions the poet, and calls him to witness all that is not himself."[29] That was certainly the intention of the lines, but there is still an unresolved (and probably unresolvable) tension between a world of play and a world of work, the world of a child and the world of an adult, the world of a daughter or son and the world of a parent, the world of Suffolk summers (nurturing memories of childhood) and the world of midwestern American winters (forcing attention to the obligations of the present moment). Karl Kroeber, you will remember, finally likened Wordsworth's relation to his valley to the manner in which "a child fits himself to, and makes fit his demands, the microcosmic environment of a garden, a farm, or a country place." This is very like the microcosmic environment of the game according to the rules of which a child plays and of the poem according to the conventions of which the poet writes. But how does it relate to a world of work and adult responsibilities and the contemporary fact that the place we find where, for a while, we can loaf and invite the soul, is almost certainly going to be some kind of temporary haven which, one way or another, is separated from the place in which we earn our living—the Wendell Berrys are certainly very rare—and which, once found, is all too likely to be lost?

Jeremy Hooker is, I think, the best British critic of literature seen in relationship to place. In his 1985 collection of essays, *The Poetry of Place*, he argues that "poetry of place after Wordsworth cannot be understood outside a context of loss"[30] and develops a paradigmatic history of post-Wordsworthian poetry by reading representative poems by Arnold, Clare, Hardy, Edward Thomas, and the tragic Ivor Gurney. Already with Matthew Arnold, Hooker finds Wordsworth's security in a shared humanity vanishing from poetry and his sense of an order embracing all mankind, along with a corresponding confidence in the spiritual and cultural centrality of poetic utterance, diminishing to an elegiac investiture of particular places "with the poet's spirit . . . [and] the localization of the poetic within an England whose dominant culture has no use for it. A resulting narrowing of focus, in poems as well as ideas of poetry, has transferred its voice from an order embracing man and nature to the hills."[31] When Arnold writes "I know these slopes; who knows them if not I," Hooker hears an expression of cultural isolation, of a culturally marginal role, more than he does an expression of a characteristic temperament. The effects of such isolation in Clare and Hardy make of place, Hooker feels, "a refuge or escape from an unmanageable or unlovable society or nation,"[32] while in Thomas and Gurney (and in Thomas's prose master, Richard Jeffries), he finds a melancholy fulfillment of these tendencies in work where the worship of nature becomes concentrated in a particular place to such an extent that, should the place be taken away, nothing will be left at all.[33]

If the poet in his place had been able to *work* and invite the soul rather than *loaf* and invite the soul (or, once utterly displaced, desperately remember), would Hooker's history look any different? Only Clare and Hardy, among comparatively recent poets, had a real and active, if "ambiguous and strained," relationship with their communities. That I respond somewhat defensively to the work of poets shown by Hooker to be cut off by their trade and their self-consciousness from the organic life of the place they love probably only means that my own experience of place is much like theirs. I arrived in Suffolk, after all, unconsciously *seeking* "a refuge or escape from an unmanageable or unlovable society or nation." And I didn't live there like a native of the place—whether a farmer, a craftsman, a doctor, or a teacher—but as a relative and friend of natives and a writer who, though he might experience and describe the place in fresh and unfamiliar ways, would never be fully integrated with its life unless he stayed there and worked there. I was more than a tourist, but less than a citizen of the place. And mightn't a poet consult more deeply the Genius of the Place in his poetry if he were constrained to consult it in every aspect of his daily life?[34]

By the time I came to write a review of Hooker's book, I was troubled and perplexed. It was 1984 and I had been commuting between the place in which I wrote in Suffolk and the place in which I worked at the University of Notre Dame for more than fifteen years. Moreover, the summer before I wrote the review I had sat at my desk within two hundred yards of the St. Joseph River in South Bend, Indiana, and written the most sustained and ambitious cycle of poems I had yet produced about East Anglia dealing in part with those three rivers in Suffolk which I loved so much, the Alde, the

Deben and the Stour. "Why not," I asked, "a poem about the St. Joseph?" The review began by trying to sort that question out.

> I think the reason is that while the St. Joseph is rich with associations that might stimulate another poet—La Salle came down this river, the Potawatomi lived nearby, the continental divide split it from the Kankakee and created a famous portage, Francis Parkman wrote about it, etc.—for me it is associated entirely with the kind of daily grind that prevents poetry from being written (or river banks from being explored). It is the river I cross in my car to go to work. Last summer was the first summer in years that I did not spend in East Anglia, that part of England where for more than a decade I have felt both welcome and free—free in the sense that Donald Hall has in mind when he speaks about emotions deriving from a "a place associated not with school or with conventional endeavor or with competition or with busyness," but a place "where we have loafed and invited the soul." I know and love the Suffolk rivers—have loafed and invited the soul on their banks—but have no feeling at all about the St. Joseph, even though I have lived beside it for most of the past fifteen years. On the banks of the St. Joseph I sought, I think, to summon back emotions I have felt on the banks of the Alde, the Deben, and the Stour. The writing, I suppose, expresses a kind of nostaligia, a compensation for loss. Loss of what? Well, of the place. A year ago we lost the house in Suffolk and it isn't clear when or if we'll be returning to East Anglia.[35]

It's interesting that in the poem I wrote, a poem exploring not only the rivers and river routes connecting locality with locality and time with time, but also the ancient paths or tracks dating back to the neolithic period known as ley lines, the chief human presences should have been Constable and Edward Thomas. I had no idea when I wrote the poem that the Constable painting I was dealing with was one of those worked up in London form the oil sketches made in East Bergholt between 1810–1811 which recalled, not a place in the Stour Valley where Constable still lived and worked, but the place he had lost by moving to London after his marriage and could only possess again through the emotional charge of his expressionistic later manner. As for Edward Thomas, his book on the Icknield Way, the chief ley line explored in the poem, was his *last* on the English countryside. I imagine him before his death in 1917.

Home, returned on leave, exhausted,
bored by prose he's published only months before
and talking with a friend who asks:
and what'll you be fighting for over there?

he picks a pinch of earth up off the path
they're walking and says: *This*
For this, he says,
This this this
For

this[36]

. . . as of course Edward Thomas *did* say before leaving to die in the war. During the Napoleonic wars, Constable painted and Wordsworth wrote poetry for much the same reason.

If my own place had been lost except in memory—one attempt to visit it found the house itself converted into a "Bed & Breakfast"—what was there to do? Making a virtue of necessity, and concerned about some of the questions I have just raised, I decided to stay in Indiana for a while and read a little history.[37] I thought I could *try* to feel "at home on the earth" even in South Bend. Moreover, as an act of will, although still believing firmly with David Jones that the poet must "work within the limits of his love," I began to write a long poem called "Facts from an Apocryphal Midwest," a section of which I intend to read to conclude this talk. I could only hope that an act of will might, in the curious processes of composition, become an act of love. At any rate, I began to grapple with some midwestern American geography, geology, prehistory, and history that parallel in many ways those with which I was working in the long East Anglian poem I had finished two years before. The chief trails this time—American ley lines, as it were—began as prehistoric paths down which Lake Superior copper was carried from the early days of the Mound Builders until the collapse of their particular economy and way of life. These trails, and especially the St. Joseph-Kankakee portage, were later used by the Potawatomi, the Miami, and other local Algonquian tribes, as well as by the Iroquois on their raids into the area, and by the French explorers, traders, and missionaries. Again, as in the East Anglian poem, three rivers figure in the topographical configuration that emerges: the St. Joseph (which the French called the River of Miamis), the Kankakee (also called the Seignelay), and the Illinois. The dominant historical figure in the poem is Réné-Robert Cavelier, Sieur de la

Salle. Ironically, once I had begun my research and composition, I found myself stimulated by exactly those things which I said in the review of Jeremy Hooker's book might stimulate "another poet"—La Salle's voyage through the Great Lakes and journey along the local rivers and trails; Algonquian (mostly Potawatomi) history and mythology; the geological and geographical transformations which occurred during the last glacial recession; and, most of all, the prose of Francis Parkman in the volume of *France and England in North America* called *La Salle and the Discovery of the Great West*. The entire poem is, in a way, a homage to Parkman.[38]

Never having walked a foot along the banks of the St. Joseph river, I now followed Parkman as Parkman—who must have trudged virtually through my back yard on his visit to the area in 1867—followed La Salle who followed his Indian guide along the portage trail to the Kankakee marsh. With respect to the self, the solution seemed to be this: that I, who had little feeling for the place I would evoke and engage, should embody myself in a figure who had great feeling for it, who in turn embodies himself in the figure who initially explored that place, contended against it, and had perforce to fit his mind to the external world to survive and the external world to his mind to prevail.

Now what about Parkman and Wordsworth? Aside from some fascinating biographical similarities—both courted in their early lives the "ministry of fear," both were cared for by their sisters, both expanded their domestic entourage to include yet other nurturing women, both grieved deeply for lost brothers who were sailors, and both were plagued by neurasthenic ailments brought on by writing (in Parkman's case, the victory of creative will over illness is nothing short of inspiring)—Wordsworth and Parkman are Romantic opposites. [39] We know that Wordsworth saw "little worthy or sublime / In what the Historian's pen so much delights / to blazon," but we should also know that this particular historian, according to his biographer, "could not abide Wordsworth and his followers." "He loved nature, " Charles Farnham tells us, "but not as a lover who sits down quietly for intimate communion."[40] He had a love, Farnham says, "of the real" and a nature which did not include "a poet's capacity for revery and contemplation." Moreover, he "deplored the modern tendency to discover objects of sympathy in vagabonds" and the like—vagrants, pedlars, shepherds, or leech gatherers—and was instead drawn to the heroic, even, indeed, the chivalric.[41] As capable as Wordsworth of sublime effects—of infusing a panoramic landscape with a light as remarkable as Turner's[42]—his sublime was anything but egotistical; he possessed, in fact, a high degree of Negative Capability and "seized with certainty the salient traits of men and women, courtiers and savages, priests and politicians, seigneurs and peasants, nuns and *coureurs de bois.*"[43] But if there is a Turner in him, there is no Constable, for he "cared not for highly humanized landscapes" and "the charms of rural England are not mentioned in his diaries."[44] Given the dual focus of his histories—the protagonists seen at first close-up and then dwarfed by the panoramic landscapes that envelop them—we need for visual analogues both paintings like West's *The Death of General Wolf* and Turner's *Hannibal Crossing the Alps*. In fact, we need a whole academy of painters that would include, along with West and Turner, such different artists as Joshua Reynolds, Thomas Cole, George Caleb Bingham, and, when we enter the Jesuit mind, El Greco.[45]

But I must soon read from the poem or I fear we'll never get there. Everyone who reads or reads about Francis Parkman understands the manner in which La Salle embodies both active characteristics of Parkman's personality and also, in La Salle's life of action, distorted versions of characteristics which would have found expression had not illness made an invalid of the author of *The Oregon Trail* and the journals which he kept of his early exploration of the Magalloway. There is something of Parkman in many of his major characters, but La Salle is an alter ego, a dark Byronic brother, a tragically flawed Coriolanus. He is one of the great characters in American literature, and one of the most troubling. Groping for comparisons, critics have mentioned Melville, Milton, and even Homer, as well as Scott, Byron, Cooper, and Shakespeare.[46] In a fascinating analysis of the psychology of composition, Howard Doughty quotes a letter to Martin Brimmer: "I conceived literary ambitions, and, at the same time, began to despise the literary life." And Doughty comments: "However inflexible he was on one level in pursuit of his chosen task, one senses a resistance to the 'calling' of authorship—to his role of artist and creator—which some subconscious mechanism of the psyche like illness was required to overcome. . . . At any rate there is something almost uncanny in the way his complex of maladies shaped his life to the best deployment of his powers."[47] This, then, is the man I follow who, in turn, follows La Salle across Lake Michigan, up the St. Joseph River, across the portage to the Kankakee, and to the Illinois within a few dozen miles of where we are this afternoon. My own language bleeds into Parkman's which in turn bleeds into La Salle's. The poem—the sixth section of *Facts From an Apocryphal Midwest*—is called "The Boat Maker's Tale."

He'd sent the Griffin on back to Niagara
loaded with the furs he thought
would pay his debts . . .
                Colbert walked in shadows

at Versailles, the river to be named for him
named otherwise by Onangizes, called
himself, like Colbert's king, the shimmering sun.

Frontenac, Onnontio to Green Bay's Ouilamette
and all the rest of Gigos clan,
dreamed a map of colonies and little forts

stretching from above St. Joseph on the lake
down the river of Miamis
to the marshy waters of that languid

tributary to be named one day for Seignelay
whose own necrology of ships
made him Minister among the idle admirals

in the shipyards and the ports of France.
Stretching farther still . . .
Stretching well beyond that river to the one

that only Joliet and Père Marquette
among the French had ever seen & named & spoken of
saying that *no land at all no*

country would be better suited to produce
whatever fruits or wheat or corn
than that along this river that the wild cattle

never flee that one finds some 400 in a herd
that elk & deer are almost every
where and turkeys promenade on every side. . . .

From the day a man first settled here
that man
could start to plow . . .
                But Cavelier, La Salle,

had sent the Griffin on back to Niagara.
He'd build a second ship
to sail down the rivers he would find. . . .

For he himself had said in Paris, sounding
just like Père Marquette, *it's all*
so beautiful and fertile, free from forests

full of meadows brooks and rivers all
abounding there in fish & game
where flocks and herds can even be left out

all winter long. All winter long!
And it was nearly winter now in Michillimackinak.
The King had said to him *We have received*

with favor a petition in your name and do
permit your exploration
by these presents signed with our own hand

but now he was in debt. Migeon, Charon—
they'd seized the beaver pelts
and even skins of skunks—Giton, Pelonquin!

Names of enemies. But there was Henri Tonty here;
there was, indeed, Count Frontenac.
These he'd name against the plotting creditors.

The Ship will fly above the crows, he'd said,
his patron governor's heraldic mast-
head besting Jesuits in a Niagaran dream of power.

He had his Récollets to do whatever of God's work
there was. Hennepin, who strapped
an altar on his back and cured the fainting

Father Gabriel with a confection of hyacinths!
And Gabriel himself; and Zénobe.
They'd sung *Te Deum* well enough upon the launching.

He'd have them sing a good deal more than that—
Exaudiat, Ludovicus Magnus!—
once they'd reached the Colbert's mouth, the sea.

The ship *had* nearly flown across the lakes.
In spite of an ungodly pilot
and in spite of god knows dreadful storms

she'd been the equal of the Erie and the Huron.
How she'd sailed out beyond Niagara!
Her canvas billowed & she fired her five small guns

to the astonishment of Iroquois along the banks.
Then a freshening northwest wind.
Down the lake and to Detroit's narrow straights

she sailed until she met a current there strong
as the bore before the lower Seine—
and twelve men leapt ashore to pull her over, through.

They marvelled at the prairies to the east & west
and stopped to hunt, and hung their
guyropes full of fowl and drying bearskins.

From wild grapes the priests prepared communion wine.
Then they were in Huron where the gale
attacked them and they brought down mainyards, tacked

with trysail, then lay long to the till.
The pilot blasphemed damnably while all the rest
cried out to Anthony of Padua

who calmed the winds and brought the ship to port
at Michillimackinak beside
the mission of St. Ignace, Père Marquette's fresh grave.

That was in the early autumn when the Ottawa
and Huron fishing fleets
were strung across the lakes from Saint Marie du Sault

to Keweenwa, from Mackinac to Onangizes' islands
in Green Bay. He'd worn his scarlet coat
with its gold lace and flown the banner of the king

while all his men fired muskets & he stepped ashore.
That was autumn, when the sun
still burned their necks & missionaries harvested.

But it was nearly winter now and he would be he said
in Illinois country when the rivers froze.
Heavy clouds blew in from Canada on northern winds.

The ship had sailed away. And so they
set forth on the lake in four canoes: fourteen men
who bore with them a forge & carpenters' &

sawyers' tools to build the Griffin's twin
beside a fort they'd also build on high ground near
the navigable lower Illinois.

They cried out to each other in the dark.
For it was dark before they were across the lake.
It stormed again as when the Griffin

rocked and shook on Huron, waves against the fragile
birchbark, rain in their red eyes.
Anvil and bellows, iron for nails and bolts,

pit-saws, arms, and merchandise for gifts
and trade when they had reached the Illinois town below
the portage weighed them down.

Gunsmith, blacksmith, joiner, mason, master-
builder Moyse Hillère—
they paddled for the further shore with Cavelier

and three priests and the guide. Half of them
were cousins to *coureurs de bois*
and would desert. Two of them were felons.

All of them washed up together with the breaking
waves beside
the mouth of the Miamis

                    and gorged on grapes, and wild haws, &
on the carcass of a deer that had been killed by wolves.

Here they stayed for twenty days, and built a tiny fort, and
spiked the hill they built it on. They took nine sondings
of the river's mouth, marking out the passage that a ship
might take with buoys and bearskin flags. The first brief
snow blew in across the lake well before December and
ice began to form along the river's edge. Occasionally, La
Salle's Mohegan guide could find a deer to kill, or bear,
and brought them meat; but food was scarce and all of them
began to urge La Salle to press on to the portage and to
Illinois or Miami camps where they might find, in covered
pits, a gleaming hoard of winter's corn. When Tonty finally came with men who had been sent ahead from Fort
Niagara but had scattered in the woods, the party numbered thirty-four. Four were left behind with messages
and maps for those who would arrive to reinforce them
when the Griffin sailed back past Michillimackinak and
down Lake Michigan & anchored here. If the Griffin
wasn't lost. If the furs to pay off creditors had not been

stolen by the pilot and his men. If all of them had not sailed straight to join the outlaw trader Dan Du Lhut at Kamalastigouia up in Thunder Bay.

Nous embarquâmes, wrote Hennepin, *le troisième Decembre. Avec trente hommes . . . Dans huit canots.* They were John Boisrondet, L'Espérance de la Brie, La Rousselière, La Violete, Picard du Gay, Etienne Renault, Michel Baribault, Bois d'Ardeene, Martin Chartier, Noel le Blanc, the nailer called La Forge, the Indian guide they called Oui-Oui-La-Meche, and those with names now known to all or names now known to none. They took up paddles once again, prepared to travel on, to shoulder their canoes along the portage trail if they could find it. Had it been spring, had it been high summer, the fields and woods that lined the river's channel would have blossomed for them, fruited like the prairies on the east and west of the Detroit straights when they pulled the Griffin through to Huron and the priests made wine. And when at last they reached the portage, they would have seen tall cedars, oaks, and water-elms; in a ravine declining from high ground they would have seen along the curving trail splashes of the reds and blues of wild forest flowers; flocks of plovers, snipe, might have flown above the trees to land beside the standing cranes in fields of wild rice in fens the far side of the of the watershed across the prairie with its elk and deer and buffalo which traders would begin to call one day the Parc aux Vaches. But it was winter; they saw none of this. They saw the skulls and bones of animals, a bleak gray plain; they lugged their eight canoes and forge and iron and anvil up the hill and then along the portage path behind La Salle who brooded on the Griffin in the melancholy, willful, isolated silence of his mind . . . La Salle whose men, with five exceptions, would forsake his vision and his surrogate at Fort Crevecoeur—39 degrees and 50 minutes latitude exactly on his fine Parisian astrolabe—and daub in tar-black letters on the planking of the half-built river boat: *Nous Sommes Tous Sauvages.*

The man who followed him in many ways was like him, and read his words, and read the words and followed all the trails of others who had passed this way before he did himself, but after him who was the first to come and was the object of his search. Charlevoix he read, and La Hontan. Tonty's own account, and Hennepin's, and all of La Salle's letters both to Canada and France. Transcripts, depositions. He, too, knew about insatiable ambition, pride and isolation, subduing all to an inflexibility of purpose. When his chronic and mysterious illness made his head swim and his joints swell, made his eyes so sensitve to light he could not read, his nights so sleepless that he could not even dream his shattered double's thousand-mile trek from the lower Illinois back to Montreal, he had his friends read *to* him, tried to comprehend their strange pronunciations of the language of the texts and maps and manuscripts de la France Septentrionale which he followed to the Kankakee or Seignelay and then beyond. . . .

Terres tremblantes, sur lesquelles on peut à peine marcher he read, and wrote how "soon they reached a spot where oozy saturated soil quaked beneath their tread. All around were clumps of alder bushes . . . pools of glistening water *une espèce de mare* and, in the midst, a dark and lazy current, which a tall man might bestride . . . twisting like a snake among the reeds and rushes and . . . *il a faut continuellement tourner* . . . They set canoes upon this thread of water and embarked their baggage and themselves and pushed on down the sluggish streamlet looking at a little distance like men who sail on land. . . . Fed by an increasing tribute of the spongy soil it widened to a river *presque aussi large que la Marne,* and they floated on their way into a voiceless, lifeless solitude of boundless marshes overgrown with reeds . . . At night they built their fire on ground made firm by frost *quelques mottes de terres glaćees* . . . and bivouacked among rushes . . ."[48]

A lecture given at the Chicago
Historical Society, Spring 1988.

Part II

৵

Others

Poetry of Place: From the
Kentucky River to the Solent Shore

Wendell Berry, *Standing by Words*, North Point Press; Wendell
Berry, *The Wheel*, North Point Press; Jeremy Hooker, *The Poetry of
Place: Essays*, Carcanet Press; Jeremy Hooker, *A View from the Source:
Selcted Poems*, Carcanet Press; Geoffrey Grigson, ed., *The Faber Book
of Poems and Places*, Faber and Faber; D. Clinton, Tom Montag and
C. W. Truesdale, eds., *An Americas Anthology: A Geopoetics Landmark*;
Ken Smith, *The Poet Reclining*, Bloodaxe Books; Gary Snyder, *Axe
Handles*, North Point Press.

I

Place can be a paradoxical business in poetry. All last summer,
for example, I sat at my desk within two hundred yards of the St.
Joseph River in South Bend, Indiana, and wrote a cycle of poems
about three rivers in Suffolk, England—the Alde, the Deben, and
the Orwell. Why not about the St. Joseph? I think the reason is that
while the St. Joseph is rich with associations that might stimulate
another poet—La Salle came down this river, the Potawatomi lived
nearby, the continental divide split it from the Kankakee and created
a famous portage, Francis Parkman wrote about it, etc.—for me it is
associated entirely with the kind of daily grind that prevents poetry
from being written (or river banks from being explored). It is the
river I cross in my car to go to work. Last summer was the first
summer in years that I did not spend in East Anglia, the part of
England where my wife was born and where my family and I, for
more than a decade, have felt both welcome and free—free in the

sense that Donald Hall has in mind when he speaks in *Goatfoot Milktongue Twinbird* about emotions deriving fom "a place associated not with school or with conventional endeavor or with competition or with busyness" but a place "where we have loafed and invited the soul." I know and love the Suffolk rivers—have loafed and invited the soul on their banks—but I have no feeling at all about the St. Joseph, even though I have lived beside it for most of the past fifteen years. On the banks of the St. Joseph I sought, I think, to summon back emotions I have felt on the banks of the Alde, the Deben, and the Orwell. The writing, I suppose, expresses a kind of nostalgia, a compensation for loss. Loss of what? Well, of the place. A year ago we lost the house in Suffolk and it isn't clear when or if we'll be returning to East Anglia. In this context, it is interesting to read the opening remarks in Jeremy Hooker's essay in *The Poetry of Place* on Geoffrey Grigson's anthology, *Poems and Places*, where he argues that "poetry of place after Wordsworth cannot be understood outside a context of loss." But Hooker has in mind something beyond the loss of place—in fact he has in mind the loss of something for which place itself becomes, in a new way, a kind of compensation. The loss, he feels, "is comprehensive, of shared belief in an ideal of order, mainly Christian in derivation, but shaped by local cultural conditions, which include a sense of nationhood, the Church, the English language," and the notion that poetry is "a central human activity, concerned with essential human experience." The intriguing claim, especially in the light of Berry's argument in *Standing by Words*, is that "as the poet's grasp on a common human world has loosened so he has sought to replace it with special relationships, with place in particular, and has come to stress the specialness of other poets, above all in their relation to place. This is both part of the movement by which the English poet has become a specialist talking to specialists, and an effort of one radically displaced within the national culture to place himself."

If Hooker restricts his diagnosis chiefly to English poets, we may rapidly extend the discussion to American poets by turning to Berry. In his longest essay, the one hundred pages of "Poetry and Place," he considers contemporary American writing in a context shaped by the work of major figures in Grigson's anthology, some of whom are also central to Hooker: Shakespeare, Jonson, Milton, Dryden, Pope, Wordsworth, and Hardy. But Berry's argument is very different from Hooker's. It is precisely, he feels, through a profound rootedness in place that the poet is likely to regain that "grasp on a common human world," avoid becoming a specialist talking to specialists, avoid the temptation of making autonomous or reflexive works, and understand that poetry can still be "a central human activity, concerned with essential human experience." History, for Berry, has not forever determined the loss of Hooker's "comprehensive, shared belief in an idea of order" because the order in question is real and present, is an order which, though we have insisted on ignoring or abusing it, must finally determine the proper place of poems and their makers, not only on the banks of Berry's Kentucky River or under Hooker's Mynydd Bach in Wales, but in the scheme of things. In his notes on "unspecializing poetry," Berry writes:

> I am endlessly in need of the work of poets who have been concerned with living in place, the life of a place, long-term attention and devotion to a settled home and its natural household, and hence to the relation between imagination and language and a place . . . To stay at home is paradoxically to change, to move. When poets—and people of any other calling—stay at home the first thing they move away from is professionalism. They move away from "professional standards." Their work begins to develop under pressure of questions not primarily literary: What good is it? Is it at home here? What do the neighbors think of it? Do they read it, any of them? What have they contributed to it? What does it owe to them . . . ? Nothing exists for its own sake, but for a harmony greater than itself, which includes it. A work of art, which accepts this condition, and exists upon its terms, honors the Creation, and so becomes a part of it.

Berry's long essay on place begins by citing four positive examples among his contemporaries—John Haines, Hayden Carruth, Donald Hall, and Gary Snyder (to whom the book is also dedicated)—who have written a poetry "formed in response to a place" which "raises frankly . . . the question of the status of poetry as a reference or response to a subject or a context outside itself, " along with a single negative example, mistakenly chosen I think, of "the poetic principle of 'autonomy' or 'art for art's sake.' " The negative example is Auden's elegy "In Memory of W. B. Yeats," the conclusion of which—"In the prison of his days / Teach the free man how to praise"—states the gist of Berry's Miltonic perspective on the poet's place not only in Ireland or England or New York or Kentucky, but in relationship to the central paradox of the human condition. For this indeed becomes part of what Berry means to suggest by the poet's place. Both in the course of his long essay and elsewhere in *Standing by Words*, Berry affirms the present relevance of the old notion of a Great Chain of Being, and of the poet's responsibility with respect to man's place on that chain. He affirms the values of propriety, temperance, decorum, just or natural hierarchies, ecological intelligence, and understanding "that one lives within an order of dependence and obligaton superior to oneself." Motivated by love—not by fame or ambition or pride—the poet should strive to make his language true to his subject while understanding that his subject will be superior to his own powers, occasion, and purpose. He must not degrade subject to "subject matter" in the same way "industrial specialists see trees or ore-bearing rocks as raw material to be subjected to their manufactured end-products." For some of the same reasons that Pope is Berry's man rather than Wordsworth, he ought to prefer Auden to Yeats (though he does not). For certainly Edward Mendelson is right (in *Early Auden*) to say that "the spirits who dictated Yeats's system bade him translate the crude contingencies of the common world into visionary patterns of cyclic history . . . [where] content is ruled by pattern, and the romantic heritage of autonomy is preserved." It is the later Auden, not W. B. Yeats, who can be accurately seen as the anti-Romantic, anti-Modernist didactic maker whose allegiance is to truth and subject and man's proper place in the scheme of things rather than to art or "manufactured end-products," singing golden birds. Auden would have been the first to agree with one of Berry's notes on unspecializing poetry: "If we don't know what poetry is inferior to, we don't know what it is superior to." But then Auden, as Jeremy Hooker makes clear, came to be conscious of a conflict between his early and virtually autistic attraction to the maternal Pennine limestone of the northern uplands and his growing "awareness of human responsibility" and therefore never became, in his mature work, a poet of place in Berry's primary sense—a poet of nature and agrarian domestic economy—or in the manner of Auden's own early masters, Hardy and Edward Thomas. To write effectively of man's responsible place in the nature of things, Auden had to divest himself of a special place in the things of nature. He felt he could unspecialize poetry more effectively in New York City than he could down on the farm. Or, in his case, up on the moors.

If Auden is an unrepresentative case, Hooker's paradigmatic history of post-Wordsworthian poetry of place can be seen in the work of Arnold, Clare, Hardy, Edward Thomas, and the tragic Ivor Gurney. The work of these poets, however, offers little to Berry's essentially hopeful and optimistic program. Already with Matthew Arnold, Hooker finds Wordsworth's security in a shared humanity vanishing from poetry and his sense of an order embracing all mankind, along with a corresponding confidence in the spiritual and cultural centrality of poetic utterance, diminishing to an elegiac investiture of particular places "with the poet's spirit . . . [and] the localization of the poetic within an England whose dominant culture has no use for it. A resulting narrowing of focus, in poems as well as ideas of poetry, has transferred its voice from an order embracing man and nature to the hills." When Arnold writes "I know these slopes; who knows them if not I?" Hooker hears an expression of cultural isolation, of a culturally marginal role, more than he does an expression of a characteristic temperament. The effects of such isolation in Clare and Hardy make of place, Hooker feels, "a refuge or escape from an unmanageable or unlovable society or nation," while in Edward Thomas and Ivor Gurney (and in Thomas' prose master, Richard Jeffries), he finds a melancholy fulfillment of these tendencies in work where the worship of nature becomes concentrated in a particular place to such an extent that, should the place be taken away, nothing will be left at all. The Whitmanesque freedom alluded to earlier which is celebrated by Donald Hall—the freedom to "loaf and invite the soul"—becomes, in Hooker's phrase, a kind of "spirtual parasitism." Wordsworth, he reiterates, "was grounded in an order, sacred and communal, whereas Gurney had nothing but place, which was absolutely his partner and his guide." Geoffrey Grigson notes in his anthology that Gurney's "The High Hills" was "written from his asylum."

> The high hills have a bitterness
> Now they are not known,
> And memory is poor enough consolation
> For the soul hopeless gone.
> Up in the air there beech tangles widely in the wind—
> That I can imagine.
> But the speed, the swiftness, walking into clarity,
> Like last year's briony, are gone.

If the poet in his place had been able to *work* and invite the soul rather than *loaf* and invite the soul (or, once utterly displaced, desperately remember), would Hooker's history look any different? Only Clare and Hardy, among comparatively recent poets anthologized by Grigson, had a real and active, if "ambiguous and strained," relationship with their communities. That I respond so readily to the work of poets shown by Hooker to be cut off by their trade and their self-consciousness from the organic life of the place they love probably only means that my own experience of place is much like theirs. Hooker describes an "egress of emotion, a bleeding away of energy, that offers in return only a fugitive—and sometimes shattering—ecstasy." One finds such fleeting epiphanies in Thomas, Gurney, the earliest Auden, and, indeed, in some of Hooker's poems set in Wales. Wendell Berry's poems have little of this ecstasy; they express a quality of emotion associated with work and rootedness rather than epiphany and sudden vision. Perhaps it is because of this that his reading of the poetry of place is ultimately hopeful and forward looking.

Writing appreciatively of the exemplary characters in Spenser's *Fairie Queen*, Berry amusingly concludes that although Spenser offers sound moral instruction and a deep commitment to the larger schemes of order, his people "are all living in Fairie Land and most of them do not have regular jobs." *The Fairie Queen*, along with most of English poetry, strikes him as "short on domestic economy." It is for this reason that he so admires Pope. Rejecting Robert Bly's contention that Pope is representative of the eighteenth century's "disdaining of nature," Berry applauds in Pope's "Essay on Man," Epistles, and certain other poems what is perhaps the last full articulation by a major poet of the notion of a Great Chain of Being. He notes that Pope understands "as clearly as any ecologist" the nature of a hierarchy which describes "a necessary kinship among all the creatures it joins," and he hears in at least one passage "the tone of a most fervent conservationist." Moreover, in "Epistle to Burlington," he finds exactly what is missing in such earlier poems of place as Jonson's "To Penshurst" and Marvell's "Upon Appleton House," something, that is, resembling *The Georgics* and *Works and Days*, which gives us a notion of how country life actually works and ought to work, something more than just the look and feel of it. Left with the look and feel of country life alone, we have the increasingly displaced and alienated poetic history discussed by Hooker. Or, perhaps, something worse. It comes as a surprise in Berry's book to find Wordsworth treated chiefly as the "ancestor of what is worst in Shelley, and in us"; as the heir of Milton's Satan determined to make "the mind its own place," to make, as he says at the end of "The Recluse," the breeding ground of fear and awe "our minds . . . the Mind of Man / My Haunt and the main region of my song." Although Berry acknowledges the existence of "a sweeter, sounder, and

more modest Wordsworth [who] turned his mind toward the shepherds, farmers and other working country people whom he knew,"
Berry's Wordsworth is a far cry from Hooker's, and he clearly finds
the Genius of the Place consulted more earnestly by Pope in his
Twickenham garden than by Wordsworth in his solitary wanderings.

A poet is perhaps more likely to consult the Genius of the
Place in his poetry if he is constrained to consult it in at least certain
aspects of his daily life. "Human work done in a place," Berry
writes, "must not affront its Genius, either as guardian spirit or as
the mostly invisible order or whole to which the place belongs, or
both." He elaborates like this:

> If the Genius of the Place is not offended, it will help; it "Paints
> as you plant, and as you work, designs." Gardening is neither
> wholly natural, nor wholly artificial, but both; it is a collabora-
> tion between the gardener and nature. Pope, I think, is allud-
> ing to the principle, commonly understood by good farmers and
> gardeners, that nature *responds* to good treatment. The gardener
> must never forget nature because nature, as much as human
> intention, indicates what must be done—that is, "designs."

I don't know how much should be made of Pope's gardening—
Berry makes quite a lot of it—but certainly something needs to be
made of Berry's farming, for example, and of Gary Snyder's day-
to-day homesteading in the Sierra Nevada foothills. Snyder and
Pope, Berry feels, in fact ask the same practical questions: "How do
we fit in? What is the possibility of a harmony within nature? These
are questions of propriety, and, between Pope and Gary Snyder, I
think that they were not much asked." Because Berry asks these
questions constantly, it follows that he also asks them about poetry:
How does *that* fit in? What is the possibility of its reflecting a human
harmony within a particular place? He begins his long essay by asking if the connection he once saw and wrote about between his
work on the Kentucky hill farm where he lives and his work as a
poet has anything to it. What he wrote was that "the place has become the form of my work, its discipline, in the same way the sonnet has been the form and discipline of the work of other poets: if it
doesn't fit it's not true." Gary Snyder said something very similar
about his work and poetry as early as 1959: "I've . . . come to realize
that the rhythms of my poems follow the rhythm of the physical
work I'm doing and the life I'm leading at any given time—which
makes the music in my head which creates the line." At the end of

his essay, Berry concludes that, in its essentials, his initial observation was sound. The farm is not, of course, a literary form, "but it is *like* a literary form, and it cannot properly be ignored or its influence safely excluded by any literary form that is made within it. Like any other form, it requires us to do some things, and forbids us to do others. Some acts are fitting and becoming, and some acts are not. If we fail to do what is required and if we do what is forbidden, we exclude ourselves from the mercy of Nature; we destroy our place, or we are exiled from it."

Berry and Snyder have each had the skill or the luck to establish an unusually integrated relationship with a place and a community. Their examples serve to show us not, I should say, that Hooker's general history is inaccurate or can easily be reversed, but rather that their own works and days are available as models of a possible, if not probable, human and poetic devolution. When Hooker writes that Edward Thomas and Richard Jeffries "find in their own work little normality, such as that found in the fellowship of a common labour, in which to recover bodily, mentally and emotionally their expenditure of energy," we understand clearly why the sometimes virtually neurasthenic emotional charge of their writing is such as it is. Berry and Snyder share "the fellowhip of common labour" in their communities. As a result, there is little of Hooker's "spiritual parasitism" about their work. Instead one finds the "symbiotic relationship," rare indeed at this date, "between the man who works the earth and the earth that works upon him" that Hooker assumes to have passed, for practicing poets certainly, into history.

To those of us who have found it difficult to integrate our writing with the place in which we live our daily lives, Berry's advice will clearly be: *Try harder; stay at home; find a way; change your life.* If my writing, I can hear him telling me, fails to name my local river until its pollution makes me ill or its waters flood my house, already, although I'll doubtless name it then, it may be far too late for the poetry or the place. And I hear him asking: *Does* my imagination—as I think it does—reside in an actual Suffolk over the sea, or only, like the characters in Spenser, in some Fairie Land? These are questions that are brought home—home!—very forcefully by reading Berry, Hooker, and the poems in Grigson's anthology. But I am also reminded of a proposition in Raymond Williams' book, *The Country and the City,* which occurs in the course of his remarks on Oliver Goldsmith. In "The Deserted Village," according to Williams, Goldsmith finds "the social forces which are dispossessing the village . . . simultaneously dispossessing poetry." This connection involves what Williams calls a "negative identification," the notion that "the exposure and suffering of the writer, in his own social situation, are identified with the facts of a social history that is beyond him . . . To be a poet . . . is to be a pastoral poet: the social condition of poetry . . . is the idealized pastoral economy. The destruction of one is, or is made to stand for, the destruction of the other." It would follow that the restitution of the one would be seen as, or would be made to stand for, the restitution of the other. Although Grigson does not, in fact, include "The Deserted Village" in his anthology, there is a good deal of the "negative identification" which Williams describes in a number of poems he does include, and there is a touch of it in Hooker and Berry. "The present is accurately and powerfully seen," says Williams, "but its real relations, to past and future, are inaccessible, because the governing development is that of the writer himself: a feeling about the past, an idea about the future, into which, by what is truly an intersection, an observed present is arranged." Berry's identification of his farm with the form of his writing, and of a certain kind of life and living with the poetics of a despecialized poetry, is in some respects not far from Goldsmith's identification of "Sweet Auburn" with, as Williams says, "a kind of community, a kind of feeling, and a kind of verse." Actually, this might well serve to remind us that "place" in poetry can be urban as well rural, and that W. H. Auden's "way of rooting himself in the modern rootless experience was," as Hooker clearly sees, "not an escape, but courageous, intellectually honest, and true to the love he consistently invoked."

II

I must now begin to make this sound more than it has so far like a proper review of the prose and poetry in hand. I have said enough, I think, about *Standing by Words* and *The Poetry of Place* to suggest something of their exceptional interest and importance, but I haven't given any sense of their structure or occasion. Hooker's book is the more miscellaneous, and consists of twenty essays written between 1970 and 1981 which range from autobiographical meditations to reviews of books like Seamus Heaney's *North*, Philip Pacey's *Charged Landscapes*, and John Riley's *Collected Works*, to fuller and more scholarly treatments of David Jones, Edward Thomas, Ivor

Gurney, and W. H. Auden. I will return shortly to the autobiographical pieces when I discuss Hooker's *A View From the Source*. With
respect to the criticism, Anne Stevenson was certainly correct when
she wrote in *TLS* that *The Poetry of Place* "presents us with an entirely fresh picture of twentieth-century writing. Hooker cuts the
cake of modernism, so to speak, as it has never been cut before."
Berry's *Standing by Words* consists of six essays written during ap-
proximately the same period as those in Hooker's book and more or
less coincident with the poems appearing in his own most recent
volume of poetry, *The Wheel*. "Poetry and Place" occupies fully half
of the volume, while among the shorter pieces the title essay and
the notes on unspecializing poetry are particularly challenging and
suggestive. Like most of the new North Point books, *Standing by
Words* is a pleasure to hold and to read. Masa Snyder, Gary Snyder's
wife, has done the calligraphy for the striking and appropriately
austere jacket—the Chinese character which so delighted Ezra
Pound, the written form of *xin*, where, as the blurb points out, one
sees a man standing beside the sign for *word*.

Geoffrey Grigson's *Faber Book of Poems & Places* is also a hand-
some volume, its jacket richly illuminated by a good reproduction of
John Sell Cotman's numinous "Study of Trees, Harrow," now in the
University of Manchester's Whitworth Art Gallery. The anthology is
orgainzed by region rather than, say, by historical period or by
grouping together all of the poems chosen from the work of each
poet included. This means that poems by Wordsworth, for example,
appear scattered throughout the volume—the poet on Salisbury
Plain, in London, residing at Cambridge, climbing Snowdon, on
Windermere, and so on—while poets who traveled less, such as
Hardy, appear in a single section. Beginning with such desirable
chestnuts as John of Gaunt's speech and Fletcher's "The Halcyon's
Nest," the anthology then moves from the South—Shakespeare's
Edgar on Samphire Cliff nicely juxtaposed with Arnold's "Dover
Beach" and Jonson's "To Penshurst"—on to the South West, Oxford and the Midlands, London, Cambridge and the Eastern Counties, Wales and the Marches, the Lakes and the North, and so to
Scotland and Ireland. The surprise of the volume—and also a particular pleasure—is that there are two further sections following
Scotland and Ireland. Grigson has also included poems written in or
about France and Italy because he feels that the emotions of British
poets have "flowed with most willingness and familiarity" to those
places across the Channel. (He asks, importantly I think, "But how
will it be later?" He might even have asked: "But how is it now?")

Having decided to include the English poems set in France and Italy, he goes on to include also a few French poems—Hugo's poems written in Lincolnshire and Bournemouth and London, along with work by Valery Larbaud, du Bellay, Ronsard, Heredia, Corbière, Claudel, and Apollinaire. Grigson eschews translation, including only one brief poem from the Irish and enough of a translation from *Sir Gawain and the Green Knight* to conjecturally locate Ludchurch in Staffordshire "as the place which the poet thought of for the site of the Green Chapel." Much to Jeremy Hooker's disappointment, no poems appear in Welsh or translated from the Welsh. Much to my own disappointment, there are only two poems by Americans—John Crowe Ransom's "Philomela" and Eliot's "Rannoch, by Glen Coe," both, I think, strange choices. Nor are there any poems written by British poets in or about America—which is where, rather than across the Channel, it seems to me the emotions of British poets have begun to flow, if not necessarily with the most willingness and familiarity, then probably nonetheless with the greatest significance, since about 1945. But *Poems and Places* is largely retrospective in its ambitions, and there are comparatively few modern, let alone contemporary, poets included. Even from Grigson's own generation there are only, along with four of his own poems, selections from MacNeice, Betjeman, and Campbell; from the next two poetic generations, he includes only Dylan Thomas's "Fern Hill" and Larkin's "Next, Please." This is a pity chiefly because of the great interest of much recent poetry responding to place. Hooker cites in his review the absence of Bunting, David Jones, Hill, Roy Fisher, Tony Harrison, Tomlinson, Davie, R. S. Thomas, Silkin, and Sisson. Leaving aside the Americans, one immediately also misses Auden, MacDiarmid, Graham, Prynne, Montague, Heaney, Mahon, Hughes, Hamburger, Ken Smith, and Hooker himself. And, if we are to have Eliot and Ransom, what about Ezra Pound's Kensington, Ed Dorn's Oxford, Zukofsky's Stratford, Richard Hugo's Skye, Lowell's late poems written from Milgate in Kent, and Ronald Johnson's remarkable *Book of the Green Man?* But already I am talking about another volume altogether, some hypothetical book of *modern* poems and places.

I think I can give a sense of the individual sections of Grigson's anthology by turning to the region of which I know something—Cambridge and the Eastern Counties. The thirty pages given over to this part of England begin with Wordsworth's "Residence in Cambridge" from *The Prelude* and continue via Tennyson's return to Hallam's rooms at Trinity from *In Memoriam,* Rupert Brook's silly cream puff on the Old Vicarage in Grantchester, John Clare on the Fens,

John Dyer on the Bedford Level, and some anonymous quatrains on
the Walsingham Priory in Norfolk before we reach a solid center
consisting of excerpts from George Crabbe's Suffolk poems, including forty of the best lines from *Peter Grimes*. The section concludes
with Swinburne on the North Sea coast and Dunwich, followed by
Jonson, Drayton, Jean Ingelow, Paul Verlaine, and Tennyson on Lincolnshire. The Tennyson pieces include the poet's farewell to the
parsonage at Somersby and the section from *In Memoriam* in which,
as Grigson reminds us in his note, Tennyson mourns his friend Hallam "whose body was coming home [to Lincolnshire] by sea from
Trieste." Although this elegiac conclusion to the section is fitting
enough, it would nonetheless have been interesting had the region's
poetry been brought up to date with something from Donald Davie's *Essex Poems* and Michael Hamburger's *In Suffolk,* along with Peter
Porter's poem on Blythburgh Church or one of Jeremy Prynne's geological meditations, or perhaps a poem on contemporary Cambridge
by Clive Wilmer or Richard Burns. Although one might want to
modify this section of the book in certain ways, what is certainly *not*
in doubt is the justice of George Crabbe's place at the center of it.

Crabbe was the complete native, utterly in place in his region,
totally rooted as person and as poet, writing the kind of poems that
Jeremy Hooker wishes he had found in the following section of
Grigson's anthology representing Wales—poems which "arrest
the . . . literary tourist and show him where he is." And Crabbe was
also "in place" in Berry's more philosophical sense. As doctor and
priest, as husband and father, his life was integrated with his community to an unusual degree; he "buried himself completely in the
obscurity of domestic and village life," his son tells us,"publishing
nothing for twenty-two years." His study of botany, an activity that
should be taken at least as seriously as Pope's gardening, issued in a
book which scholars assure us would have been significant had it
ever been published. This activity too, like his later study of geology,
rooted him firmly in his region. Here indeed we have a poet who
would "*work* and invite the soul." On the other hand, there was also
a Wordsworthian wanderer in Crabbe. Where Swinburne in "Suffolk: by the North Sea" sees "miles, and miles, and miles of desolation! / Leagues on leagues on leagues without a change!"Crabbe,
though he can see the desolation a good deal more clearly than does
Swinburne, nonetheless loved "to walk where none had walked before, / About the rocks that ran along the shore; / Or far beyond the
sight of men to stray, / And take my pleasure when I lost my way."
While Raymond Williams sees the "stretch of unproductive, weed-

ridden soil inland from Aldeburgh" as the "first general evidence"
in Crabbe's counter-pastoral, C. Day Lewis, in his Penguin selection,
asks us to appreciate a style in Crabbe's highly regular couplets
"not unlike the East Anglian countryside, where we have to look for
subtle variations of an apparently monotonous surface." Stressing
Crabbe's decorum of diction, contrasting his asperity with Pope's
wit, his frequently sardonic view of human nature with Pope's satire, Day Lewis justly observes that Crabbe's real originality was in
his subject. "Novel, highly unorthodox subjects, treated in an exceptionally sober and conservative idiom—this was surely what gave
The Village its resounding success." In many ways Wendell Berry
ought to prefer Crabbe to Pope, for the subordination of the poem to
its occasion, of style to subject, is complete and rigorous in Crabbe,
whereas it seldom is in Pope, whose subjects now and then are only
"subject matter" and whose style is sometimes on exhibit only for
the style's elegant (and even self-sufficient) sake. Raymond Williams
finds Pope, like Jonson and Marvell, still "the poet-guest of his
landed patrons," recommending "prudent productive investment
tempered by reasonable charity" in the Epistles to Bathurst and Burlington. Like that other modern Williams who resembles him in
some respects, William Carlos, Crabbe in Suffolk—leaving aside his
years as chaplain to the Duke of Rutland—is no one's guest, but
someone who as native and doctor and priest can "arrest the literary tourist and show him where he is." Through the eyes of a Peter
Grimes, from the point of view of a "low life" character, the sort
usually treated only for comic possibilities up to Crabbe's own time,
he can see and show us the River Alde as only the native perceives
it and as it runs even now beside the Maltings Opera House in
Snape where audiences for Britten and Holst and Tippett—musical
if not literary tourists—lounge beside the Hepworth sculpture or the
Henry Moore.

> Thus by himself compell'd to live each day,
> To wait for certain hours the tide's delay;
> At the same times the same dull views to see,
> The bounding marsh-bank and the blighted tree;
> The water only when the tides were high;
> When low, the mud half-cover'd and half-dry;
> The sun-burnt tar that blisters on the planks,
> And bank-side stakes in their uneven ranks;
> Heaps of entangled weeds that slowly float,
> As the tide rolls by the impeded boat.

Nothing very much like this passage appears in Grigson's section on Wales and the Marches. Instead, as Jeremy Hooker complains, Wales appears to be a "source of visionary experience for English poets"; it is exploited by outsiders for its subject matter—its natural resources, as it were—in the manner deplored by Wendel Berry in *Standing by Words*. The section begins with the Snowdon sunrise passage from *The Prelude;* includes "Tintern Abbey" and a range of other poems by English poets; but, Hooker feels, accounts only inadequately for poems written by the Welsh themselves, or by poets who lived for any length of time in Wales, with its selections from Henry and Thomas Vaughan, John Dyer, Dylan Thomas, Gerard Manley Hopkins, and W. H. Davies. This is particularly lamentable because "nowhere in these islands, and possibly in the world, [are] place and native poetry more closely identified." Even in the present century, he believes, Welsh poets embody in their work "a common world shared with their readers [which] offers an alternative relation between poet and people and place that English readers might benefit greatly from observing." Quoting Anthony Conran's translation of David Gwenallt Jones's "Rhydcymerau, " he argues that the anger of that poem "is grounded on a sharp delineation . . . of a familial neighborhood, now destroyed, in which a particular poetic tradition in the native language was the expression of a whole way of life," and he fears that Grigson's selection may in part embody "the capacity of images to obscure and even to falsify" while contributing to "an Arnoldian dissolution of Wales in the mists of English romanticism." All of this is particularly interesting seen as a background to Hooker's own poems, to which I must now turn, and to his invocation of the Welsh philosopher J. R. Jones's notion of *cydymdreiddiad*—"that subtle knot of interpenetration which grows in time (in a people's consciousness) between a territory and its people and their language, creating a sense of belonging to a particular stretch of the earth's surface."

Hooker has an attractively modest and also somewhat ambivalent attitude toward his own achievements as a poet, in large measure because he has written in Wales the poems of what he takes to be, at best, an exile from the south of England and, at worst, a kind of invader. In writing *Englishman's Road* he felt himself to be an explorer, " 'translating' the things of a particular area of Wales into an alien tongue for the first time," but also saw himself as "in some ways an enemy of the very place [he] had come to love. In this place with its native language, every thing had an otherness which I wanted to name and honour in my own tongue, yet of which I could not make a shape without helping to dishonour." In his two excellent autobiographical essays in *The Poetry of Place*, and also in the Afterword to a *A View from the Source*, Hooker explores his poetic engagement with both the *cydymdreiddiad* he shares, that of southern England in general and the Southampton shoreline in particular, and the Welsh *cydymdreiddiad* toward which he feels profoundly drawn but from which he knows himself to be ultimately excluded. As teacher and writer, Hooker has not managed to integrate his life with that of his local Welsh community in the way, for example, which R. S. Thomas has done as a member of the clergy. Nonetheless, his treatment of the things of Wales forms a fine and vivid complement to his treatment of the things of his native Solent shore, and his deep consciousness of being "an outsider on the inside" prevents his poems from ever becoming the picture postcards of the literary tourist which he criticizes in his prose. If tradition offers the Welsh poet a language of praise, a language of community, and a language of outraged nationalism, it is chiefly the first of these toward which the outsider, once he has grown inward with the spirit of the place in which he lives, might appropriately aspire. By acknowledging the difficulty of achieving in English what is natural and traditional in Welsh, Hooker makes his achievement all the more moving and his praise all the more sincerely registered and felt.

> How shall I celebrate this,
>   always present
> under our sleep and thoughts,
> where we do not see ourselves
>   reflected
> or know the language of memory
> gathered from its fall?
>
> Beidog running dark
>   between us
> and our neighbours, down
> from Mynydd Bach—
> this is the stream I wish to praise
>   and the small mountain.
>
> I am not of you, tongue
> through whom Taliesin descends the ages
> gifted with praise, who know
> that praise turns dust to light.
>   In my tongue,
> of all the arts
> this is the most difficult.

"Be secret and exult," said Yeats, rhyming his last line (which Hooker is certainly conscious of quoting here, with two small changes, in *his* last line). But surely Hooker's Welsh poems do not "come to nothing." They come, indeed, to quite a lot, especially when taken as a sequence or a cycle, with all the poems from "Under Mynydd Bach" supporting, qualifying or completing each other. While Hooker reiterates, for example, in "Brynbeidog" that "where all is familiar, around us / the country with its language / gives all things other names," he nonetheless affirms his own alien way of seeing and, by implication, of naming in "Hill Country Rhythms" where he says: "Sometimes I glimpse a rhythm / I am not part of, and those who are / could never see." In his essay "Landscape of Fire," Hooker insists that Ronald Johnson, as an American and outsider in Britain, was able to see and record the old places and the local colors with a fresh eye and in a new way, free of the familiarity that breeds, if not contempt, then blindness or boredom or oblivion. Certainly the same is true of Hooker himself in Wales. The outsider, should he be both skilled and lucky, can sometimes see and name phenomena or "rhythms" which the native—and even the native poet writing in the native language—cannot see or name for being too caught up in them. This is the strength of the outsider's oblique perspective, and it is sometimes a compensation for the more obvious disadvantages of his situation which Hooker tends to brood on.

The poems in *A View from the Source*, which were originally published in *Soliloquies for a Chalk Giant* and *Solent Shore*, are offered with far fewer hesitations than the "Under Mynydd Bach" section, which originally appeared in *Englishman's Road*. In the poems about the chalk Giant of Cerne Abbas, and especially in the evocations of the tides and shingle spits and sunken wrecks and docks along Southampton's shoreline, Hooker has written his strongest work and achieved his homecoming as a poet. By a "sleight of imagination, " he says, these poems were written as if from immediate experience and in immediate proximity to the things they remember and name, although the irony is that it was the distance from his native place and native *cydymdreiddiad*—for he wrote the poems in Wales—which sharpened his sense of both. In his afterword, Hooker writes of his determination "to give primacy to [his] subject matter or materials" in these poems; and in *The Poetry of Place*, he even says that he thinks of himself as working "not so much with words as with the materials which they name, with chalk and flint, or shingle and water and oil." Quoting and affirming David Jones's principle that "one is trying to make a shape out of the very things of which one is oneself made," he explains what he regards to be the "ground" of his poems, "a total environment, human and non-human, historical and personal, experienced through every form of relevant knowledge available to one, yet known as directly as the shock through one's whole body of treading on a stone, and through a language that was learnt there, in relation to the world it composes." If this begins to sound optimistic and affirmative, it is, and one wonders just how far these poems collectively serve to qualify Hooker's generally pessimistic picture of poetry of place after Wordsworth; a lot of this, in fact, sounds like Wendell Berry. One of Hooker's aims is clearly to "unspecialize" his poetry, although he has argued in his criticism, as we have seen, that "as the poet's grasp on a common human world has loosened" it is precisely through a preoccupation with place that he has "come to stress the specialness of other poets . . . and become a specialist talking to specialists."

The contradiction, if that is what it is, doesn't matter. What matters are the poems, and they are as vivid and alive as one could hope, as tangible and tactile as the chalk and flint and shingle they evoke, and written from an experience of the "ground" as deep as Crabbe's. Like Crabbe, Hooker sees the "gumboot-sucking ooze" at low tide, the weeds in the channel, and—coming later than Crabbe—the oil and industrial pollution. Still, as in his Welsh poems, the poems of the Solent shore constitute a poetry of celebration and praise—not of the grim present condition of the shoreline itself, but of life and work and love seen against the history and legend necessarily rooted there as deeply as a post in the harbor. And if praise can "turn the dust to light" in Wales, it doubtless can turn even oil slicks and blue-gray mud to light in Southampton. Emerging out of "water that is bottle green, with a salt crust / And an unmistakable flavour of sewage" as out of some antediluvian source of amphibious life, a characteristic poem notices "a tarred gull" floating past, "an orange box / And the helmet of a marine; a glove / With the hand still in it," as it struggles toward its (earned) vision:

> Going home,
> The view from Totton flyover
> Makes me gape
> Even now.
> The river's wedge broadens
> Seaward; a dream of cranes swims in haze;
> Everywhere, men I know work under it.
> Necessities are unladen and shipped.
> That is the root.

I think Hooker would like his poems to be as essential as the necessities unladen in the harbor, "greased with use," as he expresses it in another poem. Imagining a seagull on a post, he wishes for the gifts both of post and gull: the post's gift to mark a channel and serve as a mooring, "standing ever / Still in one place," and the gull's gift to fly "inland or seaward; settle / At will—but voicing always in her cry / Essence of wind and wave, / Bringing to city, moorish / Pool and ploughland, / Reminders of storm and sea." In the end, he sees no resolution between the gull and the post, "only the necessity of flight / Beyond me, firm / Standing only then."

That is the note, in fact, on which the "Solent Shore" poems end. But I cannot leave Hooker's work without noticing briefly "At Osborne House"—his poem about the renovated manor house on the Isle of Wight where Victoria died—which connects so centrally with the poems on great houses by Jonson, Marvell, and Pope which Berry discusses and to which I've alluded earlier. The poem should be read not only beside these celebrations of hospitality, wealth, and social or natural hierarchies, but also beside Robert Lowell's excellent "Doomsday Book" in *Day by Day*. Both Lowell's poem and Hooker's should have had a place in Grigson's anthology since, together, they bring a grand (and grandiose) tradition to an end. John Peck has memorably said of Lowell's poem that "the great house sets out a minefield of privilege ornamented with a deerpark of tricky literary precedent. Insofar as its theme is great and inescapable, the great house is the house of our culture, or part of it, and we ourselves are the house-breakers, willy-nilly." In Lowell's great house, inhabited by an American—Lowell himself!—the poet thinks on others—on Lathom House, Middleton Manor, New Hall, and Silverton—as all are "converted to surgeries, polytechnics, / cells of the understaffed asylum / crumbling on the heads of the mad." At Osborne House—now a convalescent home for military officers, but with the old royal apartments open to the public—Hooker, along with other tourists "under the cedar and ilex," walks beside the lawns as "Convalescents / watch us, / from coach and car / Mobbing their repose." Observing the statue of Victoria as Britannia to whom Neptune "entrusts / The command of the Sea," Hooker declares: "The finish is perfect, / A spectacle, / Complete . . ." And instead of imagining as he might, "innumerable salutes, the waterway / Busy with dispatches," he:

> . . . would rather look out,
> Down the terraces of statuary

Over woods of oak and beech,
Elms dying or dead,
To the blue Solent,
Spithead,
The tower blocks of Portsmouth.

For the future belongs, as Hooker knows, to the tower blocks of Portsmouth and to those who unladen the ships even as the river broadens seaward through his dream of cranes. As for a poetry of place—and in particular a poetry of place where, as in Britain, history is unavoidably part of the "ground"—Hooker explains in his prose volume what he has come to realize living in Cardiganshire and, presumably, writing the poems of *Solent Shore*. "Finding a memory, attempting to do a measure of justice to the dead," he says, "is at once to recover a part of oneself and to lose the most treacherous of all illusions, that the self is autonomous, whereas it is part of a process which it can be in touch with but not fully comprehend." And he continues, with his usual eloquence, the most far-reaching of conclusions.

But for any individual, in order to be creative this awareness depends upon his society and its culture having a future that he wants to live for; otherwise, his sense of the past will become essentially morbid, and he will retreat into it, as into childhood memories, because there is nowhere to carry its energies but back into the past. Now, perhaps more than at any other time, the economic and political powers are forcing individual growth downward, twisting it back into itself, into the darkness where it should be fed for its ascent into the human world.

Seen against this statement of our present condition, Gary Snyder's *Axe Handles* is rather slight and disappointing, and Berry's *The Wheel* is far less compelling than his prose. There is an artful artlessness to Snyder's work which, though frequently charming, is also so often blithely optimistic about everything as to become irritating. While his poems certainly never retreat into any past—whether personal or political—and while their energies engage always the things of the human or natural world, there is a kind of left-handed superficiality about that engagement that verges sometimes on self-parody. Snyder brings to bear something like Ezra Pound's ideogrammatic method on quotidian experience—memories, work, homesteading, child rearing, traveling—and even a visit to "Berry territory" in Kentucky. He writes mainly what I think Frank O'Hara used to call "now I do this, now I do that poems." The title poem about cultural traditions seen metaphorically as axes shaping axe handles—"Pound was an axe / Chen was an axe, I am an axe / And my son a handle, soon / To be shaping again, model / And tool, craft of culture"—is the most impressive piece in the book, but even it is vitiated by the breathless pretended ingenuousness of its conclusion: "How we go on." And the book ends with some cheerleading for "one ecosystem / in diversity / under the sun / With joyful interpenetration for all." This seems to me to trivialize the powerful arguments put forward in Berry's *Standing by Words*. However, if Snyder's book is perhaps too playful for its own good, Berry's is mostly flat. The title is taken from Sir Albert Howard's *The Soil and Health: A Study of Organic Agriculture*, where Howard invokes an eastern religion's "Wheel of Life"—"the successive and repeated processes of birth, growth, maturity, death and decay"—the revolutions of which "never falter and are perfect." The tone of the poems is elegiac and grave, and the subjects range from the death of a friend and teacher to the severe ecological damage being done to the Kentucky River which, "bridged and forgot . . . carries down the soil of ravaged uplands," to the growth and maturity of children and "The Gift of Gravity" itself. There are some good poems in the book, but also some writing that is bad enough to send one back to those autonomous artifacts which Berry so deplores: "Things that mattered to me once / won't matter any more, / for I have left the safe shore / where magnificence of art / could suffice my heart."

Of the two books that remain, little needs to be said of *An Americas Anthology: A Geopoetics Landmark*, and little *can* be briefly said of Ken Smith's magnificent *The Poet Reclining*. The anthology is an interesting collection of work by such as Peter Michelson, Robert Peters, Millen Brand, Lyn Lifshin, and Paul Metcalf that can be recommended for its contents in spite of Tom Montag's humorless introduction which makes up a new jargon for a not-so-new kind of practice, and reduces the implicit poetics to an eleven-step recipe that one is inclined to respond to in the way Robert Bly responded to Olson's essay on Projectivism: it is so formulaic that it suggests that good poetry can be written even by people who lack imagination and skill. Ken Smith possesses all the imagination and skill one could hope for in a poet, and *The Poet Reclining* needs to be reviewed on its own, and at length, in order to do it any justice at all. Though I hope to do just that before very long, I mention the book because it ought to be seen and read in this particular company, and because I want American readers to know of its existence. Its vision of America, contained in some of the poems in the first section, is as important as that of either Berry or Snyder—and it is the vision of an outsider. But if Smith is, like these others, a poet of place, he is also, as it were, an antipoet writing antipoems of an antiplace. I want to end by quoting one of these antiplace antipoems—a piece which, although highly characteristic of Smith's work in this mode, does not appear in *The Poet Reclining*—in order to put everything I've said in this essay into a slightly skewed (but I hope also useful) perspective, and allow myself an oblique exit. Smith writes about what the English poet's "American poem" would contain, and the assumption is that it would contain something false, stereotyped, or distorted as the result of superficial impressions acquired during too brief a stay. But the piece contains—along with the irony of its self-deflating title—all the precision of a Hopper painting. If one's first impression is that the imagery is simply dated or derives from books or photographs from the 1930s or 1940s, that is precisely what our *initial* response is intended to be. Actually, the poem is a kind of negative which, held up to the light, contains visual and spiritual lucidities which are startling.

The English Poet's American Poem

would contain a gas station and a desert. Later a single parched figure would gesture in that landscape. Or it may be corn and the long plain, like a deep well taken out of the ground and hammered flat . . .

It would go nowhere. It would admit its own defeat, a continent run out through the fingers. And weariness: it should be covered in the dust of journeys, and yellow light, the harsh terminals and the travellers' sleepy faces drawn sharply in the neon. And so on: a sign blowing in the land wind come a thousand miles to no particular purpose. It would settle for some desperate image of itself: an American railway station one hundred and fifty miles south of Chicago, like a lone ship abandoned by all but its passengers, stamping their feet in the first cold of September, their breaths turning to smoke.

From *The Southern Review*, 1985

W. H. Auden and Benjamin Britten

Edward Mendelson, *Early Auden,* The Viking Press; Humphrey Carpenter, *W. H. Auden: A Biography,* Houghton Mifflin; Donald Mitchell, *Britten & Auden in the Thirties,* Faber and Faber; Ronald Duncan, *Working with Britten,* The Rebel Press; Benjamin Britten, *Our Hunting Fathers* and *On This Island,* BBC Artium.

I

Since the death of W. H. Auden in 1973 and Benjamin Britten in 1976, an enormous amount, appropriately enough, has been written and broadcast about both of them. Initially, there were the inevitable memoirs, elegies, memorial addresses, BBC specials, and the like. Then came the extended tributes with photographs—Stephen Spender's *W. H. Auden: A Tribute* and Donald Mitchell's *Benjamin Britten 1913–76: Pictures From a Life.* As both very late and very early works by the composer and poet were published, re-published or recorded, the unofficial biographies appeared—Charles Osborne's *W. H. Auden: The Life of a Poet* and Christopher Headington's *Britten*—and the first critical essays were written which were able to consider either an entire *oeuvre,* or a particular period of writing or composition within the context of that *oeuvre.* Clearly Edward Mendelson has emerged as the leading Auden scholar. As executor, bibliographer, editor, and critic, Mendelson has worked with devoted and indefatigable energy from 1973 onward. He has given us the later Auden's version of Auden by editing the *Collected Poems* in accordance with the poet's final instructions regarding inclusions, exclusions, and revisions. But also, by editing *The English Auden,* he has made the poems from the 1930s accessible in their entirety and in their original versions. *Early Auden*—which is to be followed by a second volume on the later Auden—studies the work of the 1930s from a perspective that is largely sympathetic to the work that follows. Meanwhile, in Humphrey Carpenter's *W. H. Auden: A Biography*, we have the closest thing we are likely to get to an authorized life, unless Mendelson eventually decides to write one himself. Carpenter makes clear that Mendelson's cooperation and support have made him virtually "an active collaborator" on the book. Although Donald Mitchell has not been as prolific as Mendelson, his activities as Britten's trustee and editor, as well as administrative officer of both the Aldeburgh Festival-Snape Maltings Foundation and the Britten-Pears school of Advanced Musical Studies, make his work as a critic of Britten's music as official as Mendelson's on Auden's poetry. In his *Britten & Auden in the Thirties*, we have an anticipation of the authorized biography which is promised in the near future. Ronald Duncan's *Working with Britten*—a much more personal and even rather eccentric book—is largely a reminiscence of Duncan's collaboration with the composer as librettist of *The Rape of Lucrecia*. It also includes a highly critical portrait of Britten once he had achieved his enormous success and established the Aldeburgh Festival. Perhaps at this point, our greatest thanks to Mitchell are due for the remarkable recording of *Our Hunting Fathers* and *On This Island*, which he and the Britten Estate have evidently persuaded the BBC Sound Archives to issue as an LP. These two song cycles, and particularly the first, show the collaboration between Britten and Auden during the 1930s at its best.

II

Mendelson's *Early Auden* is many things, and one of the most interesting (and sometimes irritating) of them is a sustained polemic against modernism, postmodernism, and structuralist and post-structuralist theories of literature that Mendelson takes to have their sources in Romanticism and ultimately in the vatic, as opposed to the civil, tradition of poetry. As such, *Early Auden* takes its place alongside such recent books as Robert Pinsky's *The Situation of Poetry* and Gerald Graff's *Literature Against Itself*, and assures for its author a place in an important debate well outside the limits of Auden criticism. It is almost as if Auden and Mendelson had made a deal: Mendelson would defend the later Auden while attacking much of the poet's early work in almost exactly the later Auden's own terms on condition that Auden would help Mendelson "get that lot" in Paris and at Yale.

Beginning in his introduction with Homer's Achilles singing to himself in his tent, and ending 350 pages later with a resonant footnote on Heidegger, Mendelson makes Auden into the poet who successfully "challenged the vatic dynasty" and found a way out of his artist's isolation and "the imprisonment of a reflexive personal voice" into "the context of civil poetry that extended from Chaucer through Shakespeare, Dryden, and Pope." Arguing that the vatic and civil traditions "perennially divide literature" and have done so since before Aristophanes' Dionysus presided in the underworld over the contest between the civil Aeschylus and the vatic Euripides in *The Frogs*, Mendelson rejects an art of inner vision made of a deliberately invented poetic language which, in isolation from an audience and with the "breakdown in what might be called the symbolic contract" joining both poet and audience to the subject of the poet's poems, becomes virtually autistic. Instead of Achilles singing for himself alone, Mendelson wants a Phemius or a Demodocus singing "in service to their audience" and responding to "a specific occasion." Rather than the "extravagant modern fictions" of Euripides, Mendelson (like Dionysus) chooses the moral teaching and traditional gods of Aeschylus. Rejecting the "dislocation of language" required by Rimbaud, Pound, and the early Eliot, Mendelson looks to the formal conventions, meters, and parabolic didacticism in Hardy, Kipling, and Brecht. If later generations in the vatic/romantic/ modernist line "understood the self to be constituted *by* language, and the wordless unconscious to be organized *like* a language" then "no community seemed possible except the centerless, contradictory, unstable community of language itself." Auden, whose own earliest poems brought him up against this dead end, abandoned a poetics "that would be occupied by an avant-garde thirty years afterwards."

When he turns to Auden's earliest poems, Mendelson appears to be well aware—which he is not always later on—of John Bayley's admonition recently quoted in these pages by Austin Warren that "critics of Auden have always appeared to find it difficult to talk about his poetry, as opposed to the borrowed materials in it, and its nominal preoccupations." Mendelson succeeds in large measure in talking about the poetry, about its essential nature. He finds that nature to be of an "intensely isolated and reflexive character" which has long "been obscured by the more public character of [Auden's] later work." Auden's early poetic language, a language theoretically justified in the early essay called "Writing" with its "insistence on the antagonism and difference between language and its objects," is "nonsymbolic" and "noncommunicative." When gathered together in his first volume, however, the poems nonetheless seemed to suggest that they were "fragments of a larger whole," and yet, when they are read in sequence they do not "provide enough data to identify that whole." By "noncommunicative language" I think Mendelson really means "nonparaphrasable language," for even when one reads the poems as he suggests—on balance, a thoroughly good idea—one finds that they communicate with extraordinary energy their rhythms, images, tones of voice, and fields of force—the unique, jagged, and mysterious linguistic universe that Auden's early style creates. They communicate their *sound* as they engage the silence around them. In the end, in order to make certain key points about the central early poems, Mendelson must contradict himself to a degree by attempting to paraphrase and interpret quasi-referentially what he takes to be reflexive and "noncommunicative," and then indeed there is some talk about the "borrowed materials" and "nominal preoccupations" that John Bayley speaks of, rather than about the processes that transfigure, say, the psychological, political, or moral content of such materials and preoccupations into the nonsymbolic content of the poems themselves. Also, there is the problem of sequence and structure in Auden's individual volumes to be dealt with.

By arguing that the individual pieces in *Poems* are fragments which do not cohere to form a larger whole, Mendelson is absolved from having to make anything much of the sequence of poems that seemed, by sporting Roman numerals rather than titles, to insist on its sequential nature. His refusal to discern a pattern where he feels none exists recalls the early refusal by I. A. Richards to find "a coherent intellectual thread" upon which the items of *The Waste Land* are strung, and a recent refusal by Donald Davie to look any longer, as he had looked before, for either narrative or patterns of personae in *Hugh Selwyn Mauberley*. Finding the chronological order of composition usually more instructive than the order of poems in Auden's published books, Mendelson not only organizes his own topical discussion to take up the poems chronologically, but also publishes the numbered sections of *Poems* (as well as the poems in *Look, Stranger!* and *Another Time*) in the order of composition in *The English Auden*.

This is my one strong objection to an otherwise fine editorial job. Although it is useful to know that the poem beginning "Will you turn a deaf ear" was written immediately before the one beginning "Sir, no man's enemy," it is disconcerting to find them numbered XXII and XXIII in *The English Auden* when they were numbered I and XXX in both the 1930 and 1933 editions of *Poems*. In *Early Auden*, Mendelson does find the first poem to be an appropriate opening for *Poems* since it is "a rebuke to Auden's literary and personal isolation" while the other is a formal, although unsatisfactory, conclusion in its "appeal to some external agency to impose from without the change he could not make from within." As he also finds the poem which Auden later entitled "1929" the "centerpiece" of both editions of *Poems*, we have at least a beginning, a middle, and an end.

When it comes to the chronology of composition, Mendelson is a master of the facts. With the executor's privileged inside view, he can tell us about Auden's development almost down to the hour, as the poet worked slowly or hectically through poetic contradictions and personal reversals of fortune toward what Mendelson regards to be the achieved, mature, civil poetry of the American period. Thus, Auden wrote one poem "within a few days or weeks of his first meeting with John Layard"; certain speculations had "outgrown the confidence in which they began a few months before"; "the dire sense of evolution's indifference . . . yielded, for a month or two, to a meliorative faith out of the woozier pages of Gerald Heard"; and so on. After an impressive and elaborate interpretation of *The Orators* made possible by the fact that this book, unlike *Poems*, actually does possess a key to its obscurities in the unlikely shape of John Layard's anthropological paper "Malekula: Flying Tricksters, Ghosts, Gods, and Epileptics," Mendelson traces the emergence of a poetry in search of an audience aiming at accessibility and communication where public references replace private ones, inner divisions take outward forms, and an attempt is made to overcome personal isolation and employ a language which can be shared and which can illuminate and affect "a physical and ethical world whose order and events are not only verbal ones." This development corresponds with a decision, in 1932, "to write larger and more coherently patterned poems . . . that recommend a large social unity by embodying a large poetic unity."

Since the publication of *The English Auden*, Mendelson's biographical approach to Auden has made the second poem from the sequence *Look, Stranger!* (which Auden later called "A Summer Night") the most significant single poem of the English period if not the most significant one in the entire canon. He reads this piece in the context of Auden's 1964 essay contributed to Anne Fremantle's anthology, *The Protestant Mystics*, in which Auden describes "a fine summer night in June 1933" when he experienced what he calls "a vision of Agape." Mendelson's assumption, and the burden of his argument in the eighth chapter of *Early Auden* as well as in the introductions to *The English Auden* and Auden's *Selected Poems*, is that the poem and the relevant paragraphs in the essay are about the same experience. By the time "A Summer Night" has received its fullest treatment in the present book, it appears almost as a sacred text, with lines numbered down the left margin as if it had just stepped out of *The Norton Anthology*. The chapter title, taken from the poem's second stanza, "Lucky this Point," reminds us at once of Mendelson's observation in his introduction to *Selected Poems* that "luck eventually acquired in Auden's vocabulary almost the force of religious 'grace'." In *The English Auden*, he says in a sentence what in *Early Auden* he expands upon and explains in the book's remaining two hundred pages: "It is possible to read almost all his work during the rest of the thirties as a series of attempts to learn—or to evade—the meaning of that summer night in June 1933."

While it is certain that "A Summer Night" does indeed represent Auden's transitional style at its strongest, the poem has never seemed to me to be about the same experience treated in the 1964 essay, but always to have been more sympathetically than antithetically related to a range of poems that cluster around it in *Look, Stranger!*, some of which Mendelson, following the judgment of the later Auden, thoroughly regrets.

Although I have never experienced anything like a "vision of Agape," I have experienced the cozy sense of warm well-being—"lazy and ardent," as Barbara Everett calls it—that I think "A Summer Night" half celebrates and half condemns, in terms of the class guilt attaching to privileged complicity in an unjust social system, where other people's suffering, even nearby and on an enormous scale, does not move us to act or change or even ask "what doubtful act allows / Our freedom." Mendelson's reading of the poem (which does not, incidentally, ignore the guilt or complicity) is lovingly detailed, deeply committed to its central hypothesis, and almost convincing. It needs, however, to be absolutely convincing, given its utter centrality to the argument of *Early Auden* as a whole and the place "A Summer Night" has assumed in Auden's work as a result of Mendelson's editions and introductions. "A Summer Night" is one of the poems Auden extensively revised for inclusion in the 1945 *Collected Poems*. In the revised version, the concluding flood imagery is largely depoliticized by the loss of three stanzas, and the guilty recognition that a wall conceals the self-indulgence and petty charity of "Our metaphysical distress, / Our kindness to ten persons" from the wretchedness of gathering multitudes is lost. An attempt to clarify pronoun references and antecedents in the final stanzas alters the meaning of the poem while not entirely eliminating ambiguity. "A Summer Night" seems to have given Auden more doubts than it does his critic as he attempted to save it from the wreck of *Look, Stranger!*

All other doubts which Auden eventually had about poems from this period, however, Mendelson shares. Taking Auden more or less at his word that he never "attempted to revise [his] former thoughts or feelings, only the language in which they were first expressed," Mendelson finds that, when Auden writes badly in the mid to late 1930s, "it is generally a sign that he cannot make himself believe what he is making himself say." As a result of this, a later stylistic revision is likely also to be an ideological revision. The chief indication of a "dishonest poem"—a poem which "expresses beliefs which the author never entertained"—is found to be significant internal contradiction. Auden's attempt "to learn—or to evade—the meaning of that summer night in June 1933" involved, according to Mendelson, five essential "projects" which, after the momentary triumph of a single poem, sought permanently to resolve his divisive loneliness and overcome the frontier between himself and the world of others through a language now committed to accessibility and reference. The problem is that the new, accessible language often betrayed Auden into what he later took to be rhetorical dishonesty and what, revealed in its contradictions, Mendelson resoundingly condemns. These were the projects which occupied Auden until his departure for America in 1939: "*Erotic*—joining two worlds through sexual love and personal growth; *Redemptive*—saving mankind from its divisions by personal example and direct cure; *Didactic*—teaching an audience, through parables, to unlearn hatred and learn love; *World-Historical*—allowing the problem to be solved by determined forces working on an international scale; and *Escapist*—abandoning the problem altogether and finding comfort on an island of refuge."

Behind the incidental contradictions in many of the best known poems of this period lies the fundamental one which Mendelson again attributes to Auden's inability to make a clean break with modernist poetics. Now determined to write "in a tradition that engaged the problems of choice and action, and performed a didactic function in society," the poet continued to apply "the formal and rhetorical methods of a tradition that claimed to be independent of existing society [and] superior to its vulgar concerns." Like the critical methods of the schools Mendelson dislikes—formalist, structuralist, deconstructive, and so on—his own approach "thrives on the internal contradictions of the texts," even though its ultimate aim is to bring us—in another book—before poems in which the techniques of modernism are no longer adapted "to contexts unsuited for them." As contradictions are revealed and rhetorics explained, Mendelson's moral assessment of particular poems (as well as certain key essays) becomes more pronounced than it was in the first half of the book. Sometimes it is levelled with a vehemence exceeding Auden's own in later years. Auden was "violating his gifts. . . . Perhaps at moments he convinced himself he actually believed this wretched stuff. . . . All that is missing is the vibrato of massed violins. . . . The poem takes so much pleasure in its witty images of crisis that it manages to avoid saying what is to be done. . . . The new final stanza is the crudest and clearest example of Auden's historical double-think. . . . This contemptible idea [is] brought into the poem for the sake of a paradox. . . . This inept stanza says that what the poet's voice can do . . . is proclaim that individual acts and lies make no difference."

There are, to my mind, two rather problematic chapters and two especially successful ones in the second half of *English Auden*. The particular successes are Mendelson's treatment of Auden's love poems of the middle 1930s discussed in chapter X which, together, make up the first of those five "projects" following on the heels of "A Summer Night"; and his treatment of *Spain* and "September 1, 1939" in chapter XIV which, along with a few related poems, make up the fourth such "project"—"project," by the way, being the one annoying term Mendelson borrows from his adversaries among the currently fashionable schools of criticism. Chapter X includes persuasive readings of Auden's best love poems of the period—"A Bride in the Thirties," "Lullaby," the ballad "As I walked out one evening"—and a fascinating if overconfident reading of "Our Hunting Fathers" which, like the reading of "A Summer Night," is almost, but not quite, convincing. Dating the love poems with his usual precision from the "vision of Agape" in 1933—"by the following spring [it had] altogether faded"; "six months had passed since Auden's vision of Agape," and so on—Mendelson sees the Audenesque Eros of the period offering "a brief refuge from political chaos" but "giving no relief from the difficulties of choice." The major poems, which are really *about* choice, are seen to be largely successful in kind with their "double subject of sexual success and emotional failure." Mendelson's treatment in chapter XIV of

Auden's briefly held belief in a determined and purposeful History, along with the collapse of the notion in the self-contradictions of *Spain*, is masterful. He claims persuasively that there are two sustained and mutually exclusive arguments in *Spain*, one expository (insisting on human freedom and human choice), and the other figurative (suggesting that the central actions of the volunteers in Spain are determined rather than willed); and that, when Auden came to revise the poem, all of his changes tried to rid it of the figurative argument for a determined history. In the process, he also provides the best answer I have ever seen to George Orwell's famous objection to the poem.

Less successful on the whole, but interestingly problematic, is Mendelson's treatment of Auden's third "project," the one he calls "Redemptive," in chapter XI. My doubts here turn on the use made of an unpublished poem in regular unrhymed triplets in which Auden evidently indulges certain messianic temptations and redemptive ambitions. Written just before Poem XVII from *Look, Stranger!*— which Auden later called "The Malverns" and eventually eliminated from the canon—the poem in triplets casts the poet in the role of prophet and aims to warn and to save an entire generation. Six stanzas from the unpublished poem became that part of "The Malverns" beginning "And out of the turf the bones of the war continue," while other parts found their way into yet another unpublished poem in triplets. Transcriptions of both unpublished poems finally ended up in Michael Ransom's "most self-important and sometimes hysterical . . . speeches" in *The Ascent of F-6*, which is pretty much where Mendelson thinks they belong. Mendelson often makes use of unpublished manuscripts and drafts in his book, and there are moments when one feels that Auden should have left instructions that these, rather than his letters, be destroyed after his death. Early revisionary processes which involve these drafts are usually seen, unlike the later revisions, as a sign of confusion and contradiction rather than clarification. In the case of the messianic triplets and "The Malverns," Mendelson feels "The Malverns" to be virtually contaminated by the presence of borrowed material. Monroe Spears has written of J. W. Beach's shock at Auden's "use of the same passage in different contexts." Mendelson could hardly be more different as a critic from the literal-minded Beach, and his rather melodramatic revelation about the source of these borrowed stanzas, like his later revelation that Auden cribbed passages in *The Dog Beneath the Skin* from Anthony Collett's *The Changing Face of England*, sounds somewhat disingenuous. "The Malverns" does not say the same thing the poem in triplets says, even though it manages to incorporate six of its stanzas; and Auden, in his published work, never took on the role of messianic poet/prophet/savior. But Mendelson's real interest is in the unpublished poem itself, and for now predictable reasons: "Having begun with the purpose of saving his generation, Auden ended by writing a poem concerned reflexively with its own composition, and ultimately with preventing itself from being written."

Of the two remaining "projects,"— the "Didactic" and the "Escapist"—Mendelson's treatment of the "Didactic" is, I think, the less engaging mainly because he is obliged to provide a narrative account of theatrical and film history during the 1930s in which he does not appear to be very interested. Humphrey Carpenter's version of Auden's involvement in the hectic activities of Rupert Doone's Group Theatre and John Grierson's GPO Film Unit is a good deal livelier. Mendelson's discussion of the plays and films— poetic drama being Auden's main didactic vehicle—is chiefly important for what it has to say about *The Ascent of F-6*. Although Christopher Isherwood is given all due credit for his contributions to three of the plays—and also chided for being so silly as to think the subject of *F-6* was really T. E. Lawrence—Benjamin Britten's work on two of them is only just acknowledged. Mendelson feels that Auden solved more of the problems of writing modern poetic drama than anyone but Brecht, although the plays are seen to be full of imperfections. *The Ascent of F-6* is taken to be the appropriate focus of our attention among the plays and films for two related reasons, both of which give it the same kind of biographical prominence Mendelson attributes to "A Summer Night." As he has told us twice before in his introductions to *The English Auden* and *Selected Poems*, Mendelson takes the creation of Michael Ransom to be a kind of simultaneous externalization and exorcism of Auden's secret (because unpublished) self-deluding messianic fantasies. "The implied equation between Ransom the redemptive climber and Auden the redemptive poet would have been entirely lost on the play's audience," but there it was nonetheless. Mendelson explains that Auden understood for the first time that he would have to leave England for good while he was at work on this play. This is the second reason for its particular significance. Read with a full knowledge of Auden's subsequent career, *F-6* becomes "a parable of the fate Auden . . . avoided, the fate of the indifferent redeemer destroyed by a public role his private terrors tempted him to accept." (Humphrey Carpenter quotes from the interview which Mendelson only refers to regarding this sudden realization. The fate Auden was *conscious* of trying to avoid was not the redeemer's: "I knew that if I stayed [in England] I would inevitably become a member of the British establishment.")

Perhaps my final hesitation about this important study is suggested by the phrase "with the full knowledge of Auden's subsequent career." As we read Mendelson's excellent concluding chapter which treats the final "project" in terms of the island imagery which replaced the border "as Auden's geographical sign of entrapment and enclosure," we begin to wonder if Mendelson hasn't himself been tempted by a characteristic of the modernism which he rejects—I mean its particular rage for order, its obsession with pattern, its view of things from a very high altitude, its "hawk's vision," in fact. The modernist critic, perhaps a good deal more conspicuously than the modernist poet, is inclined to impose a grid on the material he studies—and is attacked, in fact, by the postmodernist critic for doing so. Everything must cohere; nothing can be out of place; the territory is mapped; and the map-maker, like Stephen Dedalus's dramatic artist, sits above it all paring his nails. An *oeuvre* is somehow already read, already understood, rather than encountered or engaged in the critical prose. There are moments when I think the structure of this book is much too neat to accommodate the chaotically explosive world of Auden's early poetry. Mendelson criticizes a form that "can accommodate *all* experience within itself, and can do so on its own formal and aesthetic terms." He criticizes "content ruled by pattern." Reading an essay I admire by Joseph Buttigieg— *Boundary* 2, IX, 1(1980)—that raises questions in these terms about a recent book on Samuel Beckett made me wonder if Mendelson has taken sufficient care to avoid some of the very contradictions he discusses in the early work of Auden. Annoyingly enough, one must conclude that it is too early to be certain. Although *Early Auden* is some 370 pages long, it is still only half a book, broken off just before Auden's emigration when, in a sonnet from *In Time of War*, he makes "the one discovery that will release him from his private island." But one suspects that pattern will eventually dominate the whole once we have the second volume treating Auden's later work. The desire for coherence threatens to take over, and it makes one worry about various fixed points always already on the map—especially the summer night and the decision that came with the composition of *The Ascent of F-6*.

The present volume moves toward its conclusion with a deeply appreciative reading of *In Time of War*, the sonnet sequence which

Mendelson feels to be "Auden's most profound and audacious poem of the 1930s" and "perhaps the greatest English poem of the decade." It recovers, in his view, much of the ground lost since "A Summer Night" and suggests that Auden is now ready to learn, rather than evade, its meaning. The discovery already alluded to in Sonnet XXVI that will "release him from his private island" is, not surprisingly, "the amazed discovery of love's consistency and strength," and the sequence as a whole which, like *Spain*, surveys all of human history, makes a "first gesture toward finding the ground of ethics in religion." In his discussion of what he takes to be the central sonnet (XIV), Mendelson at last concludes his debate with modernism, postmodernism and "certain schools of literary theory" in a lengthy footnote. Auden, like Heidegger, makes use of Holderlin's line *"dichterisch, wohnet der Mensch auf dieser Erde."* But, while Heidegger (inspiring those certain schools) uses the line to argue that "Being itself is founded by poetic language, with the implication that there can be no absolutes beyond the fiats of verbal imagination," Auden uses it "to expose the corruption of any system of thought that regards the ethically neutral powers of language or nature as the measure of all things."

> The mountains cannot judge us when we lie;
> We dwell upon the earth; the earth obeys
> The intelligent and evil till they die.

For the rest, Mendelson praises the poems Auden wrote in Brussels immediately before his departure for America as precursors of the later work, of the mature orientation and style. In "Musée des Beaux Arts" in particular, Auden gives notice that he has begun not only "to accept in himself the dull ordinariness of suffering," but also "responsibility for others' suffering" and, in following Brueghel's example, he refuses to be awed by the "the grand rhetoric of History" or "appeals to the autonomy of art." This, according to Mendelson, was "to the bafflement of critics who preferred bright colours and loud noises." We will doubtless be hearing more about—and from—these critics in the future. One awaits the sequel to this volume eagerly.

III

I have left myself far too little space to do justice to Humphrey Carpenter's biography, Donald Mitchell's *Britten & Auden in the*

Thirties, and Ronald Duncan's *Working with Britten*. Carpenter's book, of course, overlaps with Mendelson's in all kinds of interesting ways until his account of the morning of 26 January 1939, when Auden and Isherwood arrived in New York City. At this point, in the absence of Mendelson's second volume, we are entirely in Carpenter's hands with respect to Auden's later career.

One of Auden's best known objections to biographies of writers was that they are superfluous because "a writer is a maker, not a man of action." In the first half of his career, at any rate, Auden *was* something of a man of action, and any competent account of his activities in Berlin, Spain, Iceland, and China is bound to be interesting. Also, I suppose, the full inventory of Auden's generally unsatisfactory love affairs does illuminate a number of the poems in various ways, though Auden held that, at best, the works of a writer might "throw light upon his life" rather than the other way round.

Carpenter's treatment of the love affairs is particularly candid, and this he justifies by quoting Auden's 1969 review of J. R. Ackerley's *My Father and Myself* in which he says "Mr. Ackerley is never quite explicit about what he *really* preferred in bed. The omission is important because all 'abnormal' sex-acts are rites of symbolic magic, and one can only understand the actual personal relation if one knows the symbolic role each expects the other to play." Although Auden was inclined to boast of success and satisfaction in his emotional life, the love poems, as Mendelson has shown, tell a different and a sadder story. It was only when Auden met Chester Kallman in New York that he discovered himself really capable of loving with the "consistency and strength"—the fidelity—that Mendelson finds anticipated in Sonnet XXVI from *In Time of War*, rather than with the faithlessness proclaimed in "Lay your sleeping head, my love." The relationship with Kallman was ultimately difficult and painful for Auden, but he seems to have maintained his devotion and loyalty to the end. Carpenter tells us that the relationship provides a biographical source not only for short poems like "The Prophets" and "The More Loving One," but also for a rather unlikely range of later works including "Prospero to Ariel" and the libretto for Stravinsky's *The Rake's Progress* on which Auden and Kallman collaborated.

A good proportion of Carpenter's biography is, in fact, about collaboration with other artists on various projects, and of course Donald Mitchell's book is an extended treatment of one such collaboration over a period of several years. In *Early Auden*, Mendelson takes very seriously a review Auden wrote of Violet Clifton's *The Book of Talbot* in which Auden affirms as an implication of Lady Clifton's devotion to the memory of her husband that, as Mendelson says, "love makes possible a union of isolated perspectives in a coherent work of art, one broader and larger than any single point of view could allow." In a footnote, Mendelson tells us that, shortly after writing the review, Auden embarked on a long series of collaborations. These included work with Isherwood, MacNeice, Stravinsky, Brecht, Kallman, Henze, Nicholas Nabokov, Leif Sjoberg, and, from *Our Hunting Fathers* in 1936 to the setting of the "Hymn to St. Cecilia" in 1942, with Benjamin Britten. Collaboration is indeed a relief both to solitary artists and their biographers. For the artists, work without isolation and loneliness becomes a possibility; if there is love between the collaborators, so much the better. For the biographer, many of an artist's normally internal processes are externalized in collaboration and may thereby be more easily examined; "making," in Auden's terms, comes a few degrees closer to "action."

Britten seems to have felt intimidated by Auden from the start. Six years older than the composer, Auden approached the arts in an intellectual and theoretical way that gave Britten, what he calls in the journals quoted extensively by Mitchell, "a bad inferiority complex." Furthermore, according to Carpenter, Auden "made it his business to 'bring him out'," to make Britten admit his homosexuality and "throw aside all repression." If this sounds less high-minded and exalted than Lady Clifton's devotion to her husband, it clearly was. Britten parried, as it were, Auden's "Underneath the abject willow" with its invitation to "Walk then, come / no longer numb, / into your satisfaction" by setting the poem, as Mitchell says, "as a brisk—jaunty, even—impersonal and highly mannered polka-like dance." To the end of his life Britten found Auden to be "bossy"— "bullying" was Peter Pears' word—while Auden deeply regretted that he eventually became estranged from one of his closest friends, calling this "a constant grief." The sometimes brilliant results of this particular collaboration were produced without love between the collaborators. Mutual respect, great talent, and an edgy emotional atmosphere between them was enough to generate the work.

What I take to be the most impressive fruit of the collaboration—the genuinely strange *Our Hunting Fathers*—came almost at once. It is now at last available, along with *On This Island* and *A Charm of Lullabies*, on the BBC Artium label in a live 1961 performance by Peter Pears. Auden provided the prologue—which he wrote especially for the song cycle—and the epilogue—which gives the cycle its title and was taken from *Look, Stranger!* Britten found both of these demanding poems exceedingly difficult to set, and Donald Mitchell finds them equally difficult to understand, leaning heavily on John Fuller's interpretations, and, in his notes, on Mendelson's. Between the prologue and the epilogue, Auden placed two anonymous poems—"Rats Away" and "Messilina"—and a "Dance of Death" in the shape of Thomas Ravenscroft's "Hawking for the partridge." Although the entire song cycle is about animals—which are, according to the prologue, both "our past and our future"—it is also, in its anthropomorphic treatment of "Rats Away" and "Dance of Death," about the political vermin which had appeared on the scene by 1936 and about the way the human hawks and "the dogs of Europe," as Auden would have it in a later poem, set about to hunt their prey. The music—and the texts as well, if they were fully understood—was clearly a jolt to the very proper audience at the Norwich Festival in 1936 "supported by the local gentry whose hunting habits [came] under scrutiny." Mitchell finds that the setting of "The Dance of Death" represents "the peak of orchestral virtuosity" with its "ferocious transformation of the music hitherto associated with the hunt" brought to "the very brink of chaos and disintegration." It is tempting in this context to give the final lines of Auden's epilogue, with their quote from Lenin, the politically activist reading that Mendelson will not allow. In any case, the work must have been seen for what it essentially was: a virtuoso display of energy and panache by two enfants terribles of a new generation out to overthrow their elders.

Although the collaboration also produced notable results in *On This Island*, certain cabaret songs, at least one of the films and two of the plays, I doubt that either collaborator felt that they ever quite equalled again the initial triumph. When Britten and Peter Pears followed Auden and Isherwood to America, Auden produced a libretto for *Paul Bunyan* which suggests to Mitchell that "Auden never wholly comprehended that, while words are words, words written for transformation into and by music—for consumption by music— are something entirely different." Although Britten dutifully wrote his score for *Paul Bunyan*, he gave up in despair when Auden began to deliver installments of the enormously long and utterly unsettable Christmas oratorio, *For The Time Being*. By then, Britten was tired of feeling dominated in any case, and his longing for his East Anglian roots became as pronounced as Auden's stated desire "to live deliberately without roots." On his way back to England, Britten set the "Hymn to St. Cecilia" for unaccompanied choir. It is a formal farewell to the collaboration.

Far less formal is the extraordinary letter from Auden to Britten written at the time Britten and Pears had decided to sail for England, which is printed in Mitchell's notes. In some ways, the letter strikes me as the most important thing in the entire book. Auden suggests, in terms that parallel in lived experience Mendelson's contrast between the vatic and civil traditions in art, that "Goodness and Beauty are the results of a perfect balance between Order and Chaos, Bohemianism and Bourgeois Convention. Bohemian chaos alone ends in a mad jumble of beautiful scraps; Bourgeois convention alone ends in large unfeeling corpses." It becomes clear that Auden is really talking—in his "bossy" or "bullying" way—about the artist's need to locate and release potentially destructive energies in himself while simultaneously controlling, making intelligible, and indeed domesticating them through the imposition of form.

> Every artist except the supreme masters has a bias one way or the other. The best pair of opposites I can think of in music are Wagner and Strauss. (Technical skill always comes from the bourgeois side of one's nature.)
>
> For middle-class Englishmen like you and me, the danger is of course the second. Your attraction to thin-as-a-board juveniles, ie. to the sexless and innocent, is a symptom of this. And I am certain too that it is your denial and evasion of the demands of disorder that is responsible for your attacks of ill-health, ie. sickness is your substitute for the Bohemian.
>
> Wherever you go you are and probably always will be surrounded by people who adore you, nurse you, and praise everything you do, eg. Elisabeth, Peter (Please show this to P to whom all this is also addressed). Up to a certain point this is fine for you, but beware. You see, Bengy dear, you are always tempted to make things too easy for yourself in this way, ie. to build yourself a warm nest of love (of course when you get it, you find it a little stifling) by playing the lovable talented little boy.
>
> If you are really to develop to your full stature, you will have, I think, to suffer, and make others suffer, in ways which are totally strange to you at present, and against every conscious value that you have; ie. you will have to be able to say what you never have had the right to say—God, I'm a shit.

Neither Britten nor Auden ever submitted entirely to Bourgeois Convention, Order, or the tyranny of sheer technique. Neither Britten's Aldeburgh—his "warm nest of love"—nor Auden's Christianity were sufficient to tame altogether in either what Clive James calls in Auden "the artistic equivalent of the Midas touch." To some degree—more, I think, in Auden than in Britten—energy slowly drained from the work, and virtuosity tended to become facility. Although Auden was all his life the complete eccentric in the external management of his daily activities, he is right in the letter to call Bourgeois Convention a danger for himself as well as for Britten. If "every artist except for the supreme masters has a bias one way or the other," his bias was—at least in the organization of his mental and spiritual life—in that direction. While Britten's external life would appear to have followed the course Auden's letter predicts, his mental and spiritual life did not because it could not: its entire existence was musical. Shaw called music, in a phrase Auden quotes in one of his poems, "the brandy of the damned." It is not so easily chastened as poetry. However much *Peter Grimes* was intended to be a celebration of Britten's homecoming, the opera confirms, as Peter Conrad has brilliantly observed (*TLS*, 10 July 1981) "an outlawry from which he was seeking to be pardoned." Grimes is not Peter Pears' "ineffectual dreamer, beseeching the pity of his fellows" but Jon Vickers' "barnacled prophet, a pathological martyr who defies the community rather than imploring its aid." Similarly, beneath the etiquette of the court and the "escape from the carnal enchantments of the wood" in *A Midsummer Night's Dream*, is the music's covert life: its "audible sexual delirium." Although Britten would have been no more pleased with Conrad's observations than he was with Jon Vickers' Peters Grimes, they reinforce, I think, Mitchell's belief that Auden's letter unveils "the very topic that was Britten's concern throughout his later creative life and formed the substance—the heart—of his last opera, *Death in Venice*." Significantly, it is the menacing sound of the solo tuba that is associated with the notion of pestilence both in "Rats Away" from *Our Hunting Fathers* and in *Death in Venice*. In both, it is the music, not the words, that most profoundly acknowledges "the demands of disorder."

Mendelson, in his introduction, remarked that the vatic and civil traditions "merge at times in the work of a few great writers." Auden implies in his letter that the supreme masters achieve a "perfect balance between Bohemianism and Bourgeois Convention." If this merging and balancing is available only to the greatest writers and supreme masters, the Audens and Brittens must settle for Mendelson's despised "tension." Without such a tension there will be no art at all—or, rather, "large unfeeling corpses" or "beautiful scraps." If the business of the artist is to disenchant us, as Auden came to believe, he must necessarily enchant us first. He can never cease entirely to be that "Double Man" who says with Montaigne: "We are, I know not how, double in ourselves, so that we believe what we disbelieve, and cannot rid ourselves of what we condemn."

In their lives, both Auden and Britten "suffered and made others suffer," like all of us. Carpenter's story of Chester Kallman's infidelities that led Auden "to know what it is to feel oneself the prey of demonic powers . . . stripped of self-control and self-respect, behaving like a ham actor in a Strindberg play" is no less painful to read than is Ronald Duncan's account in *Working with Britten* where he tells us he was "not fooled by Britten's diffidence, knowing his ruthless ambition; nor impressed by his gentleness, having observed his cruelty. If he embraced anybody, it was to strangle them eventually. . . . No man had more charm, could be more generous or kind; but behind the mask was another person, a sadist, psychologically crippled and bent." Is Duncan's account true and accurate? False? A jealous exaggeration? I have no idea. What should one know and what should one say about someone else's life? And when should it be said or known? The night after Auden died, I sat in a pub in Little Shelford and listened to a minor member of one of Bloomsbury's most eminent families hold forth maliciously about Auden's frailties, repetitions, and semisenilities committed in the Christ Church Common Room during the last year of his life when he had returned to Oxford hoping to grow old there as E. M. Forster did at Kings College, Cambridge. It did not seem the right time then for telling all those stories. Now, I imagine it is. "Personally," Ronald Duncan says, "I think that a character as complex as Britten's can never be explained, only accepted; never judged, only loved." Does Carpenter love Auden's equally complex character? I suppose so, in a way. At any rate, he is not keen to judge. Randall Jarrell's judgment was stern and confident enough when, in the second of his major essays on Auden, he attacked Auden's "hysterical blindness to his actual enemies" during the war (German Nazis rather than British and American progressives) and concluded, speaking of Auden's conversion: "When the people of the world of the future—if there are any people in the world—say to us—if some of us are there, 'What did you do in all those wars?' those of us left can give the old, the only answer, 'I lived through them'. But some of us will answer, 'I was saved'." Carpenter does not tell us in his biography that Auden, who was always perplexed by the persistence of Jarrell's attacks, remarked on hearing that Jarrell had killed himself by stepping in front of a speeding truck: "He might at least have thought of the driver."

From The Southern Review, 1983

Robert Duncan and David Jones: Some Affinities

Living in London in the late 1960s, I first came to Robert Duncan's work by the unusual route of David Jones's *In Parenthesis, The Anathemata, Epoch and Artist,* and what came to be called *The Sleeping Lord and Other Fragments.* In 1967, these last poems were simply the "work in progress" published in the special David Jones issue of

---

Given the density of reference in this essay, I employ the following abbreviations in the text to reduce the number of endnotes: BB, *Bending the Bow,* by Robert Duncan (New Directions); D, *Derivations,* by Robert Duncan (Fulcrum Press); TFD, *The First Decade,* by Robert Duncan (Fulcrum Press); OF, *The Opening of the Field,* by Robert Duncan (Grove Press); RB, *Roots and Branches,* by Robert Duncan (New Directions); TLM, *The Truth and Life of Myth,* by Robert Duncan (Sumac Press); I:2, *The H. D. Book,* Part I, Chapter 2, by Robert Duncan (*Coyote's Journal,* no. 8); I:5, *The H. D. Book,* Part I, Chapter 5, by Robert Duncan (*Stony Brook* 1/2); SM, *Robert Duncan: Scales of the Marvelous,* ed. Ian W. Reid (New Directions); IP, *In Parenthesis,* by David Jones (Faber); A, *The Anathemata,* by David Jones (Faber); EA, *Epoch and Artist,* by David Jones (Faber); SL, *The Sleeping Lord and Other Fragments,* by David Jones (Faber); DG, *The Dying Gaul and Other Writings,* by David Jones (Faber); IDJ, *Introducing David Jones,* ed. John Matthias (Faber); DJ, *David Jones: An Exploratory Study,* by Jeremy Hooker (Enitharmon); Ag, *Agenda* 15, 2/3; RGR, *Religion in Greece and Rome,* by H. J. Rose (Harper); HGR, *A History of Greek Religion,* by Martin P. Nilsson (Norton); LU, *The Land Unknown,* by Kathleen Raine (Braziller); LAL, *The Lost America of Love,* by Sherman Paul (Louisiana); ET, *Englarging the Temple,* by Charles Altieri (Bucknell); LFP, *Our Last First Poets,* Carry Nelson (Illinois); TNAP, *Towards a New American Poetics,* by Ekbert Faas (Black Sparrow); HU, *Human Universe,* by Charles Olson (Grove); GI, *Geography of the Imagination,* by Guy Davenport (North Point); B2, *Boundary 2,* VIII, 2.

Agenda. I don't mean that David Jones's texts literally referred me to Duncan—I doubt Jones had ever read him. I only mean that, when I began to read Duncan seriously, I immediately recognized a deep affinity between the Anglo-Welsh poet and painter who had survived both the Western Front and the crippling neurasthenia that attacked him after the war, and his younger American contemporary who, as I was reading his early work in London, was writing those "Passages" which appear at the close of *Bending the Bow.* The late 1960s was a good period for British modernism and American postmodernism in London. Jones, Basil Bunting, and Hugh MacDiarmid were at last acquiring the readership they had long deserved, and Fulcrum Press was busy publishing Duncan, Dorn, Niedecker, Snyder, Rothenberg, and others. Although it was because a friend suggested Duncan's "Venice Poem" as an analogue to the sonata form of Basil Bunting's *Briggflatts* that I opened the Fulcrum edition of *The First Decade,* "The Venus of Lespuges," part 3 of "The Venice Poem," sent me back to the evocation of the Venus of Willendorf in Jones's *The Anathemata,* and on from there to read and re-read Jones and Duncan together. The purpose of these notes is simply to suggest some of the pleasures—as well as the critical difficulties—of doing that, of reading Jones and Duncan together.

At its most fundamental, this, it seems to me, is the common ground: For both Duncan and Jones, man is *homo faber* and art a gratuitous and intransitive activity which, embodied fully in a work, implies also an element of transitivity or sign that is sacramental in its nature and incarnational in its affirmations. The poet himself draws in his writing on at least three traditions: the Greek notion of poet as maker, the Celtic notion of poet as bard, and the Jewish notion of poet as singer of psalms.[1] The poet is also seen as analogous to the priest or magus or tribal rememberer—or a composite of all three figures. While I imagine many contributors to this issue will be making application of categories from Duncan's poetics to his own practice as a poet, I will stress rather more heavily some of David Jones's leading theoretical ideas as a kind of experiment. Much of what follows should be considered tentative, and is offered in that spirit, including this first point: I don't think Charles Olson's "wisdom as such" ever really figured as a problem in Duncan's work, no matter how often Duncan himself broods over Olson's famous essay (HU, 67–71) both in his verse and his prose. (And if God does rush in, that's no problem for the work, only for a certain kind of reader, including the kind of reader Duncan sometimes is of his own work.) I am glad, however, that Olson introduced the term "sign" so early on, because that is David Jones's word, too, and because both David Jones and Duncan would have their signs be significant. What follows can only be a sketch of some future exploration of these (and other) issues common to both poets and central to their respective traditions.

1. The Actually Loved and Known

"Our wise is not more or less than our ways," Duncan has said. And Sherman Paul has observed in *The Lost America of Love* that Duncan's ways turn on an inheritance, a poetic ground, an "essential autobiography he could not alienate" (LAL, 184). The question of Duncan's *materia poetica*, what Ekbert Faas has nicely called "an erudite conglomerate of all that was half or totally heretical in the course of Western cultural history," seems to have been, from the beginning, a question of love rather than wisdom, a "way" which, because of the manner in which the known was known, could not have been "otherwise" (TNAP, 27). In his preface to *The Anathemata*, David Jones argues that "the poet may feel something with regard to Penda the Mercian and nothing with regard to Darius the Mede. . . . No matter, there is no help—he must work within the limits of his love. There must be no mugging-up, no 'ought to know' or 'try to feel'; for only what is actually loved and known can be seen *sub specie aeternitatis*" (A, 24). Although Duncan may, of course, feel nothing in particular for *either* Penda the Mercian or Darius the Mede, and a great deal instead for Taliessen, say, or George Mac-Donald, David Jones's question is fundamental and is also Duncan's question: "What," Jones asks, "for us *is* patient of being 'actually loved and known'. . . . Where do we seek or find what is 'ours,' what *is* available as material for our effective signs?" And he answers, "Normally we should not have far to seek: the flowers for the muse's garland would be gathered from the ancestral burial-mound" (A, 25). Deferring for a moment the implications of that "normally," of that "would be," the "actually loved and known" is seen to have its source in a past both personal and broadly cultural. Duncan and Jones have both given moving accounts of how access to that past was gained in early childhood while lying in bed at night and listening to the conversation of loved adults, taking in sense impressions around them, dreaming, and making visual or verbal associations. This process—acknowledgement of a loved voice as a source, authority, or "permission," combining with sense impressions from immediate experience, dreams, and verbal or visual associations—never ceases in either poet; it is the very stuff of their poetry.

In *The H. D. Book*, Duncan remembers "his mother's voice reading the fairy tales and myths that were to remain the charged ground of [his] poetic reality" (I:2,27) and, when the stories were over, "drifting in the environment of voices talking in the next room" (I:5,4). His elders told him that his soul "went out to the stars or to other worlds"; his body in the bed sailed like a wooden shoe "on a river of crystal light, / into a sea of dew." The adults spoke of their beliefs, his parents invoking their teacher, the Hermetic Christos. His grandmother would later show him images of Thoth from *The Book of the Dead* which he would recognize at once as the bronze figure that stood on his aunt's piano. His aunt Fay—he would make the associations with *fey, fairy, fate, faith, fair,* and *feign*— would explain that his soul "was like a swarm of bees, and, at night, certain entities of that swarm left the body-hive and went to feed in the fields of helium." The lure that he felt—that he still feels—"is the lure of those voices weaving as I began to understand words." Dreams came as "instructions from angels of the Sun" or as "messages from the Underworld." Older, still listening, still dreaming, having moved from the region of San Francisco to Bakersfield where "our religion became something one did not talk about to everybody," he talked about it to himself. "There is only what I remember from childhood: the colored lithographs of Egyptian temples and the images upon the table, the voices talking of 'Logos' and 'Nous,' the old women looking wisely into the Astral Light and telling what they saw there" (I:5,4ff). Before there were any books, before *Isis Unveiled* and *The Secret Doctrine, Fragments of a Faith Forgotten* and *Echoes from the Gnosis,* before *The Zohar* (or even *The Golden Bough, Themis,* and *From Ritual to Romance*) there were the loved voices, the associations, the dreams, the voyages to be taken with Wynken, Blynken, and Nod whose shoe turned out to be, in time, the ship of Avalon and Ra-Set's boat and D. H. Lawrence's ship of death—just as the little figure on Aunt Fay's piano turned out in time to be Thoth. Speaking of his own backgrounds and inheritance, David Jones says in his preface to *The Anathemata:* "If such like motifs are one's materials, then one is trying to make a shape out of the very things of which one is oneself made . . . You use the things that are yours to use because they happen to be lying about the place or site or lying within the orbit of your tradition" (A, 10). These are the things that will be "actually loved and known." At the beginning of *The Truth and Life of Myth,* Duncan writes:

The shaping of every spiritual and psychic imagination has its ground in these things I did not originate but that came to me as an inheritance of what I was, a gift of life meanings. Today I still love, even foolishly, the signs and wonders, felt presences or nearnesses of meaning, where we must follow, in trust, having no more sure a guarantee of our arrival than does the adventurer in fairy or hero tale. . . . The roots and depths of mature thought, its creative sources, lie in childhood or even "childish" things I have not put away but taken as enduring realities of my being. The mothering and fathering voices about me conveyed a realm of pleasure and pain I was to seek not to dismiss but to deepen. (*TLM* 8,13,14)

David Jones's account of his initial access to what would ultimately become his *materia poetica* is strikingly like Duncan's. His poetry, he argues, has nothing to do with erudition and everything to do with the channels through which the ancestral burial mounds, the stratified cultural deposits, were opened. "I am speaking of channels only, but of immediate channels and such as condition all that passes through them, and which condition also one's subsequent attitude to all the rest. These I judge to be of the most primary importance. It is through them that 'all the rest' is already half sensed long before it is known" (A, 40ff). His father—Welsh, reticent, and speaking with what Jones calls "suppressed pride" for the land his son was eventually to feel he belonged to—sang, as Jones attempted to imitate the sounds, *Mae hem wlad fy nhadau* or *Ar hyd y now*, and pointed out the drawings of Welsh foot-soldiers in J. R. Green's *Short History of the English People*. His mother's reminiscence made for a living link with the last great days of the Pool of London, her father, the Ebenezer Bradshaw of Princess Stair in Jones's "Redriff" section of *The Anathemata*, having been a master mast- and block-maker. A late reader, Jones paid his sister a penny to read aloud the Arthurian stories in a series called "Books for the Bairns" and *The Lays of Ancient Rome*; he gazed at Johann Frederich Overbeck's illustrations to Keble's *Christian Year*. In a transcribed tape recording made at the end of his life and now called "In illo tempore," he dates his first memory from about 1900 when he climbed from the cot by his mother's bed to stand by the window and see and hear "a great marvel—a troop of horse, moving in column to the taratantara of bugles." (These were recruiters on a ride through the suburbs during the war in South Africa.) When his mother put him back in bed, he lay "for some time wondering who, in fact, were those strange horsemen. I had heard my sister saying something about 'the vats of Luna' and 'the Yellow Tiber.' " Decades later, writing *The Tribune's Visitation,* Jones had his Tribune speak of "some remembered fuller cup from Luna Vats," writing he says, "unconsciously and without hesitation, as though Luna was the only place in Italy for wine of good vintage"; and in *In Parenthesis* his reference to " 'Peredur of steel arms,' though quoted from Edward Anwyl's translation of the *Gododdin* fragments, also recalled the childhood glimpse of the strange riders seen through the slats of the venetian blinds, and the *At tuba terribili sonitu tarantara dixit,* many years before I had heard of Ennius" (*DG,* 19–21). In summary, he writes in his preface to *The Anathemata:*

> It may be yesterday only that you heard of the significance of *The Epistle of Clement* and but a few years back that the other Clement's *Exhortation to the Greeks* was recommended to you by a perceptive cousin. But it was very many years ago that you wondered what Clement had to do with Danes. And it was much longer still ago that an aunt initiated you into "Oranges and Lemons." She may have been evasive when asked, "Aunty, what's Clemens?" but she was handing down a traditional form and starting up in you a habit of "recalling." For names linger, especially when associated with some sort of *disciplina ludi.* They go into your word-hoard, whether or no you ever attempted to unlock it. (A, 42)

Led in *The H. D. Book* by what he loved and knew as a child to an exploration of Madame Blavatsky's *The Secret Doctrine,* and hence to the Order of the Golden Dawn and its schism between the Christian mystics and the pantheists, and from there via G. R. S. Meade to the Oxbridge world of Frazer, Harrison, and Jessie Weston, Duncan begins to uncover burial mounds, along with their channels of access, that belong to the Celtic-Christian ancestors of David Jones's imagination as well as his own imagination's Orphic, Gnostic, Kabbalistic, and Hermetic ones (well, and Celtic too—for that world he shares with David Jones, and it proves to be rich in deposits drawn upon in his poetry from very early on). The rhyme about the wooden shoe begins indeed, like the one about the oranges and lemons, "a habit of recalling." Duncan says that in "Blavatsky's theosophy the psyche inhabits every time and place," and he compares this notion with Freudian psychoanalysis in which "the individual psyche is seen to recapitulate the psychic life of the species" (I:5, 11). Turning to the bardic tradition as one channel into the past among many, and as one technique of anamnesis, Duncan quotes from the 13th century *Romance of Taliessin* in which Gwion names himself for one of David Jones's favorite figures from sixth-century Wales, the poet Taliessin whose boast at Maelgwn's court is assimilated—along with the boast of Widsith, the boast of Arthur's porter Glewlwyd, and the boast in John viii—to Dai Greatcoat's boast in *In Parenthesis*. If Duncan can begin the boast in an essay recalling theosophy, "Chief bard am I to Elphin, / my original country is the region of the summer stars; / I was with my Lord in the highest sphere, / On the fall of Lucifer into the depth of hell" (I:5, 11), David Jones can finish it in a poem recalling the Somme: "I was the spear in Balin's hand / that made waste King Pellam's land . . . / I served Longinus that Dux bat-blind and bent;

> The Dandy Xth are my regiment;
> who diced
> Crown and mud-hook
> under the Tree,
> Whose Five Sufficient Blossoms
> yield for us . . .
> I heard Him cry:
> > *Apples ben ripe in my gardayne*
> I saw him die. (IP, 79–84)

Duncan has written that he is "unbaptized, uninitiated, ungraduated, and unanalyzed," that his worship belongs to no church, his mysteries to no cult, his learning to no institution, and his imagination to no philosophical system (I:2, 27). Although David Jones, like Duncan, was a passionate autodidact—and therefore also "ungraduated"—he was baptized, initiated, and analyzed. Fully as catholic in his range of sources, allusions, and mythological references as Duncan, he was also Catholic (the Roman kind). His mysteries therefore belong ultimately to one cult, his learning to one institution, and his imagination to one philosophical system. If Duncan's syncretic religion (like his syncretic poetry—and they are really the same) is indeed that "conglomerate of all that was half or totally heretical in the course of Western cultural history," David Jones's orthodox religion (like his eucharistic poetry) can be seen at least in part as a conglomerate of all he is able to regard as half or totally predicting, prefiguring or typologically embodying the Christianity to which he eventually subscribed (and these prefigurations and types include some of Duncan's favorite gods, goddesses and heretics). The relationship between the two poetries—as between the heretic and the Christian—is symbiotic. Duncan's signs, his anathemata, signify a range of beings, powers, and energies that exist before, after, below, above, or to the side of David Jones's eucharistic center. Jones's poetry wishes, as it were, to baptize as many of those beings, powers, and energies as possible once they are embodied, incarnate. Working the other side of the street, Duncan's poetry, like Pound's, would repaganize much in their common Western tradition that is already Christian. Although many of Duncan's sources are in some way dualistic or neo-Platonic, he, like Jones, is ultimately incarnational in his beliefs and in his poetry.[2] Although he "draws utterly away from Him" in "Another Animadversion" and in other poems, he includes Christ among the gods of his pantheon.

> Divine Being shows itself
> not in the rising above,
> but embodied, out of
> deliberate committed lines of stone or flesh
> flashings of suffering shared. (OF, 84)

Or, in prose: "This non-Christian's view is just that he would not, in honoring Christ, dishonor or displace any of the other gods, dreams, goddesses, eternities of human vision" (NAP, 404).

2. The Feminine, Man-the-Maker, and Their Sign

"Not in the rising above, / but embodied, out of / deliberate committed lines of stone or flesh." As for the Son, so also for the Mother: in any of her forms and manifestations. As Michael Davidson has said, Duncan's Christ, "through his various avatars in history, is folded *into* history; his nature demands that he be revived. . . . His mystery may be found in the things of the world"[3] (SM, 72). But the mysteries of the Mother, of the Feminine, are anterior to the mystery of the Son—both in the life of the species and in the manner in which the individual psyche is seen to recapitulate that life. In Duncan's life, the feminine voices which succeeded one another—his adoptive mother's, his grandmother's, his aunt's, Edna Keough's, Gertrude Stein's, and H. D.'s—all speak of the one he never heard, his own mother's, which was stilled upon his birth. "Mnemosyne, the Mother-Memory of Poetry," he writes in *The*

H. D. Book, "is our made-up life, the matrix of fictions. . . . Freud, too, teaches that the Art has something to do with re-storing, re-membering the Mother" (I:2, 27–28).

As I mentioned at the outset, the first lines of Duncan's I can remember reading are these:

> Of first things: solid.
> Her paleolithic image
> is large. Six inches in height,
> it is monumental.
> The spirit is flung upward.
> The body remains, monumental,
> from which all spirit flows. . . . (TFD, 96)

The re-membering, the re-presentation, the anamnesis continues as "Her image looms / wherein lies the universe of felt things. . . . / the shoulders and the long neck / with the round sexual head / curved like the violin neck / of the female musical body / seem instrumental, / the deep strings of the viol / waiting for sound" (TED, 96). As the Venus of Lespuges metamorphosed into the Queen of Hearts and Eleanor of Aquitaine and Henri Rousseau's Queen of the Jungle, I can still remember turning to David Jones's *Anathemata* and reading of that other paleolithic Venus, the Willendorf, and of its maker.

> Who were his *gens*-men or had he no *Hausname* yet
> no *nomen* for his *fecit*-mark
> the master of the Venus?
> whose man-hands god-handled the Willendorf stone
> before they unbound the last glaciation. (A, 59)

It is perhaps where they are invoking and evoking the Feminine powers that David Jones and Duncan are most complementary. They are, I think, along with Pound, Joyce, and Graves, the major twentieth-century poets of the Feminine in English. The mothers, daughters, goddesses, muses, sibyls, queens, and other embodiments or voices of the Feminine proliferate in a myriad of ways through the work of both poets. All three of Duncan's major collections—*The Opening of the Field, Roots and Branches,* and *Bending the Bow*—are dedicated to the Feminine, to the Muse. She is "The Queen under the Hill" of "Often I am Permitted to Return to a

Meadow" (OF, 7); she is the one who "has a place in memory that moves language" in the first section of "The Structure of Rime" (OF, 12). She is considered "precedent to the Shekinah" in "The Maiden," and she rhymes with Dante's Beatrice, with Persephone, with Rachel, and her image can be glimpsed in Millais's painting of Elizabeth Siddal as Ophelia, or even in a photograph of Marianne Moore (OF, 27–28); Kore in "An Evocation," she shakes the earth in San Francisco (OF, 40); Sophia in "A Sequence of Poems for H. D.'s Birthday," she is "the eternal woman woven in blue. . . . the blue of the sky all around" that Solovyev saw (RB, 16); heard in "the hysterical talk of a school girl" on a bus, she is Duncan's mother herself, and then the Great Mother . . . "or metre, of the matter . . ." (RB, 76); in "Doves" she is H. D. (RB, 86). Typically a version of the mother, she is also famously manifest as Psyche, the human soul, searching for Eros and performing her tasks in "Poem Beginning with a Line by Pindar" (OF, 62). If we re-member her, recall her, she, as Isis, will re-member us even as she did Osiris, restore us to our humanity: "Our mother comes with us to gather her children" (RB, 69). Gaia, Earth—"murther, murmerer, demurrer"—in "The Continent," she is once again Mnemosyne at the beginning of "Passages," and associated, as she is in David Jones, with the campfire, the hearth stone, and the city (BB, 10); she broods over the egg from which Eros, Phanes, will emerge in accordance with Orphic cosmogony. The mother of Christ, she is also Christ Himself in His feminine aspect: "Christ was more and rare that was a maiden's babe: / He was part girl . . ." (OF, 28). Having forgotten the Lamb in "At Christmas," Duncan sees "a woman where I lookd for Him, a wounded beast upon the marriage bed / from which Love ran" (OF, 58). And in the eighth section of "Passages," at the threshold of speech, "at life's labia": "Her crack of a door opening / her cunt / a wound now / the gash in His side. . . . All maidens bear Christ's sign" just as we are "To be born again from the wound in His side" (BB, 24). Mother and daughter, goddess and mortal girl, virgin and harlot, these versions of the Feminine coalesce and disperse and coalesce again, calling us to dance. In "Reflections" (BB, 38), one of those pieces in which he answers Olson's essay on "Wisdom as such," Duncan writes that "before the righteous hearts hardened against the ease of Christendom," Christ was not only Leader of the Waltz, "But He was Himself, He said, the Waltz Itself." As early as "The Dance" (OF, 8), the voice of the Feminine answers the poet's "Where have I gone, Beloved?" by saying clearly: *"Into the Waltz,*

Dancer." But the Feminine, again, is not simply agent or mediatrix or "voice of first permission," Mary's *fiat mihi.* Looking back from the major collections to the first decade of Duncan's work, we can see much of his treatment of the Feminine anticipated in "Medieval Scenes," which, although it contains an "Adoration of the Virgin" in which the Queen of Heaven holds, wonderfully, "the Infant Wizard," begins with an epigraph from Laura Riding, the words, "so legend goes," which she "had inscribed in letters of gold" on the wall of her bedroom: *"God is a Woman"* (TFD, 51).

The drama in any attempt to re-member and restore the archaically Feminine is likely to center finally on Kore and Demeter, and I think Sherman Paul is right to regard Duncan's work "in the spirit of Eleusis" as part of a project that would "bring Kore out of the hell of war-ravaged civilization into the meadow, the open field of restored life . . ." and make for a restoration "by a saving remnant of 'the mothering Life or Great Mother' " (LAL, 179). And this activity, too, like the Waltz that is Christ, is a dance. Martin Nilsson reminds us that the Eleusinian mysteries "possessed no dogma. . . . Instead, they had certain sacred acts, which aroused religious feeling and into which every age could put the symbolism it desired" (HGR, 211). "It is not," Duncan says in "Towards an Open Universe," "that poetry imitates but that poetry enacts in its order the order of first things" (PNAP, 217). This notion comes very close to what David Jones means, thinking both of poetry and the Mass, by anamnesis. "To dance out the mysteries," H. J. Rose explains, was a phrase for a particular kind of impiety on the part of Eleusinian initiates if done in public (RGR, 70). But to "dance out the mysteries" in language *is* the enactment affirmed by Duncan and the anamnesis affirmed by David Jones. It is that method of re-calling, re-membering, re-presenting "an event in the past so that it becomes here and now operative by its effects . . ." which David Jones finds stated to his satisfaction in *The Shape of the Liturgy* by Gregory Dix (EA, 126). The Christian priest, too, must in his own way "dance out the mysteries," enact the order of first things by offering up his efficacious signs. Here, too, as Duncan says of poetry in "Towards an Open Universe," "there is no form that is not content, no content that is not form" (PNAP, 217).

While the variety of David Jones's figurations of the Feminine is as wide-ranging and impressive as Duncan's—and one thinks at once of his Queen of the Woods in *In Parenthesis,* his Gwenhwyfar and his Lady of the Pool in *The Anathemata,* his Tellus Mater and his

Tutelar of the Place in *The Sleeping Lord and Other Fragments*—I want to stress for a moment the manner in which these figures, as also all of Duncan's, manifest man's inalienable nature as a sign-making creature, as, indeed, *homo faber*.

As I have argued in *Introducing David Jones*, it is a cardinal belief of this poet that in so far as man is man—and as he developed out of other forms, so may he develop into other forms—he is a maker, an artist, capable of the gratuitous and intransitive activities which are traced in *The Anathemata* to some of their earliest manifestations. Although these manifestations include the Lascaux cave paintings, Jones's focus is on the Venus of Willendorf of the same Aurignacian culture, she whose maker's "man-hands god-handled" the stone. "Chthonic?" he asks; and answers: "Why yes / but mother of us . . . She that they / already venerate (what other could they?) / her we declare? / Who else?" (A, 60). In his note on the passage, Jones writes that the Venus is the "earliest example of a long sequence of mother-figures, earth-mothers and mother goddesses, that fuse in the Great-Mother of settled civilizations" (A, 60), while in the text of *The Anathemata* she is seen to anticipate the statue of Athena in "Middle-Sea and Lear-Sea" and prefigure the Queen of Heaven herself whose beauty outshines even that of Guenever at the midnight Mass in "Mabinog's Liturgy." Regarding man to be "a creature which is not only capable of gratuitous acts but of which it can be said that such acts are this creature's hallmark and sign-manual," he writes that "it is the intransitivity and gratuitousness in man's art that is the sign of man's uniqueness . . . ," that "man is unavoidably a sacramentalist and . . . his works sacramental in character," and that "palaeolithic man, whatever else he was, and whatever his ancestors were," juxtaposed marks and made shapes "not with merely utile, but with significant intent; that is to say a 're-presenting,' a 'showing again under other forms,' an 'effective recalling' of something was intended" (EA, 148ff).

In *The Truth and Life of Myth*, Duncan, too, affirms the element of the gratuitous or extra-utile as, in his case, *play*. "We play in art, yes; and as artists show how much of the Father—even the ruthless mad old Father of the Old Testament—there is in Man as Maker, *homo faber*" (TLM, 75). And if the sanction of the Feminine is again required for such father's play, Jones delivers it from both the Old Testament and the New. "Holy Wisdom herself says *ludo*. In the famous passage in the Book of Proverbs she is made to say *ludens in orbe terrarum*. She was with the Logos when all things were formed, 'playing before him at all times' and as the Knox translation puts it:

'I made play in this world of dust, with the sons of Adam for my play fellows' " (EA, 154). And in a letter to René Hague, Jones calls the enactment and anamnesis of the Roman liturgy itself, "as it stood with the Chant," a "stupendous art work—as inutile as Mary Maudlin's precious unguents poured out from the fractured alabaster" (Ag, 44). [4]

If it is fair to say that the complex metamorphosis of the Feminine in David Jones's work, as also in Duncan's, is a myth, one must go on to say at once that Jones means by myth pretty much the same thing that Duncan does in *The Truth and Life of Myth* where he quotes Milton's extraordinary paragraph on Isis and Osiris from *Areopagitica* and argues that Milton is "not illustrating a principle with a figure of speech" but recalling to the conscience and consciousness of the Puritan parliament "the meaning of what they do as revealed in a myth that is also the true history hidden in history. . . . The mythological mind . . . hears this not as fable or parable but as the actual drama or meaning of history, the plot and intention of Reality" (TLM, 61). Jeremy Hooker reminds us that for Jones, "the fact that Christianity is myth makes it, if possible, more rather than less true," for Jones "invariably uses the word myth to mean a true story"—Duncan's history hidden in history, his "plot and intention of Reality" (DJ, 28). The metamorphosis of the Venus Genetrix in his work through the earth-mothers and mother goddesses to Mary herself is a "true myth," a "history hidden in history."[5]

Perhaps one could find no better representation of the composite figure which one is dealing with in the works of both David Jones and Duncan than in the former's paintings of *Aphrodite in Aulis* (at the Tate) and *Y Cyfarchiad I Fair* ("The Greetings to Mary," at the National Museum of Wales)—for we must remember that David Jones was a visual artist long before he ever wrote a book. The myths embodied in these paintings, these things *made*, these collages of signs, correspond in intention and execution to the treatment of the Feminine in the poetry. Iphigenia becomes Aphrodite because Jones's intention was "to include *all* feminine cult-figures . . . wounded of necessity as are all things worthy of our worship" (Ag, 76). Nails have pierced her hands and feet; without her sacrifice there will be no wind, no incarnation without her *fiat mihi*. As a Welsh girl in *Y Cyfarchiad I Fair*, she is visited by a Gabriel who is clearly also Mercury; the enactment of the Annunciation unfolds in a context of Celtic myth drawn from the *Mabinogion* and alluding to Culhwch's quest, itself an allegory of Christ's passion. If the painting could speak, it might address Duncan in the words of the second century Justin: "In this we agree with you in that we both look on the Logos, whom you call Hermes, as the messenger of God" (Ag, 75).

3. Sign, Hearth, Meadow, Cave, and "Requisite Nowness"

It is important for me to state clearly that, in spite of the fact that Duncan's texts are often self-interrogating and sometimes self-referential or reflexive (especially in "The Structure of Rime" sequence),[6] and, in spite of many things he has said about the absence of reference in his poetry, I find his work as fundamentally committed to sign and sign-making as that of David Jones, the master of the Venus, the painters of the Lascaux caves, and, let us say to complicate the matter, Rodilla in his Watts towers. In the first of the Ekbert Faas interviews, Duncan meets Faas's observation that Robert Creeley maintains that his (Creeley's) poems have no referential meaning with: "Well, but then that's balderdash" (TNAP, 74). Although the situation may be more complex in Duncan's own work, I do think his poems usually refer in obvious ways to the myths, figures, friends, art works, texts, wars, houses, animals, and so forth that they are re-membering, re-presenting, and embodying in the course of the enactment which is their formal unfolding.[7] Even Rodilla's Watts towers, celebrated with another nod at Olson's "Against Wisdom as Such" in "Nel Mezzo Del Cammin Di Nostra Vita" as "Art, dedicated to itself!" (RB, 22) are, through the gratuitousness and intransitivity embodied in the objects themselves, lent an element of transitivity: they become the effective sign, after all, of the gratuitous and intransitive nature of the gesture that gave them being, and therefore become the sign of man-as-such, of homo faber, and his connection through time all the way back to the prehistory of his species and the identical gesture of "the master of the Venus" and the painters in the Lascaux caves. They are an assertion, as in much contemporary abstraction,[8] of man's sign-making nature per se, and, therefore, a sign and affirmation of the extra-utile in a world of utilitarian instrumentality in the Spenglerian civilization that has grown out of the primitive matriarchy, the culture of the hearth presided over by the mother goddess, whatever her name. Or, at any rate, that is the way I think David Jones would see and describe them. For Jones, the paradox is this: if such art is truly "dedicated to itself" it is, by the nature of that dedication, "made over to the gods." God does rush in. Or myth.

> . . . a fairy citadel,
> a fabulous construction out of
> Christianity where Morgan le Fay
> carries the King to her enchanted Isle . . . (*RB*, 23)

Shortly after I first met Robert Duncan—when he spoke enthusiastically about David Jones both as poet and painter—I received a letter in which he said, among other things: "More than philosophy I think I still love curiosity. And my own poetry (like my house—ours, for both Jess and I have that bent) is a curiosity shop."

Although I have never visited Duncan's home, the descriptions I have had of it from mutual friends remind me of the three homes I associate most profoundly with the work of David Jones—Jim Ede's Kettle's Yard in Cambridge, and Helen Sutherland's two houses, Rock Hall and Cockley Moor. Both Jim Ede and Helen Sutherland were early collectors of David Jones's visual work, and Jones himself worked for various periods at Rock Hall and Cockley Moor. I have elsewhere described Kettle's Yard as a visual, tactile equivalent for Jones's accumulating written works, while Kathleen Raine, who knew Jones and stayed with him at Cockley Moor, calls Helen Sutherland's home "a house which seemed to me then more like a place of the imagination—some castle in Spenser . . . one of those places of arrival where treasures are shown to pilgrim or traveller, and wounds are healed" (*LU*, 128).[9] A curiosity, if it is curious enough, becomes a treasure, a wonder, and I cannot help thinking of Duncan's house not only as a formal analogue to his poetry (for which he gives me permission), but also of both the house and the poetry as repositories of signs and anathemata which can perhaps be evoked by David Jones when he explains what the title of his own book might, however obliquely, suggest.

> The blessed things that have taken on what is cursed and the profane things that somehow are redeemed: the delights and also the "ornaments," both in the primary sense of gear and paraphernalia and in the sense of what simply adorns; the donated and votive things, the things dedicated after whatever fashion, the things in some sense made separate, being "laid up from other things"; things, or some aspect of them, that partake of the extra-utile and of the gratuitous; things that are the signs of something other, together with those signs that not only have the nature of sign, but are themselves, under some mode, what they signify. Things set up, lifted up, or in whatever manner made over to the gods. (*A*, 28)

In such homes and around such hearths as Duncan's, Jim Ede's, and Helen Sutherland's, "all the signs rime" as Duncan has it in a section of "The Structure of Rime" (BB, 4) or, to paraphrase his favorite text from Heraclitus, one understands that, being at variance, they accord with each other. Michael Davidson's excellent essay on *The Opening of the Field* makes much of the fact that Duncan was establishing a new household in San Francisco while writing many of the poems that engage "the mythology of the primal hearth as a source of cultural origins" (SM, 60). He tells us that Duncan read Fustel de Coulanges's *The Ancient City* during this period which "provided a description of Greek and Roman law, having its base in the household—literally beneath the hearth where the ancestors were buried" (SM, 61). This notion returns us at once to the question I left hanging about why *normally* the flowers for the muse's garland *would be* gathered from such a place—the implication being, of course, that we live in abnormal times, that we come very late indeed into the world of our ancestors.

When Davidson writes of Duncan's use of the *Zohar* by Moses de Leon where he found a description of "the field of Machpelah and its adjacent cave . . . holding the beginnings of civilization in the form of its first parents" (SM, 61), I think at once of *In Parenthesis* where John Ball, entering the trenches by night, is assimilated into what was, paradoxically, David Jones's most profound experience of the hearth, where "you know the homing perfume of wood burned, at the termination of ways; and sense here near habitation, a folk-life here, a people, a culture already developed, already venerable and rooted" (IP, 49). Beneath this hearth is, as it were, the cave on the field, the ancestral burial mound buried itself under the phantasmagoric system of trenches and defenses, what Jones calls in his notes "the tumbled undulations and recesses, the static sentries, and the leaning arms that were the Forward Zone" which called up an "abiding myth of our people." Here lie the barrow sleepers . . . the *fer sidhe* sleepers "under fairy tumuli, fair as Mac Og sleeping." Here lie Mac Og, Arthur, Owen of the Red Hand, the Cumberland Sleepers, even Plutarch's Cronus—"imprisoned with Briareus keeping guard over him as he sleeps" (IP, 51 and 198). This, like Duncan's meadow, is Jones's "place of first permission" his "everlasting omen of what is." Like Duncan in Part IV of "The Structure of Rime," he finds "the kin at the hearth, the continual cauldron that feeds forth the earth, the heart that comes into being through the blood" (OF, 17). He finds, indeed, a version of the matriarchal hearth and culture in the total absence of women, but under the sponsorship of moonlight—"that perbright Shiner stood for Her rod-budding"—and of the earth.

If the appearance of the Queen of the Woods following the terrible slaughter in the seventh section of *In Parenthesis* corresponds in many ways to Duncan's attempt, as Sherman Paul expresses it, "to bring Kore out of the Hell of war-ravaged civilization into the meadow, the open field of restored life" (LAL, 179), still there is evidence in the workings of that civilization that any making dedicated to the muse is gravely endangered, that the signs may cease to signify and rhyme, that the meadow and the field will be flooded, the ancestral burial mound levelled to build parking lots and airports. The restoration "by a saving remnant" of "the mothering Life or Great Mother" may be only "*for* a saving remnant." As Jones writes in "The Tutelar of the Place," his great hymn to the mother: "set up the hedges of illusion round some remnant of us, twine the wattles of mist, white-web a Gwydion-hedge / like fog on the *bryniau* / against the commissioners / bringing writs of the Ram to square the world-floor and number the tribes and write down the secret things and take away the diversities by which we are" (SL, 63). Thus we gather from "Passages 29" they might have prayed among the Cao-Dai in Viet Nam (and among the Albigensians at Montségur); thus might any poet pray in his way from the hearth that is his trench or dugout. Even in "Often I Am Permitted To Return To A Meadow" there is an allusion to Duncan's particular nightmare of universal unmaking, his Atlantis Dream, which his mother thought was the memory of a past life but which seemed to him to be "a prediction of what life will be . . . a showing forth of some content of what life is" (I:5, 19).

If the goddess who would restore us does appear, but calls herself Rhiannon, what if no one acknowledges that name? And if she says her name is Kore, are the chances really better? In his preface to *The Anathemata*, Jones argues that the signs offered up, the names incanted, must not only express "the mythos, deposits, matière, ethos, whole *res* of which the poet himself is a product," not only be "a recalling of something loved," but must possess what he calls "a requisite nowness." "The sign," he says, "valid in itself, is apt to suffer a kind of invalidation" due to the acceleration of change in our time. "This presents most complicated problems to the artist working outside a reasonably static culture-phase" (A, 20ff). It is interesting to watch a reader as subtle and learned as Ian W. Reid struggle with "Gassire's lute" and "the song of Wagadu" in "Passages 20," observing that "access to proper comprehension is not made easy" because the references "cannot reasonably be thought to belong to the generally recognized repository of Western literary culture" (SM, 172). Such references may indeed belong exclusively now to the poet's hearth; but so may many that have for centuries belonged to Western literary culture. "If the poet writes *wood*," Jones asks, "what are the chances that the Wood of the Cross will be evoked? Should the answer be 'none,' then it would seem that an impoverishment of some sort would have to be admitted." (And if a man build three bejewelled towers in Watts . . . ?) "The arts abhor any loppings off of meanings or emptyings out, any lessening of the totality of connotation, any loss of recession or thickness through" (A, 23). Guy Davenport, whose essay "The Symbol of the Archaic" in *The Geography of the Imagination* celebrates modernism's recovery of Persephone as Eurydice, and of the city as culmination of works by those who worshipped Cybele-Demeter, ends by depriving the poet even of his hearth: "Our poets are gypsies camping in the ruins again. Persephone and Orpheus have reverted to footnotes in anthologies" (GI, 28). Although David Jones has shown that even a camp in the ruins can be a hearth, he has had to compose his own footnotes—an acknowledgement of the precarious state in which he finds the signs and anathemata he would make over to the gods and share with an audience.

While Duncan refuses to be deprived either of his hearth or the resonance of his signs even in his most problematic, painful, and ambitious book—*Bending the Bow*—he is also keenly aware of the difficulties which Jones articulates. Imagining as "Readers" lines of advancing police or guardsmen during a Viet Nam protest in the 1960s, he writes from the perspective of a demonstrator who is also a poet stubbornly holding the ground of his testimony: "We ourselves are the boundaries they have made against their humanity" (BB, ii). And Jones, writing in an allegorical letter of man-the-technocrat whose civilization follows the culture of man-the-artist, imagines a burying party and a salvage squad attempting to decipher "what were still valid as signs, for some of us, when our front was finally rolled up." He says of them, "No matter how metamorphosed by a technocracy the full ramifications of which we cannot as yet guess, in so far as they are still men they will not altogether escape the things of man" (EA, 141). It is very nearly the same point. In the final paragraph of "The Readers," Duncan turns from the advancing lines to "those alike in soul," and in "It" he reestablishes his household—precariously "high on the ground of a history written in earthquakes"—affirming "an almost womanish tenderness in orders we are fierce to keep" (BB, vi). In "Passages 1" the "poet's voice speaks . . . from the hearth stone, the lamp light, the heart of the matter where the / house is held" (BB, 9). But in the hearth itself, in this book, burns the fire of Heraclitus.[10] If Duncan's signs are to achieve in his own terms the "requisite nowness," the contemporary validity, that David Jones insists upon, he understands that they must be transfigured by that fire and submitted to the workings not only of the Christian Logos but, as Charles Altieri has said, also of the Greek Logos "conceived as a mode of violence continually unsettling what is and re-creating it."[11] Where this is so, both in *Bending the Bow* and more generally, Duncan and David Jones part company, although both maintain in their work the sacramental ethos which I claimed for them at the outset.

Leaving for another occasion what might prove to be an interesting discussion of the fundamental *differences* of orientation in David Jones and Duncan, let me conclude with two final quotes, one from *The Anathemata* and the other from "Passages" which, as it were, answer each other from the sacramental depths of each poet's tradition.

We already and first of all discern him making this thing other. His groping syntax, if we attend, already shapes:
    ADSCRIPTAM, RATAM, RATIONABILEM . . . and by preapplication and for *them*, under modes and patterns altogether theirs, the holy and venerable hands lift up an efficacious sign. (A, 49)

The Orphic Xristos descends in the magic rite—
        the driving of the nails into his hands and feet,
    the briar crown, and, before: the sweating, stumbling
        destitute carrying of the instruments of his death
            to the place of His death

Her death he comes to   to unite   Kore and Xristmas (BB, 60)

From *Ironwood*, 1983

Dai Greatcoat

René Hague, *Dai Greatcoat: A Self-portrait of David Jones in His Letters*,
Faber and Faber.

In *Dai Greatcoat: A Self-portrait of David Jones in His Letters*, the
maker of *In Parenthesis* and *The Anathemata*, of the *Vexilla Regis* and
The Four Queens, has once again been loyally served by his old friend
and colleague, René Hague. Hague has drawn before on his correspondence with David Jones, both for biographical and exegetical
purposes in his essential and meticulous volume of 1977, *A Commentary on the Anathemata of David Jones*, as well as in his earlier mono-
graph in the "Writers of Wales" series and his essays on Jones in
periodicals. Readers of David Jones will doubtless have savoured
these excerpts, and they will also very likely know the *Letters to Vernon Watkins*, edited by Ruth Pryor; the *Letters to William Hayward*,
edited by Colin Wilcockson; and certain important letters published
singly or in small groups, such as those to Saunders Lewis in the
1973–74 David Jones issue of *Agenda*. Even so, few readers will be
fully prepared for the sustained experience of reading the nearly
fifty years of correspondence gathered together in *Dai Greatcoat*.

Hague tells us in his preface that his early plan for the book
"changed as it was being put together." He had at first intended
something more in the nature of a proper biography which was to
have been generously illustrated by the letters. As he worked away
at the mass of correspondence, "the material itself took control and
determined the form. It very soon became clear that, left to himself,
David would both record the progress of his life . . . and at the same
time portray his character and personality." What we have in *Dai
Greatcoat* is, therefore, very much "a self-portrait" rather than a bi-

ography—but "a self-portrait" with some considerable stress on the article. The letters, with several important exceptions, are addressed to four correspondents: Hague himself; Harman Grisewood, editor of Jones's two volumes of essays, *Epoch and Artist* and *The Dying Gaul;* Tom Burns, the publisher; and Jim Ede, an early collector of Jones's visual work and, following his years at the Tate, founder of Kettle's Yard, Cambridge. The letters to Hague and Grisewood dominate the selection. There are forty-six letters to Grisewood and thirty to Hague, while there are only thirteen letters to Ede and twelve to Burns. Having recently read through the one hundred letters of the Ede correspondence at Kettle's Yard, I can see that even an adjustment in the volume of the proportion of letters to these four old friends—forty-six to Ede, for example, and thirteen to Grisewood—would alter the features of the self-portrait to some subtle degree. *Dai Greatcoat* is not *just* a matter of leaving David Jones to himself to "both record the progress of his life . . . and . . . portray his character and personality." That would be the achievement of a Collected Letters. Hague's shaping hand—and not *just* "the material itself"—is very much at work in this book, and, although Hague is not quite a biographer here, he is perhaps a kind of artist. The final effect of the volume, read straight through, is deeply moving and essentially aesthetic. Hague's explanation of his sharp focus occurs early in the preface.

> What is printed concentrates on a single aspect of the man. He may well (indeed, I know that he does) speak in a different tone, and so present a different person, to others with whom he had a different relationship. I felt, however, that I could not bring myself to copy and print anything which I could not fully understand, could not fully get the feel of, because it went into intellectual, emotional, literary, historical or religious fields, and attitudes to those fields, that were in any degree foreign to me. I wished to print only what was said in a tone of voice that was completely familiar to me. I could feel sure of my ground only if I knew David's correspondent well enough to understand how what David wrote would be received and understood. Had I felt otherwise, a vast range of correspondence would no doubt have been open to me. . . .

This paragraph is candor itself, and I do not wish in the slightest to fault the volume in hand by speculating for a moment about what might be missing from the point of view of a hypothetical biographer or an editor of a hypothetical Collected Letters. Indeed, Hague discusses these matters himself, referring his reader to Tony Stoneburner's *List of Letters by David Jones* (Granville, Ohio: Limekiln Press, 1977) which catalogues some seven hundred letters addressed to some seventy-five correspondents, an inventory which, although very useful, is by no means definitive or complete. A quick glance at Stoneburner's compilation shows many letters written to women—letters, for example, to Petra Tegetmeier (née Gill), to whom David Jones was briefly engaged; Nancy Sandars; Janet Stone; Kathleen Raine; and Helen Sutherland, the chief patron of David Jones's painting and to whom there are 136 letters—more than to anyone else on the list. Surprisingly, there are no letters listed to Prudence Buhler (née Pelham), to whom David Jones must certainly have written many times. Hague calls this relationship "the most important . . . in David's life."

My point is that the chief omission in *Dai Greatcoat* is certainly of representative letters written to women, letters which would reveal, as Hague says, "a very different aspect of the writer." This is important both because Jones's notion of "the feminine" is of such central significance in his work, and because one of the foggy areas of the self-portrait in *Dai Greatcoat* has to do with Jones's relationships with women—both those with whom he was in love ("I believe in the reality of 'Romantic Love.' I always have"), and those with whom his relationship was of a different kind altogether—literary, artistic, scholarly, or what have you. It is not a question of Hague being too fastidious to print letters in which Jones writes of his emotional turmoil. Enough time seems to have passed, in fact, that he feels free to disregard Jim Ede's note "not for publication" written in the margin of the letter to him in which Jones expresses his great distress when Prudence Pelham decides to marry Guy Branch. But the relationships with women friends—and especially the relationships with those whom Hague calls Jones's "cult figures"—are necessarily pretty dimly outlined in the book in the absence of letters actually written to some of them.

Related to this matter is perhaps also the question of Hague's interpretation of David Jones's several psychological breakdowns and the severe psychological stress with which he had to deal throughout most of his life and which, for long periods of time, made work, particularly painting, a near impossibility. Hague's theory is surprising at first, but it would seem to be supported by most of the letters he prints which deal with what Jones usually calls simply "neurosis" or "neurasthenia," and what at first Tom Burns, and later Jones himself, began to personify as "Rosy."

What surprises one is Hague's belief that David Jones's war experiences had virtually nothing to do with his breakdowns, and, to a lesser degree, that the loss of Petra Gill and Prudence Pelham to other men figured only insofar as marriage was finally seen by Jones as necessarily incompatible with the practice of the artist's vocation in the civilizational phase in which he found himself. Whether the publication of further correspondence or other biographical investigations will lead to any sort of qualification of Hague's analysis and the evidence of the letters at hand remains to be seen. For a long time now, I think it has been assumed by readers of David Jones—and asserted by many—that Jones's war experiences were the central causal factor in the breakdowns and protracted illnesses. Douglas Cleverdon, for example, says in his essay on "David Jones and Broadcasting" that it was specifically the "vivid externalisation of the horrors of trench warfare" brought about when Jones heard the November 1946 BBC performance of the radio version of *In Parenthesis* that "precipitated an illness that lasted for several weeks" and led Jones eventually to Bowden House and the care of the sympathetic and gifted psychiatrist, Dr. Stevenson. But Hague is adamant that:

> David enjoyed the war. He loved soldiering and comradeship . . . *In Parenthesis* . . . is not an exposition or condemnation of the horrors of war, even if it is concerned with them. A careful reading of the Preface shows a pride and delight in the type of war that, by David's reckoning, ended in 1916; and the core of the book is the goodness of "the intimate, continuing, domestic life of small contingents of men, within whose structure Roland could find, and for a reasonable while, enjoy his Oliver" . . . Stronger confirmation comes from David's conversation and letters. . . . There were no nightmares, no horrors that could not be mentioned, no noises, smells, scenes that made wounds bleed afresh. . . . On the other hand, the difficulties he met in his work, and the accompanying at times paralysing mental and spiritual stress, will be patent to every reader of his letters and published work.

Before Dr. Stevenson and Bowden House, Jones had been treated in 1932 by a neurologist specializing in the treatment of shell-shock who advised "masterly inactivity"—in particular no painting if painting brought on the illness—and a long sea voyage to Cairo and Jerusalem. Although the voyage was temporarily helpful, the "masterly inactivity" was ultimately an impossible prescription, for, as Jones later recognized, "the unconscious demands a higher and higher blackmail—less and less activity as a price, so that the *only* way is to beat the unconscious in open war." Stevenson, says Hague, understood when treating Jones after his 1946 breakdown "what David meant when he spoke of the difficulties that present themselves to the artist in this 'age of steel', and made David himself see that they could be solved only by frontal attack. After a first period of rest and gentle recreation, he was ordered to paint. He obeyed, and he won."

Some of the most interesting "letters" in the entire collection are not, properly speaking, letters at all, but rather what remains of the series of notes which Jones wrote to Dr. Stevenson during his treatment acknowledging "the ramifications of the sexual impulse" and "the findings [of the doctors] . . . about my fear etc. with regard to sex," but going on beyond such an acknowledgement to argue that the fundamental cause of his illness was to be seen, as Hague says, "in the tension which arises when the artist has to accommodate himself to modern civilization." The notes are remarkable and fascinating, and they have nothing to say about life on the Western Front.

> It is difficult to see how the peculiar qualities that characterize the art of painting can continue to coexist with a civilization such as our own is, or is becoming. (The root trouble about a materialistic conception lies here—if things are thought of as simply utile—as for instance a radiator or a gas-fire or an electric bulb—then a kind of conflict arises in the mind of the artist with regard to them, and he tends to go to earlier forms of light and heat, as candle and woodfire, when he is expressing the universal concepts of fire and light. This in turn creates a kind of loss of touch with the contemporary world—his world, after all—and a kind of invalidity pervades his symbols—it sets up a strain. However unconscious, it produces a neurosis. Previous ages did not know this tension.)

An aspect of the artist's essential vocational problem presents itself in terms which Jones feels to be "completely defensible and reasonable" even though they *may* be interpreted, in his own case, as a "rationalization" of his inhibitions.

> I do emphatically say that over and beyond those symptoms of imbalance in my own make-up, there is the concept of "not

marriage" as a perfectly rational desire in order to pursue what appears to this or that person to be a great good. Here it seems to me the whole of history bears witness. . . . I should also like to mention that I feel that the "contemporary situation" has a real bearing here—it seems to me (and I have all my life been aware of it) that at the breakdown of a culture (bringing great abnormality at all levels and very great divergence of standards of every sort, and economic pressure—all detrimental to mating and normal marriage even for tough and resilient persons) many people who otherwise in a normal world would get married, quite logically avoid doing so if they feel they have some vital work to do, because the conditions of their time make it virtually impossible for them to marry and bring up a family without at the same time prostituting (or something like it) the work they do. . . . I think perhaps psychology as such is less concerned than are religion and metaphysics with hierarchies of perfection. What may be an admirable and salutary thing at one level may be unsatisfactory at another level. Whatever our psychic make-up, we all desire perfection, even at the expense of great misery.—This gets one into difficulties . . . "Why do you want the moon when you have the stars?"

I quote at length because these notes to Dr. Stevenson stand at the very center of Hague's book and appear to define the central problems of David Jones's life and work, at least as he saw them at the time. If Yeats was right and "The intellect of man is forced to choose / Perfection of the life, or of the work," David Jones chose perfection of the work. Making that choice, he suffered out the consequences in his life with an ever increasing understanding of his predicament and an ever increasing ability to articulate his situation—a situation which he took to be representative—in letters, essays, and sometimes poems. The struggle against the dominant pressures of the age, however, against the "utile infiltrations," the "root trouble," the internalized demands for "less and less activity" as an artist had to be fought out initially in the arena of his painting, the activity in which what he calls his "major conflict" first and most radically displayed itself. The decisive battle against his furies was waged and won in the completion of the *Vexilla Regis* in 1947.

Throughout the period of extreme adversity, and throughout the rest of his life, Jones was able to count on the devoted friendship of the four men to whom he writes in *Dai Greatcoat*. "How bloody lucky one is to have such nice friends," he writes to Ede. And to

Grisewood he says: "O dear, it's nice to talk to someone whose brain is the right *kind*—that's what one sighs for —the disagreements don't matter—but the *temper*—the *kind*—the *sort* of thing that a chap regards as *significant*—that's what one wants—and that is hard to come by." Hague says that Jones's friends—all with the kind of brain and temper that Jones sought, all taking the same sort of thing to be significant—"regarded it as a privilege to help in any way the man whom they loved and respected above all others." After the breakdown in 1946–47 and the determination to engage and defeat "Rosy" by means of frontal attack, Jones began, says Hague, "to carry out what he regarded with almost evangelic fervour, unwilling though he might have been so to express it, as the poet's mission." This involved the conviction that it was "quite just and reasonable that any friends who were able to help him should do so. He served society—indeed, he gave his health and his whole working life to what he regarded as that service, and it was proper that society should recognize this through the medium of his friends."

Hague is writing here about the financial contributions which came at regular intervals from certain friends (initially organized by Jim Ede in the early 1940s) and helped to solve the severe money worries from which Jones suffered. But this generosity is almost as nothing in comparison with the loving attention and response his correspondents clearly gave to Jones's ideas in the letters after 1947 about painting, poetry, theology, sign, sacrament, and his characteristic distinction between the nature of the utile and the extra-utile or the gratuitous, an attention which must have been infinitely valuable to Jones in the lamentable absence of sustained and serious public discussion of his essays, and, indeed, of *The Anathemata* itself, the late paintings, and the final poems and fragments.

> . . . dearest Harman, *why* oh why, in all the varied stuff from "fans" or from those hostile or most critical, is this pivot round which all one has ever stated depends, this utterly crucial matter, the distinction between the utile and the extra-utile, between, at its highest conceivable level (for Catholics, anyway) the *Oblatio* at the Supper, a ritual act and words wholly extra-utile, and the entirely utile acts whereby he who was already self-oblated was made fast by iron hooks to the wood of the *stauros* [not acknowledged or understood]. . . . *Now* among our mates and contemporaries, this business of utile and inutile is virtually impossible to get across. . . . All the bloody sweat of *Epoch and Artist* simply evidently had no meaning. You will re-

member how we were surprised at the time that no one took up the questions raised. They are or are not real questions. . . . They say, Well, of course man is a maker and a user of *signs* with a small "s"—but they *don't seem to have grasped the actual situational fact* that technological man is fast losing that habit of thought, or at *every* level the capacity to understand what one is talking about.

There is an increasing intensity (bordering sometimes, as above, on desperation) in Jones's expression in these letters of his dilemma as an artist which corresponds to the increasing intensity of the expression given to that dilemma in his introductions, essays, and letters to the press. Hague writes that the final stage of the difficulties which Jones met in his work "was the attempt to find an historical and philosophical justification for his view of the function of the artist in every society; to explain it to countless correspondents; and, what caused him endless worry and disappointment, to present it to a wider audience in his published essays." If the wider audience was not listening, the correspondents clearly were—listening, says Hague, to letters dealing with Jones's fundamental preoccupations running sometimes to more than nine thousand words. "He was anxious to know that he was understood, and would . . . take great pains to explain himself, and would be immensely grateful when a friend or stranger found some key to what the poet feared might remain a puzzle—even if the key was not, at times, a very good fit." Such letters—and, as Hague suggests, the responses which they elicited—doubtless constituted an important aspect of Jones's general mobilization of forces against the threat of further incapacitating illness. Still, his late and obsessive doubts—"I do feel that 'our attitude' is now something of a 'lost cause'. The temptation is to feel that it is useless to proceed . . ."—along with his extreme isolation, make it clear that "Rosy" remained a near neighbor from 1947 onward.

By focusing on what I take to be the central issues of *Dai Greatcoat*, I do not want to give the impression that Jones's letters are inevitably grim and solemn essays on aesthetics, theology, and his personal psychology. Far from it. With the exception of several letters written around the times of the 1932 and 1946–47 breakdowns, along with certain others written during the Munich period and toward the end of his life, the letters are characteristically witty and joyous—even when they touch upon extremely serious and painful subjects. While a certain sense of responsibility must have qualified the pleasure of receiving a nine-thousand-word letter about art and society, a more spontaneous response must surely have greeted the more typical (and generally earlier) letters in which, says Hague, "the excellence depends to some degree on the mixture of the apparently trivial and the profound," where the " 'Thank Auntie for the dripping and we hope her leg is better' is as important as a discussion of Marcion's distortion of Pauline theology." Some of the earlier letters are all play and game, like this one to Hague himself:

> Hi hold up what's this I say speak up what is this says where is this so-called Hague's letter in retorts to your loving thoughts; *it is not come* is the retorts of this meager chambermaid says where is this postman God damn his sole. Says here is this *Times* newspaper to get on with and a gralie fruge and a egg Christ what mores do you want. Says I know all about that which what does this meager maid replie you know fuck-all about it, I've brought the *Telegraph* by mistake—sorry sir.

Even in the midst of a quite painful meditation on his extreme loneliness during a low period in the middle 1930s his unique humor at his own frustrations can enter parenthetically and wonderfully.

> I think if I could only get not having the worse type of nerves and could work at painting or writing (Bugger—I did not know this had a drawing on the back—it is my leg. I drew it as a study for a thing I'm doing—bugger! I want it, but can't write this letter again—well, I shall have to send it as it is and do my leg again if I want it) I should be quite happy alone always.

Hague suggests that the two happiest periods of David Jones's life were his two Chelsea periods (when he was by *no* means alone)—the first in the late 1920s, and the second during the early phases of the war when he was living in Tom Burns's house in Glebe Place. Hague's memory of Jones in the 1920s "is one of great gaity and energy," and he is inclined "to minimise the distress" caused by Petra Gill's decision to marry Dennis Tegetmeier. This period included the first exhibition of Jones's paintings at St. George's Gallery in 1927, and a second, more successful, exhibition at the same gallery two years later. It also included the beginning of *In Parenthesis*. The letters of this period are much less dense with ideas than they were to become, and more concerned with what he is doing, where he is living, and whom he is seeing. They include sketches, inscriptions, and rude jokes in the margins. As the first Chelsea period ended in the early 1930s, Jones began to spend a good deal of time with Hague and his wife at Pigotts near High Wycombe in Buckinghamshire, and it is here, after finishing his last engraving, *He Frees The Waters* (which "shows the marks of angry jabs with a tool that refused to express his intention"), that Jones's first breakdown occurred. "Gaity fled," says Hague, "but a wry and rueful humour remained." Because of his illness, and because of the interruption caused by the prescribed voyage to Cairo and Jerusalem, the completion of *In Parenthesis* was delayed until 1935 and its publication until 1937. By 1934, Jones had returned to England, staying mostly at the Fort Hotel in Sidmouth, but able to do very little work. Many of the letters from this period, especially those to Ede, lament his inability to paint, or, as he says to Grisewood, "to hold to one's General Line . . . I should not mind other types of unhappiness if I could work properly, because it is all I really want to do, or ever have wanted to do . . . What a real sod and bugger this neurosis is for this generation—it is our Black Death, all right."

Around the time of the Munich Crisis, some rather disturbing letters on politics appear—letters which coincide with Jones's anguish over the marriage of Prudence Pelham, and which must, I am afraid, provide a kind of gloss on essays such as "Art and Democracy" and "Art in Relation to War." He tells Ede that he feels "personally so sophisticated and decadent and ill a person" that, if there were a "real showdown," he doesn't see what he would do, and he wishes he were "young and knew *nothing* like I was in 1914." Withholding from publication a letter to Chamberlain sent along with a presentation copy of *In Parenthesis*, Hague remarks that it would be "unfair to print it" because it shows "the rule of illusion was as effective in 1939 as it was in 1914". By June 1939, Jones is telling Grisewood that he "can't cope" with "that political stuff" and wants to "get back to [his] own 'art work', which is all [he] really care[s] for," but feels "bewildered with the noise of contrary ideas and the infernal complexity of religion, sex, the structure of society, the arts and everything." The several letters written just before, during, and immediately after the Munich period proper include the hope that "Hitler and Musso and Schuschnigg arrange the affairs of Austria between themselves," some considerable praise for Chamberlain, attacks against the left and the League of Nations, and a very confused and quite nasty paragraph written after a reading of *Mein Kampf* in which a series of qualifications and hesitations do not fully diminish a momentary enthusiasm for the book and the author.

"Anyway," he concludes, "I back him still against this currish, left-ish, money thing, even though I'm a miserable specimen and de-pendent upon it." I quote out of context, of course, but these observations do, I think, connect with the crisis in Jones's writing, painting, and personal life in an alarming subterranean way. This was clearly another very bad period for Jones, and he longed for "a more settled world." Several of the letters from the late 1930s con-tain fascinating glimpses of *The Book of Balaam's Ass*, a work Jones finally abandoned. Hague prints, in fact, an unpublished portion of the manuscript, a passage inspired by Prudence Pelham, which is utterly different in character from the fragment which appears in *The Sleeping Lord*. If more of this work were to be published—and there are indications that this may come about before too long—some of the letters from this period would be seen in a fuller context.

Instead of to a "more settled world," Jones returned from Sid-mouth to London just in time for the blitz—and evidently rather liked it. "Like all immediate things (e.g., the front-line in the last war)," he writes to Ede, "it had its points." This was the second of the Chelsea Periods when he was living at Tom Burns's house in Glebe Place. He was able again to see friends regularly, he became more active, and he even did a certain amount of painting, finishing the fine *Aphrodite in Aulis* in 1941. "He was not," says Hague, "so overwhelmingly oppressed." His chief worries between 1940 and 1946, the war aside, had to do with the uncertainty of his financial situation and with Prudence's debilitating, mysterious, and ulti-mately fatal illness (complicated by the loss of her husband in the air war in August 1940). Most of the letters published from this period are to Tom Burns, who was working at the British Embassy in Madrid, describing life in London and Jones's response to the raids. The letter of 14 September 1940 is particularly interesting.

> There is a raid on and shrapnel bursts very high up and a good way off. It is a funny world and no mistake. . . . To me it is all a kind of resuscitation, under vastly different and weird circum-stances, of the last war—all very different in every way except this reaction of different temperaments—there is a "social" thing in it too—

His consideration of this " 'social' thing in it" anticipates an-other dimension of his self-analysis at the time of his notes to Dr. Stevenson, and one that Hague does not rule out of court. Indeed, he argues that Jones's sense that he "had no defined social position, that he had moved away from the social level of his childhood and felt an alien in the supposedly higher levels" constituted "another form of estrangement." The letter continues:

> I feel it in *my own self*—being neither flesh, fowl, or red herring, socially—but by having become by one accident or another "supernumerary, attached, pending allocation to unit" (as the military jargon goes) to the upper classes—yet with my roots among the lower orders (of whom I have a *great fear* and whose reactions I *hate*, but for whom I feel a deep *understanding* at the same time). I feel *quite different* in morale, for instance, when I am with Harman, for instance, from when I am trying to disentangle the reactions of the suburbs, servants, etc. That is why the excellent anonymity of the army is good. Rosy herself resides a lot in the complex maladjustments of the social order. . . . Death, mutilation, deprivation of every sort comes with a singular disparity on the "rich" and "poor." The very nature of their fear is of a subtly different character. I see this very clearly. That is really what this war is about, a good bit. There are truly a *million* and *ten million* variations and seeming contradictions in this, but it becomes increasingly clear to me, as in peace so in war, the Ritz and the Doss House, so far from being united in death, face death with utterly other emotions. And that is one of the basic problems of our age. The cat is creeping (rather than leaping) out of the bag.

Jones goes on with his letter two days later, beginning, not uncharacteristically, "What a lot of balls the old whiskies tell—anyway I'm sober now."

As *The Book of Balaam's Ass* ground to a halt and as *The Anathemata* and the later poems were begun and concluded, Jones lived first in what Hague calls "a small shelter at 12 Sheffield Terrace" and then, after the breakdown of 1946–47, at two addresses in Harrow. (Following his stroke and fall in 1970, he was cared for until his death at the Calvary Nursing Home on Sudbury Hill.) Of the period from 1947 to 1964, Hague writes that "in spite of his ever-increasing dissatisfaction with the world in which he lived, in spite of his entrenchment in his own small fortress, of his exasperation as he sought to pack more and more into both his written and plastic work, of his indecisions, his increasing fastidiousness, of his immobility . . . of at least one new emotional disturbance—in spite of all these he held his own and never sank back into helplessness." As proof of this, Hague cites Jones's extremely impressive productivity during these years. *The Anathemata, Epoch and Artist,* and *The Sleeping Lord,* he says, make up only about one-twentieth of what Jones actually wrote, and the correspondence amounts "to well over a million words." We have seen that the letters from the postwar period keenly engage—sometimes at great length and always with considerable rigor of thought and analysis—many of the same issues taken up in his essays. They also, toward the end, begin to tunnel more and more deeply into the past. "If David's letters can be regarded as providing a life of the poet . . . the life they provide," says Hague, "is written almost in reverse."

Hague achieves a powerful and sensitive conclusion for *Dai Greatcoat* simply by following the chronology of the letters which he has at hand right on through to the end when Jones is writing, partly stimulated by Colin Hughes's research on the London Welsh Battalion, about the Great War. Two particularly fine late letters written from the Calvary Nursing Home in 1973 and 1974 deal at length with his wounding in the assault on Mametz Wood during the Battle of the Somme, and with his first sight of a Mass shortly after the Somme campaign when he had returned to France following his recovery. I think it is appropriate, given the eucharistic center of all David Jones's later work, to conclude by quoting from the numinous evocation—indeed the memory, almost, of a kind of vision—of the Mass into which Jones nearly stumbled searching for wood on the Western Front. He was, he tells Hague, looking for some decent firewood between the support trench and the reserve line when he noticed "what had been a farm building now a wreckage in the main, owing to shell fire." He saw nobody around the place and, thinking he might well find a store of dry wood or at least some discarded wooden objects, walked up to investigate the one bit of wreckage with its walls still standing and its roof still intact.

> When I came close to the wall I found there were signs of its having been more knocked about than appeared from a few hundred yards away, but there was no door or opening of any sort on that side, but I found a crack against which I put my eye expecting to see . . . empty darkness and that I should have to go round to the other side of the little building to find an entrance. But what I saw through the little gap in the wall was not the dim emptiness I had expected but the back of a sacerdos in a gilt-hued *planeta,* two points of flickering candlelight no doubt lent an extra sense of goldness to the vestment

and a golden warmth seemed, by the same agency, [lent to] the white altar cloths and the white linen of the celebrant's alb and amice and maniple. . . . You can imagine what a great marvel it was for me to see through that chink in the wall, and kneeling in the hay beneath the improvised *mensa* were a few huddled figures in khaki.

I have extended this review to some length mainly because I have been unable to refrain from long quotations, but I hope I have given the reader a sense both of the variety of subjects and the various textures of the letters in this book. For anyone with an interest in David Jones—whether as writer, painter, thinker, or survivor of the Great War—the volume is well worth its rather high price. "Dai de la Cote Mal Taile"—a figure taking his name from Malory and from Jones's own boaster in *In Parenthesis* (as also from Joan Hague's comical drawing of a "Greatcoated Lurker" from which the boaster got his greatcoat to begin with)—comes vividly to life in these pages. Until there is a biography of David Jones or a volume of collected letters, this ample selection of his correspondence to four old and devoted friends will tell us more about the man and the artist than does anything else in print.

From *PN Review*, 1981

The Later Poetry of David Jones

David Jones, *The Sleeping Lord and Other Fragments*, Faber and Faber.

There is a house in Cambridge called Kettle's Yard where, if you should want to look at several representative examples of David Jones's visual art, you can ring a bell and meet a Cambridge undergraduate who will show you—along with pieces by Gaudier-Brzeska, Ben Nicholson, Henry Moore, and others—H. S. Ede's collection of Jones's woodcuts, drawings, and watercolors, including the extraordinary *Vexilla Regis* of 1948 and the *Flowers* of 1950. The house is a visual, tactile equivalent for David Jones's accumulating written works. It is not exactly a gallery—are David Jones's writings exactly "poems"?—but, as Mr. Ede says in his introduction to the handlist of paintings, sculptures, and drawings, "a continuing way of life from these last fifty years, in which stray objects, stones, glass, pictures, sculpture, in light and in space, have been used to make manifest the underlying stability which more and more we need to recognize if we are not to be swamped by all that is so rapidly opening up before us." These stones, pictures, sculptures, and objects which he has assembled in his house are Ede's *anathemata*. He felt strongly, he says, a need "to give to others these things which have been given to me; and to give in such a way that by placing and by a pervading atmosphere one thing will enhance another, making perhaps a coherent whole." He has given his house and his collection to the university and now lives in a small cottage in Scotland. The handlist, set in Monotype Perpetua, a typeface designed by Eric Gill, has for a cover David Jones's inscription *Quia Per Incarnati.* . . . In this house and in this context, if anywhere, the author of *The Sleeping Lord* does not appear to be, as the *Guardian's* poetry critic had it a few years back, "an eccentric figure on the periphery of English poetry."

Which is why I went there to think about what I should say about this book. The temptation, to which I think I ought to succumb, is to be uncritically partisan, to try and find readers for the book, to praise and praise. And why not, given my admiration for the poems? Only because that kind of thing always has its strident side, and because stridency is pretty alien to David Jones's sensibility. As if one should stand outside Kettle's Yard and shout to passersby: "Go inside and look at the *Vexilla Regis!*" But what if no one does? And only because the artist is generally thought to be an eccentric figure on the periphery of English painting? One of the great lessons we can derive from David Jones's career will come from the thought of his nearly infinite patience.

All but one of the pieces in *The Sleeping Lord* have been known to David Jones's admirers at least since the 1967 special issue of *Agenda*, in which they appeared along with some reproductions of his visual work and essays by several hands both on his earlier books and on what was then called his "work in progress." "The Wall" was first published as early as 1955, "The Tribune's Visitation" in 1958, "The Tutelar of the Place" in 1961, and "The Dream of Private Clitus" in 1964. The poems, having been around for a while, have occasioned useful commentary from some who have seen and admired them. *Poetry Wales* published a special David Jones number in 1972 which contains essays on the "work in progress," and now *Agenda* has produced a second Jones issue to coincide with the publication of the new book. Also, there is David Blamires's *David Jones: Artist and Writer* which appeared in 1971 and discusses the pieces under review.

I mention these publications for a good reason. If I am to recommend a serious reading of the poems, I should acknowledge their difficulty and say where to go to find help. A good deal of help is provided in Jones's own notes and glosses, and still more in his collected essays brought together under the title *Epoch and Artist*. The notes and essays, in fact, are an organic part of the corpus of his work. It is all one: *In Parenthesis, The Anathemata*, the *Vexilla Regis*, the recent watercolor drawing *Trystan Ac Esyllt, Epoch and Artist, The Sleeping Lord*, the note on the Catuvellaunian King Cunobelinos and the note on the pronunciation of the Welsh word *gwaundir*—all the poems and essays, all the drawings, etchings, watercolors, inscriptions and notes—part of a continuing way of life from these last fifty years.

How does this continuing way of life touch ours? It is not everyone who can say with Stuart Piggot, the archaeologist, that Jones's emotive referents are his own—"from Mesolithic to Mabinogion." Much of our response to Jones, in fact, is conditioned by an encounter in his work with sheer *otherness*, things otherwise opaque made numinous by the craft of the maker. But, along with materials which derive from the "unshared backgrounds" about which Jones has often written in his essays, are those deriving from certain backgrounds which he can safely assume are shared by many readers, American as well as British, and which, as the strange therapy of his language works against our amnesia, we begin to remember. In remembering, and in encountering things *other*, we are changed.

And if the questioner is king? Listen to this tapestry of sound. Who can equal it?

> Do the celestial forechoosings
> and the hard journeyings
>
> come to this?
>
> Did the empyreal fires
>
> hallow the chosen womb
>
> to tabernacle founders of
> emporia?
>
> Were the august conjoinings
>
> was the troia'd wandering
> achieved
>
> did the sallow ducts of Luperca
>
> nourish the lily white boys
>
> was Electra chose
>
> from the seven stars in the sky
>
> did Ilia bear fruit to the Strider
> was she found the handmaid of the Lar.

Did the augers inaugurate, did the Clarissimi steady the transverse rods, did they align the plummets carefully, did they check the bearing attentively, was the templum dead true at the median intersection

> did the white unequal pair
>
> labour the yoke, tread the holy circuit
>
> did they, so early
>
> in the marls of Cispadana
>
> show forth, foretoken
>
> the rudiments of our order

when the precursors at the
valley-sites made survey of the loam, plotted the trapezoids on the
sodden piles, digged the sacred pits, before the beginning . . .
did they square the hill-sites
for the hut-circles, did the hill-groups look to each other, were the
hostile strong-points one by one made coordinate

did Quirinal with Viminal
call to the Quadrata
did the fence of Tullius
embrace the mixed kindreds
did the magic wall
(that keeps the walls)
describe the orbit

did that wall contain a world
from the beginning
did they project the rectilineal plane upwards
to the floor of heaven
had all
within that reaching prism
one patria:
rooted clod or drifted star
dog or dryad or
man born of woman

did the sacred equation square the mundane site
was truth with fact conjoined
did the earth-mother
blossom the stone lintels
did *urvus* become *urbs*
did the bright share
turn the dun clod
to the star plan
did they parcel out
per scamna et strigas
the *civitas* of God
that we should sprawl
from Septimontium
a megalopolis that wills death?

Prophecies and myths, a supernatural birth, surveying and
building, a history and a way of life issue in a question—rhetorical

for Jones and the reader, real for the perplexed legionary who asks it, who guards a Jerusalem wall at the time of the Passion. The megalopolis wills the death of the *other*, the death of a troublesome Jew full of disruptive parabolic talk. But it also wills the death of Empire as the speaker has understood it and lived it. "They used to say we marched for Dea Roma behind the wolf sign to eat up the world . . . but now they say the Quirinal Mars turns out to be no god of war but of armed peace." The world of Jones's Roman poems is familiar enough: from the *Pax Romana* to the *Pax Americana* the distance is not very great. We are clearly in an area of backgrounds shared by any westerner, Christian or otherwise. A mile away from where I write runs the Roman road to Colchester down which Boudicca travelled to sack the Empire's British capital. On the same road, in the opposite direction, travelled the Christian religion out of Roman Jerusalem. Over my head fly the American jets from Bentwaters Air Base.

> Does the pontifex, do our lifted trumpets, speak to the city and the world to call the tribes to Saturnalia to set misrule in the curule chair, to bind the rejected fillet on the King of the Bean?

The pontifex does, the lifted trumpets do. But if we say so, we say so—like the legionary himself—entangling ourselves in a network of history and signs which, although we only half remember (as he only half anticipates), involves us, while we lament with him bad government, in the Twelfth-Night feast, the cutting of a very special cake, the election of a lord, the adorning of a sacrificial victim.

Four of the nine poems in *The Sleeping Lord* are on Roman themes, all of them deriving from Jones's enforced visit to Jerusalem in 1934 as a convalescent. This was the period of the British Mandate. Singly, the British personnel recalled figures that this veteran of the Western Front had seen twenty years before in France, the men and shades who march through *In Parenthesis* from Calais to King Pellam's Launde. But, as he says in a letter to Saunders Lewis, "in their full parade rig . . . the riot-shields aligned to cover the left side and in each right fist the half-grip of a stout baton [they] evoked not the familiar things of less than two decades back, but rather of two millennia close on. . . ." Because of this association, Jones's legionaries often talk like cockneys. More importantly, because of the association, his sympathy is extended to these uncomprehending agents of Imperial power so far from their homes (in Greece, in Rome, in Gaul) and so caught up in the convolutions of history. But the Empire and the megalopolis it spawns, their technology and their emporia, do will death—the death of things *other*,

things "counter," "pied," and "several." In spite of what Imperial
unity, the heterogenous composition of the Roman forces, or the key
word *sacramentum* in the enlistment oath might prefigure, the things
of Caesar are the things of Caesar, a boot is always a boot. In a beautiful and moving prayer to "The Tutelar of the Place," a place dear to
the poet at the very edge of the Empire, a voice resists the Ram.

Queen of the differentiated sites, administratrix of the demarcations,
let our cry come unto you.
                  In all times of imperium save us when the
mercatores come save us
            from the guile of the *negotiatores* save us from the *missi*,
from the agents
                who think no shame
by inquest to audit what is shameful to tell
                        deliver us.
When they check their capitularies in their curias
                     confuse their reckonings.
When they narrowly assess the *trefydd*
                 by hide and rod
                 by *pentan* and pent
by impost and fee on beast-head
                  and roof-tree
and number the souls of men
                notch their tallies false
disorder what they have collated.
When they proscribe the diverse uses and impose the
rootless uniformities, pray for us.
              When they sit in *Consilium*
to liquidate the holy diversities
              mother of particular perfections
              queen of otherness
              mistress of asymmetry
patroness of things counter, parti, pied, several
protectress of things known and handled
help of things familiar and small
              wardress of the secret crevices
               of things wrapped and hidden
mediatrix of all the deposits
              margravine of the troia
empress of the labyrinth
              receive our prayers.

This from the least "political" of poets, but also the one who has written that "there is a sense in which *Barbara Allen* is many times more 'propagandist' than *Rule Britannia*" and that "the more real the thing, the more it will confound their politics." May this prayer confound! Because the Wales of the supplicant is also the Wales of the poet, the Wales of Saunders Lewis and R. S. Thomas and Dylan Thomas, of Ceri Richards and Vernon Watkins, of William Mathias and Osian Ellis—the Wales of the present and the recent past. A land threatened by Roman bureaucrats has become a land occupied by legions of tourists and rendered by modern industry and its masters less every year a "differentiated site" of "holy diversities."

It is probably the Welsh material (beginning with the Welsh words themselves) which will present the most immediate difficulties for most readers of *The Sleeping Lord*. The title poem especially is studded with words like *trefydd* and *pentan*. In general, Jones would stress—as he does in his preface to *The Anathemata*—the impossibility of achieving in English an identity of content and evocation for the words he prints in Welsh before going on—as he does in a headnote to *The Sleeping Lord*—to consider the musical function of the words, or any desire for a rich and dense texture, or a craftsman's determination to use a word as a *thing*, as an object to be moved here or there, to be seen in relationship to this or that. But his willingness so often to think out his music in terms of the nominative, of the-word-as-a-noun, produces a texture which is wonderfully knitted with the stuff of otherness. We want to run our fingers over the page. At the same time, I imagine, the Roman leveller in most of us hopes his trigonometry will serve.

> . . . and the hundreds and twenties
> of horsed *palatini*
> (to each *comitatus*
> one Penteulu)
> that closely hedge
> with a wattle of weapons
> the firsts among equals
> from the wattled *palasau*
> the torqued *arglwyddi*
> of calamitous jealousy. . .

Which poet is it, we might ask Wallace Stevens, who "tries by a peculiar speech to speak / The peculiar potency of the general, /

To compound the imagination's Latin with / The lingua franca et jocundissima"? If we substitute "the imagination's Welsh," the poet that emerges writes something very like the poems on Welsh themes by David Jones—although, of course, he uses the imagination's Latin too (not to mention the imagination's Anglo-Saxon!).

> Does he lap
> the bruised *daudroed* of his lord . . .
>
> as did Mair Modlen
> the eternally pierced feet
>   of the Shepherd of Greekland
>   the Heofon-Cyning
> born for Y Forwyn Fair
>   lapped in hay in the ox's stall
> next the grey ass in the caved *stabulum*
> *ad praesepem* in heye Bedlem
>   that is bothe bryht and schen.
>
> Does he lean low to his high office
>   in the leafy hollow
>   behind the bare *rhiw*
> where the sparse hill-flora
>   begins to thicken
> by the rushing *nant* where the elders grow
> and the talled-stemmed *ffion*
>   put on the purple
> to outbright the green gossamer fronds
> of the spume-born maiden's hair.

I suppose you either like it or you don't. I do. There are certainly easier ways to write a poem. If I had space to argue the point, I would argue what I only have space to suggest: that once one enters fully into Jones's world, once one is no longer merely a tourist in the strange country of his poems, the full and cumulative effect of context on details may well work the way in which the dream-logic of Private Clitus's dream does for the dreamer on the dream-speech of his Welsh friend Lugobelinos:

> And now (in my dream-now that is), from his side our gestatorial marble, Lugo cried out a name: Modron! he cries, and then,—but very low-voiced though: Porth-Annwfyn. Some numinous, arcane agnomen, but which to my dream-cognition

was lucid as moonshine and did plainly signify: Gate of Elysium . . . So, as I figure it, his Modron and our Matrona are one, and his *porth* that shadowy portal beyond which Proserpine abides, from fall till crocus-time.

But if this is only dreaming, I should say as well that all the words are glossed and all the sounds spelt out phonetically—and beautiful sounds they are. Will it come as a surprise to some that Jones is an English monoglot? He is insistent on the point. "I mean this in the literal sense: I have at my command no language but English" (*Epoch and Artist*). For the poet, too, these words are things which are in some sense profoundly *other*. Could he love them as much if they weren't?

There are two main groups of poems, then—the Roman and the Welsh. "The Tutelar of the Place," falling in the middle of the book, is pivotal. There is a door in, "A, a, a, Domine Deus," a poem of only a page (very short for this maker of long poems), and a door out, a passage from the abandoned *Book of Balaam's Ass*. The latter makes a good ending for it sends one straight back to Jones's beginnings in *In Parenthesis*, dealing as it does with the First World War by way of a myth taken over from the Old Welsh *Y Gododdin* (and thereby linking it with "The Hunt," "The Sleeping Lord" and "The Tutelar of the Place").

The Roman poems, with the exception of two thirds of "The Fatigue," are monologues spoken either by low-ranking legionaries (identified in Jones's mind with cockney privates or NCOs) or, in the case of "The Tribune's Visitation," by a Military Tribune who admits to his men that he too "could weep / for these Saturnian spells / and for the remembered things," the "known site" and "vintage hymn," but goes on to say that he and they are detailed "to discipline the world-floor / to a common level / till everything presuming difference / and all the sweet remembered demarcations / wither / to the touch of us / and know the fact of empire." In "The Dream of Private Clitus," Clitus's dream animating the relief carving of Tellus Mater, a version of the mother goddess addressed in "The Tutelar of the Place," is interrupted by Brasso, the "fact man," who would "knock sideways and fragmentate these dreamed unities and blessed conjugations" and call the names of those, including the dreamer, who must stand the Middle Watch, while in "The Fatigue" the unfortunate legionaries involved find themselves detailed to supervise the Crucifixion of Christ.

It is quite impossible to give a short and simple account of what is going on in the Welsh poems. They are full of wonders. "The Tutelar of the Place" anticipates "The Hunt," and "The Hunt" is really the first part of "The Sleeping Lord." The chief figure in these last two poems—the dominant and disquieting presence—is that of Arthur. Jones has been a devoted Arthurian from *In Parenthesis* onward, and his long essay on "The Myth of Arthur" is one of those pieces, like Charles Olson's *Call Me Ishmael*, that beats the academic competition by a mile. The Arthur of these poems is positively haunting—and, of course, given Jones's orientation, he is a complex and composite figure in whom the "holy diversities" find their unity in "blessed conjugations" and their embodiment in the hunter of the boar Trwyth and the Lord whose sleeping body is his land. Hero, King, and Lord, attended by his candle-bearer, his poet, and his priest, he is everything our megalopolitan technological society denies. Most of all he is *other*. He is not, as one critic has hopefully suggested, our imagination. He is the Sleeping Lord. The voice that issues from these poems—and particularly from the title poem—is, for one reader anyway, absolutely compelling. It is a voice that seems to speak simultaneously from the very depths of the abyss of time and from our own moment as well, from our precarious ledge—linguistic, cultural, and social—on the edge of that abyss. It is the voice of a visionary in an age when we seem to want our poetry to skate over the surface of our desperate urban lives and number the pigeon shits on the asphalt—an age when we need vision desperately but habitually settle, in our poetry as in our philosophy and our politics, for hopelessly meager and impoverished substitutes. *Poiesis*, making, is for Jones a high calling—in fact it is *the* human calling, it is definitive. As a Christian he can write: "Unless man is of his essential nature a *poeta*, one who makes things that are signs of something, then the central act of the Christian religion is totally without meaning" (*Epoch and Artist*). This in spite of his deeply tragic sense of a profound diminution in our ability to respond to sign, symbol, allusion, analogy, and what he regarded as the sacramental nature of all artists' juxtaposed forms in a time when, as he says in *The Anathemata*, "the utile infiltration . . . is coming through each door."

Perhaps the gods have abandoned England. Evidently, they have returned to Wales. Sleeping there, they may wake. And our reasonable sentries at the gate of the city (at the mouth of the skull) had better spread the news:

                when he shifts a little in his fitfull
slumber does a covering stone dislodge
              and roll to Reynoldstone?
When he fretfully turns
              crying out in a great voice
              in his fierce sleep-anger
does the habergeon'd sentinel
              alert himself sudden
from his middle-watch doze
              in the crenelled traverse-bay
of the outer bailey wall. . . .

Does he cock his weather-ear, enquiringly
lest what's on the west wind
              from over beyond the rising contours
may signify that in the broken
              tir y blaenau
these broken dregs of Troea
              yet again muster?
Does he nudge his drowsing mate?
              Do the pair of them
say to each other: 'Twere not other
than wind-cry, for sure—yet
              best to warn the serjeant below . . .
you never know *what* may be
              —not hereabouts.
No wiseman's son *born* do know
              not in these whoreson March-lands
of this Welshry.

                        From *Poetry,* 1975

Such a Kingdom:
The Poetry of Geoffrey Hill,
1952–1971

Geoffrey Hill, *Somewhere Is Such a Kingdom: Poems 1952–1971*.
Introduction by Harold Bloom. Houghton Mifflin.

For the Unfallen, *King Log*, and *Mercian Hymns*, Geoffrey Hill's
three previous books, his poems from 1952–1971, are now gathered
together under the title *Somewhere Is Such a Kingdom*, with an introduction by Harold Bloom. When the frogs in Aesop's fable asked for
a king, Jove dropped down a block of wood. It lay inert as the frogs
sang out "God save King Log." They complained. Jove sent down
King Stork—who devoured them all "with a greedie maw" (Ogilby's
translation and Pope's source in the *Dunciad*). King Bloom? Aesop is
silent. It seems perhaps a little dangerous to risk an introduction by
someone whose critical obsessions are so specialized, whose private
pantheon is so fixed, and whose appetite is so ravenous.

But he is right, of course. We *do* come late, and Hill *is* "strong"
in his belatedness. We see him lifting weights on a desolate northern beach; he will wrestle William Blake in the Newcastle gym.
Blake's seconds are Coleridge and Wordsworth; Hill's are Ashbery
and A. R. Ammons—flown over especially for the match on Gnostic
Airlines, Ltd., if I may be allowed my joke. Geoffrey Hill is, as anyone who has made the effort to read him understands, a magnificent
poet. Harold Bloom knows this, and knows many of the reasons
why. In America, outside of a few now fairly standard anthology
pieces, Hill's work has been little read. Although I would have preferred to see Jon Silkin's long, subtle, and discriminating essay on

Hill (available in Michael Schmidt's *British Poetry Since 1960*) as an introduction, Bloom's will serve. For a body of work as difficult and, to an American audience, as foreign as Hill's, some sort of map is useful. There will certainly be others in time.

I say "foreign" and mean "English." Perhaps it's come to that, as Donald Davie keeps telling us. Including Bloom and Davie, there are now perhaps seven people in North America who read contemporary British poetry. The names must be withheld to protect the innocent. Houghton Mifflin, under the circumstances, is to be congratulated for publishing this brilliant, fierce, and unsellable book. Not that Hill hasn't got an audience in mind, whether in England or America, when he writes. It is Coleridge's "clerisy." In an essay on T. H. Green published in the English journal *Poetry Nation* (number four) and written in a prose nearly as dense as his verse—delivered initially, incredibly, as a lecture at Leeds—Hill writes that:

> The original subscribers to Coleridge's *The Friend* numbered just under four hundred. He was satisfied, we are told, "to direct his remarks to the 'learned class' he was later to call the 'clerisy.' " He required "the attention of my reader to become my fellow-labourer," but from the surviving comments of several self-assured readers . . . it is evident that some of them considered that he asked too much. His readers, with few exceptions, rebuffed his attempts, finding him "abstruse and laboured" as others, later, found Green "cruelly inarticulate."

I am no self-assured reader of Geoffrey Hill. I suppose I understand about two-thirds of what he has written—enough, at any rate, to make me read on and reread; enough for me to wish to become a fellow-laborer; enough for me, like several others, to have been influenced by some of his more characteristic methods. I find that I know several of his poems by heart. While I'd be pleased and able to stand on a stage and recite them, I would be rendered, were I asked to say very much about them, "cruelly inarticulate." Still, discriminations are possible. It is fair, for example, to say that sometimes Hill is too "abstruse and labored." And it is possible to demonstrate that—on the balance—Hill's work, which was impressive to begin with, has been getting even better. Bloom says that there are no "bad" poems in the canon, and he is right. But some are better than others, and the best are the more recent ones.

Bloom discounts "what is superficially judged to be poetic influence"—the "transmission of image, idea, diction, and metric." In his eagerness to talk about "deep or true influence, or Blake's Mental Warfare," he has very little to say in his introduction about craftsmanship in the work of this most craftsmanlike of poets. But poems succeed or fail at the level of image, idea, diction, and metric—at the level of form, style, and technique. Hill worries, you understand, over these things. In reprinting a poem he doesn't like—"In Memory of Jane Fraser" from *For the Unfallen*—with a revised final stanza in *King Log*, he calls the act "a necessary penitential exercise"—a matter of one punctuation mark, six words, and a spondaic foot. Any sophomore, if I can intentionally misprize Mr. Bloom, can struggle with William Blake in heaven. Lines of poetry either work or fail to work. These, from "The Bidden Guest," for example, seem to me at one moment awkward, at another very nearly banal.

> But one man lay beneath his vine
> And, waking, found that it was dead.
> And so my heart has ceased to breathe
> (Though there God's worm blunted its head
> And stayed.) And still I seem to smile.

The much admired "Genesis" begins like this:

> Against the burly air I strode,
> Where the tight ocean heaves its load,
> Crying the miracles of God.

I would fault the second line. "The tight ocean heaves its load" is either a bad joke or a mistake. The first quatrain below (from part III of "Metamorphoses") is too painfully concentrated and worked over; the second (from "Ovid In The Third Reich") is honed to perfection—one of Hill's best.

> A shark hurricaned to estuary-water,
> (The lesser hunter almost by a greater
> Devoured) but unflurried, lies, approaches all
> Stayers, and searchers of the fanged pool.
>
> *
>
> I love my work and my children. God
> Is distant, difficult. Things happen.
> Too near the ancient troughs of blood
> Innocence is no earthly weapon.

One could go on. The point is that Hill's intense concentration, his power, and his learning tend to leave one intimidated. But our obligation as readers is to attempt to assess Hill's own extraordinarily fastidious, his absolutely scrupulous assessment of his own subjects and of himself as poet in relation to these subjects and the ambiguous act of writing about them. This must be done at the level of image, idea, diction, metric, and so on. My guess is that the prose poems in *Mercian Hymns* imply a temporary dissatisfaction on Hill's own part with the dense and clotted style of his first two books. But only temporary. His recent poems in magazines have returned to the earlier modes.

Enough if I have made my point. Hill, since the death of David Jones, carries almost alone the burden of maintaining in the teeth of unsympathetic times—and very profoundly too against his own inclination to remain silent—a visionary poetics in England. After *The Anathemata, Mercian Hymns*. David Jones, like Hill and Hill's King Offa of the *Hymns*, "exchanged gifts with the Muse of History." Hill, unlike Jones, feels that his gifts, at least in his first two books, may be merely "the tongue's atrocities": "Poetry / Unearths from among the speechless dead / Lazarus mystified. . . . The lily rears its gouged face / From the provided loam." And the dead are dead, whether recently in Terezin Camp or in 1461 on the field of the Battle of Towton. Hill, risking "the tongue's atrocities," will write their "funeral music"—"a florid grim music broken by grunts and shrieks," he says of his gorgeous and terrifying sequence of unrhymed sonnets on "the period popularly but inexactly known as the Wars of the Roses." The inference of a narrative in these poems has a value, he says in a note on the sequence, "if it gives a key to the ornate and heartless music punctuated by mutterings, blasphemies, and cries for help"—a music not entirely unlike that which he hears in *Biographia Literaria* and *The Friend*, where there are "interpolated cries and groans" and "flashes of grotesque comedy." There is, in fact, little narrative in "Funeral Music," *Mercian Hymns*, or the other poems on historical subjects, except by way of minimal statements of fact or allusions supported by a footnote (the longest of which is called an "essay," called indeed *King Stork* in the first printing of *King Log*), or an ironic headnote ("born 19.6.32—deported 24.9.42"). Instead, there is the music—"heartless," florid or austere—a "key" for which is provided (sounded?) in a narrative of real human suffering which we must infer. "It is . . . worth remarking," Hill writes in the essay on Green, "that 'music' is a term which can

be exploited both ideally and empirically. It is the 'still, sad music of
humanity' and it is the precise detail of articulation, the 'difficult
music' of communication." It is also the music which we in America,
in our longing or our lust, make it our business to "detect."

> The provident and self-healing gods
> Destroy only to save. Well-stocked with foods,
> Enlarged and deep-oiled, America
> Detects music, apprehends the day-star

> Where, sensitive and half-under a cloud,
> Europe muddles her dreaming, is loud
> And critical beneath the varied domes
> Resonant with tribute and with commerce.

A serious source study of Hill's work would be fascinating. (Is
he as pedantic as he now and then appears to be, or is he putting us
on? "To the best of my recollection, the expression 'to invest in
mother-earth' was the felicitous (and correct) definition of 'yird'
given by Mr. Michael Hordern in the programme *Call My Bluff* tele-
vised on BBC 2 on Thursday January 29th 1970.") The tension between the scholar and the visionary, on the whole, is fruitful. It
gives us form. Just as the tension between the moralist and the
"connoisseur of blood" (more about this in a minute) gives us energy. Adrienne Rich has a poem called "Readings of History," which
begins: "Is it in hopes / to find or lose myself / that I / fill up my
table now / with Michelet and Motley?" The answer, for a poet like
Hill, is *neither*. It is in the hope (and the horror) of finding vehicles
for poems, materials to exploit in "the provided loam": "At night-
fall . . . I leaned to the lamp . . . Words clawed my mind as though
they had smelt / Revelation's flesh . . . So, with an ease / That is
dreadful, I summon all back." Hill goes to his sources—"with a
duty to acknowledge that the authorities cited . . . might properly
object to their names being used in so unscholarly and fantastic a
context"—as passionately as Van Gogh went into a sun-drenched
pasture, easel and canvas on his back, brushes all abristling—and
then nearly collapses in a fit of fastidiousness, reticence, or guilt,
saving himself by an irony or a "flash of grotesque comedy" or
some "interpolated cries and groans" impacted in six or eight tortured and searing lines. For Hill will wound. Wound himself and
wound the reader. Not for nothing is his favorite subject martyrs.

For the reading I can recommend
   the Fathers. How they
cultivate the corrupting flesh:

toothsome contemplation: cleanly
   maggots churning spleen
to milk. For exercise, prolonged

suppression of much improper
   speech from proper tombs.
If the ground opens, should men's mouths

open also? 'I am nothing
   if not saved now!' or
'Christ, what a pantomime!' The days

of the week are seven pits. Look,
   Seigneur, again we
resurrect and the judges come.

This in memory of Robert Desnos, who died in Terezin Camp in 1945. "Artistic men prod dead men from their stone," Hill writes in a poem on Auschwitz. In still another on the camps, he concludes, as if he had intended to say much more and is suddenly brought up against his own "improper speech," "This is plenty. This is more than enough."

Flesh of abnegation: the poem
Moves grudgingly to its extreme form,

Vulnerable, to the lamp's fierce head
Of well-trimmed light. . . .

In the essay on T. H. Green, Hill writes that "the distinction between rigorous abnegation and easy abdication, so keenly asserted [by Green and Sidgwick] in principle, is not always marked in their own practice." It *is* marked in Hill's. His apocryphal Spanish poet, Sebastian Arrurruz, says of himself in his *Songbook:*

Already, like a disciplined scholar,
I piece fragments together, past conjecture
Establishing true sequences of pain;

For so it is proper to find value
In a bleak skill, as in the thing restored:
The long-lost words of choice and valediction.

It is "proper to find value / In a bleak skill"; true sequences of pain may be established as "the poem / Moves grudgingly to its extreme form." "If the ground opens, should men's mouths / open also?" Perhaps they should if they can distinguish rigorous abnegation from easy abdication (and "acknowledge that the authorities . . . might properly object to their names being used in so unscholarly and fantastic a context." Said Brecht: "The basis of just about every great age in literature is the force and innocence of its plagiarism." But we come late: *Call My Bluff . . .*). In the essay on Green, Hill quotes the following lines from Wordsworth: "She ceased, and weeping turned away, / As if because her tale was at an end / She wept;—because she had no more to say / Of that perpetual weight which on her spirit lay." Wordsworth, says Hill, "implies that words are 'in some degree mechanical' compared to the woman's action and suffering. But in order to bring out the difference Wordsworth puts in a collateral weight of technical concentration that releases the sense of separateness: the drag of the long phrasing across the formalities of the verse, as if the pain would drag itself free from the constraint. In 'as if' and 'because,' pedantically isolating her, we glimpse the remoteness of words from suffering and yet are made to recognize that these words are totally committed to her existence. They are her existence. Language here is not 'the outward sign' of a moral action; it is the moral action."

Bloom makes great play on this idea in his introduction (although he makes no reference to the essay on Green, an enormously valuable resource for readers of Hill), and so does Jon Silkin in his admirable piece in *British Poetry Since 1960*. Hill, says Bloom, brings to his poems "his power, his despair, and (in spite of himself) his Word, not in the sense of Logos but in the Hebraic sense of *davhar*, a word that is also an act, a bringing-forward of something previously held back in the self." Silkin, who would agree with this formulation (although he considers the idea in somewhat different terms), says at the end of his piece that "one should avoid the impression that there is relish in Hill's re-creation of cruelty." Personally, I think there is (among other conflicting emotions) relish in Hill's re-creation of cruelty. That is what some of the poems are about. The side of him which insists upon rigorous abnegation is in constant tension with the side of him (and of any poet, of any human being) which is, as he has put it in the fourth section of "Of Commerce and Society," a "connoisseur of blood." Such connoisseurship is perhaps the end of the euphoric state against which T. H. Green, thinking he understood the susceptibilities of poets, warned. This tension provides, as I said earlier, the extraordinary energy behind these poems. The energy, in turn, generates a language which is moral action, a Word which is, indeed, *davhar*. Without it, we would have the later Wordsworth—or maybe "easy abdication," or *difficult* abdication, an Abyssinian career.

But perhaps it is only you, *hypocrite lecteur*, fellow member of the clerisy, who is a connoisseur of blood? *Il faut être toujours ivre?* You and I together? *De poésie?* And do the poems provide?

> Prodigal of loves and barbecues,
> Expert in the strangest faunas, at home
> He considers the lilies, the rewards. . . .
> For his delight and his capacity
> To absorb, freshly, the inside-succulence
> Of untoughened sacrifice, his bronze agents
> Speculate among convertible stones
> And drink desert sand. . . .

"Make intercession," Auden prayed to the ghost of Henry James (Reinhold Niebuhr presiding), "for the treason of all clerks." In his own poem in homage to James, Hill meditates upon the figure of St. Sebastian, and upon a painting of his martyrdom (probably Pollaiuolo's in the National Gallery in London). "A grotesque situation, / But priceless, and harmless to the nation." The price, of course, *is* harm—"the cold blood of sacrifice." Conversely, the harm is that history can appear to be "scraped clean of its old price." Hill will not allow this to happen in his own work, precisely because he keeps implying that it *is* happening. This is the price *he* must pay. Since he pays, we, perhaps, are inclined to pay as well and attempt to come to terms with harm rather than, as he often intentionally tempts us to do, savor it. As he says of Green's lectures, Hill's own poems in *For The Unfallen* and *King Log* may be, in their completely different way, "an act of atonement, in the arena of communication, between the 'unconscious social insolence of the listener' and what Coleridge termed the seeming 'assumption of superiority' on the part of the speaker."

Hill has earned his *Mercian Hymns*, where, to some degree, both poet and reader may, having reached something of an understanding, relax and enjoy the view: *Somewhere Is Such a Kingdom*. No longer is the reader invited into a poem with an initial line like this: "Slime; the residues of refined tears." No, his attention seems positively to be solicited along with Offa's, "the presiding genius of the

West Midlands from the middle of the eighth century until the middle of the twentieth (and possibly beyond)."

> King of the perennial holly-groves, the riven sandstone: overlord of the M5: architect of the historic rampart and ditch, the citadel at Tamworth, the summer hermitage in Holy Cross: guardian of the Welsh Bridge and the Iron Bridge: contractor to the desirable new estates: saltmaster: moneychanger: commissioner for oaths: martyrologist: the friend of Charlemagne.

> 'I liked that,' said Offa, 'sing it again.'

When Robert Lowell looked back at some of his early poems after finishing *Life Studies*, he remarked (in *New World Writing* 21) that his early style seemed "distant, symbol ridden and willfully difficult. I felt my old poems hid what they were really about, and many times offered a stiff, humorless and even impenetrable surface. . . . [They] seemed like prehistoric monsters dragged down into the bog and death by their ponderous armor." It is perhaps in terms such as these that an unsympathetic (and not necessarily uncomprehending) reader might object to some of the poems in *For The Unfallen* and *King Log*. Lowell went on to say that he "began to paraphrase [his] Latin quotations, and to add extra syllables to a line to make it clearer and more colloquial . . . I felt that the best style for poetry was none of the many poetic styles in English, but something like the prose of Chekhov or Flaubert." As I have said, if Hill felt anything like a reaction against the dense and clotted style of his first two books, which was in any way like Lowell's reaction against *his* early style, it was temporary. The evidence is in "Lachrimae," a sonnet sequence printed in the Spring 1975 issue of *Agenda*. Although it may be only a temporary concession to the reader (and while Hill's "prose" is a good deal more austere and demanding than the "verse" in *Life Studies*), the style of *Mercian Hymns* makes Hill's vision potentially available to more readers than he has had in the past. While Bloom is certainly right when he insists upon the subtlety and oblique character of this work, there is no underplaying the importance of what he calls "the limpidity of its individual sections." Robert Bly has said that "the prose poem appears whenever a country's psyche and literature begin to move toward abstraction." That may be very true. In any case, we are inclined, like Offa, after hearing that first hymn, to "like it." I'm certain that Hill, like T. H. Green, objects to "the citing of 'agreeable sensations and reflections' as supposed criteria for determining the value of literature," and would like to see an alternative "to the spasmodic 'I like' and 'I don't like'" of our habitual responses. Still, like Coleridge's harper in the second essay of *The Friend*, Hill's tuning of his instrument is "attributable both to his own professional conscience and to his servitude to those who can call the tune." When Offa says, "sing it again," Hill sings it, if a little more darkly, a second time.

> A pet-name, a common name. Best-selling brand, curt graffito. A laugh; a cough. A syndicate. A specious gift. Scoffed-at horned phonograph.
>
> The starting-cry of a race. A name to conjure with.

From Poetry, 1976

Poet-Critics
of Two Generations

John Berryman, *The Freedom of the Poet,* Faber and Faber with Farrar, Straus & Giroux; Robert Pinsky, *The Situation of Poetry: Contemporary Poetry and its Traditions,* Princeton University Press.

John Berryman's *The Freedom of the Poet* is pretty much the brilliantly exuberant, but carefully discriminating, long, scholarly, sometimes dark and portentous, tough and often dead-accurate, evolving and passionate miscellany one had been expecting. In the wide range of its subject matter and learning—if not in its idiom—it recalls *The Dyer's Hand,* about the author of which book Berryman once said: "his opinions are important because they are his." One can say a good deal more about *The Freedom of the Poet* than that, but that to begin with: the opinions are important because they are his. Also, that it represents the concerns and commitments of Berryman's exceptional generation of American poets better than anything to come into print since the criticism of Randall Jarrell. It is a formidable performance and, immediately upon its publication, historical. The book will be read for a long time, in part because of its prose.

Anyone with sufficient energy will profit from reading Robert Pinsky's *The Situation of Poetry* directly after *The Freedom of the Poet.* There is an excellent and sympathetic discussion of Berryman's work in the book, as there is also of Lowell's, and Pinsky no less than Berryman goes unerringly for what is authentic, unique, and excellent, determined to "take up contemporary work and deal with it in the harsh perspective of history." His book is decidedly *not* a miscellany, although not quite a single sustained argument either, and is perhaps most interesting at its conclusion where he develops an entirely convincing defense of the discursive poetry and what he calls its "prose virtues" which he himself has practiced with conspicuous success in his recent volume of poems, *Sadness and Happiness*. Pinsky's immediate generation includes that group of American poets who were, along with himself, among the last students of Yvor Winters at Stanford University between 1963 and 1967—Robert Hass, John Peck, James McMichael, Igor Webb, Kenneth Fields, a couple of others. (The hypothetical graduate school essay, circa 2001: "The *Other* Wintersians?" "The *Anti*-Wintersians?" Only Fields is anything like a true disciple.) Like Berryman, Pinsky honorably acknowledges his masters and teachers—the book is dedicated "in memory of A. Y. W."—while usefully calling attention to some of the best work of his contemporaries, notably McMichael's long poem, "Itinerary." Amusingly, and accurately, having come from where he's come from, Pinsky can compare Robert Creeley with Barnabe Googe and Allen Ginsberg with George Gascoigne, employ comfortably the characteristically Wintersian adjective *bardic* in the same sentence with some of his favorite Walt Disneys like *oddball* and *dopey* and *daffy*, and refer to a tone that "wobbles" (Pound?) or to a problem out of which he must "slither." The sometimes strange combinations help to make for a style, both here and in his poems. In both *The Situation of Poetry* and *The Freedom of the Poet*, in fact, the reader is gratefully in the presence of a poet's increasingly familiar, persuasive, and compelling style. That is their first pleasure, although certainly not their last.

The style is perhaps not as instantly apparent in Berryman's work as his editor and old friend, Robert Giroux, suggests in his preface. In *Love and Fame*, Berryman writes of the earliest essay here collected, saying: "My girls suffered during this month or so, / so did my seminars & lectures & / my poetry even. To be a *critic*, ah, / how deeper & more scientific. // I wrote & printed an essay on Yeats's plays / re-deploying all of Blackmur's key terms / & even his sentence-structure wherever I could." This was a good many years before Berryman farted famously over "Rich Critical Prose" in Dream Song 107. But the style is there, in snatches anyway, in the prose as in the verse, from pretty early on. The prose is rich, critical, his. It also sidles up pretty close to the idiom of the mature poetry. By the time one gets into the middle and later essays, not to mention the several excellent short stories, there is some temptation to paste together a do-it-yourself Dream Song.

Friends, the hovering and plunging grief
Exceptionally sings. Wow! We put
Against it, then, a pretty
Round-faced wench, who, with Alfred Kazin
And his wife, edited
Her fiction—ah! I thought—

And missed the boat. God amuses himself;
Then man. Both these facts have been forgotten.
Windmills grind wheat
From which, Sir Bones, our bread is made. Irony
To the end. Fair enough!
You may wonder whether I dislike aestheticians.

A high and prolonged riskiness? The later
Men just drudged along: Lowell into spondees
And humped smash. Hardy's
Reputation has been furiously unstable.
Tell you a story. Until
A writer begins to bore us, O, it is . . .

. . . a matter of supreme importance that he handle characteristic materials characteristically." This from seven essays dated 1948, 1953, 1960, 1965, 1966, and 1967 (with a little help from a quote out of Nashe's *Unfortunate Traveler*). Along with the Boneses and the Os, you may include in your kit the following free-floating adjectives and adverbs: *delicious, adorable, spectacularly, American, ferocious, hallucinatory, intense, painful, marvelous, superior, sharply, foolish, irresistible, heavily, suicidal, little, ridiculous, ravishing, ominous, exquisite, brilliant, tumultuous, gigantic, radiant, Christian,* and *free.* It is mostly a vocabulary of praise, but a somewhat eccentric vocabulary. Add to that the somewhat eccentric syntax, which usually occurs when emotion is intense, along with the depth charges of emotion themselves, and you have the ingredients of the style.

"Most of us," Berryman writes, "never get to know many other human beings very well . . . We know people, perhaps, chiefly by their *voices*—their individual, indescribable, unmistakable voices." We can sympathize with Saul Bellow, who knew Berryman's voice as well as anybody, when his friend Dennis Silk asks him, while he's off in Israel writing *To Jerusalem and Back,* to "read some of [Berryman's poems] in Berryman's own manner." Says Bellow: Well, he can *try.* The manner, the voice, was disconcerting and

was meant to be; difficult to reproduce or imitate, it was unforgettable once actually heard. It *is* unforgettable. Thinking about the occasionally eccentric syntax of the prose, I realize that, in part, I'm
remembering certain exaggerations of pause, pitch, and pace—of
rhythm and punctuation—which Berryman was inclined to impose
on any text at all, whether it was the first paragraph of Stephen
Crane's "The Open Boat" (which is the first thing I ever heard him
read), or one of his own poems, or somebody else's poem, or an
essay. There are strange hesitations; periodic sentences are drawn
out oddly or else rushed along; unstressed syllables sometimes get
stressed. In the Library of Congress recording you can hear two
statements became quasi-questions in Berryman's reading of Dream
Song 4, as well as the audience's response—a confused response? It
is nervous laughter—following his reading of the last stanza of the
terrifying (and funny?) Dream Song 29. I'd have given a lot to hear
Bellow's reading of that one. Berryman worries over the poem in his
essay about his own stylistic development.

Some reviewers have found the Elizabethan essays which constitute the first eighty-seven pages of *The Freedom of the Poet* somehow unimportant, the work of a scholar who is not necessarily a
poet. They are certainly wrong. These essays seem to me absolutely
central both in terms of their scholarly and critical merit as excellent
and useful studies of writers who matter intensely to Berryman—
Marlowe, Nashe, and Shakespeare—and, even more importantly, as
angles on certain characteristics of Berryman's poetry which begin
to show themselves as early as the "Nervous Songs" and the
sonnets.

Before any of these essays was written, Berryman had come in
1936 to Clare College, Cambridge, "a burning, trivial disciple of the
great Irish poet William Butler Yeats," as he called himself at the
time. At Cambridge, along with the *Fitzwilliam Virginal Book*, he
stumbled on to Brian Boydell who, as he says in *Love and Fame*, "introduced me to the music of Peter Warlock // who had just knocked
himself off, fearing the return / of his other personality, Philip Heseltine. / Brian used to play *The Curlew* with the lights out, voice
of a lost soul moving." What Warlock, the arch-Elizabethan among
modern English composers, once Heseltine, alias Rab Noolas, alias
Huanebango Z. Palimpsest, set from the poems of W. B. Yeats for
the ears of his burning, trivial disciple was, among other lines, these:

No boughs have withered because of the wintry wind;
The boughs have withered because I have told them my dreams.

You can hear that last line—first sung, but afterward whispered—on the E. M. I. recording by Ian Partridge. It will break your heart, as doubtless it did Berryman's. In an excellent essay in *Cambridge Review* for May 1974, Kevin Barry, commenting that "a more apt description of Berryman's achievement in *The Dream Songs* would be hard to find," quotes Wilfred Mellers writing on Warlock in *Scrutiny* for March 1937.

> The songs have passed beyond any mere self-expression. There is, therefore, nothing fantastic in the fact that Heseltine should have been able, as no one else has been able, to reinterpret the Elizabethan art song and the English folk song on which that art form depended, in purely modern terms . . . Whereas the technique of the "Elizabethan" or folky song is comparatively straightforward and diatonic, here the melodic lines are twisted and contorted.

By the time he writes *The Dream Songs*, Berryman is as much a contemporary Elizabethan among poets as Warlock was among composers. (It is odd, in passing, that no composers—have they?—have gone to work on *The Dream Songs*.) The distance between Warlock, Boydell, and the Cambridge of 1936 and the essay introducing Thomas Nashe's *Unfortunate Traveller* of 1960 is not very great. In that essay Berryman distinguishes between two kinds of style.

> The notion "style" points in two contrary directions: toward individuality, the characteristic, and toward inconspicuous expression of its material. The latter is the more recent direction (George Orwell a superb practitioner); we may range it with T. S. Eliot's intolerable and perverse theory of the impersonality of the artist; it may have something wrong with it. Nashe is an extreme instance, perhaps the extreme instance, of the feasibility of the first theory.

Berryman likes the first theory, likes extravagance, likes the abundant energy—held just in check by convention or contrivance or will—of the impetuous stylists from Dekker and Nashe all the way up the line to Pound and Dylan Thomas. (I will qualify this in a moment.) Quoting a passage from *The Unfortunate Traveller* which Berryman regards, in fact, as relatively tame, "a suggestive but median passage, though exalted in the close," he appreciates: (1) "Inversion or rearrangement for rhythm, emphasis and simulation of an (improved) colloquial"; (2) physicality and active verbs; (3) a self-consciousness which is "alert" rather than "laboured"; (4) an "anti-pedantic" (apparent) spontaneity which is, however, "showmanlike"; (5) a "queerly schizophrenic" division between the Marlowe side of image patterns, representing "Learning," and the Shakespeare side, representing "Daily Life"; (6) a "complicated simultaneous double movement" worked out in terms of a tension between democratic and hierarchical values; and (7) "a peroration at once highly rhetorical and rather casual, pathetic, and joyous." An enthusiasm for such a style as he here describes brings him at least half-way to his own, in verse as in prose, if not the whole way. Now the qualifications. He can also admire and practice himself, restraint, austerity, delicacy, and inconspicuous expression of material. In a "period as licentious as our own," he can admire a Waller or a Henry Reed, though he is "far from wishing to produce" either of them. He can even admire some of Dreiser, "who wrote like a hippopotamus," observing that "no style may on occasion be preferable to some aspects of Melville's lengthy and deplorable affair with Shakespeare."

Still, his own affair is with Shakespeare—and Marlowe and Nashe and Cervantes and Monk Lewis and Whitman and Yeats and Pound and Lowell—with writers who have produced at some point in their careers, early, middle, or late, sustained displays of prodigious energy. *The boughs have withered because I have told them my dreams.* It all depends on what you dream, and on what you tell about what you dream, and with how much power. "To be free of unruly and discreditable desire," he writes of *The Tempest*," is the heart of the play's desire, and even in this does Prospero participate, released from the intoxications of hatred and might." But Marlowe dreams otherwise: Marlowe who "wrote simply to gratify himself . . . whose mind had no popular cast . . . who flaunted himself . . ." Marlowe, says Berryman, "twice at the summits of his art" damns himself for his two favorite and finally fused obsessive vices for either of which, indeed, he could have been burned. "The impression is unavoidable that he *enjoyed* writing these scenes, *and* was excoriated. His sinister art ran exactly with his life."

W. H. Auden, whose last great poem, *The Sea and the Mirror,* is about *Tempest,* came to believe that it is the business of art to disintoxicate and disenchant rather than the reverse. But the artist is extremely likely to be self-intoxicated and enchanted by his own work. So Auden wrote the "Horae Canonicae," brought down the curtain on magic, wrote bad poems on purpose, wrote libretti, wrote light verse. Berryman, tossed back and forth between the Marlowe and

Prospero sides of himself, also wrote a *Horae Canonicae* (which fails, certainly, to sustain a comparison with Auden's), taught *Job* to his seminar, taught *Luke*, taught Freud's *Civilisation and its Discontents* and Herman Feifel on the meaning of death. Although he is moved beyond words by Prospero's "retirement" (in the 1962 essay and later, always), he did not, on the evidence, exorcise the Marlowe from his make-up, or disenchant and disintoxicate himself. In many of the tortured later poems, he tried to. (And in "Eleven Addresses to the Lord," he nearly wrote his Canto CXVI, a poem fit to retire on, ripe, serene, transcendent.)

There is a retrospectively sad paragraph from the 1962 essay in which Berryman wonders how it is "that Stephano and Trinculo have or can have no part in this general redemption" at the end of *The Tempest,* and remarks: "Possibly it is because they are drunk . . . Irrational, self-set outside reason, they stand beyond the reach of the ruler's redemptive design. *They* think they are 'free,' of course." In a very late interview which might have been a part of this book, Berryman says (not *intentionally* parodying Alvarez parodying Berryman): "The artist is extremely lucky who is presented with the worst possible ordeal which will not actually kill him . . . And I think that what happens in my poetic work in the future will probably largely depend . . . on being knocked in the face, and thrown flat, and given cancer, and all kinds of other things short of senile dementia . . . I hope to be nearly crucified." This sort of intoxication would not seem to be a condition of freedom either.

But was it? Can it be? Given a certain theology, a teleology, a necessity requiring recognition perhaps different from that impinging on, though ignored by, most men? And given the habitual practice from an early age of what Berryman calls "a terminal activity, taking place out near the end of things, where the poet's soul addresses one other soul only, never mind when"? And if this activity aims, as he says, "—never mind *either* expression or communication—at the reformation of the poet, as prayer does"? In the face of such a conception of poetry one had better, until all the evidence is in, if it ever is, reserve the matter.

There are less than ultimate reasons for writing poetry, too, and, mostly, *The Freedom of the Poet* has to do with those. "Love of the stuff and of rhythm, the need to invent, a passion for getting things right, the wish to leave one's language in better shape than one found it, a jealously for the national honor, love for a person or for God, attachment to human possibility, pity, outletting agony or disappointment, exasperation, malice, hatred." It is a fine list. As

Berryman moves from one of these reasons to another, as each of them in turn becomes his subject, there is much talk along the way about pronouns. Berryman regarded himself, rightly, as a master of the pronoun, which "may seem a small matter, but she matters, he matters, it matters, they matter." His discussion of his own ambiguous pronouns in the concluding essay of part 4 of his book, following the loving consideration of Whitman's "Song of Myself," Pound's masks and personae, "J. Alfred Prufrock," and Lowell's "Skunk Hour," illuminates what is for him far more than a useful convention or powerful tradition, what is indeed "a necessity in a period inimical to poetry, gregarious and impatient of dignity." That is beautifully put, and he's certainly right about the period. The gregarious and impatient citizen is also right to feel that Berryman, like most modern poets, wants it both ways: (1) "That's good-old, charming-old me talking there, sweetheart"; and (2) "I didn't say that, officer! *Persona* said it. Let me alone." (I've noticed while looking into Warlock/Heseltine/Noolas/Huanebango's setting of Yeats in *The Curlew* that this exemplary heteronymic composer pressed D. H. Lawrence for libel, or, at least, forced a change in the travesty of himself—himselves?—which we get in *Women in Love*. Sometimes these things are at least legally more simple than meets the critical eye.) Introducing "Skunk Hour," Berryman says: "One thing critics not themselves writers of poetry occasionally forget is that poetry is composed by actual human beings, and tracts of it are very closely about them. When Shakespeare wrote 'Two loves I have,' reader, he was *not kidding*." Four pages later, he says: "The necessity for the artist of selection opens inevitably an abyss between his person and his persona . . . The persona looks across at the person and then sets about his own work." So Lowell; so "I." He doesn't tell us if the fairy decorator or the summer millionaire or the hermit heiress have any rights; nor whether Shakespeare's two loves had or have. It is an interesting problem.

For the rest—and there is *so much* in this nervous, jagged, and problematic book—I should point at least to these things: the excellent discussions of Isaac Babel and Stephen Crane; the treatment of "enslavement" in the lives and work of Fitzgerald, Dreiser, and Ring Lardner—an enslavement which Berryman finds to be the result of typical vague yearnings on the part of an outsider for whatever object, love or fame or money, in a culture disastrously split between the intellectual and the popular; the powerful justification—I was almost going to say the redemption—of "new critical" methodology in his often stunning, detailed, and moving readings of poems, stories, passages, novels, lines; the excellent fiction, suggesting that if Berryman had not become Berryman he might have become, say, Peter Taylor instead; and his omnivore's ability to call up all opinion and scholarship on a subject, sort it out, compare everything with everything else—was there any book he hadn't read?—eliminate what didn't matter to him, make the unusual or unforeseen point, and, in a word, teach.

In 1959, at the University of Utah in the early days of what Donald Hall calls *poëbusiness*, Berryman found it hilarious when the administrator of one of those summer "writers' conferences" told him he must call all of us "members" rather than "students." If *we* were members, *he* certainly wasn't; but he, if anyone, knew what it meant to belong to the unregistered guild from which all but the truly gifted are barred. We can profit from being his students. Out in Salt Lake City, he quoted Ralph Hodgson, who figures in the last Dream Song, as he quotes Ralph Hodgson in *The Freedom of the Poet:* "I don't try to reconcile anything; this is a damned strange world." And then he went on and tried.

❧

Robert Pinsky's book overlaps in many respects with Berryman's. When he begins his defense of discursive poetry, he quotes a snatch from a Berryman interview about the difficulties of finally abandoning "Henry" and the Dream Song idiom, and remarks that "Henry and the special manner of *The Dream Songs* are 'marvellous' and useful to the poet because of what they let him say, and not as complex dramatic screens or personae." Berryman had called Henry an "outlet," a "way of making my mind known." What Pinsky calls for is as simple (and difficult) as this:

—the right to make an interesting remark or to speak of profundities, with all of the liberty given to the newspaper editorial, a conversation, a philosopher, or any speaker whatever . . .

And this:

—talking, predicating, moving directly through a subject as systematically and unaffectedly as [one] would walk from one place to another.

If language in poetry as anywhere else, given its nature, must be abstract—and Pinsky lines up with the philosophical realists and against the philosophical nominalists—then this sounds a sensible enough program, and simple enough. But there are grave difficulties for someone who might need "to speak of profundities" rather than chat, or like a philosopher rather than a journalist, and maybe even be eloquent *in order* to make his mind known in a period, as Berryman says, "inimical to poetry, gregarious and impatient of dignity." The results in such a case might look at first to be affected, unsystematic, and very clumsy indeed in getting from one place to another. In such a situation, Pinsky observes in an earlier chapter on Berryman, "a contemporary poet has adopted an elaborate mannerism in order to speak simply." In what is surely the best thing on Berryman's style since Berryman's essay on Nashe, Pinsky writes:

> Perhaps the most important point to be made is that the colloquial words and the gag-words are not the words for which the extravagant style provides a kind of license or passport. Rather, the colloquial words help the syntax, the gags, and the personae in a general effort to admit another kind of phrase—like "a smothering southern sea"—just as in ordinary talk tough-slangy tag lines such as "all that jazz" often excuse and qualify a phrase the speaker fears may seem too elevated or pretentious.

Then he quotes the conclusion of Dream Song 75 and goes on:

> It is precisely only the context that is ironic, the weird manner. The irony is only that of a man in pain assuming dialects and self-effacing tones in torments of embarrassment and diffidence, as to distract himself. That is, the phrases of celebration, and the poet's phallic pride in his book, are meant; the irony constitutes a sort of request for permission to use such phrases and to express such pride.

The main theme of Pinsky's near-polemic for discursive poetry, however, has to do with less complicated and ambiguous practitioners of it than Berryman sometimes is. The main theme, in fact, has to do with the implementation of what Pinsky calls the "prose virtues" in poetry, "a drab, unglamorous group, including Clarity, Flexibility, Efficiency, Cohesiveness . . . a puritanical assortment of shrews . . . [which] do not as a rule appear in blurbs." Having no sympathy for the "quasi-political terms by which practice in the art is spuriously divided," he praises poets as different from each other as J. V. Cunningham, Frank Bidart, and James McMichael. He is also enormously interested in poets like John Ashbery and A. R. Ammons and Frank O'Hara who, as it were, *negotiate* with the prose virtues and the discursive manner in their poems—and two of these three he clearly wants back from Harold Bloom, as examples for practicing poets, for *use*. Among poets of the modernist tradition more or less committed to what he regards to be an unsound nominalist orthodoxy, he finds "overwhelming moments . . . when a poet breaks through into a kind of prose freedom and prose inclusiveness," transcends his anti-verbal prejudice in a "generosity of movement," and writes "with the freedom and scope of speech . . . inquiring, expanding." His examples include Eliot's passage on History in "Gerontion," the autobiographical and moralizing sections of Canto LXXXIII, and Williams's poems which are organized around "remarks." (It's a pity, in passing, that there is almost no discussion of contemporary British poetry in the book—Tomlinson gets a stanza quoted and Hughes gets a parenthesis—as there is much in Auden, Roy Fuller, Larkin, Davie, Tomlinson, Turnbull, Fisher, Prynne, Silkin, Tarn, and many others which would broaden and complicate the terms of his discussion. And what of MacDiarmid's later poems as some kind of test? Of patience and stamina, anyway. But Pinsky allows there is boredom even in Ammons.)

But I have been discussing the conclusion of *The Situation of Poetry*. The "situation," the problem of poetry in the modernist and postmodernist period is, according to Pinsky, chiefly to be seen in terms of a deluded nominalist orthodoxy among poets which, paradoxically, has continued to produce masterpieces for sixty years. Interested in "affinity" and "tradition" rather than "influence" (a concept which has recently taken on a Romantic meaning: "the irresistible force of one personality upon another"), Pinsky discusses "a climate of implicit expectation and tacit knowledge" which has changed and grown, and "technical means which may be shared." The cost to a contemporary of not sufficiently understanding his tradition will be conventionality and mannerism; the price of understanding it too well may be a compulsion to disown it, or silence.

Pinsky does not disown it. He does disown the conventionality and mannerism of certain of his knee-jerk contemporaries who have not struggled to understand the tradition in which they are writing. Tracing that tradition back to the Romantic period by way of a detailed reading of "Ode to a Nightingale," he concludes:

. . . the Romantic poet regards the natural world nostalgically, across a gulf which apparently can be crossed only by dying, either actually or through some induced oblivion. The gulf is closely related to the gulf between words and things. Various philosophical descriptions might apply to the situation. The broadest of these . . . stems from the terms "nominalism" and "realism." Nominalism can be defined loosely as the doctrine that words and concepts are mere names, convenient counters of no inherent reality, though they may be useful means for dealing with the atomistic flux of reality. I understand philosophical realism as the opposite doctrine that universals—and therefore, concepts and words—embody reality. The Romantic poet tends to look for values to emerge from particular experiences—associated sense perceptions and states of mind at particular moments—and insofar as that is true, he is a nominalist. But insofar as he is a poet he must to some extent be a realist, for those reasons which may bear repeating: words are abstractions, sentences are forms disposing their parts in time, and rhythm is based upon the concept of recurrence or pattern.

Finding, therefore, "the ultimate goal of the nominalist poem . . . logically impossible"—and telling us in a footnote that, when Pound said "go in fear of abstractions," he was speaking rhetorically and not philosophically: he was calling for concrete referents—Pinsky concludes rather surprisingly: "But the pursuit of the goal, or the effort to make the gap *seem* [my italics] less than absolute, has produced some of the most remarkable and moving poetry in the language." *Seem.* Pinsky is, in fact, passionately in love with poem after poem which his theories call profoundly into question. True, as I said earlier, nearly all of these poems are concerned with defining the dilemma itself, and he is not much amused by "vulgarisations" of the tradition where the dilemma becomes obscured ("A poem should be wordless / as a flight of birds"), or by various reductions (a poem appearing in *The Paris Review* which reads entire: "Bananas are an example"). Although it would be rash to say that Pinsky clearly prefers poems to principles (Winters: "We shall scarcely get anything better unless we change our principles"), the poems do absolutely come both first and last, providing both the source and a rigorous test of the principles. It is obviously safer (I don't say better) to proceed like Berryman, who is all scholarship and electric response, and to avoid being too concerned with theory.

What does Pinsky like coming out of this tradition? Those poems which demonstrate that the poet understands the bind he is in by making clear that he can't possibly write the poem he has written, or, better, those that demonstrate by their very existence that the poet can't possibly think what he seems to think, or, best of all, appreciates the terrible cost of thinking it, which sometimes leads to his abandoning the idea or hypothesis as a delusion: ". . . the fancy cannot cheat so well / As she is famed to do, deceiving elf."

> My proposition is that the difference between the dross and vulgarization on the one hand, and genuine work on the other, is a sense of cost, misgiving, difficulty . . . The peculiar, somewhat paradoxical project—to make an art's medium seem less what it is—produces brilliant techniques and new assumptions. Then, as generations pass, those techniques and assumptions come to seem the only way of writing. The original premises and difficulties of the style, and the original dilemma of mind, become obscured.

The modern poems against which he tests the work of his contemporaries are Williams's "The Term," Frost's "The Most of It," and, supremely, Stevens's "The Snowman." Later on, there is much praise for A. R. Ammons's "Motion." Against these poems which he admires, Pinsky ranges work by poets both familiar and unfamiliar from the second-best all the way down the line to the absolutely awful, formulaic poems from what he calls the "surrealist-jackanapes" school and things like Lawrence Raab's "The Word," about which he says: "Without flying too far off the handle, I suggest that, in its oblique way, this is cant."

Yvor Winters begins a famous chapter by saying that "a poem is a statement in words about a human experience," and, in one of his poems which Pinsky has had occasion to quote elsewhere against the sort of work he doesn't like, writes of "Something one would never say / Moving in a certain way." But some of the finest poetry of the century has been written by people who believe that a poem is not a statement in words about a human experience at all, but, elusively yet triumphantly, an object made out of words that provides a human experience, and that poets are makers rather than sayers. Pinsky allows this, as I've said, investigates the assumptions and the work resulting from the assumptions, praises and censures, then sticks to his realist guns. It's very interesting that, in a passage on John Ashbery, he is willing to say this: "The language comes closer than one might have thought possible to being, itself, a nominalistic particular: pure, referring to nothing else, unique." The language is used, he says, like paint in a nonrepresentational painting. There is abstraction and then there is abstraction. This is the point at which another kind of book by another kind of poet might begin.

Pinsky is an eminently sane, enormously helpful and lucid critic of poetry. As the major poet of John Berryman's generation enters his sixties, one begins to look around hopefully for some younger talents who are able to take on the high responsibility of continuing the practice and criticism of the art in increasingly difficult times (in which, if for no other reason, no poet is free because his book of 176 pages is likely to cost £9.70). Pinsky and a handful of other poets of his immediate generation—Hass, Peck, McMichael—promise and have indeed already accomplished a great deal. I would stress, precisely, the wholeness and tenacity and coherence of their work—which implies no sacrifice of energy, vision, or invention—after a period which has seen important poetry published which is sometimes seriously unhinged or severely misshapen or obsessively violent. As I must end this, however, I think I should do so with a quote from Pinsky which has to do with unusual clarities which can be achieved "out near the end of things," as Berryman has it. Taken broadly, what he says of sanity at work in poetry—even when emotion is nearly intolerable or "wonder interacts with a deranged or neurasthenic aspect of personality"—describes some of the highest achievements of Berryman's work as well as the strangely descriptive poems by Roethke, John Clare, and Sylvia Plath, which he discusses in the chapter this passage introduces, and which he admires.

A "sane" work of art . . . is one which accomplishes its meaning consciously. Otherwise the meaning is the reader's creation, the art a symptom; sanity in writing is the tonal adjustment that changes confession into character-making. Authentic clarity is the style's proof that the fiction is true: not a patient's tortured, oblique version of a dream, but the authoritative dream itself, naked and magisterial.

From *The New Review*, 1977

An Afterword for Paul Mariani*

I arrived at the University of Utah straight from my high school graduation ceremony in June of 1959. I was seventeen years old and utterly unprepared to meet a man like Berryman. On the first day of the fiction workshop—the course he taught during the first week of the conference, taking over poetry from Stephen Spender in the second week—he passed out copies of three brief stories which I had submitted a few weeks before arriving. Having always been praised by my indulgent high school teachers for whatever writing I produced, I of course assumed that my genius was about to be proclaimed by this strange, intense man who placed the accents of words on unusual syllables and immediately struck an aggressive posture toward the small auditorium full of would-be writers by saying that, although he had just been told by Brewster Ghiselin, the conference administrator, to refer to us as "members" rather than as "students" he thought, nonetheless and on the whole, that "students" would do just fine. I can still remember my folly of leaning over to my right and proudly identifying myself to a fellow "member" as the author of the pages that were, alas, about to be annihilated. The job done on the stories was as unremitting and detailed as it was devastating. I don't think a single sentence escaped his censure or ridicule. Though I was not so young as to be unable to weather this storm and profit from the beating that it gave me, a number of the more matronly "members" took it upon themselves to protest in various ways against what they took to be, I suppose, an inappropriately fierce critique of the naive scribblings of a high school senior. One of the ladies drew up a statement and tried to collect signatures; another left an anonymous letter under Berryman's door. The whole thing was terribly embarrassing. One of my defenders was a science fiction writer who was into Dianetics and Scientology. She encouraged me to come to her room and throw pillows at the wall while repeating some kind of Scientological incantation.

When Berryman finally left my poor stories behind and turned to something more substantial—a positive rather than a negative example of style—we were treated to another sort of incantation entirely, and one I've never forgotten. Berryman had asked us to read Stephen Crane's "The Open Boat" and, when he began to discuss

---

*This is a letter written to Berryman's biographer answering his request for information about the poet during the summer of 1959.

the story, asked us in his rhetorical manner what the different nuances seemed to be if we chose to place a primary stress on one word rather than the others of the opening sentence. For an entire morning he worked away on that sentence:

"*None* of them knew the color of the sky."

or

"None of *them* knew the color of the sky."

or

"None of them *knew* the color of the sky."

or

"None of them knew the *color* of the sky."

or

"None of them knew the color of the *sky*."

Did it matter which word took the chief stress in this pentameter line of Crane's? Should one write pentameter lines in sentences of fiction, especially in first sentences? Did Crane do anything to curb our inclination to stress rhetorically a word on which a metrical stress might not fall? (This last was a question I found myself asking about Berryman's own work years and decades later.) Anyway, it was a marvelous display of pedagogical virtuosity and critical ingeniousness, and it was only a taste of what was coming. In spite of the shock of the opening day's workshop, I found myself warming to the man tremendously. On the whole, he let me off the hook after that first blast, although, from time to time, he would remark that the only person who had learned anything from him so far was "young Mr. Matt-i-as" (as he insisted on pronouncing my name both then and when we met again later on).

By the time I finally had a private meeting with Berryman in order to discuss my work, he had clearly become a little perplexed by the anonymous letters, petitions, and so forth on my behalf. I think he tried to apologize in a way by trying to find a few lines and images and sentences he could call "promising." I remember his urging me to read D. H. Lawrence's "The Rocking Horse Winner" and Jon Silkin's "The Death of a Son," a poem he had also been pressing on Stephen Spender. He said he would tell me at the conference picnic why he wanted me to read the Lawrence story and why he thought it was a masterpiece. In fact, he never returned to the subject, and I was too shy to bring it up again myself. At the conference, he also remarked that someone had told him that we looked alike. I can't think that we *did* look very much alike in 1959, but it's certainly true that we did later on—after my own features had begun to mature a bit and when we both were wearing beards. By the middle and late 1960s, this similarity in our appearance was something nearly everybody noticed and something that seemed to bother him. It was not just a matter of facial features, but a question of characteristic gestures, mannerisms, personal tics. Much of it was in the hands—both their shape and length, and the way we used our hands when we talked. Years later a student of mine wrote and published a poem beginning:

> You, John, look like John. Matthias resembles a Berryman.
> Weary hair that sprawls like a hanging
> Garden of King Neb's dead grass.
> Vaulted forehead, wrinkles, fluting, the shrine
> Of a developed brain . . .
> Proud, dripping eyes . . . the schizoid clergyman
> Buried under one too many vows . . .

By the time of the conference picnic, all of the visiting writers—Berryman, Spender, and Herbert Gold—had begun to call Brewster Ghiselin "Mother Gooselin." Evidently, he took the personal welfare of his writers very seriously, felt that they should get to bed at a decent hour, and tried to keep them sober and respectable. I retain two images from the picnic: the tall and enormously ungainly Stephen Spender trying to play volleyball—always leaping in the air when he should have been firmly on the ground, and on the ground when he should have jumped—and Berryman, presumably pretty drunk, trying to run a straight line in the footrace he had organized, and running instead at a diagonal virtually tangent to the volleyballers and almost into a tree. Mother Gooselin was dismayed.

Berryman and I met again from time to time as we both grew older and as he became more and more famous. I saw him for the last time when he came to Notre Dame to read in May of 1969, just before my own first book was published. The students who sponsored his reading didn't tell me that he had checked into the Morris Inn on campus two days before the scheduled reading. For two days, they had left him alone in his hotel room without realizing what that might mean. By the time I got to him he was in dreadful shape. His suitcase was full of cigarette cartons and bottles of Jack Daniel's, and he had been smoking and drinking alone for a long time. I managed to get some food into him and we took a walk around the Notre Dame lakes talking about Yvor Winters (under whom I had studied at Stanford) and Hugh MacDiarmid, whose *The Drunk Man Looks at the Thistle* Berryman admired and which seemed to me to be a possible source of influence on *The Dream Songs*. This he acknowledged. By the time of his reading, Berryman was in pretty good shape and read very well, dedicating the evening to my wife with whom he had flirted in his courtly way during dinner. Afterward, we had a small reception for him at our house. When everyone had left, I asked if I could read some poems to him to make up for the juvenilia he'd been obliged to endure in 1959. He listened attentively and made some acute observations. Then he signed two of my Berryman books. For my daughter, then less than a year old, he signed Dream Song 385, the beautiful conclusion to *His Dream, His Toy, His Rest*, that poem of thanksgiving which begins "My daughter's heavier." For me, he signed the page facing his earlier signature in my old copy of *Homage to Mistress Bradstreet*. The first signature is dated "Salt Lake City, 19 June 1959" and the second, "Notre Dame, 5 May 1969." Just a few weeks less than an even decade.

Some Notes on the English Poetry
of Göran Printz-Påhlson

Göran Printz-Påhlson, *Gradiva och andra dikter, with a summary in English*, Bonniers; *The Green-Ey'd Monster*, Michael Smith; *Säg Minns Du Skeppet Refanut?*, Bonniers.

Shortly after I first met Göran Printz-Påhlson in 1973, he and I and the British poet Richard Burns gave a reading together at Clare Hall, Cambridge, where Printz-Påhlson is a Fellow. We all read from our translations that evening, as well as from our own poems, and Printz-Påhlson amused the audience enormously by reading a poem from *Gradiva* three times—twice in English and once in Swedish. "When Beaumont and Tocqueville First Visited Sing-Sing" was, in fact, originally written in English. It appears in *Gradiva* translated by Printz-Påhlson himself into Swedish. Discovered there by an American reader of Swedish poetry, it was translated back into English and published in a literary journal. The new English version, obviously enough, was quite different from the first. Printz-Påhlson's reading of the three poems that night formed a comic triptych with an elusive moral. But the adventures of the Beaumont and Tocqueville poem do not end there. A year ago, I picked up Lars Gustafsson's *Forays Into Swedish Poetry* and discovered that the one poem chosen from Printz-Påhlson's work to represent him among his Swedish forbears and contemporaries was the ubiquitous "När Beaumont och Tocqueville först besökte Sing-Sing"—translated back into English for the American edition of the book, this time presumably by Gustafsson. Such are the hazards risked by extraterritorial types who are determined to write memorable work in more than

179

one language. The fate of this poem is almost worthy of an extended treatment by Nabokov—or of a short one by Borges.

The Beaumont and Tocqueville poem is not the only curiosity to be found in *Gradiva*, for it is surely not typical—or so I must assume—for a volume of Swedish poetry to conclude with a "Summary" which, in fact, consists of three poems in English on the subject of American comic strip characters. In a note on the "Summary," Printz-Påhlson says that he has so named the section "in order to show that you don't have to be less serious when you write about Superman . . . than you do when you write about the Rosenbergs." Like several of the Swedish poems in *Gradiva*, the three concluding poems in English are written in rigorously metrical rhyming quatrains, and it is in the making of these quatrains that much of the "seriousness" to which Printz-Påhlson refers in his note resides. But there is another kind of seriousness involved here as well which goes beyond the seriousness of good craftsmanship—a reorientation of imaginative energies which was perhaps stimulated when Printz-Påhlson began translating English and American poets and took up residence in English-speaking countries, initially in America (1961–64) and afterward in England. In a very interesting poem addressed to the American mathematician Newcomb Greenleaf, Printz-Påhlson writes:

> . . . When I met you & Connie
> I was ambitious, crisp, refractory, European. You & America
> taught me to flatten my desire onto the untoward topology
> of the ingenuous . . .

The English poems in *Gradiva* may well represent an early meeting of sorts between the ingenious mind of the poet and the ingenuous American phenomena he has come to love—a "flattening," as it were, of an ambitious theme to occupy the two dimensions of the quintessentially unambitious comic strip. At any rate, the poems about "Superman," "Bringing up Father," and "The Katzenjammer Kids" make use of a highly idiomatic American English with great energy and authority when they are at their most knockabout and boisterous—slapping together rhymes like "mad pursuit" and "doesn't care a hoot," "something cute" and "He is a fruit," and so on—and then suddenly sound rather British when they grow reflective. These concluding quatrains of "Bringing up Father," for example, remind me of the early work of Donald Davie (which Printz-Påhlson has translated) in such representative poems as "Remembering the Thirties" and "The Garden Party."

We can forgive our ancestors the mere
Deception of their ruthless living lie
But hardly the brutality to leave us here
And rot away and stink and simply die.

This goes to show that feeling is without pretence,
Construing the unbearable (as our pun gets slyer)
In bringing up our fathers in the awful sense
Of exhumation of a dreaded sire.

Ambitious, that. Perhaps even crisp, refractory, European. It is
good for the poems that they can accommodate both the sophisticated thought and craftsmanship of the poet as well as his exuberant
response to what is actually a kind of folk art.

It is folk art, in fact, which has recently come to occupy Printz-
Påhlson a good deal whether he is on his British or his American
turf. Between the publication of *Gradiva* in 1966 and (in English) *The
Green Ey'd Monster* in 1980, Printz-Påhlson has written considerably
more than I suppose most Swedish readers are aware of. And yet
there was indeed a dry period, a time when perhaps the question of
whether to write in Swedish or English became sufficiently problematic that the flow of poems in both languages all but ceased. I can
imagine Printz-Påhlson during this fallow period waiting for the
tardy arrival of his muse while the music of Scott Skinner or Dock
Boggs wailed on that scratchy old machine in Stapleford. While I've
been treated to many recordings both in Stapleford and Cambridge,
I have trouble remembering who's who among Printz-Påhlson's
elect of hillbillies and highlanders. I do, however, have a letter in
my files telling me that "the fiddler James 'Scott' Skinner is the in-
ventor of a very influential cross-bowing plonking, drawing-room
style of fiddling." I think it is safe to assume that Skinner's fiddling,
like Printz-Påhlson's wonderful poem in homage to his style, *takes
off*. The piece is short enough to quote in its entirety.

The kelp is not enough. Two hundred
thousand wet sea-birds every
minute serve the mind with writs of constraint
in *pizzicato* dancehalls all over
the moody crags. A lonely kipper
is seen to flounder in the volatile traffic
leaving his ladder, embarking

for France, land of *cotillons* and plenty,
prognathous and proud in the strathspey
prattle of little Jacobite girls in terror.
Far, far away, o dominie, from
glamour-grammar grit and the sweet
mountain smell of mossy socks in Allenvale!

If Skinner's invented technique stands, say, in a relationship to traditional fiddling somewhat analogous to Eliot's "individual talent" and *that* tradition, it is probably more important to note that *any* Scots fiddling, however sophisticated or exportable, will be "connected with the unchanging flow of life, accepted values, rustic stability, indigenous belonging and such"—a point Printz-Påhlson makes about the pre-Eliotic received sense of the word *traditional* in a recent essay on Tranströmer. But if all kinds of traditional or folk or ethnic music are in one sense deeply conservative, they are in another sense radical and subversive in an age of centralized economies, political control from distant capitals, pressure of all kinds for social uniformity, and an international style in painting, literature, and music (whether of the symphony orchestra, the jazz band, or the rock group). If that lovely kipper—taking off like Skinner's fiddling—must sojourn in France for a while, prognathous and proud as any Stuart Pretender, he may well return strengthened by his flight to the valley of the Spey to work with all those other trouts and herrings for Scottish devolution (while, doubtless, dancing the Birks of Invermay or the Braes of Tullimet with many a pretty Jacobite). Skinner's style, like the Scots poetry of Hugh MacDiarmid, has a political as well as a strictly aesthetic meaning. It is interesting in this context to remember that Printz-Påhlson and Jan Östergren have, for several years, discussed the possibility of translating Mac-Diarmid into the Scanian dialect, and that Printz-Påhlson's long poem in Swedish, *"Gläd Dig, Du Skåning,"* can be seen, as he has written in a recent letter, as "a kind of Scanian version of *A Drunk Man Looks at the Thistle"*—MacDiarmid's most successful and sustained poem in his unique synthetic reinvention of the Scots vernacular.

Though the nitty-gritty of the mountain moss in Allenvale may be "far, far away, o domine," from the hills of Dock Boggs, the poem in homage to Boggs' music makes a point not unrelated to the Scott Skinner piece. The tone, too, is similar in many respects to that of "Scott Skinner," as is the character of the humor. It is the idiom, of course, characterized by those "sourmash blandishments" and "gridiron reverberations," that bluegrass "bushwhacking" of God's melodies, and the "clodhopper shovel / smack in the kisser," that measures the distance between the two.

> There are gridiron reverberations
> in the hills, sourmash
> blandishments bleating
> from the sheriff's office.

> Ah, the *gavroche* innocence of a barnyard rape!

> He offers a smile, mild
> as pick-axe handles a
> mile wide which kindles
> the hide of rutabagas:
> their red necks swabbed
> by cool, pale blue grass
> in the abstracted stare of poverty.

> Bushwhacking the melodies of God
> for the breakdown of brushfires,
> he nurtures illustrious health
> with the grating pap
> of pink indigence,
> plucking the lure of life
> from the audible *mouchoir* moment
> when distant authority suppurates
> the blueridge landscapes of childhood.

> Raw death: a clodhopper shovel
> smack in the kisser.

While the region festers in the "benign neglect" of a centralized political system, Boggs' music is efficacious. For the staring poor, he nurtures health with the pap of indigence itself—his singing. Even raw death, like raw music, has something to be said for it, the contrast being (to use Robert Lowell's distinction between two kinds of poetry) the "cooked" death of the modern urban hospital with all life-support systems buzzing and blipping until the last mechanically assisted breath and artificially stimulated heartbeat. This is another good poem, by the way, as confident in its (highly idiomatic!) dealings with America as the Scott Skinner poem is in its dealings with Scotland. It is itself, however, "cooked" rather than "raw."

Nothing could be more carefully contrived (in a totally nonpejorative sense) than that marvellous imagery of the rutabagas having their red necks swabbed in the pale blue grass. Printz-Påhlson, though often drawn to the down-home subject, is always, as a poet, crafty and sophisticated and urban. He loves Dock Boggs—not, however, close-up in the local sheriff's office, but from the relatively safe distance of a speaker system in Cambridge, London, or Lund. Nor is this in any sense hypocritical. The politics of the poem are deeply felt in part *as a result* of the distance.

When the politics gets closer to home, however, the distance disappears. "Odradek," a frightening and brilliant poem based in part on Kafka's little parable, "The Cares of a Family Man," is dedicated to Printz-Påhlson's old friend and publisher, Bo Cavefors, who was, at the time, the target of civil and criminal proceedings by the Swedish authorities which were interpreted by many in Sweden as a kind of legal harassment aiming at censorship. In a letter to me dated 28 April 1980, Printz-Påhlson breaks off at the bottom of one page only to begin again in great consternation at the top of another. "Next morning at 7. Awakened by an express letter. It contained clippings from Swedish newspapers telling us that Cavefors was convicted in the proceedings for 'obstruction of fiscal control and suppression of documents.' As Bo had been detained on suspicion of much more serious crimes, the judge very generously considered it quits. But nobody offered to give him restitution for the unfounded slur on his reputation that any conviction in a criminal court entails." "Odradek" arrived in the mail a few days later.

In Kafka's parable, Odradek is the name of the strange mechanical creature representing all sorts of obscure and seemingly benign forces of denial that lurks in the house of the narrator—in the garrett, the stairway, the lobby, the entrance hall. Initially, it appears to be "a flat star-shaped spool for thread." But it is "not only a spool, for a small wooden crossbar sticks out of the middle of the star, and another small rod is joined at a right angle. By means of this latter rod on one side and one of the points of the star on the other, the whole thing can stand upright as if on two legs." The thing is "extraordinarily nimble and can never be laid hold of." Also, it can talk. In Printz-Påhlson's poem the "cases"—locative, instrumental, and accusative—are intended to have both a linguistic and legal meaning, as well as the more general sense of sets of circumstances or affairs and the informal one referring to peculiarities or eccentricities. Here is the poem:

Odradek

Es klingt etwa so wie das Rascheln
in gefallenen Blättern

Their cases are locative or instrumental.
Here, in this place, I see the leaves falling
on the fabulously stayed crosses and inscriptions,
as they fell on the Homeric simile of generations.
You have heard them, the little dissuaders,
whispering in the attics, or from behind the creaking stairs,
with their busy spools and laughter, seemingly
from no human lungs. You proceed to ask:
What's your name? Answers: Odradek.
Where do you live? *Unbestimmter Wohnsitz.*
They cannot die but cease to exist
when you do not listen. In another place,
in Paris, a car is stopped: a little dog
in the lap of a young girl exploding
like a ripe autumnal fruit in her hands. Her
lover is already carved in half by bullets.
There are cleaner cases, more winsome
uses for the accusative. Do not heed them anymore.
Here we all die, in bits and pieces.

For Bo Cavefors

Although in these brief remarks I have felt I should limit my commentary to those of Printz-Påhlson's poems which are short enough to be quoted in full, it would be entirely misleading to leave the impression that all of his work in English is in the mode of "Scott Skinner" and "Dock Boggs" or in the mode of "Odradek." Along with "Acrobats on the Radio," the letter-poem to Newcomb Greenleaf from which I quoted a few lines earlier, there are three other middle-length poems of an epistolary and/or discursive kind: "To John at the Summer Solstice" (the companion piece for the Greenleaf poem), "My Interview with I. A. Richards," and "Comedians" (dedicated to Kenneth Koch). All of these are, to some extent, poems about poetry (or at least about language), and therefore all of them lead very naturally to Printz-Påhlson's most ambitious poem in English, *The Green Ey'd Monster*, a poem that Richard Burns has accurately called "a playful, witty, profound, sad, funny, serious poem, which combines all the Swedish, American, and English influences on his earlier work in a brilliant synthesis." It is, he says, "one of the finest long poems written in English (and what is more, in England) which I have read in the last ten years." Poems about poetry. . . . Well . . .

> Before it had become fashionable to write poetry
> about writing poetry, it was considered
> so exceedingly difficult that it was next
> to impossible,

. . . begins the poem to Kenneth Koch. By the end, however, through the agency of a little girl who learns in the course of the poem to swim without water-wings and then "without air, / without rhythm, without metaphors" . . . and who says " 'Wait a minute, / I am being used as a metaphor now,' " "Comedians" concludes:

> But there she is wrong. The poem, if it is any good at all,
> is never about writing poetry: but rather about
> making jokes, or love; or deceit; once again she (in
> spite of her perky independence of mind) and the reader
> have together been lead up that proverbial old
> garden path. But, in that case, consider a boy
> on the first day of spring when the rain has just stopped,
> playing with marbles up that old garden path,
> water-logged still by the rains . . .

. . . and we must return again to the beginning. The conclusion of *The Green Ey'd Monster* is similar.

> My song is
> soon to end, but don't mistake
> my placid tone for equanimi-
> ty. Most of all it is itself
> a metaphor, in which the
> vehicle is missing but the
> tenor, in wonderful belcanto warblings
> goes on and on and on.

And then, *Encore, da capo*, the voice sings. There is no way for me to give any brief sense of the complexity of *The Green Ey'd Monster*. Formally, it may be even more ambitious than the title poem of *Gradiva*. In a letter of 14 January 1980, Printz-Påhlson wrote: "I do hope that you can see what I am trying for in the new poem: in the intersection between the farcical and the pathetic for instance, in the constant worrying about synchronicity (in a strictly non-Jungian and nonsuperstitious sense) and diachronicity—alternative worlds, but more in the strictly logical meaning of the phrase. I tried to clarify it in my poem 'Comedians' (which should be the writer-reader relation) and I am using it on a grand scale in *The Green Ey'd Monster*." This will indicate at least some of the poem's essential preoccupations—although, of course, it gives little account of its shape or movement.

The first section of the *Monster*, "The Mezzotint," is, in fact, my favorite. We are asked again and again to "imagine a picture." Again and again, the picture dissolves. "But this is not the picture," we are told. It is not the "manor-house in Salop. or Derbyshire"; it is not the "Italian villa on the bleak Dalmatian shore"; it is not the "mandala / of Oriental opulence and splendour / straddling the world"; it is not even the work of the "mimeobionic, infraquarcine, microplane android artist" whose crime is re-creation of the Past, the "palinpoietic activities" which are, "as every callow space cadet will know, punishable / by Eternal Life." But . . .

> imagine two lovers who have long since ceased
>   to talk
> to one another, or who will go on talking to them-
>   selves, whispering *quarrel, gauntlet, equinox, soon, same, graves.*

> This is the same picture, the same
> treasure-filled *Spelunca,*
>   darkness scratched from the dry copper plate.

> Every conversation is inbetween these two,
>   not between the maiden and her ravisher, nor the child
>   and God, nor the artist and his shrunken world.

It strikes me that what Lars Gustaffson wrote in conclusion about the much-travelled Beaumont and Tocqueville poem also applies to the world of *The Green Ey'd Monster* opened up by "The Mezzotint." I want to conclude these notes by quoting it. Gustaffson argues that the Beaumont and Tocqueville poem sees the entire modern world as a prison:

> The poem is part of a sequence entitled *Carceri Suite*. This name alludes to a series of engravings by the eighteenth-century Italian artist, Piranesi, a remarkable suite of gigantic,

labyrinthine prisons, an indoor universe of deep arches and endless cavities of hewn stone. Printz-Påhlson's work has the same melancholy authority, the same desolate, windy dream quality—*dream* and yet, *reality*.

There are other qualities, as Richard Burns suggests, which are also characteristic of *The Green Ey'd Monster,* but in the end I feel it is the "melancholy authority" and "desolate, windy dream quality" that Gustaffson finds both in Piranesi and the *Carceri Suite* that continues to dominate.

From *Tärningskastet,* 1981

Part III

Three Poems On Poetics

Turns: Toward a Provisional
Aesthetic and a Discipline

(i)

The scolemayster levande was the toun
and sary of hit semed everuch one.
The smal quyt cart that covert was and hors . . .
to ferien his godes. To ferien his godes
quere he was boun.

The onelych thyng of combraunce (combraunce)
was the symphonye
(saf a pakke of bokes)
that he hade boghte the yere
quen he bithoght
that he wolde lerne to play.

But the zele woned (zele woned).
He neuer couthe ani scylle.

(ii)

And so the equivalent
              (the satisfactory text.
squ'elles sont belles
              sont pas fidèles. rough
west-midland, hwilum andgit
of andgiete: the rest is not
              a word for word defense . . .

(iii)

And make him known to 14th-century men
Even when everything favors the living?
Even if we could reverse that here
I know you've read and travelled too.

So Destination or Destiny: *Quere He Was Boun!*
And yet to introduce the antecedent place.
Restrictive clause; sense of the referent noun.
A tilted cart is a cart with an awning.

              Langland has it "keured"
              John of Mandeville "coured"
              Wycliffe "keuered"

But "covert" in Arimathaea

Personal luggage: not the same as merchandise.
Cursor Mundi's "gudes"; Purity's "godes"

This is personal luggage / destination / travel

    Harp and pipe and symphonye

    (saf a pakke of bokes)

(iv)

Where dwelle ye if it tell to be?

    at the edge
        of the toun?
    at the edge
        of the toun?

Levande was.
He Levande Was The Toun.

Reason the nature of place
Reason he can praise
Reason what the good-doing doctor said

    Rx.: cart (that covert was & hors)

Dull ache in the hip is probably gout.
Painful nodes of calcium—(neck & in the ears).
Palpitations, flutters. Stones in the gland.

    food to avoid? drink

    (put him in the cart)

    Rx.: bibliography
    Rx.: map

(v)

The metaphysicality of Hermetic thought—
Let him think o' that! (Problem is he
Still enjoys cunt . . .)

    . . . instrument was ay thereafter
Al his own combraunce . . .

Sary of hit semed everuch one.

Torn between disgust & hope
He simply never couthe . . .

antiquorum aegyptiorum
oh, ... imitatus . . .

(vi)

All day long it rains. He travels
All day long. Wiping water from
His eyes: and twenty miles? and
Twenty miles? Fydlers nod & smile.

Cycles pass him. Cars pass him.
Buses full of tourists . . .
Dauncers & Minstrels, Drunkards
And Theeves. Whooremaisters,
Tossepottes; Maskers, Fencers
And Rogues; Cutpurses, Blasphemers
Counterfaite Egyptions . . .

Greek, Arabic, Medieval Latin,
Mis-translated, misconceived.
More than just for his disport

who loveth daliaunce

who falleth (o who falleth)

far behinde . . .

(vii)

That supernatural science,
That rare art should seem . . .

here among
a randy
black-billed

ilk

Les traductions sont comme les femmes. And time to get off of her
toes. Idiomatic: toes. Lorsqu'elles sont belles. I should apologize,
then: to apologize. The schoolmaster was leaving the village, and

everybody seemed sorry. Simple as that. The miller lent him the cart and horse to carry his goods. Simple as that. And no particular trouble with the words. Scolemayster: 1225 in the *Life of St Katherine*. But you change the spelling, see, to conform with the dialect. Levande was: *The Destruction of Troy,* "all the Troiens lefton." But use the participial construction. Sary of hit: see the *Lay Folks Mass Book*. The city of his destination. Twenty miles off. Quite sufficient size for his effects. The only cumbersome article (save the pack of books) was: count on the medieval mind to be sympathetic. Though I come after hym with hawebake / I speke in prose and lat hym rymes make. My general principles I take from the King (and his Queen). Tha boc wendan on Englisc. Hwilum word be word. Hwilum andgit of andgiete. Swa swa ic hie geliornode. It would be idle and boring to rehearse. Here what is available. Let me simply indicate the manner. Take sulphur from Sol for the fire and with it roast Luna. From which will the word issue forth . . . *If* the given appeared in a verifiable text. *If* the given was truly equivalent.

The usual procedures are the following: (1) To ignore altogether: "make no effort to explain the fundamentals"; (2) To drop apologetic footnotes: "I'm sorry, but I simply cannot understand this esoteric sort of thing"; (3) To make suggestive remarks while hurrying on to something else: "*If* the given appeared in a verifiable text. *If* the given was truly equivalent." But the schoolmaster was leaving the village, and everybody seemed sorry. *Jude the Obscure,* paragraph one, a neat linguistic exercise. Written by Thomas Hardy in 1895. And such a revelation makes the art available to the vulgar. Who will abuse and discredit? *Keeper of secret wisdom, agent of revelation, vision, and desire:* THIS IS THE QUESTION WE MUST ALWAYS RAISE.

Now some of the obscure, like some of the lucid, do not become proletarianized. Unlike the majority of their kind, they are not cast down from the ruling class to produce a commodity which both enslaves them and enslaves the exploited labourers with whom they are objectively allied. Perhaps they hold teaching jobs in public schools or universities; perhaps they have an inherited income. In any case, some maintain their Hermetic privilege. They are not obliged to live by their art or to produce for the open market. Such unproletarianized obscure are revolted by the demands of a commercialized market, by the vulgarity of the mass-produced commodity supplied to meet it. And revulsion ultimately tells (1) on their sex life (2) on their health.

While a relationship of cause and effect is established between obscure and lucid organizations emerging from the division of labour and the consequent dialectical evolution of social reality, such becomes, we know, increasingly separated from the actual productive function of society, from sleep. This gives us pause. "The point is that the notion of invariancy inherent by definition to the concept of the series, if applied to all parameters, leads to a uniformity of configurations that eliminates the last traces of unpredictability, of surprise." This gives us pause.

And so the system and its adherents are the villains; license, conspiracy, and nihilism are the virtues of the heroes: *or*: The system itself becomes a context for heroics; license, conspiracy, and nihilism become the crimes of the villains; acceptance of convention and austere self-discipline become the virtues of the heroes. The schoolmaster is forever an intermediary: the shape of his life is determined by the nature of society: the nature of his art seeks to determine the shape of society by administering to its nature. And intermediacy ultimately tells (1) on his sex life (2) on his health.

But make him known to 14-century men even when everything favours the living. Reason the nature of place. Reason he can praise. Reason that he travels in a cart. With Cursor Mundi's "gudes"; with Purity's "godes". With Joseph of Arimathaea, turns: to elliptically gloss.

Double Derivation, Association, and Cliché:
From The Great Tournament
Roll of Westminster

(i)

The heralds wear their tabards correctly.
Each, in his left hand, carries a wand.
Before and after the Master of Armour
Enter his men: three of them carry the staves.
The mace bearer wears a yellow robe.
In rigth & goodly devysis of apparyl
The gentlemen ride.
The double-curving trumpets shine.

Who breaks a spear is worth the prize.

(ii)

Or makes a forest in the halls of Blackfriars
at Ludgate whych is garneychyd wyth trees & bowes,
wyth bestes and byrds; wyth a mayden
syttyng by a kastell makying garlonds there;
wyth men in woodwoos dress,
wyth men of armes. . . .
                              Or Richard Gibson
                                    busy
with artificers and labour, portages and ships:
busy with his sums and his accounts:
for what is wrought by carpenters & joyners,
karrovers & smiths . . .
(Who breaks a spear is worth the prize)

Who breaks a schylld on shields
a saylle on sails
a sclev upon his lady's sleeves;
who can do skilfully the spleter werke,
whose spyndylles turn

Power out of parsimony, feasting
Out of famine, revels out of revelation:—
Out of slaughter, ceremony.
When the mist lifts over Bosworth.
When the mist settles on Flodden.

Who breaks a spear is worth the prize.

(iii)

The double-curving trumpets shine:
  & cloth of gold.
The challengers pass. . . .

Well, & the advice of Harry Seven:—
(or the Empress Wu, depending
where you are):
We'll put on elegance later.
We'll put off art.
No life of Harry the Seven
    there in the works of the Bard . . .
(No Li Po on Wu)
An uninteresting man? Parsimonious.

Wolsey travels in style . . .
              & on the Field of Cloth of Gold
    & in the halls at Ludgate
a little style . . .
Something neo-Burgundian
(Holy, Roman, & bankrupt) illuminating
Burgkmairs in *Der Weisskunig & Freydal.*
Rival Maximilian's mummeries, his
dances and his masques, his
armouries & armourers the mark.
Hammermen to King, his prize; King
to hammermen: guard, for love of progeny,
the private parts!
           (*My* prick's bigger
than *your* prick, or Maxi's prick,
or James')

(iv)

          & like the Burgkmairs
these illuminations:—
where, o years ago, say twenty-two or
say about five hundred,
cousins in the summertime would
ritualize their rivalries

in sumptuous tableaux.
Someone holds a camera. Snap.
In proper costume, Homo Ludens wears
Imagination on his sleeve.

But chronicle & contour fashion
out of Flodden nothing but the truth.
The deaths, in order & with dignity,
of every child: I remember that.

Who breaks a spear is worth the prize.

(v)

Who breaks a schylld on shields
      a saylle on sails
a sclev upon his lady's sleeves . . .
And in the north, & for the nearer rival.
Who meteth Coronall to Coronall, who beareth
a man down:—down the distance to Westminster,
down the distance in time.

For the pupil of Erasmus,
for the rival of the Eighth,
a suitcase dated Flodden full of relics.
Shipped Air France, they're scattered
at the battle of the Somme.
It intervened, the news:
it intervenes

As, at the Bankside, Henry makes
a masque at Wolsey's house and, certain
cannons being fired, the paper
wherewith one of them is stopped
does light the thatch, where being
thought at first but idle smoke,
it kindles inwardly consuming
in the end
the house
the Globe

          The first & happiest hearers of the town
          among them, one Sir Henry Wotton

Largely Fletcher's work

(vi)

O, largely spleter werke
that certain letters could be sent
unto the high & noble excellent Princess
the Queen of England from her dear & best beloved
Cousin Noble Cueur Loyall with knowledge of
the good and gracious fortune of the birth
of a young prince:
     & to accomplish certain
feats of arms the king (signed Henry R)
does send four knights . . .

  & sends to work his servant Richard Gibson
on the Revels and Accounts
& sends the children in the summertime to play
& sends the rival Scot a fatal surrogate
from Bosworth, makes an end
to *his* magnificence.

Slaughter out of ceremony, famine
out of feasting, out of power
parsimony, out of revels
revelation . . .

   As an axe in the spine can reveal,
  as an arrow in the eye.

Who breaks a spear is worth the prize.

(vii)

And what is wrought by carpenters & joyners,
by karrovers & smiths, is worth the prize;
and what is wrought by labour.
For those who play. Of alldyr pooles & paper,
whyght leed and gleew, yern hoopes of sundry
sortes; kord & roopes & naylles:—
All garneychyd at Ludgate. With
trees & bows. All garneychyd with
cloth of Gold.

    The challengers pass

And deck themselves outrageously
in capes & plumes and armour . . .

And out to play: making in the Summertime
a world against all odds, and with
its Winter dangers.

    In a garden, old men play at chess.
    In the Summer. In the Winter, still.

Who will decorate the golden tree,
Employ properly the captive giant
And the dwarf? Who will plead
His rights despite decrepitude . . . ?

    I reach for words as in a photograph
    I reach for costumes in a trunk:

An ancient trunk (an ancient book)

    a saylle, a schylld, a sclev

  a yellow robe, a wand—

    pipes & harpes & rebecs,
    lutes & viols for a masque.

Where double-curving trumpets shine
The challengers pass.

Who breaks a spear is worth the prize.

Clarifications for Robert Jacoby: "Double Derivation . . . ,"
part iv, ll. 1–10; part vii, ll. 1–15, 22–28

A moment ago, Robert, I thought I was watching
    a wren, the one which nests
By my window here, fly, dipping & rising,
    across this field in Suffolk
So like the one we used to play in, in Ohio,
    when we were boys. But it was
Really something that you, Dr. Jacoby, would
    be able to explain by pointing out
To me in some expensive, ophthalmological text
    the proper Latin words.

It was no wren (still less the mythological bird
    I might have tried to make it)—
But just defective vision: one of those spots
    or floating motes before the eyes
That send one finally to a specialist. Not
    a feathered or a golden bird,
Nothing coming toward me in the early evening
    mist, just a flaw, as they say,
In the eye of the beholder.

Like? in a way?
    the flaw in the printer's eye
(the typesetter's, the proof-
    reader's) that produced and then
Let stand that famous line
    in Thomas Nashe's poem about the plague,
"Brightness falls from the air,"
    when what he wrote was, thinking
Of old age and death, "Brightness
    falls from the *hair*."

I wonder if you remember all those games
    we used to play: the costumes,
All the sticks & staves, the whole complicated
    paraphernalia accumulated to suggest
Authentic weaponry and precise historical dates,
    not to mention exact geographical places,
All through August and September—the months you
    visited. You wanted then, you said,

To be an actor, and your father—a very practical
     lawyer—said he found that funny, though
I think we both intuited
     that he was secretly alarmed.

With little cause. You were destined—how obvious
     it should have been!—to be professional,
Respectable, and eminent. Still, you put in time
     and played your child's part
With skill and grace.

There is a photograph of us taken, I believe,
     in 1950. Your plumed hat (a little
Tight) sits sprightly on your head, your cape
     (cut from someone's bathrobe) hangs
Absurdly down your back, and in your hand you
     brandish the sword of the patriarch
Himself, grandfather M., Commander in Chief
     of the United Spanish War Vets.

                                        My
Plumed hat is slightly better fitting, if less
     elegant, my sword a fencing foil with
A rubber tip, my cape the prize: something from
     the almost legitimate theatre, from
My father's role in a Masonic play where he spoke,
     once each year before initiations
On some secret, adult stage, lines he practiced
     in the kitchen all the week before:
Let the jewelled box of records be opened
     and the plans for the wall by the
Southwest gate be examined!

The photographer, it seems, has irritated us.
     We scowl. The poses are not natural.
Someone has said Simon says stand here, look
     there, dress right, flank left;
Someone, for the record, intervenes. Or has
     James arrived? Our cousin from the
East side of Columbus who, with bicycles
     and paper routes and baseballs
Wanted you in time as badly then as I could
     want you out of it. A miniature
Adult, he looked askance at our elaborate

rituals. He laughed outright,
Derisively. No mere chronicler, he was reality
    itself. I hated him.

Of whom I would remind myself when asking you:
    do you remember? a world of imagination,
Lovely and legitimate, uncovering, summer after
    summer, a place that we no longer go,
A field we do not enter now, a world one tries
    to speak of, one way or another,
In a poem. Robert! Had the jewelled box
    of records been opened and the plans
For the wall by the southwest gate been examined,
    news: that he, not you and I, made
Without our knowledge, without our wigs and
    epaulets, with bricks he had a right
To throw, binding rules for our splendid games.

How remote it all must seem to you who joined
    him with such dispatch. One day, I
Suppose, I'll come to you in California saying
    to you frankly: cure me if you can.
Or to some other practicing your arts. Until then,
    what is there to talk about except
This book of photographs? And what they might
    have made of us, all those aunts,
Clucking at our heels, waddling onto Bosworth field
    or Flodden with their cameras. And why
They should have come, so ordinary and so mortal,
    to bring back images like this one
Turning yellow in a yellow book. Brightness fell
    from the hair

Of whom I would be worthy now, of whom I think
    about again as just outside my window
A child plays with a stick. And jumps on both feet
    imitating, since she sees it in the field
(With a stick in its beak), a wren. She enters
    the poem as she enters the field. I will
Not see her again. She goes to her world of stick
    and field and wren; I go to my world
Of poem. She does not know it, and yet she is here:
    here in the poem as surely as there

In the field, in the dull evening light, in the world
    of her imagining, where, as the mist descends,
She is a wren.

As I write that down she is leaving the field.
    She goes to her house where her
Father and mother argue incessantly, where
    her brother is sick. In the house
They are phoning a doctor. In the poem—
    because I say so,
                because I say once more
That she enters the world of her imagining
    where, as the mist descends,
She is a wren—
    She remains in the field.

Part IV

Not For Sale in USA:
Some Poets of the 1980s

Anthologies of Contemporary British Poetry

Blake Morrison and Andrew Motion, eds., *Contemporary British Poetry*, Penguin Books; Michael Schmidt, ed., *Some Contemporary Poets of Britain and Ireland*, Carcanet Press.

I have been asked by the editors of *Another Chicago Magazine* to contribute what will become a regular column on the subject of British poetry. This is a welcome but unusual request. American readers of poetry have taken very little interest in the work of British poets for some time now. It was not always like this. When my generation of American poets was growing up in the Fifties we all, I think, quite naturally read the Brits along with the natives. We all cut our teeth on the anthologies then available—those old Oscar Williams and Louis Untermeyer books where you found Hardy toward the beginning and maybe Hughes or Larkin or Tomlinson at the very end, after some Hecht or Snodgrass. Thumbing in Williams's *Pocket Book of Modern Verse*, the first book of poetry I ever owned, I still find it natural to see the poems of D. H. Lawrence beside the poems of Ezra Pound, the Penn Warren just before the Vernon Watkins, the Delmore Schwartz after the F. T. Prince. And yet, familiar as these juxtapositions are, I know the book is from a vanished world. It is dedicated "To the memory of Dylan Thomas—major poet, great man and immortal soul." And not only are there thirty pages of Thomas's work—as against, significantly, just one poem by William Carlos Williams—but also nearly as much of George Barker's. Oscar Williams prints almost as many poems by Edith Sitwell as by Marianne Moore, and he includes substantial chunks of Graves, Auden,

207

Spender, and MacNeice beside his Tate, Roethke, Lowell, and Wilbur. If the old anthologies seem now to come from a vanished world, they also seem to come from one which had produced a range of poets who maintained, in a variety of styles and idioms, a fundamental transatlantic unity. I suppose we had a vague sense in high school of T. S. Eliot sternly blessing this Anglo-American union from the Faber and Faber offices in London—Eliot, who, ironically enough, wasn't even in the Williams book because of Faber's comical prohibition against publication of his work in paperback anthologies. For Eliot, you had to go to Untermeyer. There you also found a format which anticipated things to come. My copy of the massive Untermeyer anthology is a two volume affair, "new and enlarged." The American poets are in one volume, the British in the other. Before very long, even this style of anthological marriage had, as it were, broken down. The British half retired to her island feeling insufficiently desirable in America and, as a result of that, made herself unavailable as well, stamped on the back beneath her prices in Australia, New Zealand, South Africa, and Canada: *Not for sale in the USA.*

Well, I exaggerate. A little. Donald Hall—a wonderful advocate of the best British poetry for many years—kept the Atlantic route open in both directions with his two *New Poets of England and America* anthologies edited in 1957 and 1962, first with Robert Pack and Louis Simpson, and then just with Pack. It was here, I suppose, that most of us first read Donald Davie, Thom Gunn, Michael Hamburger, Geoffrey Hill, Jon Silkin, Christopher Middleton, George MacBeth, and a range of other poets just too young for, or excluded from the final pages of, the Williams and Untermeyer books. But Hall's first anthology was countered by that defiantly and exclusively American book edited by Donald Allen, *The New American Poetry.* After that, it was all but over for the British in America. Never mind that certain of the most innovative British and Irish poets might actually have been themselves included in Allen's book had he admitted any un-American activities. David Jones, Basil Bunting, Hugh MacDiarmid, Gael Turnbull, Roy Fisher, Peter Whigham, John Montague, Christopher Logue, and others (including Tomlinson and Middleton) had deep affinities with the Pound-Williams strain of American poetry represented by Allen and had done significant work by the time of *The New American Poetry*'s publication. Trying to redress the balance and argue for a viable and active modernist tradition in Britain, I entered the fray myself with 23 *Modern British Poets*, an anthology including the British poets listed above, together with others whose work matured during the 1960s: Tom Raworth, Lee Harwood, Matthew Mead, Ken Smith, Nathaniel Tarn, Harry Guest, Ian Hamilton Finlay, and Gavin Bantock. (I didn't know, sadly, the work of J. H. Prynne or John Riley, two enormously interesting poets whose work has affinities both with Donald Allen's Americans and some of the British 23.) My book remains the last exclusively British anthology to be published in America, and it is both out of date and out of print. Sales never justified a second edition.

Meanwhile, in England, a variety of sometimes antagonistic movements and individual talents continued to emerge and develop. Hall and Pack had been able to draw on work included both in Robert Conquest's polemically conservative *New Lines* anthology of 1956, which represented work by "The Movement" poets, and also poems by those appearing in the anthologies published partly in reaction to *New Lines*—Lucie-Smith's *A Group Anthology*, Howard Sergeant's and Dannie Abse's *Mavericks*, and, most importantly, A. Alvarez's Penguin volume called *The New Poetry*.

These anthologies, of course, were not available in America, and the Hall-Pack volume doubtless suggested a greater degree of fellow-feeling and common-cause than actually existed among the poets on their home turf. Alvarez—whose introduction, "Beyond the Gentility Principle," became widely known in America even though most of his poets didn't—began his selections with work by two Americans, Lowell and Berryman (adding Plath and Sexton in the second edition), as a lesson in intensity to the British. The influence was meant to produce more Ted Hugheses in England and fewer Philip Larkins. The chief alternative to the influence of the American confessional poets, or, as Alvarez called them, the "extremists," seemed also to be American. The Black Mountain, Beat, and New York School poets gathered in Donald Allen's book took hold in England for a decade and helped spawn an opposition both to the *New Lines* or "Movement" poets and to those championed by Alvarez. The results ranged from the distinguished work of Prynne and Riley to the lesser lights of the left fringe gathered in Michael Horowitz's rather gaga book, the Penguin *Children of Albion*. The point is that any real dialogue between British and American poets largely disappeared in the Sixties. Influence, where it existed, was that of the Americans on the British. No one in New York or San Francisco thought it useful to learn a trick or two from Geoffrey Hill or Tomlinson, Sisson, Graham, or Davie; nor even from those aging modern masters, David Jones and Basil Bunting. All eyes were turned on South America—or was it Eastern Europe? The British, in any case, were just genteel. That's what A. Alvarez said.

Which brings us to the Seventies and Eighties. The Seventies saw the publication in England of Philip Larkin's eccentric and provincial *Oxford Book of 20th Century English Poetry;* Edward Lucie-Smith's eclectic *British Poetry Since 1945;* Alan Bold's *Cambridge Book of English Verse 1939–1975;* John Heath-Stubbs's and David Wright's *Faber Book of 20th Century Verse;* Frank Ormsby's *Poets from the North of Ireland;* Jon Silkin's *Stand* anthology, *Poetry of the Committed Individual;* the continuing series of Penguin Modern Poets, three poets per volume, which faded out with number 27 in 1979; and four Faber *Poetry Introductions,* which, like the Carcanet *Ten English Poets* and *Ten Irish Poets,* offered more poets per volume than did the Penguin series, but fewer poems per poet. There were other anthologies published during the period, but these in particular fairly represent the fluctuations of a decade's taste and talent. Most of the books were not available in America, and those few that were rarely got reviewed, distributed, or read.

The most important development during the 1970s, however, was probably the emergence of *PN Review* and Carcanet Press, both edited from Manchester by Michael Schmidt. Like his colleague at *PN Review,* Donald Davie, Schmidt manifests a fruitful tension between his commitment to British poetry where it is least influenced by American or continental modernism—the tradition leading from Hardy through Edward Thomas to Philip Larkin—and a wary fondness (which he often tries to stifle) both for some American writing in the Pound-Williams (or even Stevens-Ashbery) tradition and for British poets such as Tomlinson, Middleton, Jeremy Hooker, and John Ash who have produced a body of interestingly related work.

This tension makes for a healthy catholicity in Schmidt's editing and publishing. His *Eleven British Poets* (published by Methuen, in fact, rather than Carcanet, and of course not for sale in the USA) represents this catholicity, but also suggests its limits. Although the book ranges from work by R. S. Thomas, Elizabeth Jennings, Philip Larkin, and Donald Davie through the riskier and more adventurous contributions of W. S. Graham, C. H. Sisson, Tomlinson, Hill, Hughes, and Heaney, there was no room for a Jeremy Prynne, a Roy Fisher, or a Matthew Mead. Nor, after Heaney, were there other Irish poets included. Irish poetry—and this news *does* seem to have reached America—was forged anew in the crucible of a decade's troubles in the north. If Schmidt, both in *Eleven British Poets* and the anthology under review, takes some notice of this renaissance, Irish poetry provides the cutting edge for Blake Morrison and Andrew Motion in their *Penguin Book of Contemporary British Poetry*. The Seventies in "British" poetry was, to some considerable degree, an Irish affair. Heaney's work, in particular, acquired a readership probably larger even than Hughes's and Larkin's. In the Eighties, the Irish contribution seems to be as strong or even stronger. By contrast, the new London movement which has so captivated journalists and even serious critics in England, the movement which may have motivated Penguin Books to issue their first major anthology since Alvarez's *The New Poetry*, looks superficial. Craig Raine's little poem, "A Martian Sends a Postcard Home," gave this group its name: The Martians.

> Mist is when the sky is tired of flight
> and rests its soft machine on ground:
>
> then the world is dim and bookish
> like engravings under tissue paper.
>
> Rain is when the earth is television.
> It has the property of making colours darker . . .
>
> . . . time is tied to the wrist
> or kept in a box, ticking with impatience.
>
> In homes, a haunted apparatus sleeps,
> that snores when you pick it up.

Well, you get the idea. This is the Martian style, from the now famous postcard. Other practitioners, along with Raine, represented in the Penguin anthology are Christopher Reid, David Sweetman, and, to some extent, Mabdh McGuckian. The movement, if that is what it is, strikes me as having produced some of the thinnest and most foppish poetry in England since the Sitwells. It is also likely to remind the American reader of a recent and very un-English category of composition: the writer's workshop poetry assignment, second month, third week—"Write a poem which seeks to make something familiar very strange by way of exploiting a sequence of unusual metaphors or similes." Raine's dogs "shit like weightlifters, and relax / by giving each other piggy backs"; his corpses in the mortuary bulge "like soft cheeses . . . / sideways on the marble slabs"; his small daughter's cunt is a "neat button-hole." One of his poems is dedicated to Ian McEwan, and indeed Raine's poems at their strangest make the reader uncomfortable in some of the same ways McEwan's fiction does. But the poems do not, in my view, make us see more clearly. Nor in Michael Schmidt's view. In an essay written with Peter Jones introducing his critical survey, *British Poetry Since 1970*, Schmidt anticipates one of the chief tensions between the reading of British poetry represented by his own anthology and that represented by the Motion/Morrison Penguin. Referring to Morrison's essay in the same critical survey, Schmidt and Jones remark, "Morrison contends that such poetry requires that we look; it seems to us that it provokes puzzlement, rather. What we are supposed to *see* becomes more remote." Quoting Houseman on the Metaphysical poets, they continue, "The essential limitation of the 'movement' represented by Raine and Reid . . . is the mechanical nature of its means. . . . Remote metaphors are 'no more poetical than anagrams; such pleasure as they give is purely intellectual and amused.'" Schmidt and Jones conclude that the public which has sponsored the success of the Martians—"professors, lecturers and dons"—does not realize that "their entertainers degrade the reality they pretend to illuminate." This is very harsh, and Schmidt has, to some extent, modified his views, at least about Raine. For me, Raine's strongest poem in the Penguin is "A Walk in the Country," which is his most recent poem among those anthologized and also the least characteristically Martian. It indicates that his work is capable of development, and that it may now be moving in an entirely new direction. Whether Reid's and Sweetnam's work is likely to develop in less restricted and more promising directions is difficult to predict on the strength of the Penguin selections. Raine, at any rate, appears to be the most interesting poet of the three, while McGuckian, although she shares some characteristic techniques with the Martians, ought properly to be read beside the other poets from Ulster.

Morrison and Motion are conscious of representing four fairly coherent groups in their anthology, all of whom, they argue, seek to "extend the imaginative franchise." Along with the Martians, whose work appears at the end of the book, come the Ulster poets, poets who write from a provincial and working-class background, several poets who work in a narrative mode, and women poets—one hesitates to say feminist. Among these groups, the Ulster poets are both the best known and the most impressive.

"The new spirit in British poetry began to make itself felt in Northern Ireland during the late 1960s and early 70s," Morrison and Motion declare. But if "making the familiar strange" is to be the formula for this new spirit, I wonder if the poems from Ulster don't rather, in some sense, make the strange all too painfully familiar. Daily reality in Belfast didn't have to be made to look bizarre by its poets; its strangeness had to be endured and understood and maybe even changed by the poems that risked engaging it at all. (Part of the risk was always that the subject lent itself to opportunistic exploitation in unsuccessful poems.) In any case, Heaney and Mahon make most of Raine and Reid look trivial. Or compare those Martian couplets quoted above with this by Tom Paulin.

> . . . streetlamps
> Light up in the glowering, crowded evenings.
> Time-switches, ripped from them, are clamped
> To sticks of sweet, sweating explosive. . . .
>
> Or, in a private house, a Judge
> Shot in the hallway before his daughter
> By a boy who shut his eyes as his hand tightened.

In such a situation, neither the Judge nor the boy had occasion to think the daughter's cunt might resemble "a neat button-hole." Moreover, the exile's stance of Heaney (having left the north for Dublin) or Mahon (now living in Kensington) has less in common with "the attitude of the anthropologist or alien invader" than Morrison and Motion suggest in their introduction. While there may be something quizzical about Heaney's inner émigré as wood-kerne, the political context of poems such as "Exposure" distance them considerably from the Martians' often frivolous examination of their cultural and social surroundings.

> I am neither internee nor informer;
> An inner émigré, grown long-haired
> And thoughtful; a wood-kerne
>
> Escaped from the massacre,
> Taking protective colouring
> From bole and bark, feeling
> Every wind that blows;
>
> Who, blowing up these sparks
> For their meagre heat, have missed
> The once-in-a-lifetime portent,
> The comet's pulsing rose.

If Derek Mahon sometimes seems more bemused by what he observes around him than does Heaney—and Mahon *does*, in fact, imagine one life among several in which a torc become an oar become a lump of clay become a stone becomes an anthropologist—he also soberly reflects in "Afterlives" that, had he stayed in Belfast "and lived it bomb by bomb / I might have grown up at last / And learnt what is meant by home." Mahon is a marvellous and necessary poet, as fine a poet, I think, as Seamus Heaney. If Michael Longley and Tom Paulin are not as obviously virtuoso craftsmen, they too have produced notable work that American readers ought to know. Longley's "Wounds" and several of Paulin's poems both in the Penguin and the Carcanet anthologies rank with Mahon's "A Disused Shed in Co. Wexford" and Heaney's famous bog poems. I am personally not persuaded by the Paul Muldoon selections—especially not by the interminable "Immram." Medbh McGuckian, the youngest poet in the Penguin anthology, is interesting, with a sympathetic and winning sensibility, but her mostly domestic poems are rather slight and perhaps somewhat vitiated by their Martian affinities.

Among the poets writing directly out of a provincial and working-class background, the most interesting is Tony Harrison. Harrison's open cycle of Meridithian sonnets, *Continuous*, may in its serial structure and its combination of eloquence, learning, humour, pathos, and jagged rhythms held together by a nervous and edgy northern working-class idiom remind the American reader of John Berryman's *Dream Songs*. One of the chief differences, of course, is that while Berryman's minstrel show blackface is put on for the occasion, Harrison's northern dialect is the language he grew up speaking in Leeds. The tension in the sequence derives in large measure from Harrison's sense that, in acquiring a classical education and leading the life of a writer, translator and opera librettist, he has betrayed his class origins and is responsible for the breakdown in communication with his family. "You're like book ends, the pair of you," Harrison's mother says of Harrison and his father in one of the sonnets, and the poem concludes with the recognition that "what's still between's / not the thirty or so years, but books, books, books." Working-class (and sometimes revolutionary) values are not, however, just a matter of family and regional background in the cycle, but a verbally and politically active force in the dialectic which develops as *Continuous* progresses. Sometimes, as in the first poem of the group, "On Not Being Milton," these values are expressed with a concentrated energy recalling Geoffrey Hill. (An "Enoch," Harrison tells us in a note, "is an iron sledge-hammer used by the Luddites to smash the frames which were also made by the same Enoch Taylor or Marsden.")

> The stutter of the scold out of the branks
> of condescension, class and counter-class
> thickens with glottals to a lumpen mass
> of Ludding morphemes closing up their ranks.
>
> Each swung cast-iron Enoch of Leeds stress
> clangs a forged music on the frames of Art,
> the looms of owned language smashed apart!

Much the same orientation characteristic of Harrison's work finds expression in the earlier poems of Douglas Dunn and in the oblique historical refractions of Jeffrey Wainwright's excellent twelve-part sequence on the radical reformer and visionary, Thomas Muntzer. Geoffrey Hill would again seem to be an influence on Wainwright's poem, and I find myself responding to its tough and elegant concentration much more readily than to the pentameters of Dunn's "An Artist Waiting in a Country House" or the diffuse long lines of his "Remembering Lunch," poems which break with the early manner and connect Dunn's work with certain poems by Muldoon, Paulin, James Fenton, and Andrew Motion himself. These poems form the third informal grouping in the Penguin book, those which Motion and Morrison call narrative—Michael Schmidt insists they are merely anecdotal—but narrative "which draws attention to the problem of perception," fictionalizing poems where "fictionalizing is relished as it is performed," story telling with more reference than in the past "to what the process involves."

Among the narrative poems, Motion's own "Bathing at Glymenopoulo" and James Fenton's "A Vacant Possession" and "A Staffordshire Murderer" strike me as the most interesting. But neither Motion nor Fenton restricts himself to the narrative mode, and indeed in Fenton—a poet very widely praised in England for the last several years—one finds a political poet writing about post-war Germany and his own experiences as a journalist in Cambodia with an intelligence and precision the equal of the best of the Ulstermen. A kind of triple threat in this anthology, Fenton is the man initially responsible for grouping and naming the Martians in a book review, and he shares in some of his poems certain preoccupations common to Raine and Reid. He is at his best, however, in "A German Requiem," a poem which has been often quoted and anthologized, and

which deserves to last. Some eighty lines long, and divided by asterisks into nine sections, it begins like this:

> It is not what they built. It is what they knocked down.
> It is not the houses. It is the spaces between the houses.
> It is not the streets that exist. It is the streets that
> no longer exist
> It is not your memories which haunt you.
> It is not what you have written down.
> It is what you have forgotten, what you must forget.
> What you must go on forgetting all your life.

There remain from the Penguin anthology poems by Peter Scupham, Hugo Williams, and all of the women other than Medbh
McGuckian. Hugo's work is sufficiently slight that its omission
would have been no great loss to the book, and Scupham, as
Michael Schmidt has pointed out, is badly served by the Penguin
selections. (He appears as a much stronger and more important poet
in the Carcanet volume.) Meanwhile, one simply longs to find some
women writing important poetry in England, but there appear to be
very few. When I edited *23 Modern British Poets* in 1970, I couldn't
manage to include a single woman, and, of course, I was vigorously
attacked for this. In retrospect, I can see that I should have anthologized some of Elaine Feinstein's work, but she is now too old, well-
known, and widely published to be included in anthologies
representing chiefly new British poets. The sad fact is that Fleur Ad-
cock, Carol Rumens, and Penelope Shuttle do not appear in these
selections to be writing very interesting poetry. I am partial to some
of Anne Stevenson's work, but she is really an American (although
she has now lived a long time in England), and her most lively
book, *Correspondences*, is a sequence of interlocking epistolary poems
that resists excerpting. While it appears that every third woman one
meets in America is able to produce a notable poem, in England
the women all write fiction. If only there *were* a woman writing
verse the equal of Doris Lessing's or Margaret Drabble's prose! Even
Elaine Feinstein now concentrates her energies on writing novels.

❧

The Penguin anthology makes large claims for the radical and
innovative nature of the work it represents. Not quite certain

whether to attribute the innovations they perceive among their contributors to "a degree of ludic and literary self-consciousness reminiscent of the modernists" or to "the spirit of postmodernism," Morrison and Motion nonetheless declare confidently that "there are points in literary history when decisive shifts of sensibility occur. . . . Such a shift has taken place very recently in British poetry." (Back in 1980, Morrison thought the work of the 1970s was fathered neither by modernism nor by postmodernism, but by *anti*modernism: "The fathers of the 70s generation of poets have not been the Modernists, but the dominant figures in British poetry since 1945 . . . Larkin in particular.")

Michael Schmidt's anthology not only resists making such large claims, but also explicitly questions those of the competition. "Anthologies of contemporary poetry," he says, "often flatter their readers with promises of radical novelty, new beginnings, even 'decisive shifts of sensibility.' Yet what strikes me most about the work of my contemporaries is how readily it accommodates itself within the English traditions." In spite of the very real points of contention and divergence between Schmidt and Morrison/Motion, it may be that the common ground is more important. The two anthologies represent, mostly with quite different selections, seven of the same poets—Peter Scupham, Tony Harrison, James Fenton, Derek Mahon, Tom Paulin, Jeffrey Wainwright, and Andrew Motion. If the American reader is looking for something like consensus about the major single poems of the last fifteen years, he would do well to pay particular attention to those several occasions where not only the same poet appears in both books, but also the same poem. This brief list includes Harrison's "The Nuptial Torches" and four sonnets from *Continuous;* Mahon's "The Snow Party" and "A Disused Shed in Co. Wexford"; Wainwright's "Thomas Muntzer" and "A Hymn to Liberty"; Fenton's "A German Requiem," "In a Notebook" and "The Kingfisher's Boxing Gloves"; Paulin's "The Harbour in the Evening" and "A Lyric Afterwards"; and Motion's "Anne Frank Huis" and "One Life." Most of these poems are, in fact, very impressive. But, again, the focus of the two books is quite different. Schmidt represents no Martians (although Craig Raine was asked to participate and refused), he includes fewer women—only Gillian Clarke and Alison Brackenbury—and he does not regard the Ulster poets to be, as a group, nearly as significant as do Morrison and Motion. Schmidt, in fact, comes rather close to sharing the position that one of his contributors, Andrew Waterman, an English poet living in Ulster, expressed in a controversial *PN Review* article a few years back called "Ulsterectomy." In *British Poetry Since 1970*, Schmidt remarked that "London critics have a soft-spot for Ulster. The metropolitan enthusiasm for Ulster has been rewarded of late by two poets—Seamus Heaney and Tom Paulin. Otherwise the province remains, like any other, and like the capital itself, a hive of essentially local activity, locally interesting, which does not transcend locality. The inflation of the 'Ulster school' has occurred for quite understandable extra-poetic reasons." Although Heaney does not appear in the Carcanet anthology, that is only because his work was already included in Schmidt's earlier *Eleven British Poets*, a collection in which Heaney was the youngest in a group of older poets and in relation to which the present book is intended to function as a sequel. With the addition of Mahon in the new anthology, Schmidt adds a third name to those whose work he was willing to applaud in 1980. But there is no Longley, no Muldoon, no McGuckian. It is also fair to say that Schmidt's controversial English Ulsterman, the same Andrew Waterman, has produced one of the most interesting poems from the region in "From the Other Country."

Against the London-Ulster bias of the Penguin, then, Schmidt gathers a group of poets associated from early on with *PN Review*, none of whom appear in the Morrison/Motion book, and, thinking chiefly of their work, outlines in his introduction a kind of provisional poetics for a period he finds characterized by a "degree of positive incoherence" and "the absence of general poetic trends." He argues—sadly and wrongly in my view—that "the great Anglo-American modernists . . . have not been, and now perhaps never will be, assimilated into the 'mainstream' of British writing." Objecting to the term "post-Modernist" being used "in anything but chronological terms" (and perhaps to describe the work of John Ash), he discerns "a distinctly Victorian spirit" in the poetry he admires. His poets, he says, "have lived among ruins rather than monuments," and, in some of them, he finds "an Arnoldian earnestness—committed, secular, at odds with the age and its intractable forces and puzzled at their place in it." Invoking the notion of civic responsibility which has characterized the editorial position of *PN Review* from the beginning, he honors a representative poem for "its desire to speak for, as well as to speak; to be responsible and be seen to be so in a very specific, civic sense." (I wonder if he still feels, as he did in his introduction to *British Poetry Since 1970*, that the best political poetry being written during the period will prove itself to be "durable because not useful." Surely there must be more to cause and effect in the matter than that.)

In the absence of modernist or postmodernist influences, Schmidt cites the importance for his poets of, variously, Ruskin, Hardy, Houseman, Edward Thomas, Auden, Browning, and Clough. A decidedly odd group. Neither Hughes nor Larkin, among the major talents of the previous generation, are found impinging on the present one. I am surprised that Schmidt does not cite Yvor Winters as a formative influence, for his example, more than any other, animates much of what is going on in the work of Dick Davis, Clive Wilmer, and Robert Wells. As a former student of Winters, I have always been both interested and perplexed by his powerful hold on this group. The combination of Wintersian and Victorian influences is particularly strange, given Winters' loathing for almost every nineteenth century British poet. (Much of the Wintersian influence at work on these poets gets filtered, I think, through Donald Davie and Thom Gunn.) Anyway, these are the main points of the introduction. What about the work itself?

The most important poets not also in the Penguin anthology whose work Schmidt's introduction seems designed to forward are Wilmer, Davis, Wells, David Constantine, and Andrew Waterman. It also accounts for some of what is going on in Scupham, Harrison, Mahon, Wainwright, Fenton, and Paulin. Where the anthology is most interesting, however, is in the work of those few poets who, in many ways, seem not to fit Schmidt's program. It's difficult to see what John Ash and Michael Hofmann have to do with poets like Davis and Wilmer, and Frank Kuppner's strange "Svensk Rapsodi" is totally off the wall in the context of this book. In many ways, my favorite poet of all is the quiet and delicate Jeremy Hooker, a poet American readers will like, I think, and one whose work has deep affinities with the Pound-Williams tradition in spite of what Schmidt implies to the contrary. Although I would prefer to quote something from Hooker or Ash in conclusion, I had best end with a poem more representative of the kind of work Michael Schmidt has consistently supported. The second of Clive Wilmer's two "Antiphonal Sonnets" about John Taverner is very impressive. If there is a point at which the Victorian influence, the Wintersian influence, and the influence of a major writer from the previous generation—in this case Geoffrey Hill—come together, this is it:

This was the world: the word.
                                        Gratuitous day,
Stained by a red or a blue glaze, confined
By aspiring stone to space with no horizon:

Earthly things that composed an allegory
Which guessed at heaven. He cast given speech
Against the bossed and starry vaults, shattered it
To falling fragments, harmonies—a fertile
Resonance, as much like beauty as like that
It seemed at length to mask: in empty space
A simple disembodied word, the truth.
Then beauty was the hoofbeats in the nave,
The radiant shower of glass, a mace that knocked
Devotion from her pedestal, the flames
That burnt the rood in the broad light of day.

One last point. Anthologists like to represent "new" or "young" poets and thereby attempt to define what might constitute an emerging generation of writers in a region, a nation, a language. But the best work of a particular period is likely to be produced, not by the young or the new poets, but by older, more experienced ones. (This is something that Michael Schmidt understands clearly and has often asserted.) The present period is no exception, and the best work of the last fifteen years has not been produced by Raine or Reid, or even by Fenton, Harrison, or Paulin. It has been produced by Geoffrey Hill, Charles Tomlinson, Christopher Middleton, Donald Davie, Roy Fisher, Michael Hamburger, Jon Silkin, John Montague, and Christopher Logue (in *War Music*). More than that, even within the time-frame of these two anthologies, a number of the best poems of the period by poets under fifty are missing. I limit myself to a list of five poems, all of them problematically long, but three of them no longer than Muldoon's "Immram" and the others organized in excerptable sections. They are all exploratory poems which take great formal risks. (Most of the poems in both anthologies play it safe formally.) I think I know what Schmidt, Morrison, and Motion would have to say about some of these titles, but I would make large claims for all of them: Richard Burns's "Angels," J. H. Prynne's "News of the Waring Clans," Ken Smith's "Fox Running," Tom Lowenstein's "La Tempesta's X-Ray," and John Riley's "Czargrad." John Riley is dead (tragically murdered in Leeds in 1978), and I suppose, on those grounds alone, he was excluded from both of these anthologies which represent the work of his living contemporaries. But the seriousness of Riley's example continues to inspire many in Britain who knew him and his work. I will try to talk about some of these excluded poems and poets in future contributions to *ACM*.

Neither the Penguin nor the Carcanet anthology is, of course, available in the USA. Both, however, can be ordered either directly from the publishers or from British bookstores which are accustomed to filling orders from abroad, such as Blackwell's in Oxford and Heffer's in Cambridge. It is not much of an effort to order the books, and both of them are certainly worth having. The Carcanet anthology can also be obtained inexpensively by ordering issue No. 36 of *PN Review*. The contents are identical to those of the hardback version, and all one misses in the journal format is the durability of a book and a slightly longer introduction.

From *Another Chicago Magazine*, 1985

Poet-Translators and Translator-Poets

Christopher Logue, *War Music*, Penguin Books; Tony Harrison,
Selected Poems, Penguin Books; Tony Harrison, *The Orestia*, Rex
Collings; Peter Levi, *Collected Poems 1955–1975*, Anvil Press; Peter
Levi, *The Echoing Green*, Anvil Press; Peter Levi, *The Lamentation of
the Dead*, Anvil Press; Peter Levi and Anne Pennington, *Marko the
Prince*, Duckworth; Peter Russell, *All for the Wolves*, Anvil Press;
Peter Russell, *The Elegies of Quintilius*, Anvil Press; Seamus Heaney,
Sweeney Astray, Faber and Faber; Seamus Heaney, *Station Island*,
Faber and Faber.

Shortly after I delivered my initial *Not For Sale in USA* column
to the editors, several events occurred or came to my notice which
have modified in one way or another the British poetry scene and
which might properly be observed before turning to the books at
hand. Although John Betjeman would have made a perfect *last* Poet
Laureate, Lord Gowrie, the Thatcher government's Minister for the
Arts, evidently persuaded the powers that be to perpetuate this embarrassment to British poetry by installing Ted Hughes, of all poets,
in the office. Everyone has been calling this decision "bold." "An
appointment that has confounded the prophets, who had assumed
that the post was going to Philip Larkin, but one which has been
wisely welcomed as a bold and imaginative move," wrote John
Gross in the *Times Book Review* as he swept for a week through the
London literary scene and wrote about its "hoopla and hullabaloo,"
its prizes, and its gossip. But why would Ted Hughes want this
anachronistic office, and what on earth will he write for all those
Royal births, baptisms, and marriages? One can only begin to imagine the expression on the cunning face of Crow as he sips cham-

pagne in Kensington beside the princely prams. (On the positive side, one can recommend without reservation Hughes's most recent book, *River*, a volume which *is* available in this country from Harper and Row. It contains some of his best work in many years, especially the fine "October Salmon," a poem which should immediately join the Hughes selections in all the major anthologies.)

A position which can be taken a good deal more seriously, although it too has its comical aspect, has recently been filled by Peter Levi. Levi was elected Oxford Professor of Poetry and gave his inaugural lecture, which has been published by Anvil Press and will be discussed below, on October 25th, 1984. Levi is an excellent poet, translator, and critic. Little known in America, he has published five volumes of poetry with Anvil Press, including his *Collected Poems*. Levi's translations from the Greek are masterful and, although I am going to express some reservations about *Marko The Prince*, his work on the Serbo-Croatian oral poems with Anne Pennington is very important. Formerly Peter Levi, S. J., he has now left the Jesuit order and is married. One of his more remarkable experiments is a series of verse sermons in rhyming couplets first published in a volume called *Death is a Pulpit*. Will the Oxford Professor turn to verse at some point in his series of lectures? He has demonstrated, at any rate, that something analogous to the verse lecture is possible by writing his sermons. And perhaps life is a lecturn, as another earlier Levi title almost had it—"Life," he said, "Is a Platform"—though I notice he has wisely amended this rather rash observation in a note to his *Collected Poems* which declares, "Life must be what it can."

The comical element, by the way, which attaches to the Professorship has to do with the manner in which the new poet is elected. All Oxford MAs are permitted to vote, but they must vote in person. The successful candidate needs to muster his forces from all over the country and persuade them to visit Oxford on the day of the election. Since not many MAs are willing to make the trip for an occasion which doubtless seems to many of them rather frivolous, the election can be won by a few votes cast by some last minute recruits dragged from a punt or discovered drowsing over their pints in the nearest pub. It's a chancy business, and the whole enterprise is capable of being sabotaged. One year, a group of undergraduates nearly succeeded in electing Muhammad Ali. Anyway, Levi's election is, on the whole, to be welcomed. On the evidence of his first lecture, and certainly on the evidence of his previous work, he will prove to be a distinguished Oxford Professor whose complete lectures, after a term of five years, will be published by OUP.

224   Reading Old Friends

Although it will be my practice to concentrate on small press publications in these essays, it would be inappropriate not to call attention to the new order of things at Penguin Books and Faber and Faber given the fact that some important changes have taken place in these powerful and taste-making houses. In *ACM* 12, I talked about the influence of the so-called "Martian" school of poetry and the centrality of Craig Raine, the leading Martian, both to the school and to the Penguin anthology, *Contemporary British Poetry*, edited by Blake Morrison and Andrew Motion. Raine turns out to be just as central to the new Faber poetry program and what can only be called a kind of blitz which has produced a 37 percent increase in Faber poetry sales, a new Faber poetry format and logo, and a sense of vitality and youth in the venerable offices at Queen's Square. As poetry editor at Faber, Raine will ultimately be judged by the quality of new work he brings to the press. My guess is that he is thus far responsible only for bringing Michael Hofmann and Philip Gross to Faber, and, while Hofmann's *Nights in the Iron Hotel* and Gross's *The Ice Factory* are interesting volumes, only time will tell if they, and, indeed, if Raine himself, are remotely in the company of Seamus Heaney and Tom Paulin, Ted Hughes and Thom Gunn, Louis Mac-Neice and W. H. Auden. What *can* be said of the new Faber poetry program is that the full backlist is suddenly available in an inexpensive run of paperbacks and a format which is more attractive and better produced than what one was accustomed to in the past. The paper is excellent (and *doesn't* turn yellow in six weeks like the paper on which Carcanet prints its books), the jackets are firm and the books well bound. The two Faber books which I'll be looking at— Heaney's *Sweeney Astray* and *Station Island*—have, of course, American editions. Seamus Famous, as Clive James called him, has a very considerable American readership. Still, with his new books at present selling here in cloth editions only, and given the strength of the dollar against the pound, these and other Faber volumes might well be found sufficiently desirable to be ordered directly from British booksellers at a price of only a little more than $3.50 per copy— an excellent bargain, even with air mail postage added in.

The new poetry program at Penguin Books is also very promising. Abandoning the old Penguin Modern Poets format which I discussed in my survey of anthologies in *ACM* 12, Penguin is now presenting very substantial selections by single poets in place of the long-familiar three poets per volume. Tony Harrison's *Selected Poems*, for example, is virtually a *collected* poems. It contains *The Loiners*, an expanded *Continuous*, his Palladas translations, and a hefty selection of new work. It runs to two hundred pages and costs only £3.95 (about $4.80 if you're spending dollars). Harrison's book, James Fenton's *The Memory of War and Children in Exile,* and Christopher Logue's magnificent *War Music* are all part of a large format series called King Penguin, a series in which one initially found only novels. The titles chosen thus far for the series have all been of the highest quality (and surely everyone remembers what an odd mixture of the good and bad appeared, sometimes in the same volume, in Penguin Modern Poets). I don't know who's responsible for the change of focus at Penguin Books, but clearly Craig Raine has an energetic rival with a distribution network in his hands outstripping even Faber's. Another recent Penguin project of nearly incalculable importance has been the publication in two inexpensive volumes of the complete poems of Hugh MacDiarmid. I will discuss MacDiarmid's work in a future issue of *ACM.*

❧

The books to which I am now going to turn are all the work of poet-translators—poets who are also translators, translators who are also poets, or writers for whom the act of translation and the act of original composition are sometimes all but indistinguishable. Of this last sort, Christopher Logue in *War Music* is perhaps uniquely exemplary among his contemporaries.

Critics have been at a loss to know exactly what to call *War Music* ever since its first section, "Patrocleia," was published by Scorpian Press back in 1962. Logue now calls the three sections which comprise his work—"Patrocleia," "GBH," and "Pax"—"An Account of Books 16 to 19 of Homer's *Iliad.*" An "account," however, sounds too much like journalism or literary criticism to be properly suggestive. George Steiner has no hesitation in his magisterial *After Babel* in calling Logue's Homer a translation, even though there are often passages of many lines with no precise equivalent in Homer's Greek. Steiner seems fairly comfortable assigning the work to Dryden's category of "metaphrase," calling it a sequence of "licentious but numbingly powerful variations" which produce a "shock of contemporaneity," and observing that Logue's ignorance of Greek may be a paradoxical advantage. Steiner is clearly a fan of *War Music* (and, in fact, he is acknowledged for his "critical support" in Logue's introduction). Ringing some changes on the *Iliad* in *After Babel* by quoting a range of translators from Chapman to the present, he concludes by contrasting a passage by Richmond Latimore, whose work embodies "the sum of modern textual and historical scholarship" but whose attempt to achieve a "timeless,' unobtrusively lucid idiom" produces "the persistent impression of flattening" and a strange cadence which Steiner calls "part Longfellow, part Eisenhower," with this from Logue on Achilles' helmet:

> though it is noon the helmet screams against the light,
> scratches the eye, so violent it can be seen
> across three thousand years. . . .

Steiner comments: "This trick of blinding vision across time is both a definition of the classic and of the task of the translator. To make visible in its own light. Not to dim to our own."

Back when I edited 23 *Modern British Poets*, I simply included as much of "Patrocleia" and "Pax" as I dared, hoping that someone would notice what I took to be some of the finest writing in English achieved during the period. Evidently some reviewers of the present volume have decided not to read the work as translation at all. Derek Mahon wrote in the *Observer* that *War Music* is "less translation than an adaptation . . . less an adaptation, in fact, than an original poem of considerable power;" and David Wright has called it "a remarkable contemporary poem . . . its oblique analogues comment effectively, not to say devastatingly, on our day and age." Logue's own description, in his introduction, of working on the literal translations made for him by Donald Carne-Ross (and also, early on, by Peter Levi) sounds uncannily like the manner in which the Homeric oral poets (or the South Slavs who sang their epic songs to Vuk Karadzhich and later on to Milman Perry and Albert Lord) worked on *their* material. "As the work progressed beyond its original limitation I paid less attention to my guides. . . . I would concoct a storyline based on [the] main incident; and then, knowing the gist of what this or that character said, would try to make their voices come alive and to keep the action on the move." Licentious procedures indeed! And to those who disparage them, Logue might well retort with a comment attributed to Chapman when he was accused of basing his translation on a French crib. "Envious Wind-Fuckers," he said.

The reader must not expect to find the whole of the *Iliad* translated (adapted, metaphrased, recreated) in *War Music*. The book is only eighty pages long and has the kind of power it possesses in part because Logue never had any intention of rendering the whole of the epic, just some of its most intense and numinous episodes.

He chose Book 16 at the suggestion of Carne-Ross and because the Patroclus episode seemed to represent the *Iliad* in miniature. It had, Carne-Ross reminded him, "a quarrel, a making-up, a concession, several battles, the death of a famous leader (Sarpedon), disagreement in Heaven, a human cheeking the Gods, and, as a result of that human's death, an irreversible change." Logue found in Book 19 the opposite of all this—"disaffected allies settling their differences in order to avoid defeat at the hands of a mutual enemy" and exemplification of "the public confession of common sins righted by material compensation and absolved by formal sacrifice." Looking for a quote, I'm tempted to represent Logue's most violent manner from the most recent section of his poem, "GBH" (or "Grievous Bodily Harm"), in which Logue realized, as he tells us in his introduction, "that conflating books 17 and 18 . . . would allow [him] to try [his] hand at something new—600 odd lines devoted almost entirely to violent, mass action—which, once done, would unite 'Patrocleia' and 'Pax' into a narrative capable of being read independently of its guessed-at parent." But I think I'd better quote instead the ending of "Pax," and hence the ending of *War Music* as a whole, where Achilles, reconciled with Agamemnon and the other Greeks, mounts his chariot and returns to battle:

He mounts.

The chariot's basket dips. The whip
Fires in between the horses' ears;
And as in dreams, or at Cape Kennedy, they rise,
Slowly it seems, their chests like royals, yet
Behind them in a double plume the sand curls up,
Is barely dented by their flying hooves,
And wheels that barely touch the world,
And the wind slams shut behind them.

"Fast as you are," Achilles says,
"When twilight makes the armistice,
Take care you don't leave me behind
As you left my Patroclus."

And as it ran the white horse turned its tall face back
And said:
                    "Prince,
This time we will, this time we can, but this time cannot last.
And when we leave you, not for dead—but dead
God will not call us negligent as you have done."

And Achilles, shaken, says:
"I know I will not make old bones."

And laid his scourge against their racing flanks.

Someone has left a spear stuck in the sand.

❧

As I devoted a certain amount of space in *ACM* 12 to Tony Harrison's work anthologized in the Penguin *Contemporary British Poetry* and the Carcanet *Some Contemporary Poets of Britain and Ireland*, let me only stress again in passing the importance of his *Selected Poems* and, in particular, the open sequence of Meridithian sonnets published first in *The School of Eloquence* and then in *Continuous* which is here augmented by a selection of new poems appearing for the first time. What he aggressively writes in the first of those sonnets must have been said, in so many words, to the National Theatre's cast in *The Oresteia* for whom he translated Aeschylus into what he calls "a text written to be performed, a rhythmic libretto for masks and music": "The stutter of the scold out of the branks / of condescension, class and counterclass / thickens with glottals to a lumpen mass / of Ludding morphemes closing up their ranks. / Each swung cast-iron Enoch of Leeds stress / clangs a forged music on the frames of Art, / the looms of owned language smashed apart!" Or, as he writes in "The Rhubarbarians":

Those glottals glugged like poured pop, each
rebarbative syllable, remembrancer, raise
'mob' *rhubarb-rhubarb* to a tribune's speech
crossing the crackle as the hayracks blaze . . .

. . . and extends to explain his translations of Smetana's *Prodana Nevesta* for the Metropolitan Opera:

Crotchets and quavers, rhubarb silhouettes,
dark-shy sea-horse heads through waves of dung!
Rhubarb arias, duets, quartets
soar to precision from our common tongue.

For Harrison, the common tongue is Northern, the speech of Loiners. What he stuffed into the mouths of those National Theatre actors, then, was something intended to *open* their mouths, slow down their delivery, and make them hear and speak each word as a barbed rebarbative thing of rhubarb syllables. If it's not all glottals glugged, it certainly is native, Northern, and as alliterative as *Piers Plowman*. What he wanted to get away from was the actor's besetting sin of empty-headed euphonious delivery. This is the sort of thing he writes:

> No end to it all, though all year I've muttered
> My pleas to the gods for a long groped for end.
> Wish it were over, this waiting, this watching,
> twelve weary months, night in and night out,
> crouching and peering, head down like a bloodhound,
> paws propping muzzle, up here on the palace,
> the palace belonging the bloodclan of Atreus—
> Agamemnon, Menelaus, bloodkin, our clanchiefs.

So speaks the Watchman, and the Chorus intones: "Apollo he-god healer your she-kin / Artemis intervene prevent her / sending winds on the fleet," and then sings this refrain: "Batter, batter the doom-drum, but believe there'll be better." For me the effect of this over the whole of *The Oresteia* is too thunderous to be other than slightly deafening. It seems to be an approach one might approve of on principle rather than in practice; or, as Harrison insists, something that must actually be heard on stage rather than read in a text. Since I have not, in fact, seen the National Theatre's production, not heard the "rhythmic libretto" spoken through masks to the music, I feel that I should not express a judgment of this *Oresteia*. At the very least, it is a fascinating experiment, and doubly fascinating read directly after Logue's *War Music*. Harrison has proven himself to be one of the best translators in the business—witness his *Misanthrope* and his *Phaedra* for the National Theatre, his work in opera, his selections from Martial, the Palladas included in *Selected Poems*—and must always be taken very seriously indeed, his new work awaited with great anticipation.

🙠

Peter Levi discusses both *The Iliad* and *The Oresteia* in his inaugural Oxford lecture, "The Lamentation of the Dead." He finds that "lamenting the dead has usually, perhaps always, been the role of women," and he thinks that Homer is adapting women's poetry at the end of *The Iliad* when Andromache, Hecuba, and Helen—the widow, the mother, the sister-in-law—wail for Hector along with the "singers," the "leaders of laments." And yet he says that neither in *The Iliad* nor *The Oresteia*, do we have a clear sense of what the antiphonal songs for the dead must have been like. "Aeschylus has some antiphonal lamentation in *The Oresteia*, but that is little help. Perhaps a dirge was always a passionate conversation of laments with a background of weeping and wailing." Still, however modified by its multiple roots and its professional tradition, epic poetry (and also some tragedy) makes a special place for lamentation. Levi finds at least remnants of the primitive art of lamenting in all epic poetry, and he finds them profoundly central to the epic fragments which comprise *The Battle of Kosovo*, the Serbo-Croatian poem which he has translated in collaboration with the late Anne Pennington. In the section of *Kosovo* called "The Mother of the Jugovichi," Levi finds "an epic swiftness, and sinuousness, and force. It flickers as Homer does between formality and the most daring originality, with no disruption of its lucid, traditional language." I truly wish the Kosovo cycle had found its Christopher Logue in the Levi/Pennington collaboration, for the poems—and also the cycle that follows them about Marko Kraljevich, the "prince" who gives his name to the book—certainly does constitute, as Levi says in his preface, "one of the strongest and most unregarded rivers of verse in Europe." Readers of *AMC* 12 may remember the epigraph from Vladeta Vucković's *The Dimensions*, a poem that draws heavily on the Kosovo fragments as must inevitably any work by a Yugoslav poet (witness both Vasco Popa and Ivan Lalić) who wishes to tap his region's deepest traditions: "Hail, Milosh! friend of mine and traitor! / Tomorrow you'll betray me on the field of Kosovo."

"At a stroke," writes Levi, "everything was seen in terms of the lost battle of Kosovo. To generations it was like the fall of Troy, intensely and personally felt." And lest we think this dusty history concerns only a handful of nostalgic Serbs, Rebecca West reminds us in her great book *Black Lamb and Grey Falcon* that "it is probable that the battle of Kosovo deducted as much from civilization as the sum of England after the Tudor age." Milosh, in fact, is not the traitor in the poem, but rather its hero; the traitor is the deceptive Vuk Branković. At the supper in Krushevatz before the battle, Milosh defends himself against the accusations of his Tzar and tells him: "I am sworn / to die for you at Kosovo / For you / and for the Christian faith . . .

But treason, Lazarus,
　　　　sits beside you now—
The traitor sips his wine
　　　　right up your sleeve . . .
And when on Vitus-day
　　　　tomorrow morning
We make our dawn attack
　　　　upon the Blackbirds' Field
We'll see right there
　　　　at bloody Kosovo
Who is loyal to you
　　　　and who is not!

Now this, I confess, is not a quote from the Levi/Pennington translation, but from a version which Vladeta Vucković and I made some years ago. I introduce it in order to suggest an alternative to what is basically prose written out in lines with what E. D. Goy has called "some rhythmical echoes." The Levi/Pennington passage goes like this:

I have never been any traitor,
never been one, never shall be one,
at Kosovo tomorrow I intend
to die for the Christian faith.
The traitor is sitting at your knee
drinking cold wine under your skirts:
Vuk Brankovich, I curse him.
Tomorrow is lovely St. Vitus day
and we shall see in Kosovo field
who is faithful, who is the traitor.

This strategy makes for a clear and workmanlike rendering, but not for a poem that sings. And when "The Maid of Kosovo" and "The Mother of the Jugovichi" lament their dead, the poems must sing.

O pity, pity!
　　　　I am cursed so utterly
That if I touched
　　　　a greenly leafing tree
It would dry and wither,
　　　　blighted and defiled.

The poems, of course *were* originally sung to the accompaniment of a single stringed instrument called a gusle. Our own decision was to break the original line into halflines, vary the position of the caesura (to coincide with the line-breaks, which in fact sometimes make for only a visual pause in reading), and strive for a flexible iambic rhythm (instead of the trochaic of the original which is impossible to sustain in a long poem in English without sounding like Longfellow). In the original, each line is end-stopped, and there is invariably a pause after the fourth syllable of the decasyllabic line. When sung by the guslar, however, the very regular verbal rhythm is in counterpoint with a second, more complex rhythmical pattern. Though one cannot provide the guslar's playing and incantation on the page, one might strive to attain, at any rate, something like variety and flexibility within a norm. But a prose version is not the solution. It is nonetheless extremely important to have the Levi/Pennington in print simply because at the moment there is nothing else. It may some day provide a Christopher Logue with a place to begin.

Levi writes in his inaugural lecture that "elegy is a lament that has strayed from its pure origins." As an elegist, Levi proves himself to be a master in *The Echoing Green*, a sequence of three elegies written for dead friends, one of whom was his collaborator on *Marko The Prince*. These poems extend an elegiac strain which can be found in a number of the *Collected Poems 1955–1975* beginning with the early "In Memoriam C. W." and "Elegy for Richard Selig" and concluding with " In Memory of George Seferis." As a classicist, Levi is perhaps somewhat more at home in the Greek Balkans than the Yugoslav. He was a friend of Seferis, has translated George Pavlopoulos, and has dedicated one of his best and most ambitious poems to Nikos Gatsos. He has also written a guide to modern Greece. In the Oxford lecture, he remembers getting very close to the elegy's "pure origins" in the Mani country of southern Greece. "I heard an old woman on a cross-country bus sing a lamentation for the dead Christ that lasted something like an hour." In this part of the country, the art of lamentation survived, evidently, until very recently, and professional lamenters could still be found in the villages. The true style of lamentation sounds, he tells us, much like this (translated from *The Tachydromos* collection, *Ta Demotika Mas Tragoudia*):

> Wake, though you have not had enough of sleep,
> this sleep is heavy, it will bring you harm,
> your youth spoils in your sleep and beauty spoils,
> youth runs to earth and beauty runs to grass.

Am I mistaken in hearing in Levi's beautiful elegy for Seferis a language and orientation which have not strayed *too* far from such origins?

> Who thought deeply, loved also what was living.
> Virtue was in the mountains, in the stony villages,
> magpie in meadow,
> swiftly the shade, swiftly the afternoon.
> The shepherd sees the city it is in his eye.
> The oracle is water. Stone shall prophesy.
> I am lost in this deserted extent.

"Grief is the principal leavings of time," the elegy concludes. Although I do not wish to give the impression that the elegiac occasion dominates Levi's *Collected Poems*, I do feel, especially returning to the volume after *The Echoing Green*, that Levi is at his very best as an elegiac writer. I have earlier indicated something of the diversity of form and content which can be found in *Collected Poems*. Along with the experiments in very public poetry—the rhyming couplets of the verse sermons—the most varied and expansive writing occurs in a series of cycles, notably the ten poems dedicated to Gatsos, "Ruined Abbeys," "Canticum," and the peculiar and interesting "Pigs." But it is chiefly to the elegies that I find myself returning.

🍃

A very different kind of elegy entirely proves to be the major interest of Peter Russell's selected poems, *All for the Wolves*. These elegies were "translated" by Russell from the work of one "Quintilius," all of whose poems—save for two late pieces written "in his madness"—appeared previously in Russell's *The Elegies of Quintilius* (Anvil Press, 1975). This earlier volume contains six elegies (the fourth in two versions, one "made after Mr. Pound's *intervento*"), endless notes and appendices, and a biographical introduction about Quintilius himself, "a figure of admitted obscurity." Here are some of the facts about our poet:

> Cittinus Aurelianus Quintilius Stultus (AD 390–427) was the son of a Transpontine freedman (cf. fragment of Lib. I, Ode IV in Schlugel, *Spicilegium Facetiarum* [1881], vol. IV, pp. 703–704). His early studies, if Lib. II, Ode IV—again, a disjointed fragment—be borne in mind, would appear to have been exclusively legal. Later he became an intimate of Verus and his

circle, dying, according to Flavianus Adeodatus, of a surfeit of lentils (*Scandals and Importunities of the Grammarians*, Lib. V, Cap. III); although, in view of Flavianus' marked antipathy to all but Montanist literature, this account must be accepted with the most severe reserve. Of Quintilius' writings we possessed until recently six Elegies and two complete Odes only (Lib. I, Odes I and II), together with a few additional fragments from the first and second books. There were, it appears, four books originally. Flavianus mentions also an heroic poem with the medical subject: *Ars Vomitoria*. Among the MSS which the noted humanist, Guarino Veronese, lost when he was ship-wrecked, was a copy of the *Odes* Book II, recensed from a Mandean transcript. It will be remembered that Savonarola is reported to have said when he heard the news: "The Church can afford the loss." The two extant Odes (*Codex Ureglius*) formed the favourite early morning reading of the Supreme Pontiff himself, at the time Alexander VI. The text is not given, as it is still being freed from interpolation (University of Tucson: *Studies in Early Romantic Philology* XI, III [1938]).

It is very difficult to stop quoting this marvelous spoof of classical scholarship, a parody which rises to new heights (descends to new depths?) in the notes on the two new elegies. The poems themselves are in part a pastiche of late Latin poetry which might profitably be read beside Tony Harrison's translations of that *actual* late poet of Greek paganism, Palladas. But Peter Levi is certainly correct when he writes in a very sympathetic review of *All for the Wolves* that, while the poems *are* a matter of brilliant pastiche and parody, they are also "passionately convincing. They are an extremely funny learned joke, Quintilius being an invention, but they are full of truth to life, being based on real characters, conversations and places, particularly Santayana, the Ligurian coast of Italy, and Cagnes-sur-Mer, where Peter Russell used to bicycle through forest fires to drink in the vast and rancorous learning of Quintilius from Richard Aldington and Roy Campbell. I do not think either of those writers, or Santayana himself, need be displeased if they are best remembered one day through the *Elegies of Quintilius*." That last seems an extraordinary statement. But Levi is deeply convinced by Quintilius and the rest of Russell, claiming that to praise his book "is to invest in one's own future reputation as a critic." (And yet he finds Russell to be so little known that, in writing about him, he feels as though he had virtually "invented such a poet.") The poet's

most engaging persona writes from Cagnes-sur-Mer about The
Golden Age, but also about aspects of that age when all is for the
wolves:

Times there have been when in Ligurian hills
Quintilius dreamed a space and all was changed—
The learned Muses on their sacred mountains praised
And Arts and Sciences pursued for Virtue's cause
(Not the foundations of rich merchants or the schools
Open to all and propped up hypocritically with funds
Extorted from the purse of each unthinking citizen):
Here in the little oppidum of Cagnes all trace of human crime
Shall disappear; a leader shall arise
To teach each Province of the weary world its way
To a new age when wars shall cease and harsh times grow
     gentle . . .

    If something of Ezra Pound (and something too of Pound's pol-
itics) both engages and troubles the reader behind the pastiche and
parody in this passage, he should know that he is reading not a
minor disciple, but a truly important Poundian, editor of the journal
Nine (precursor, really, of *Agenda*), and *An Examination of Ezra Pound*
published in 1950 when most of the world had either forgotten
Pound or felt that he deserved to stay precisely where he was. And
that parenthetical passage on the schools anticipates the strange sojourn of Quintilius to Canada—a journey documented meticulously
in the notes—where, disguised perhaps as Mr. Russell, he had
about as fine a time at the University of Victoria as Pound's old colleague, Wyndham Lewis, had while disguised as René Harding in
the Ontario of *Self-Condemned*. It was during the period in Victoria
that Russell "translated" the poems of Quintilius "written in his
madness," arguing that "incontrovertible evidence of an archaeolog-
ical, that is, a material nature of Quintilius's actual presence at Cultus Lake may persuade the incredulous that Canada existed in the
cultural sense before the establishment of the Canada Council. It
should however be emphasized that the name 'Cultus,' misunder-
stood by the early settlers around A.D. 1956 as having something
to do with culture in the modern Canadian sense, is in fact a very
ancient Interior Salish word originally meaning 'bear's excrement'
(*cul*-toos)."
    Readers of Seamus Heaney (or of *ACM* 12) will remember
Heaney's metamorphosis into "an inner émigré, grown long-haired /

And thoughtful; a wood-kerne / Escaped from the massacre, / Taking protective colouring / From bole and bark. . . ." Quintilius makes *his* escape as Brock the Badger in a poem of his madness "found inscribed on the winding sheet of the corpse of a sacred prostitute in the recently excavated Temple of Isis in Mestre." It is impossible to read this poem without thinking of its desperately sad ancestor in the work of John Clare.

> A badger, they call me, the priests and the military tribunes,
> The *rufuli*, rhetors and noisome rhapsodes,
> The lying scribes in their scribaria
> And the advocates in their short greasy togas
>
> Of a Sabbath they will come together
> And put on the tunics of hunters
> And come to my house-door with logs and with sulfur,
> And spinning the oaken stick
> In the deep groove of my mother's womb
> Set fire to birch twigs and then to the musty pile,
> And smoke me out
>
> But I am wily—I have three back doors
> (For borrowed wives and other emergencies)
> And I know better than to leave my precious belongings
> Unprotected in an empty house
>
> *Vamus*
>
> Into the virgin forests where badger dreams
> Hang from the white undersides of the alders
> By the side of shining nymph runs. . . .

One wishes Brock the very best of luck.

I can be brief about Seamus Heaney, his two new books having received so many reviews in this country already. I cannot, however, ignore these books in an essay that aims to talk about the relationship between poet and translator in work of recent poet-translators. Heaney has produced the first complete English version of the Gaelic *Buile Suibhne* since 1913, and for that reason, if for no other, the work has a kind of objective importance analagous to the Levi/ Pennington translation of the Kosovo poems. His first impulse seems to have been to translate only the most intensely lyrical sections of the work and to ignore the prose narrative which links lyric moment to lyric moment. In the end, however, he felt he had "to earn the right to do the high points by undertaking the whole thing." But much of *Sweeney Astray* seems to me more an act of will than an act of love, and I wonder if his initial impulse mightn't have been the right one. On the other hand, had he followed that impulse and presented the fragments of greatest intensity out of their narrative context, perhaps the last section of *Station Island*, "Sweeney Redivivus," would never have been written, for here a sequence of lyrics "voiced for Sweeney, the seventh-century Ulster king who was transformed into a bird-man and exiled to the trees by the curse of St. Rowan," develops in a manner which might have been obviated by a selective approach to the translation of *Buile Suibhne*.

Two versions of Purgatory haunt the poems in *Station Island*—Sweeney's in an ancient kingdom which is now partly County Antrim and partly County Down, and Dante's. I think Heaney must at some point have considered translating *The Inferno*. A fine version of the Ugolino canto concludes *Field Work*, the volume he published in 1979, and there has been a fairly consistent range of Dantesque allusion in his work for some time. What he did instead was to write the "Station Island" poems, a cycle where, as pilgrim on an island which has been a site of pilgrimage for a millenium, he encounters figures from his past who remind him of things he has chosen to forget and accuse him of offenses he both is and is not guilty of. Much has been made by reviewers of Joyce's appearance at the end of the cycle, and his advice that Heaney should give up tormenting himself with "that subject people stuff," his "peasant pilgrimage," and the obsessive matter at the end of Stephen Dedalus's diary. "The English language / belongs to us," he says.

> You lose more of yourself than you redeem
> doing the decent thing. Keep at a tangent.
> When they make the circle wide, it's time to swim
>
> out on your own and fill the element
> with signatures on your own frequency,
> echo soundings, searches, probes, allurements. . . .

Swim out or fly out. Such advice could be practiced less well by the wood-kerne of *North*, the familiar "inner émigré," than by that more Daedalus-like figure, the Sweeney/Heaney bird-man who speaks the final poems of the new book. Heaney has written in his introduction to *Sweeney Astray* that "insofar as Sweeney is . . . a figure of the artist, displaced, guilty, assuaging himself by his utterance, it is possible to read the work as an aspect of the quarrel between free creative imagination and the constraints of religious, political, and domestic obligation." It would be a great mistake to read *Station Island* in such a way as to assume that the order of the sections in some way or another resolves this quarrel. For whether as inner émigré, Joycean artificer, or mad and singing Sweeney, Heaney will continue to hear the purgatorial accusations and, in one way or another, make his oblique or direct response. In the most profound dialectical tension with the Joyce passage is section VIII of *Station Island* in which the cousin whose death in sectarian violence so beautifully elegized in "The Strand at Lough Beg" from *Field Work* accuses Heaney of a terrible complicity:

> The protestant who shot me through the head
> I accuse directly, but indirectly, you
> who now atone perhaps upon this bed
> for the way you whitewashed ugliness and drew
> the lovely blinds of the *Purgatorio*
> and saccharined my death with morning dew.

The original poem drew on one of the most gorgeous moments in all of Dante: "I turn because the sweeping of your feet / Has stopped behind me, to find you on your knees / With blood and roadside muck in your hair and eyes, / Then kneel in front of you in brimming grass / And gather up cold handfuls of the dew / To wash you, cousin." *Ambo le mani in su l'erbetta sparte / soavemente 'l mio maestro pose: / ond' io, che fui accorto di sua arte, / porsi ver' lui le guance lagrimose.* The problem is, as artists, we are in Purgatory for good. Perhaps, with Quintilius, and even with Marko the Prince, we must learn a way to laugh there as well as cry.

From *Another Chicago Magazine*, 1985

Of Publishers, Readings, and Festivals, Circa 1986

> The question is
> How does one hold something   To sell? The question is
> In the mind which he intends   When will there not be
>   a hundred
>
> To grasp and how does the salesman   Poets who mistake that
> Hold a bauble he intends   gesture for a style.
>
> —George Oppen

When I was in England to attend the Cambridge Poetry Festival last summer, I decided to investigate some of the things I had heard and read and reported about Faber and Faber by paying a visit to the offices at 3 Queen Square, London.

My own contacts at Faber have been pretty much with the old regime. *Introducing David Jones,* my one bit of editorial work for them, was among the final projects supervised by Peter du Sautoy before his retirement. I was especially interested to meet Desmond Clarke, the man I understood to be responsible for the extraordinary increase in Faber poetry sales in the course of the previous year. Clarke reviewed the recent developments at Faber and anticipated future plans with an outline of strategies both past and present which struck me as being simultaneously visionary and grotesquely inappropriate to the marketing of serious literature. Can you, after all, sell poetry the way you might sell soap or soup or dog food? Yes, he thought, you can. He looked me in the eye and said, "For the first time in the twentieth century we are selling poetry successfully from the point of view of the consumer."

Clarke's promotional blitz has increased Faber and Faber's poetry sales by 37 percent in 1985 and is projected to increase those sales by another 25 percent or more in 1986. In just twelve months, the retail sales value of Faber poetry amounted to 1.7 million pounds. Well, I had a lot of questions which he'd clearly heard before. First of all, wasn't there a difference between a reader who might want to buy a book of poetry and a "consumer"? He shrugged. I tried the question in another way. Didn't he think that certain kinds of promotion were perhaps inappropriate when it came to selling poetry, that maybe books by Faber poets could be so misrepresented as to have their natures truly violated by advertising and promoting them as if they were hack novels, picture books of royalty, or rock 'n' roll cassettes? He did not. He said, in fact, "Has Rosemary [Goad] shown you the cassettes?" She had indeed. By Hughes and Heaney. But the issue is real. To be specific: Should, for example, Douglas Dunn's painful elegies for his wife be promoted in the idiom of advertisements launching the confessions of a third-rate movie star?

Clarke's promotional innovations have taken several forms. The initial move must have been the decision to change the format and design of Faber poetry volumes in order to market them as a coherent group of titles where the whole might be perceived as greater than the sum of the parts but where each part, each single book, would still be seen as an expression of an individual poet's particular personality or signature. The jacket design, in which dark and light repetitions of the "ff" logo surround a white rectangle on which the title and the author's name are quite austerely printed, reminds me of the old postwar Penguins. I think this is intentional. Anyone old enough to remember these initial volumes of the paperback revolution will make the following associations at one level or another almost immediately: quality, economy, democracy, and a canon in the making which is asking for one's trust. The chief difference between the new Fabers and the old Penguins comes in the character of the drawing or photograph or etching underneath the title. This is the manifestation of personality in the design's impersonal context. (The individual talent working through tradition? It's Eliot's old firm, after all.) And then these books are priced from £1.95 (for Heaney's *Field Work* or Larkin's *High Windows*) to £4.00 (for Paulin's *Liberty Tree*) and advertised not only in literary publications, but in the daily press, the Sunday supplements, on radio and T.V., through mass mailings and elaborate displays, and even with unlikely promotional stunts (two Faber poets, for example, flying all over the country in a helicopter followed by a flock of journalists who cover their readings in the provinces).

It's hard to believe that all of this has happened first in England rather than America. For American poetry publishers not to have been first in the field with such impressive hype seems almost unpatriotic. The evidence in America, after all, has been in for a long time. With enough hard sell you can make the public pay for anything. Acknowledging the early successes of Faber's publicity effort, I asked Mr. Clarke how on earth they were paying for it all, for clearly all this advertising and promotion was expensive. "Cats," he said. I must have looked confused, because he smiled and said a little louder: "Cats." In fact I knew what he meant. Only a few days before I had clipped the following from *The Bookseller*:

> Thanks to the *Financial Times*, we now have some means of gauging how huge a windfall *Cats* has been for Faber. *FT* correspondent Gay Firth reported that Andrew Lloyd Webber's musical earned Faber royalties of £650,000 last year. She suggested that earnings for 1985–86 would "certainly be twice that sum" and added, probably conservatively, that earnings over the next 10 years would probably bring Faber around £12 m altogether.

For that kind of money, you can advertise a lot of poetry. And why not, Old Possum himself being the source of this fortune?

When Mr. Clarke handed me the large new brochure titled "The Best of Poetry Today" with its photographs of all twelve living Faber poets, I was prepared for its announcement that there was to be "a major promotion of the best work of twelve outstanding contemporary poets . . . linked to a week's nationwide tour by the Poet Laureate, Ted Hughes, starting on Sunday 20th October 1985" and that the campaign "will be supported by national advertising and extensive media coverage throughout the country." I had read about the Hughes tour in a *Sunday Times* article called "Laureate set for Poetry Roadshow" which had quoted Desmond Clarke himself. "But surely," I said, "no one in England takes this Poet Laureate nonsense seriously." Mr. Clarke fixed me again with that stare of his and said, "After the week of October 20th the Poet Laureateship will never be perceived again the way it has been for the last hundred years. Did you read the article in *The Times*?" As I've said, I had. This is what it said:

> Six months after being appointed Poet Laureate, the shy and retiring Ted Hughes is being hauled out of his Devon farmhouse into the hard-sell marketplace. Still unused to the glare of spotlights and the responsibility of royal office, Hughes will

be brandished about in October by his publisher as the spear-head of a campaign to convince readers that living poets are livelier than the immortal dead. The Laureate will introduce and recite his poems at six public meetings from Folkestone to Glasgow and back through Cambridge, Sheffield, Buxton and Cheltenham. Unlike his gregarious predecessor, Sir John Betjeman, Hughes shuns the media. . . . Protecting him from their unwanted attentions on the week-long tour will be Desmond Clarke, sales and marketing director at Faber and Faber, who convinced Hughes to emerge from rural seclusion. . . . He will use Hughes as the focus of a £22,000 national promotion of 12 contemporary poets, featuring displays in bookshops and a mailing bombardment of schools and universities. "The public is beginning to realize that poetry did not end with Auden and Dylan Thomas," says the ebullient Clarke. . . . People are reading and writing more poetry. The elevation of Ted Hughes has provided a great stimulus. . . ."

The ebullient Mr. Clarke told me that the shy and retiring (and the elevated?) Mr. Hughes would certainly be reading to the largest audiences that had assembled to hear poetry readings since the heady days of Royal Festival Hall's first Poetry International festivals in the 1960s. An arrangement had been made with W. H. Smith's—England's equivalent of Dalton Books—to display Faber poetry during the week of the readings in hundreds of those cardboard "dumpbins" up in the front of their shops where you usually find the latest schlock. Here, under the benign gaze of a cardboard cut-out of the Laureate, would rest "The Best of Poetry Today," titles by Hughes, Heaney, Gunn, Dunn, Philip Gross, Philip Larkin, Paul Muldoon, Norman Nicholson, Tom Paulin, Craig Raine, and two visitors from Trinidad and the USA: Derek Walcott and Amy Clampitt. Well, the show is on even as I write this notice.

In a memo sent to members of the Faber and Faber board and later sent to me by one of them, Clarke rehearses the "crescendo of media activity" which will accompany the readings: several features in *The Sunday Times* ("with a readership of four million"); possible articles in *The Sunday Telegraph* and *Financial Times*; advertising featuring "a powerful shoutline" and "photographs of all our living poets [which] will grasp the attention of the reader;" support from Alan Giles, W. H. Smith's Merchandising Controller; possible consumer advertising backing from Blackwells and Hatchards; and Lord Gowrie's "important speech about poetry at the presentation to the winner of the Arvon Competition." This last to be judged by two Faber poets and the award to be presented to the winner by a third.

❧

The Cambridge Poetry Festival did not draw the crowds anticipated by Desmond Clarke for the Hughes extravaganzas. Nonetheless, it was a serious and successful week. Anyone who's interested in reading work both by and about the poets who attended this year's festival should send for a copy of PN Review No. 46, a special issue guest edited by Clive Wilmer, whose editorial is a good antidote to Desmond Clarke's euphoria over the state of poetry. Taking off from yet another article in the Times, Wilmer takes issue with the unidentified journalist's contention that poetry is a minor art. "If poetry is a minor art," he says, "then the state of our whole culture is unprecedented. For poetry has always been the central, focusing art—not necessarily the most important at any given time, but the one which has been thought of as standing at the threshold of a culture and calling it into being; and then sustaining it by continually renewing the instrument—language—with which the social animal understands and communicates experience."

To stand at the threshold of a culture and call it into being. Is that what Desmond Clarke has in mind for Ted Hughes on his roadshow? Or does he simply equate the possibility of popular success with literary excellence? The distance between "selling poetry from the point of view of the consumer" and *writing* poetry from the point of view of the consumer is not very great. We saw a countercultural parody of this economics of value, after all, in the 1960s. Mr. Wilmer continues in his editorial to put the question of popular appeal in the right perspective:

> Must we really now accept the correlation of cultural centrality and popular success that the Times headline implied? Seminal work has been written before in the narrowest of circumstances. The literary movement that eventually gave birth to The Divine Comedy, for instance, was a private coterie, esoteric and patrician in its outlook. Much the same can be said for the poets surrounding Sidney and Donne. In our own age of notorious inaccessibility, the influence of Hardy, Eliot, and Lawrence on our language and culture is a continuing phenomenon, though rarely recognized as such. This is not to argue that in a mass democratic society like our own the

maintenance of a tiny clerisy is adequate, or that the situation of poetry is satisfactory. It is rather to suggest that the art is far from dead and that we have a basis on which to build a wider understanding of its role and function.

Certainly one of the aims of the Cambridge Poetry Festival from the time of its founding a decade ago by Richard Burns has been to establish a public forum which does not misrepresent the art it celebrates but becomes, indeed, part of that very basis on which to build a wider understanding of poetry's role and function that Clive Wilmer affirms. The festival is simply more interesting and more important than the poetic entertainments put on at the old London Poetry International or anticipated in the Ted Hughes road-show. Although the Cambridge Festival aims to be festive and *not* dully pedagogical, it celebrates the poetry it sponsors in a spirit of critical attentiveness and a context of dialogue and discovery among the poets themselves and the audience.

The poets participating this year included Yves Bonnefoy and Jacques Dupin from France, Attilio Bertolucci from Italy, Miodrag Pavlović from Yugoslavia, Lauris Edmond and Bill Manhire from New Zealand, Vyacheslav Kuprianov from the Soviet Union, John Ashbery, Denise Levertov and Amy Clampitt from the US, and a range of poets from Britain: Charles Tomlinson, Norman Nicholson, Carol Rumens, Alison Brackenbury, Seamus Heaney, Christopher Middleton, and Jeffrey Wainwright. The program included a series of readings and concerts to observe the centenary year of Ezra Pound, performances of music by Ivor Gurney and new settings of Geoffrey Hill's poems by Robin Halloway, exhibits at Kettle's Yard of visual art championed by Ezra Pound and at the Cambridge Union Society of photographs based on landscapes evoked in poems by Welsh poets, and finally a very rare bird indeed—a full performance of Ezra Pound's opera, *Le Testament de Villon.*

The *PN Review* issue on the festival—this also served as its official program—includes excellent new translations of Bonnefoy, Dupin, Bertolucci, and Pavlović; new poems by Ashbery, Tomlinson, Levertov, Wainwright, Manhire, Rumens, and Brackenbury; essays by and about Bonnefoy and Pavlović; and brief considerations of work by Ashbery, Heaney, Clampitt, Dupin, Wainwright, Rumens, Brackenbury, three New Zealand poets, and Holloway's settings of Geoffrey Hill. The issue concludes with seven essays on aspects of the work and career of Ezra Pound by, among others, Pier Paolo Pasolini and Donald Davie. Like most issues of *PN Review*, it is well worth the price of admission.

It is always easy to make a transition from *PN Review* to Carcanet Press, both operations being run by Michael Schmidt in Manchester. Schmidt has decided in the last year or so to offer some competition to the new Faber and Faber regime with his own series of uniform format volumes called "Poetry Signatures." This is an impressive series of books and one which makes for an impression of coherent editorial strategy and development at Carcanet, coming as it does hard on the heels of Schmidt's *Some Contemporary Poets of Britain and Ireland*, the anthology which I discussed in contrast to the Morrison/Motion Penguin in *ACM* 12. The books are all bright red paperbacks with a design or drawing or photograph appearing in a circle underneath the title looking somewhat less elegant than the corresponding images in the Faber and Faber series. All are volumes of selected poems and all cost £2.95. The length ranges from 79 to 139 pages. Among the initial seven poets in this series, only Donald Davie and Elizabeth Jennings are well known in this country. The other poets are Iain Crichton Smith and Edwin Morgan from Scotland, Gillian Clarke from Wales, and, from England, Jeffrey Wainwright and the late Sylvia Townsend Warner.

I do not have space in this brief survey of recent publishing activities to review properly any of these volumes, but I will choose one or two of them to discuss in *ACM* 16. In many ways, my favorites on a quick read through the series are the shortest and the longest, the Wainwright and the Morgan. They are in most respects utterly different from each other. Wainwright publishes very little and writes with an austerity and scrupulosity reminiscent of his old teacher at Leeds, Geoffrey Hill. Morgan probably publishes too much and is something of a joker. On the other hand, his wonderful energy and versatility make him a very healthy influence on the British poetry scene, and one welcomes his benevolent presence heartily. His book includes, as the blurb tells us, "poems of city life, science-fiction, visions, concrete and sound poems, songs and lyrics, character studies ranging from Marilyn Monroe to Jack London and from Ramses II to Cinquevalli." Surprisingly, only the Davie and Jennings volumes in the Poetry Signatures series are listed in Carcanet's most recent US catalogue—and these are the two *least* necessary books for us to have in this country. It would be very good to have the Morgan and the Wainwright volumes here. I had occasion to mention Wainwright's "Thomas Muntzer" and his "Mad

Talk of George III" in my discussion of anthologies in *ACM* 12. "To His Lover" is a very different kind of poem from these, but it suggests something of Wainwright's power and concentration:

> At the dead of night he breaks in upon her.
>
> The room he knows so well,
> That they have shared alike,
> Is to him now the globe of his own eye
> That he stumbles inside.
>
> The bed-light flashes on and she is there,
> She and some other friend, limbs thus and thus,
> The sheet roped across them,
> Pulled out of sleep.
>
> —This is *love* he feels, something he *knows* he feels,
> The best we can do, known to us by jealousy.
>
> He leaves them, shoulders the laurel at the gate,
> The wrought iron dragging at the paving stone,
> And is back to the street,
> Its heavy trees,
> Pools of rigid light.

To cheer himself up, Wainwright's stricken poet-lover might sign on for a holiday trip with Edwin Morgan. This stanza from Morgan's *Itinerary* is characteristic of his verbal games playing and his mercurial imagination.

> We went to Oldshoremore.
> Is the Oldshoremore road still there?
> You mean the old shore road?
> I suppose it's more an old road than a shore road.
> No more! They shored it up, but it's washed away.
> So you could sing the old song—
> Yes we sang the old song:
> We'll take the old Oldshoremore shore road no more.

I want to conclude these notes by listing four more books which have come to my attention and which I'd liked to recommend. From Anvil, Peter Whigham's *Things Common, Properly* selects his poems from 1942–1980. Whigham is probably still best known for his Catullus translations, but his own poems—especially "The Ingathering of Love"—will amply reward the reader's attention. Whigham was a post-war British Poundian, and his book might well be read alongside Peter Russell's *All For The Wolves*, the selected poems by that other maverick Poundian which I reviewed in *ACM* 14.

From Carcanet, but not a volume in the Signatures series, John Ash's *The Branching Stairs* prints over 150 pages by a poet whom American readers will find it difficult not to compare with John Ashbery (and not just because of the similarity of the names). I suppose some of the work is actually derivative of Ashbery. On the other hand, it would not be the first time that derivative work turned out to be superior to that from which it derived. Ash is a marvelously inventive poet. His use of narrative and pseudonarrative, to cite just one of his several strengths, is much more interesting than the narrative strategies praised by reviewers of *The Penguin Book of Contemporary British Poetry* in the work of James Fenton and Andrew Motion. "The effect [of Ash's poems] is rather like reading Nabokov versified by Supervielle," Dana Gioia remarked in *The Hudson Review*. That's pretty close.

From Faber and Faber, not a book of poems, actually, but Tony Harrison's *The Mysteries*. This is an amalgamation and adaptation of the York, Wakefield, Chester, and Coventry cycles of medieval mystery plays which, when I saw them performed last summer, struck me as the most remarkable thing I'd seen on the British stage since Peter Brook's productions of *Marat/Sade* and *US* in the late 1960s. As a text, *The Mysteries* is more persuasive than Harrison's *Oresteia*. This is a poet constantly and rapidly moving from strength to strength, and one hardly knows what to expect from him next.

Finally, a Penguin. Penguin Books celebrates its fiftieth birthday this year. Although the King Penguin series of paperbacks does not seem to originate its own titles, the work reprinted in this inexpensive format—and I have mentioned before the books by MacDiarmid, Fenton, Logue, and Harrison—clearly makes a continuing contribution to the cause of making important contemporary work available to as large an audience as possible. Just published in King Penguin as part of the fiftieth birthday celebrations is the *Collected Poems* of Geoffrey Hill, a volume which reprints all of *For the Unfallen, King Log, Mercian Hymns, Tenebrae*, and *The Mystery of the Charity of Charles Péguy*. No book of poetry published in the next several years, and perhaps not in the next several decades either, is likely to be any more important than that.

From *Another Chicago Magazine*, 1986

Anglo-Welsh Poetry

Roland Mathias and Raymond Garlick, eds., *Anglo-Welsh Poetry 1480–1980*, Poetry Wales Press; Roland Mathias, *Burning Brambles: Selected Poems 1944–1979*, Gomer Press; Roland Mathias, *A Ride Through the Wood*, Poetry Wales Press; R. S. Thomas, *Ingrowing Thoughts*, Poetry Wales Press; Gillian Clarke, *Selected Poems*, Carcanet Press.

Wales this time. And next time Scotland. I may have appeared to indulge in what has looked like a special pleading on behalf of certain little-known British poets in the past, but this is going to seem ridiculous: three books by someone named Mathias. But look again—there is only one *t*, and I promise you that we are in no way related to one another save through a few years of sporadic correspondence and one long conversation on a visit to the grave of Henry Vaughan and over coffee afterward at one *t*'s home in Brecon. I tried to argue in one letter that the Welsh Mathiases must have come, like the American Matthiases, from Germany. But I was firmly told that this was not the case. The one *t*s are indigenous to Wales.

Also indigenous to Wales is poetry in Welsh. Mathias and Garlick argue in the introduction to their anthology of Anglo-Welsh poetry that "what opera is to Italy, ballet to Russia, theatre to England, symphonic music to Germany, and painting to the Netherlands, poetry is to Wales: the supreme and defining art form." Saying that, however, they must immediately qualify the claim with respect to poetry written in English—the Anglo half of the Anglo-Welsh equation—by saying this: "No one who has any acquaintance with the ultimately untranslatable splendours of Welsh-language poetry, and

its millenium and a half of magnificence, will entertain for one moment any notion of Anglo-Welsh poetry as a possible rival."

Although the reader of *Anglo-Welsh Poetry 1480–1980* will not
find Taliesin or Aneirin, Gruffudd ab yr Ynad Coch or Dafydd ap
Gwilym, or even the contemporary Welsh poetry of Saunders Lewis,
David Gwenallt Jones, or Waldo Williams, he *may* find an English-
language poetry in which, the editors argue, quoting Anthony Conran, "a 'seepage' has taken place between the two language-groups
of Wales," and between poetry written in Welsh and poetry written
in English. In 1894, Sir O. M. Edwards called for "a literature that
will be English in language but Welsh in spirit," and Glyn Jones in
the middle of the present century stated what the editors call "the
classic Anglo-Welsh position" with "characteristic commonsense
and urbanity" when he said: "While using cheerfully enough the
English language, I have never written in it a word about any country other than Wales, or any people other than Welsh people."

The problem is that sense in this matter of the two languages,
the two poetries, and the two cultures may be neither very common
nor very urbane. In a probing and provocative review published in
Poetry Wales (Vol. 20, No. 2), John Barnie questions the notion of
"seepage" from Welsh to Anglo-Welsh poetry and argues instead
that the influence of English poetry and its traditions on Anglo-
Welsh poetry has been direct and definitive: "English is not just a
neutral medium for communication, but a subtle and pervasive car-
rier of cultural attitudes and values . . . steeped in associations of
Englishness." He feels that Anglo-Welsh writers hesitate to admit a
fundamental truth, namely "that the loss of the Welsh language is
an irreparable loss to Welshness and Welsh sensibility. As if, after a
thoroughgoing conquest, French poets spoke and wrote in German,
yet claimed that their sensibility as Frenchmen had not been im-
paired in the process."

As a complete outsider to this debate, I am in no position to
adjudicate or reach any confident conclusions of my own. What does
seem clear is that the linguistic issue itself—along with related historical, political, and cultural issues—lies at the heart of some of the
best poetry anthologized by Mathias and Garlick and often provides
a tension not unlike that found in the work of Paul Celan, to take an
example not so very far removed from John Barnie's hypothetical notion of a French poetry written in German, where the language of
destroyers must serve to manifest the poetics and racial consciousness of survivors. In their introduction, Mathias and Garlick quote a
stanza from R. S. Thomas's poem "What is a Welshman?" in which,

as they acknowledge, "English is seen as the destroyer of Wales and Welsh, the language of commerce and the industrialists who came . . ."

> burrowing
> in the corpse of a nation
> for its congealed blood. I was
> born into the squalor of
> their feeding and sucked their speech
> in with my mother's
> infected milk, so that whatever
> I throw up now is still theirs.

As for Welsh, Sam Adams, writing about a Celtic hill fort in Caerleon, finds the path blocked by a sentry whose "spear-tip sparks with sunlight."

> He challenges in accents I know well;
> The words I recognise, but the sense eludes.
> I am ashamed and silent. He runs me through.

Such fairly typical lines as these suggest that some Anglo-Welsh poets, at any rate, are acutely aware of their ambiguous and paradoxical position as Welsh poets writing in English, and that they understand it more or less in John Barnie's terms. It is really only very recent poets, such as Peter Finch and John Davies, who write in English casually enough to remark that "A heritage / . . . is taking / a long time to learn / that yesterday cannot be today," or make extravagant comedy out of a recipe for "How to Write Anglo-Welsh Poetry."

> First, apologise for not being able
> to speak Welsh. Go on: apologise.
> Being Anglo-*any*thing is really tough;
> any gaps you can fill up with sighs.
>
> And get some roots, juggle names like
> Taliesin and ap Gwilym, weave
> a Cymric web. It doesn't matter what
> they wrote. Look, let's not be naive. . . .

Mathias and Garlick have managed to locate nine English-language poems worth printing before the Anglo-Welsh tradition really gets going with George Herbert and Henry Vaughan in the seventeenth century. Most of these are curiosities, although Hugh Holland's three poems are certainly impressive, and it is interesting to find the first English-language *englynion*—often discrete quatrains with something of the feel of the Greek epigram or the Japanese Hokku, but also used as stanzas in longer poems—appearing as early as the fifteenth century in a hymn to the Virgin by one Ieuan Ap Hywel Swrdwal. The editors regard eight of their first nine poems to be "in some sense praise-poems," thereby linking them to the most characteristic of traditional Welsh poetic practices, as well as to the religious poetry—poetry which substitutes the praise of God for the praise of prince and patron—of Henry Vaughan and Thomas Herbert. Actually, I find both the Vaughan and Herbert selections a good deal less impressive than they might have been. Although Herbert's greatest poems—"Church Monuments" and "The Pulley"—are readily available elsewhere, it is a pity not to find Vaughan's poem on the river Usk (which is not so readily available) or "Upon the Priory Grove, His Usual Retirement," a poem which actually does suggest an analogue to, if not a seepage from, the poems on groves and bowers by Dafydd ap Gwilym. One would also like to find "The Lamp" and "To His Books" by Henry Vaughan, and, from the work of his mysterious twin brother Thomas, the excellent couplets on the Usk—better I think than Henry's—which he inserted in his *Anima Magica Abscondita*. Here he vows to "dress my soul by thee as thou dost pass / As I would do my body in a glass." This is the river which, once polluted by the industry that R. S. Thomas sees "burrowing / in the corpse of a nation," drains the wounds of David Jones's Sleeping Lord in what, to my mind, is the greatest Anglo-Welsh poem of the twentieth century, and, indeed, one of the greatest modern poems in English.

Not much seems to happen in Anglo-Welsh poetry between the brothers Vaughan and the great generation of Glyn and David Jones, Idris Davies, Vernon Watkins, R. S. and Dylan Thomas, Alun Lewis, and Roland Mathias himself. In the eighteenth century there is John Dyer's pleasant chestnut, "Grongar Hill," and there is the work of William Williams, called Pantycelyn, who wrote his remarkable hymns both in Welsh and English and who has been claimed by Saunders Lewis, according to Anthony Conran, to be "the first great Romantic poet in Europe." During the Romantic period proper and immediately after there is, alas, almost nothing of any interest. In *A Ride Through The Wood*, Roland Mathias's volume of essays on Anglo-Welsh literature, Mathias says that "the consideration [Anglo-Welsh

poets of the nineteenth century] best deserve is . . . not one of literary evaluation so much as social and historical exegesis. In other
words, they have views and attitudes, even if they rarely express
them memorably." Memorable expression returns impressively to
Wales with modern and contemporary poetry, and it is chiefly the
work of Anglo-Welsh poets born after 1895 that will engage the
reader of *Anglo-Welsh Poetry* and stimulate an interest in the essays
gathered in Mathias's *A Ride Through The Wood*.

While more than half of the poets represented by Mathias and
Garlick up to the twentieth century were Welsh-speaking, and more
than one third also wrote in the language, this bilingualism becomes
less and less pronounced in the modern period while, feeling either
guilty or relaxed about their lack of Welsh, English-language poets
perfect their medium and their craft and produce, between the early
work of Glyn Jones and the recent work of Roland Mathias and Leslie Norris, what looks to be the best Anglo-Welsh poetry since
Vaughan and Herbert. "What brought about the twentieth century
flowering of Anglo-Welsh writing," the editors explain, "was a factor directly related to English immigration and an education in English for all Welsh children." They continue their analysis like this:

> It was a blow that immigration and its consequences in Welsh
> industry and society had administered to the confidence of
> Welsh-speaking parents in South Wales: their children, often
> brought up to believe that English was the only language of
> opportunity, were still impregnated with the radical values in-
> herent in a Welsh-speaking society and were sad enough, re-
> sentful enough, conscious of the difference enough, to use the
> English language in an un-English way and proclaim their dif-
> ference confidently to English readers. It was, first with Glyn
> Jones about 1934, and then with Dylan Thomas, Vernon Wat-
> kins, Keidrych Rhys and Idris Davies, that the new Anglo-
> Welsh, freed from the echoing classicism of their predecessors,
> made their mark.

It is surely on the strength of work by these five poets and
their contemporaries or immediate successors—David Jones, Alun
Lewis, R. S. Thomas, Roland Mathias, and Leslie Norris—that the
reader is likely to form an impression of Anglo-Welsh poetry at its
best and an opinion as to whether he thinks this writing constitutes
part of a national literature—something analogous to Irish and Scottish poetry—or merely, as John Barnie argues, a provincial litera-

ture. A serious student of the question will want to supplement his reading of the anthology and its introduction with the essays on Watkins, Dylan and R. S. Thomas, Alun Lewis, and David Jones in *A Ride Through the Wood*. Interestingly, the first casualty resulting from a reading of this book is Dylan Thomas—almost every American's sentimental image of what an Anglo-Welsh poet should amount to—who is shown pretty clearly to be the most Anglo of the generation, and the least Welsh. Even Thomas's precocity is called into question—Welsh poets typically develop slowly in the fullness of time—not to mention his total lack of contact with the Welsh-speaking community, his eagerness to get to London, and his determination to imitate the prototype of the isolated, self-consuming English romantic. Thomas, Mathias argues, accepted an alien model. Welsh poets "were almost always part-time poets, farmers, shop-keepers, shepherds, preachers, teachers: they did not see themselves as individualists and romantics because they had another position from which to see the community and contribute to it."

Take away Dylan Thomas and all is not lost. Although I am not, myself, wholly persuaded by the work of Alun Lewis and find the claim that R. S. Thomas is "one of the most distinguished living poets in the English language" to be greatly exaggerated, clearly both Lewis and Thomas have written notable poems which American readers should know. Thomas's *Ingrowing Thoughts*, his new book based on a range of mostly surrealist paintings, does not, however, add significantly to his body of work. The anthologized selections are much stronger and much more compelling than these recent poems, most of which are overwhelmed by the reproductions of the paintings with which they aim to enter into dialogue. Idris Davies—a poet totally unknown to me before I read the poems in this anthology—is something of a primitive, but no less original for that, and in David Jones we have, as I have argued elsewhere, one of the absolutely necessary poets of our time. (Mathias's essay on David Jones effectively demonstrates the error of René Hague's contention that Jones's attempt to Cambrianize his work was somehow insincere.) Glyn Jones, Vernon Watkins, and Leslie Norris have all written major modern poems, and Watkins has produced an *oeuvre* which many would regard, like R. S. Thomas's, to be international in stature. On the strength of *Burning Brambles*—Roland Mathias's selected poems 1944–1979, good selections from which appear in *Anglo-Welsh Poetry*—Mathias himself clearly takes his place among the major Anglo-Welsh poets of the century. Jeremy

Hooker, perhaps the best younger critic of Anglo-Welsh literature, has written that "memory and guilt are the main springs of Mathias's poetry," and concludes his essay on Mathias in the twentieth anniversary issue of *Poetry Wales* by quoting the last stanza from "Brechfa Chapel," the bleak but beautiful poem that concludes both the selections from *Snipe's Castle* in *Burning Brambles* and the Mathias section of *Anglo-Welsh Poetry*. Hooker also remarks, however, that when Mathias's strong impulse as a praise-poet is released—an impulse "partly thwarted by his Puritan consciousness of sin"—it flows "with a singular purity and force." The following lines conclude "Laus Deo," the tenth part of "Tide-Reach," a sequence of poems anchored in Pembrokeshire and evidently intended to be set to music:

> It is one engrossing work, this frail
> Commerce of souls in a corner,
> Its coming and going, and the mark
> Of the temporal on it. It is one
> Coherent work, this Wales
> And the seaway of Wales, its Maker
> As careful of strength as
> Of weakness, its quirk and cognomen
> And trumpet allowed for
> The whole peninsula's length.
> It is one affirmative work, this Wales
> And the seaway of Wales.

"These States!" cried Whitman. And D. H. Lawrence added (*not* parenthetically, somewhere in his *Studies in Classic American Literature*)—"Whatever that meant!" "This Wales!" Among the recent Anglo-Welsh poets anthologized by Mathias and Garlick—those born after 1935—a good number seem more perplexed, and even vexed, by Wales than confident that they know what Wales means, either to themselves as English-language poets or to the bilingual community living within its borders. Among those providing continuity between the senior generation of Anglo-Welsh poets—Gwyn Williams, Jean Earle, Glyn Jones, Thomas, and Mathias—and the younger poets who have recently emerged, a group born in the 1920s would seem to engage many of the themes and issues familiar to a reader of Vernon Watkins or R. S. Thomas while also employing some of the traditional strategies and means. I have mentioned Leslie Norris and Anthony Conran—whose *Penguin Book of Welsh Verse* contains not only excellent translations of the full range of Welsh-language poetry, but also a superlative introduction—and should add the names of John Ormond, John Tripp, and Dannie Abse, a poet whose work most readers will associate more with his medical practice in London than with his residence near Cardiff. Perhaps Gillian Clarke, born in 1937, is the last poet anthologized whose work feels to an outsider fully committed to its engagement with Welsh tradition, history, community, family life, and the genius of the place. Roland Mathias's successor as editor of *The Anglo-Welsh Review*, Clark, while adequately represented in the anthology, makes a far better showing in the selection of her work published by Carcanet Press in their "Signatures" series. This is in part because there is room for "Letter From a Far Country," a poem originally written, like Dylan Thomas's *Under Milkwood*, for the radio. The poem is valuable for a good number of reasons, not the least of which is its concern for the history and experience of women in a western rural parish where Clarke writes her apologia to "husbands, fathers, forefathers," calling it her "letter home from the future, / [her] bottle in the sea." Greedy circling gulls put to her their "masculine question:" "Where," they ask, "are your great works?" And from the daily, ordinary routines of obscure women—wives, mothers, and grandmothers—Clarke constructs her reply:

> It is easy to make of love
> these ceremonials. As priests
> we fold cloth, break bread, share wine,
> hope there's enough to go round.

As is the case with modern English poetry, Anglo-Welsh poetry does not seem to have produced many poems of merit written by women about the lives of women. This is an impressive instance of one such poem (there are others in the Carcanet selection), and one applauds with equal enthusiasm its clear vision and accomplished craftsmanship.

John Barnie finds that the most recent Anglo-Welsh poetry has begun to exchange its dependence on England for a dependence on an international style which he associates with the influence of American poetry and poetics. Finding the twin curse of contemporary Anglo-Welsh writing to be the Georgian voice (which he hears in Norris and in Clarke) and the "style that is confessional, domestic, and sired by late-Romanticism on American poetry of the 60s," he calls for English-speaking Welsh poets to have the courage, like certain Australians, to "create in the desert of the imagination." He would like to see the emergence of a Welsh Les A. Murray, a poet he believes to have created a style which is uniquely Australian. Answering Barnie from America in *Poetry Wales* (Vol. 20, No. 4), Joseph Clancy, a Welsh-American poet who is himself represented in the anthology, hopes that "from the tension during the last three decades between a sometimes over-anxious effort to achieve Welshness and a sometimes equally excessive straining to be 'modernist' and 'international' will come an Anglo-Welsh poetry sufficiently self-confident to draw on whatever may be useful in English or European or Latin-American, in Welsh-language or American-language poetry to explore what it means to be human now and in Wales." I don't see, in the present circumstances, that one can really hope for anything other than this, eclectic and syncretistic though the results must be.

As for all attendant anxieties about deracination—and all the versions of exile, internal or external, that seem to obsess Anglo-Welsh poets—certainly John Ormond's very funny poem, "Lament for a Leg," has said something like the last word on the subject. "Near the yew tree under which the body of Dafydd ap Gwilym is buried in Strata Florida," Ormond tells us in a note, "there stands a stone with the following inscription: 'The left leg and part of the thigh of Henry Hughes, Cooper, was cut off and interr'd here, June 18, 1756.' Later the rest of Henry Hughes set off across the Atlantic in search of better fortune." After describing his accident and the "short service . . . with scarcely half a hymn," Henry explains how he set out with his only, his best foot, forward to America

> Where, with my two tried hands, I plied
> My trade and, true, in time made good
> Though grieving for Pontrhydfendigaid.
> Sometimes, all at once, in my tall cups,
> I'd cry in *hiraeth* for my remembered thigh
> Left by the grand yew in Ystrad Fflur's
> Bare ground, near the good bard. . . .
>
> 'So I bequeath my leg,' I'd say and sigh,
> Baffling them, 'my unexiled part, to Dafydd
> The pure poet who, whole, lies near and far
> From me, still pining for Morfudd's heart,'
> Giving him, generous to a fault
> With what was no more mine to give,
> Out of that curt plot, my quarter grave,
> Good help, I hope.

It seems to me that Ormond and the younger poets who follow him in this anthology contribute,whether with one foot or both feet in their native land (which, let us hope, is *not* a grave), in unexpected ways to a body of work which, however essentially Welsh it may or may not be, is consistently interesting and will repay the attention of American readers.

From *Another Chicago Magazine,* 1986

Hugh MacDiarmid and
Scottish Poetry

Michael Grieve and W. R. Aitken, eds., *The Complete Poems of Hugh MacDiarmid*, vols. I and II, Penguin Books.

In my last column, I promised I would undertake a survey of modern Scottish poetry on the order of my survey of the Anglo-Welsh. I had in mind placing at the center the successive anthologies edited by Maurice Lindsay which represent the stages of the Scottish Renaissance initiated by the early poetry of Hugh Mac-Diarmid and branching out from them to consider books by some of the more interesting recent Scottish poets—W. S. Graham, George MacKay Brown, Ian Hamilton Finlay, Iain Crichton Smith, Douglas Dunn, and others. But Lindsay and the rest must wait for separate treatment in a continuation of this column in *ACM* 18. There is no way to begin talking about modern Scottish poetry without talking first about MacDiarmid. He is that rare thing in the twentieth century—a truly national poet in the manner of a Yeats, a Neruda, a Whitman, or a Pushkin. He is also such demanding and annoying company that I want him off my back. I have been reading in the two volumes and 1,194 pages of *The Complete Poems* ever since I first mentioned the books back in *ACM* 14.

In talking about Anglo-Welsh poetry, I was obliged to engage the questions of nationality and language. Is there really, in fact, a Welsh nation? If so, can its identity and the character of its consciousness be expressed in a language other than Welsh? Similar questions arise when one turns from Wales to Scotland. What, precisely, did Scotland become after the Battle of Flodden? After the accession of James I? After the Act of Union? What was Scotland after Culloden? James himself began the great tradition of poetry forged from the variant of northern English dialect spoken in the Lowlands by the nobles, burgesses, and peasants alike. Was this tradition—which has given us Robert Henryson, William Dunbar, Gavin Douglas, the border ballads, and Robert Burns—completely played out by the end of the nineteenth century? Could it be revived? Or should modern Scotland's poetry speak southern English, as Edwin Muir believed? Or maybe even Gaelic, as Sorley MacLean has shown that it can?

MacDiarmid has answered these questions differently at different times. As a Scottish Nationalist and, at one time, even a candidate for parliament running against the Prime Minister, he believed in Scotland as a political entity with an independent future. His Nationalism, however, was obliged to reach an understanding with his Communism—a distinct possibility in the complex dialectic of his poetry, but difficult for fellow Nationalists and fellow Communists to understand. MacDiarmid was thrown out of the Nationalist Party for being a Communist and out of the Communist Party for being a Nationalist. And what about the linguistic question? How best to express the character of Scottish consciousness, the Scottish soul? MacDiarmid (as C. M. Grieve) began in English, switched to Scots, and then returned to English. Along the way he made his peace with Gaelic by translating the major poems of Alexander MacDonald and Duncan MacIntyre, "Birlinn of Clanranald" and "Praise of Ben Dorain." In the view of most MacDiarmid readers, the Scots poetry from *Sangschaw* (1925) to *A Drunk Man Looks at the Thistle* (1926) is his greatest, and indeed the deepest expression of the Scottish genius since Robert Burns. But the serious reader of MacDiarmid has got to take him whole, and that means coming to some kind of terms with the later poems in English, what he called his "poetry of fact" or "mature art," in both the largely successful *Stony Limits* (1934), and the hugely problematic *In Memoriam James Joyce* (1955), *The Kind of Poetry I Want* (1961), and *Dìreadh* (1974).

There is no denying the freshness, charm, and vitality of the Scots lyrics in *Sangschaw* and *Penny Wheep*. It has been said that Christopher Murray Grieve, author of a volume in English called *Annals of the Five Senses*, dove in one side of John Jamieson's *An Etymological Dictionary of the Scottish Language* and came out on the other side as Hugh MacDiarmid. The young C. M. Grieve wrote about how "shining passions stilled / Shone in the sudden peace / Like countless leaves / Tingling with the quick sap of Immortality." MacDiarmid, on the other hand, sounds like this:

> Ootside! . . . Ootside!
> There's dooks that try tae fly
> An' bum-clocks bizzin' by,
> A corn-skriech an' a cay
> An' guissay i' the cray.
>
> Inside! . . . Inside!
> There's golochs on the wa',
> A craidle on the ca',
> A muckle bleeze o' cones
> An' mither fochin' scones.

"Country Life," it's called, and those *dooks* are ducks, the *bum-clocks bizzin'* are beetles buzzing, the *corn-skriech* is a corncrake, the *cay*'s a jackdaw, *guissay*'s a pig, *cray*'s a sty, and mother is *turning* those scones on a muckle bleeze of her fire while someone's rocking a cradle. But could you use that kind of language to talk, let's say, about Solovyev's philosophy or Dostoyevsky's fiction? MacDiarmid thought you could. From pretty early on he began to mutter darkly: "Not Burns, Dunbar . . ." and "Precedents, not traditions." There could not be a viable revival of the vernacular, he felt, unless the tendencies making for it were "a revival of spirit as distinct from a mere renewed vogue of the letter—unless these tendencies [were] in accord with the newest tendencies of human thought." There is, of course, *plenty* of Burns in the early MacDiarmid, but he stresses Dunbar as a precedent in reaction to the insipid verse of the Kailyard School which had vulgarized and sentimentalized the Burns tradition to the point that an entire generation had forgotten that a poet could *think* in Scots, and think moreover in the most demanding forms about the most arresting and most difficult ideas, and make that thinking relevant to all of Europe. Although these ambitions are not fulfilled until *A Drunk Man Looks at the Thistle*, the vivid metaphysical symbolism of "The Eemis Stane" takes him more than halfway there.

> I' the how-dumb-deid o' the cauld hairst nicht
> The warl' like an eemis stane
> Wags i' the lift;
> An' my eerie memories fa'

Like a yowdendrift.
Like a yowdendrift so's I couldna read
The words cut oot i' the stane
Had the fug o' fame
An' history's hazelraw
No' yirdit thaim.

Read it aloud. Read it aloud twice or three times, slowly. Surely
we would need to search in all the books by all the best lyric poets
of the century to find something as perfect. And Kenneth Buthlay's
prose translation makes one wonder if any English at all, in whatever hands, could say what this poem says in Scots: "In the still
centre of the dead of night, cold at harvest time, the world like a
teetering stone sways in the sky; and my eerie memories fall like
snow driven by the wind. Like snow driven by the wind, so that I
couldn't read the words cut out on the stone, even if the moss of
fame and lichens of history had not buried them." True, we need a
glossary to read "The Eemis Stane." But the poem is as good as
anything by Yeats on roughly its own scale before *Responsibilities.*
    By the time MacDiarmid came to write *A Drunk Man,* he had
synthesized not only a language both from the contemporary spoken vernacular and from poems and reference works of all kinds
and periods, but also a fairly systematic set of ideas that would allow him to undertake successfully a poem of some 2,700 lines that
could compete with Dunbar's longer poems and Burns's "Tam o'-
Shanter." In the act of composing in Scots he had discovered
"names for nameless things," as he says in "Gairmscoile," or, as he
has it in his prose, "lapsed or unrealized qualities which correspond
to unconscious elements of distinctively Scottish psychology." Chief
among the enabling ideas at work was G. Gregory Smith's notion of
"The Caledonian Antisyzygy." This doctrine holds—as MacDiarmid
was later to explain in his essay on "The Caledonian Antisyzygy
and the Gaelic Idea"—that "the prime quality of Scottish literature,"
a quality which MacDiarmid would like to perpetuate in his work, is
"a zigzag of contradictions; a reflection of the contrasts which the
Scot shows at every turn, in his political and ecclesiastical history, in
his polemical restlessness, in his adaptability." MacDiarmid celebrates "the power of entertaining all sorts of irreconcilably opposed
beliefs at one and the same time," a freedom "of passing from one
mood to another," and the "antithesis of the real and fantastic"
which cannot be explained by any rules of rhetoric but where "one
simply invades the other without warning." It is not surprising,

therefore, that his Drunk Man, gazing at the thistle, symbol of Scotland caught in moonlit metamorphosis upon a hillside, should declare early in the poem:

> I'll hae nae hauf-way house, but aye be whaur
> Extremes meet—it's the only way I ken
> To dodge the curst conceit o bein richt
> That damns the vast majority o men.

When the poem takes a medieval, and then immediately a slapstick, turn, the antisyzygical idea gets expressed like this:

> Grinnan gargoyle by a saint,
> Mephistopheles in Heaven,
> Skeleton at a tea-meetin,
> Missan link—or creakan
> Hinge atween the deid and livin. . . .

> (I kent a Terrier in a sham fecht aince,
> Wha louped a dyke and landed on a thistle.
> He'd naething on ava aneth his kilt.
> Schonberg has nae notation for his whistle.)

By the fifth stanza of this long poem, MacDiarmid's Drunk Man has explained exactly what he intends to do to prove his soul is Scots. He will begin, he says, with what is conventionally understood to be Scottish—he begins with alcohol and Robert Burns!—and then soar up "by visible degrees / To heichts the fules hae never recked." But once he gets them there, he says, "I'll whummle them"—turn them over—"And souse the craturs in the nether deeps." Just as a fit reader of Keats must himself possess to a degree the Negative Capability of the poet, so the fit reader of MacDiarmid must possess an Antisyzygical Capability. This poem would make Caladonians of us all. We must learn to enjoy being "whummled."

But I don't mean to give the impression that this poem is all a matter of upset inner tubes, farting cushions, and exploding cigars. MacDiarmid does indeed take us to the heights he promises—philosophical, visionary, even erotic—and to that place "whaur / Extremes meet" for which we must abandon our "hauf-way house." As the poem veers from passages of intense lyricism through passages of Anglophobic satire, traditional Scottish "flyting," translations or adaptations of Russian and German poems, parodies of Eliot, a ballad on the General Strike of 1926, and evocations of the figure of Sophia out of Soloviev and the Yggdrasil out of Celtic mythology, the logic of MacDiarmid's drunkenness is seen to be essentially Baude-lairian (or Nietzschean): "It maitters not what drink is taen, / The barley bree, ambition, love / Or Guid or Evil workan in's / Sae lang's we feel like souls set free / Frae mortal coils and speak in tongues / We dinna ken and never wull." On the other hand, in the central address to Dostoyevsky, and in other passages that anticipate the concluding vision of The Great Wheel, there is a movement toward both sobriety and the discursive mode.

In MacDiarmid's later work, it is certainly a discursive poetics which is at issue (along with some of the characteristic attitudes and ideas which accompany it), and often enough one wishes for a bit of the old drunkenness while plowing through the facts, lists, cita-tions, arguments, scientific theories, philosophy, political propa-ganda, philology, and linguistics of *In Memoriam James Joyce, Three Hymns to Lenin, The Battle Continues, The Kind of Poetry I Want,* and the *Dìreadh* poems. If MacDiarmid's aims in *A Drunk Man* are in some sense Faustian—"Hae I the cruelty I need . . . / And still con-tempt in endless meed / That I may never yet be caught / In my sat-isfaction?"—he also runs the danger of concluding his work, like Faust, draining swamps as a kind of cosmic sanitary engineer (as I think W. H. Auden had it). While no cultural bureaucrat could ever commission the likes of *In Memoriam James Joyce* and no theory of Socialist Realism ever accept or comprehend it, many of MacDi-armid's later poems are in negotiation with orthodox 1930s Marxist prescriptions for literature. In "Dìreadh II," for example, MacDi-armid eagerly writes that he feels he has Dmitry Furmanov beside him to help him with his poem, "Furmanov, with that special quality he had / Of being able to see himself objectively, / To weigh himself in the scales of the Communist Cause / As I here my devotion to Scotland / In the balance of the whole world's purpose." Furmanov, MacDiarmid reminds us in a note, was the First Secretary of the Moscow Association of Proletarian Writers "which gathered under its wing the overwhelming majority of the growing proletarian cad-res of Soviet literature." But if one wants the advice of a Furmanov, one will soon be knocking at the door of Zhdanov—if Zhdanov is not first knocking at one's own. And eventually the Ode to Stalin will follow, as it did at some point before 1945 when MacDiarmid shouts out the battle-cry of the MacDonalds at Tippermuir and In-verlochy, "Lamh dearg aboo!"—"The Red Hand to Victory"—and says:

Ah, Stalin, we Scots who had our first home
In Caucasian Georgia like yourself see how

The processes of history in their working out
Bring East and West together in general human triumph now.

Tell that to Gumilev, Akhmatova, Mandelstam, and Tsvetayeva.
I don't mean to suggest that MacDiarmid hardened into a strictly
ideological position. The old Antisyzygy saved him from that, and
he is capable, to the utter consternation of Marxist critics like David
Craig, of expressing the most pristine idealism even in the last of his
hymns to Lenin: "Only one or two in every million men today /
Know that thought is reality—and thought alone!" and saying quite
clearly in "Talking With Five Thousand People in Edinburgh" that
he "must be a Bolshevik / Before the Revolution, but I'll cease to be
one quick / when Communism comes to rule the roost / For real literature can exist only where it's produced by madmen, hermits, heretics, / Dreamers, rebels, sceptics, / And such a door of utterance
has been given to me / As none may close . . ." The fact is, however,
that at least from the time of *First Hymn to Lenin and Other Poems*
(1931), that door MacDiarmid speaks of so proudly has a guard
standing in it.

During the period when MacDiarmid was failing to produce in
To Circumjack Cencrastus the work which was intended to be an even
more ambitious and comprehensive poem in Scots that *A Drunk
Man*, a whole series of personal misfortunes occurred which took
him out of the mainstream of Scottish literary and political life and
isolated him in the Shetland Islands. There MacDiarmid stayed, on
the little isle of Whalsay, from 1933 to 1942. He had suffered a serious fall from a London bus in 1929, and his first marriage had broken up shortly afterward. A regular job fell through in London and
another in Liverpool lasted for only a year. MacDiarmid and his second wife, Valda Trevlyn, then left for the Shetlands. After two years
of grinding poverty living in the most austere conditions imaginable
on barren, stony Whalsay, MacDiarmid suffered a complete nervous
breakdown and was obliged to spend six weeks in hospital in Perth.
After that, he wrote almost exclusively in English and in modes
and forms very different from those to which his readers were accustomed.

In an excellent recent study, *Hugh MacDiarmid: The Man and His
Work*, Nancy K. Gish clarifies something that the publication history
of MacDiarmid's books—and also the dates in *The Complete Poems*—
totally obscures. *All* of MacDiarmid's later work, and not just those
poems and books published during the decade in the Shetlands,
was written before 1942. This explains a great deal. It explains, for

example, the very strange feeling one has encountering poems about the Spanish Civil War, tirades against Roy Campbell, hymns to Lenin, odes to Stalin, and the desire for the presence of Furmanov beside the writing desk in books published in the 1950s, 1960s, and 1970s. It is as if W. H. Auden, instead of revising the political sentiments of his early poetry when it reappeared in his collected and selected volumes, had instead left it untouched and unpublished until twenty or thirty years after it was written—then offering the public, say, "Spain 1937" or "A Communist to Others" as new poems in the middle of the Viet Nam war. At least there now seems to be an explanation for the anachronistic and often embarrassing rhetoric, tone and political context of much of the poetry in Volume 2 of *The Complete Poems*. There is, in fact, no "later" MacDiarmid. There is only early and middle MacDiarmid.

If most of the overtly political or propagandistic poems written in the Whalsay exile fail to convince by the standards, say, of Brecht's best work, poems such as "On a Raised Beach" and "Lament for the Great Music" more than make up for this failure. When the practical Marxism of the propaganda poems becomes the philosophical materialism of "On a Raised Beach," MacDiarmid, in fact, is capable of producing in English work which equals in its power of expression and depth of vision the best of his work in Scots. In contrast to his great poem of philosophical drunkenness, this grappling with matter in the form of Whalsay rocks and stones is appalling in its sobriety and stone-like austerity. Life in the Shetlands, MacDiarmid wrote in an article, was a "splendid discipline." In a pitiless place he disciplined himself to write an increasingly pitiless poetry. He describes his situation in "Lament for the Great Music," his poem about the pibrochs and the pipers of the Ceol Mor:

> I am as lonely and unfrequented as your music is.
> I have had to get rid of all my friends,
> All those to whom I had to accommodate myself.
> If one's capital consists in a calling
> And a mission in life one cannot afford to keep friends.
> I could not stand undivided and true amongst them.
> Only in the solitude of my thought can I be myself
> Or remember you clearly . . .

Undivided, lonely and unfrequented in the solitude of his thought, MacDiarmid contemplates the stones in "On a Raised

Beach." I must quote at length to do anything remotely like justice to
the character of the writing here:

Deep conviction or preference can seldom
Find direct terms in which to express itself.
Today on this shingle shelf
I understand this pensive reluctance so well,
This not discommendable obstinacy,
These contrivances of an inexpressive critical feeling,
These stones with their resolve that Creation shall not be
Injured by iconoclasts and quacks . . .

Bread from stones is my sole and desperate dearth,
From stones, which are to the Earth as to the sunlight
Is the naked sun which is for no man's sight . . .
I must begin with these stones as the world began.

This is no heap of broken images.
Let men find the faith that builds mountains
Before they seek the faith that moves them. Men cannot hope
To survive the fall of the mountains
Which they will no more see than they saw their rise
Unless they are more concentrated and determined,
Truer to themselves and with more to be true to,
Than these stones, and as inerrable as they are.
Their sole concern is that what can be shaken
Shall be shaken and disappear
And only the unshakable be left.
What hardihood in any man has part or parcel in the latter
It is necessary to make a stand and maintain it forever.
These stones go through Man, straight to God, if there is one . . .
These stones will reach us long before we reach them.
Cold, undistracted, eternal and sublime.
They will stem all the torrents of vicissitude forever
With a more than Roman peace.

What happens to us
Is irrelevant to the world's geology
But what happens to the world's geology
Is not irrelevant to us.
We must reconcile ourselves to the stones,
Not the stones to us . . .

Conjure a fescue to teach me with from this
And I will listen to you but until then
Listen to me—Truth is not crushed;
It crushes, gorgonises all else into itself.
The trouble is to know it when you see it?
You will have no trouble with it when you do.
Do not argue with me. Argue with these stones.
Truth has no trouble in knowing itself.
This is it. The hard fact. The inoppugnable reality,
Here is something for you to digest.
Eat this and we'll see what appetite you have left
For a world hereafter.
I pledge you in the first and last crusta,
The rocks rattling in the bead-proof seas . . .

And all who speak glibly may rest assured
That to better their oratory they will have the whole earth
For a Demosthenean pebble to roll in their mouths.

Several years ago in a review of Robert Pinsky's *The Situation of Poetry*, I proposed MacDiarmid's long poems in English as a test of Pinsky's theories of discursive poetry, his enthusiasm for a poetry which manifests the prose virtues of clarity, flexibility, efficiency, and cohesiveness, along with "the freedom and scope of speech." Pinsky had asked for a poetry capable of "talking, predicating, and moving directly through a subject as systematically as one would walk from one place to another." Poems like "On a Raised Beach" and "Lament for the Great Music" contain passages that more than justify arguments in favor of a discursive poetics—Pinsky's or anyone else's. But MacDiarmid wrote thousands of lines on Whalsay which, as G. S. Fraser has pointed out, are not written in imitation of discourse—like Dryden's "Religio Laici" or Pope's "An essay on Criticism" where "the real thinking has been done in prose, or silently, before the composition of verse starts"—but which exist as true, naked discourse itself and include "a sense of fumbling and groping with an emphasis not on the poetic product but on the poetic process." The reader must struggle with this issue himself in *In Memoriam James Joyce, The Kind of Poetry I Want, Dìreadh*, and other poems from which short (or even long) quotations are virtually without meaning. I hope I have not given the impression that these poems should be avoided. My actual feeling about the matter is, quite the contrary, that they represent a challenge to many of our preconceptions about poetry which critics such as Pinsky, Fraser and Nancy Gish have only begun to engage.

Volume 2 of *The Complete Poems of Hugh MacDiarmid* runs to more than 750 pages of closely printed lines, just less than the length of *The Cantos*. With all of its fumbling and groping, the volume contains passage after passage of enormous interest, and it certainly focuses the reader's attention on the question of poetic process. Everyone should at least have a go at *In Memoriam James Joyce*. I fear I can only report that, in my own case, I have not yet made up my mind about the poems. They are simultaneously fascinating and infuriating. It is extraordinary to think that they were all written in less than ten years. I would say that the characteristic pitilessness of the best poems from the Whalsay period—and the writing from this period includes about a third of Volume 1 as well as everything in Volume 2—is both its strength and its weakness, and here the inevitable contrast *is* with *The Cantos*. MacDiarmid would clearly second Pound in the complaint which Artemis raises against pity in Canto XXX:

> Pity spareth so many an evil thing.
> Pity befouleth April,
> Pity is the root and the spring.
> Now if no fayre creature followeth me
> It is on account of Pity,
> It is on account that Pity forbideth them slaye.

But Pound's pitilessness broke down in Pisa, at St. Elizabeth's, and in the "Drafts and Fragments." When pity flows into the poem, *The Cantos* are transfigured: "Ysolt, Ydone, / have compassion, / Picarda, compassion / By the wing'd head, / by the caduceus, / compassion; / By the horns of Isis-Luna, / compassion . . . J'ai eu pitié des autres. / Pas assez! Pas assez!" From the early "What maitters 't wha we kill" (cf. Orwell's objection to Auden's famous phrase, "necessary murder") to the characteristic later expressions of complete contempt for the masses who cannot share the poet's heightened historical and cosmic consciousness, MacDiarmid's pitilessness is unrelenting. It is difficult to be certain whether in other circumstances this would have made him a Stalinist commissar or gotten him shot. Possibly both. At any rate, the steely gaze in this mostly unread work both gives it a commanding claim on our attention and diminishes it as human utterance.

From *Another Chicago Magazine*, 1987

Scottish Poetry after MacDiarmid

Maurice Lindsay and R. L. Mackie, eds., *A Book of Scottish Verse*,
Robert Hale; Maurice Lindsay, ed., *Modern Scottish Poetry: An
Anthology of the Scottish Renaissance*, Carcanet Press; Sorley MacLean,
Spring Tide and Neap Tide, Canongate; Sorley MacLean, *Poems to
Eimhir* (translated from the Gaelic by Iain Crichton Smith),
Northern House; Iain Crichton Smith, *Selected Poems*, Carcanet
Press; Iain Crichton Smith, *A Life*, Carcanet Press; Duncan Glen,
Realities: Poems, Akros Publications; Duncan Glen, ed., *Akros 50* and
51, Akros Publications; W. S. Graham, *Collected Poems*, Faber and
Faber; Sorley MacLean, *Barran Agus Asbhuain: Poems by Sorley
MacLean Read by Himself*, Claddagh Records.

Having tried in my last column to grapple with the full career
of Hugh MacDiarmid in about ten manuscript pages, I must now go
on as promised and attempt the perhaps even more daunting task of
surveying the poetry written during the Scottish Renaissance (as
critics have called it) initiated by MacDiarmid's work and speculate
a bit about contemporary Scottish poetry as represented in the
books and journals listed above.

This task is made easier by the fact that the most recent edition
of Maurice Lindsay's *Modern Scottish Poetry* really does aim to be
"definitive and representative," as the blurb-writer has it, and because contributors to numbers 50 and 51 of Duncan Glen's *Akros*, for
many years the most distinguished of Scottish poetry magazines but
sadly ceasing publication after number 51, enter into dialogue with
Lindsay and the poets he anthologizes. A very useful feature of *Akros 51* is the series of brief essays by twenty critics about twenty
modern Scottish poems, nearly all of them to be found in *Modern*

Scottish Poetry. It also contains reviews of collected and selected volumes by Robert Garioch, G. S. Fraser, Edwin Morgan, and Iain Crichton Smith. *Akros 50*, meanwhile, contains interviews with Duncan Glen, Donald Campbell, and George Bruce, as well as extended statements on Scottish poetry from 1965–1981 by Ian Bowman, Ruth McQuillan, Ken Edward Smith and Geddes Thomson. And should the particularly zealous reader want something like the *full* context (from King James and Henryson) for MacDiarmid and his successors, that is available in the Lindsay/R. L. Mackie *Book of Scottish Verse*, a St. Martin's title recently remaindered in this country but still for sale from Robert Hale Ltd. in England.

From the first edition of *Modern Scottish Poetry* (Faber and Faber 1949) onward, Lindsay's reading of the Scottish Renaissance included major work in three languages: Gaelic, Scots and English. Arguing at that time that "for many reasons English cannot and must not ever be allowed to supplant Scots," he put forward "the Scots of MacDiarmid and the Lallans of [Douglas] Young and [Sydney Goodsir] Smith" in representative poems which expressed "nuances in Scottish life and thought" which English poems could never express. For the sake of similar nuances and subtleties—as well as for their quality as poetry—he included selections from the Gaelic work of Sorley MacLean. By 1965, however, in his preface to the second Faber edition, Lindsay was writing that "few writers of any consequence today employ Lallans" and that "every new census reveals a further decline in the number of those who speak, let alone read, the Gaelic." Whatever the achievements of certain individual poets—the unique work of MacLean, and the Scots poems of MacDiarmid, Garioch, Young, Sydney Goodsir Smith, and others—the Scottish Renaissance, if it was still alive, looked as if it were becoming an affair of the English language. Although the most recent edition of the anthology (now published by Carcanet) includes five poets born after 1940, Lindsay clearly now regards the movement in historical perspective. "It seems," he says, "that the impetus of the Scottish Renaissance—though not, of course, the continuing validity of its achievement—may be on the wane." If the original aim of the Renaissance implied, as Lindsay says in his second edition, "close association with efforts to revive and strengthen Lallans and Gaelic," and if, as he said in his first edition, the poet's "Scottish psyche must feel, in some degree, frustrated" unless he can use Scots, Gaelic, and English "with equal skill," then the work of younger poets in the third edition would seem to mark an end of a late stage of the Renaissance, and perhaps of the real vitality behind its initial impulse. More than half a century, after all, has passed since MacDiarmid published his first Scots poems. His most important successors are themselves now passing from the scene. And Sorley MacLean—a conundrum among anachronisms—can claim as successors only Crichton Smith and Derick Thomson.

Which does not mean that we have an excuse not to try (at least in translation) to read him. As Tony Harrison has written in "Art and Extinction," "Silence and poetry have their own reserves. / The numbered creatures flourish less and less. / A language near extinction best preserves / the deepest grammar of our nothingness." And if we can't *read* Gaelic, then at least we can *hear* it—brilliantly read by the author himself on MacLean's Claddagh recording (the same company that offers the complete reading by MacDiarmid of *A Drunk Man Looks at The Thistle*). Listening to the recording, those of us without Gaelic can understand the enthusiasm, indeed the wonder, expressed by MacDiarmid, Douglas Young, Crichton Smith, and others over the astonishing emergence of a Gaelic poetry of European stature two hundred years after Alexander MacDonald and Duncan Ban MacIntyre. The sounds of the language are gorgeous and the incantatory power of MacLean's voice emerging out of the oral Highland tradition will hold the listener spellbound through poem after poem. Along with the two LPs, one finds the texts of all poems read both in the original and in English translations by Crichton Smith and MacLean himself. MacLean's translations also appear in the generous bilingual selected volume, *Spring Tide and Neap Tide*, while thirty-five of Smith's are printed (this time without the originals) in the Northern House *Poems to Eimhir*. The available combination of original texts, translations by various hands, and the recordings give one, surprisingly, much greater access to MacLean's work than one might initially have imagined possible. We really do begin to gain a feeling, after a while, for MacLean's language and forms as he engages subjects—including the contemporary politics of the period when most of these poems were written—never before taken up in Gaelic poetry. As for the available translations, it may be that the most valuable and interesting are neither MacLean's own or Crichton Smith's English versions, but the Scots translations made by Douglas Young, some of which are printed in Lindsay's anthology. I reproduce below both the original of MacLean's "Calbharaigh" and what John Herdman calls in *Akros* 51 "one of the most completely successful examples of the translator's art that I know."

Cha n-eil mo shùil air Calbharaigh
no air Bethlehem an àigh

ach air cùil ghrod an Glaschu
far bheil an lobhadh fàis
agus air seòmar an Dun-éideann,
seòmar bochdainn 's cràidh
far am bheil an naoidhean creuchdach
ri aonagraich gu bhàs.

My een are nae on Calvary
or the Bethlehem they praise,
but on shitten back-lands in Glesca toun
whaur growan life decays,
and a stairheid room in an Embro land,
a chalmer o puirtith and skaith
whaur monie a shilpet bairnikie
gaes smoorit doun til daith.

John Herdman is certainly right to find in this Gaelic lyric the influence of MacDiarmid's early work and to find in its subject matter a good reason for it to be translated into Scots rather than English. The poem, he argues, "registers the shock experienced by the Highland poet on becoming immediately aware of slum conditions in the industrial Lowlands of the Thirties." Young's translation captures both the lyric simplicity of the original and its deeply felt outrage at the poverty encountered in Glasgow and Edinburgh. In Scots, it sounds like MacDiarmid. In Gaelic it sounds like nothing else at all.

Iain Crichton Smith has an excellent poem in his selected volume "For Poets Writing in English over in Ireland" who "have chosen with youth's superb confidence" not to write in Irish. Crichton Smith—older, visiting the Irish poets at Connemara, and understanding that "a different language is a world / we find our way about in with a stick"—prepares to go home. "To English? Gaelic?" He is permanently torn between them, unlike the Irish poets who, like Seamus Heaney at the end of "Station Island," must have decided that "the English language belongs to us." But does Crichton Smith, born on the Gaelic-speaking island of Lewis, belong to the English language? Never entirely, never without compromise, and only as one who has learned English as a second language and who understands that the readership for his poems in Gaelic is depressingly small and threatens to cease existing altogether. So he writes both in Gaelic *and* English, not feeling entirely comfortable with either, and not willing, like MacLean, to make the radical gesture of restricting himself to his native and dying tongue, but also unable to write in English without feeling about Gaelic as the Irish poet who wrote (in Irish) about his wife who had died: "Half of my side you were, half of my seeing, / half of my walking you were, half of my hearing." So it must be for the Crichton Smiths of Scotland, if not for the Sorley MacLeans.

If the future of Gaelic poetry looks utterly bleak, what about poetry written in Scots? There is no question about the recent past of this poetry, about the authority and vitality of work in Scots published in the three editions of *Modern Scottish Poetry* by poets born in the first two decades of the twentieth century. The work of Robert Garioch, Douglas Young, and Sydney Goodsir Smith is especially impressive. Garioch, in particular, seems to be sometimes a better comic and a less uneven poet in Scots than MacDiarmid. Critics have often stressed the influence on his own writing of the translations he had made of Giuseppe Gioacchino Belli's Roman sonnets, an influence that has led his Scots poems away from the synthetic Lallans of MacDiarmid and Sydney Goodsir Smith in the direction of what Ken Edward Smith calls in *Akros* 51 something "nearer home, not so much the Edinburgh of the poets as a poet's Edinburgh, Rose Street without rose-coloured spectacles." Garioch, he believes, creates a persona "which gives the poet a genuine social role" in a poetry which, though always local, is never parochial. On the opposite side of town—in the Edinburgh of poets—Sydney Goodsir Smith was making in the late 1940s the twenty-four elegies published in *Under the Eildon Tree*, a tour de force which, with its explosive sexual energy and verbal invention, can compete with MacDiarmid's *Drunk Man* on some of the latter's own terms. Tumbling all over itself, the well-known thirteenth elegy sounds like this:

> I got her in the Black Bull
> (The Black Bull o Norroway),
> Gin I mynd richt, in Leith Street,
> Doun the stair at the corner forenent
> The Fun Fair and Museum o Monstrosities,
>   The Tyke-faced Loun, the Cunyiars Den
>   And siclike.
> I tine her name the nou, and cognomen for that—
> Aiblins it was Deirdre, Ariadne, Calliope,
> Gaby, Jacquette, Katerina, Sandra
>   Or sunkots; exotic, I expeck.
> A wee bit piece

> O' what our faithers maist unaptlie
> But romanticallie designatit 'Fluff'.
> My certie! Nae muckle o Fluff
> About the hures o Reekie!
> Dour as stane, the like stane
> As biggit the unconquerable citie
> Whar they pullulate,
> Infestan
> The wynds and closes, squares
> And public promenads
> —The bonnie craturies!
> —But til our winter's tale.

Meanwhile, both Tom and Alexander Scott were producing notable work in the vernacular, while Edwin Morgan eventually turned to Scots for his remarkable translations of Mayakovsky, *Wi the Haill Voice*.

So much for the past. Against Maurice Lindsay's present feeling that "few writers of any consequence today employ Lallans" stands the vigorous optimism and, until very recently, the editorial energy of Duncan Glen. In an interview published in *Akros* 50, Glen argues that "it just happens to be a fact that some form of Scots remains the mother tongue of the masses of Lowland Scots." Glen believes in the future of a poetry written in what he takes to be a living, changing language; he writes in this language himself (allowing some older words from literary Scots to be introduced into poems essentially based on contemporary spoken Scots if this can be done "without putting a strain on the poetry"), and he provided between 1965 and 1983 the leading forum in *Akros* for other poets doing the same thing, or at any rate something similar. It is interesting that George Bruce—a poet who writes in English and whose initial response to MacDiarmid's Scots lyrics was "This can't possibly be true and even if it is true I doubt if it is desirable"—affirms the "closer-to-speech verse of Alexander Scott" as "the kind of thing which it is really possible to build on," and finds a natural outcome of Scott's way with the vernacular in the work of Duncan Glen. "Here," he says in an *Akros* 50 interview, "was a kind of reliance which related to the everyday world outside, close to the way people would speak, and suggested that the identity was not something struggled for or created. It was in [Glen's work] and in these other people and therefore quite important things were happening at a level whereby the whole thing could spread. I couldn't see it spreading from MacDiarmid. I certainly couldn't see it spreading from Sydney Goodsir Smith." It is true that Glen, however devoted he may be to the legacy of MacDiarmid—and he is *very* devoted to that legacy—writes a poetry sounding quite different from that of his master. He describes his literary Scots as "generally more anglicized in vocabulary than the spoken Scots of my grandfather . . . but still Scots." He claims the right to draw upon both old and new words depending upon his intention in a particular poem, but always remains true . . .

> . . . to a modern anglicized Scots because it is my language, rather than to some false-to-me Scots of the past or of areas foreign to me. In my head Scots and Scottish English with a Scottish pronunciation and twist are inseparably intertwined and in being true to myself I am true to that leid, even if I draw in some literary Scots as well as the Scots I spoke as a boy, so creating my own distinctive literary language. As Donald Campbell said in his poem "Bilingual Manifesto" . . . he, like me, is looking for "an unkent airt whaur baith leids mell and meet." There is no pessimism there in Donald's poem and none in my poetry. We believe in a Scots leid of the present and the future, not of the past.

Although "an unkent airt whaur baith leids mell and meet" sounds suspiciously like the kind of thing MacDiarmid might have dismissed contemptuously with sentiments like those expressed in his famous lines, "I'll hae nae hauf-way house, but aye be whaur / Extremes meet," the position of Campbell and Glen nonetheless strikes me as the one most likely to result in a contemporary Scots poetry with at least a chance of proving Maurice Lindsay wrong. American readers, I think, will respond to Glen's work with some enthusiasm. Much less dense and crabbed than much of Mac-Diarmid, it appears to have been influenced, like George Bruce's English poetry, by Whitman, Williams, and other American poets. As Glen says of *Akros*, his own poetry "takes its Scottishness and its internationalism for granted without needing to prove either." It is difficult to quote effectively from his work since his strongest writing comes in extended cycles and book-length poems. (*Realities*, which I list but cannot quote from, is an extremely rewarding single poem of 190 pages in fifteen parts.) Lindsay's selection, however, is instructive even if not altogether typical. Glen's short lyric on his father's death certainly will be compared by anyone who knows it to

MacDiarmid's "At My Father's Grave"—and not, I would say, to the disadvantage of the former.

> Staunin noo aside his braw bress-haunled coffin
> I mind him fine aside the black shinin range
> In his grey strippit trousers, galluses and nae collar
> For the flannel shirt. My faither.
>
> I ken him fine thae twenty and mair years ago
> Wi his great bauchles and flet auld kep;
> And in his pooch the spottit reid neepkin
> For usin wi snuff. My faither.
>
> And ben in the lobby abune the braw shoon and spats,
> Aside the silk waistcoat and claw-haimmer jaicket
> Wi its muckle oxter pooch, hung the lum hat.
> They caa'd him Jock the Lum. My faither.
>
> And noo staunin wi thae braw shinin haunles
> See him and me baith laid oot in the best
> Black suitin wi proper white all weel chosen.
> And dinna ken him. *My father.*

"My faither." Or *My father.* Writing in English doesn't necessarily mean that the Scottish poet appears "laid oot in the best / Black suitin wi proper white all weel chosen." For many poets, and increasingly so as the years go by, English is clearly the only option, and is naturally and natively spoken by poems wearing, as it were, "galluses and nae collar / For the flannel shirt." Maurice Lindsay's most ardent attempt to redefine the Scottish Renaissance to give prominence to poetry written in English occurs not in the third edition of *Modern Scottish Poetry,* but in his 1983 introduction to *A Book of Scottish Verse* in which he says that the Scottish Renaissance has now turned out to be essentially "a new mood of questioning sensibility applied throughout the breadth and substance of modern life, and set down in three languages . . . but, above all, in English tuned and tempered to reflect the overtones and traditions of the older tongues whose daily use and impact unfortunately dwindles from year to year." The reader of this column will remember similar arguments having been advanced on behalf of Anglo-Welsh poetry, but he will also remember various rejoinders to those arguments. But so be it. We return, again in the footsteps of MacDiarmid, to the English language. Edwin Muir had argued from the beginning that a modern poetry in Scots or Gaelic made no sense, that Scottish poets ought to write in English. And yet how utterly dark, as of 1941, was his English version of the state of Scotland:

> Now smoke and dearth and money everywhere,
> Mean heirlooms of each fainter generation,
> And mummied housegods in their musty niches,
> Burns and Scott, sham bards to a sham nation,
> And spiritual defeat wrapped warm in riches,
> No pride but pride of pelf. Long since the young
> Fought in great bloody battles to carve out
> This towering pulpit of the Golden Calf.
> Montrose, Mackail, Argyle, perverse and brave,
> Twisted the stream, unhooped the ancestral hill.
> Never had Dee or Don or Yarrow or Till
> Huddled such thriftless honour in a grave.

And this view of Scotland is not at all uncharacteristic of later poets who follow Muir and write in English.

My guess is that the reputation of some of the best Scottish poets writing in English is more secure in the United States than is that of those, with the exception of MacDiarmid, writing in Scots. For this reason, I think I need only affirm the great interest of work by W. S. Graham, Edwin Morgan, George Mackay Brown, Burns Singer, Robin Fulton, and Douglas Dunn. Several of these poets have London publishers—Graham and Dunn being major presences on the Faber and Faber list—and most are available, from one distributor or another, in this country. It is also worth noting that three of these six poets have lived mostly outside Scotland, Graham having settled until his death last year at the opposite end of the island, in Cornwall. In spite of his exile, Graham's work maintained certain quintessential Scottish characteristics, and, in fact, one might invoke, as I did when discussing MacDiarmid, G. Gregory Smith's notion of "The Caledonian Antisyzygy" in order to describe some of its most salient features. Without employing the term itself, Michael Schmidt (in *Eleven British Poets*) has appreciated "the skill with which Graham can change tone, in a single line, from raucousness to tenderness, from hectoring to a whisper. This skill," he rightly observes, "is characteristic of verse in Scottish dialect: to achieve it in standard English is no mean feat. It depends very much on the presence of a defined voice behind the poems." When the voice speaks—in the last poem of his *Collected Poems*—it sounds like this:

> Did I behave badly
> On the field at Culloden?
> I lie sore-wounded now
>
> By all activities, and
> The terrible acts of my time
> Are only a distant sound . . .
>
> Nessie Dunsmuir, I say
> Wheesht wheesht to myself
> To help me now to go
>
> Under into somewhere
> In the redcoat rain.
> Buckle me for the war.

The occasion is in fact domestic, Nessie Dunsmuir being the poet's wife, and the reference to the Battle of Culloden functions, as Schmidt says, "with tender and ironic intent in an apology." But one might ask, with respect to Scottish poetry in general, are all Cullodens now domestic, personal? Certainly one reason for the attention paid to Irish poetry written in the course of the last two decades has had to do with the skill with which the best poets have been able to grapple with public and political subjects while locating the values of the private (including the domestic) life in the larger contexts of history. Quoting Yeats's "Easter 1916" (and he might have quoted something by Heaney or Montague) in his review of Crichton Smith's *Selected Poems*, Geddes Thomson writes that "no Scottish poet has had a chance to echo the communal consciousness in such ringing tones for hundreds of years"—not since, perhaps, Culloden! And Thomson finds an awareness of this problem at the heart of Crichton Smith's work, the work of a poet who has said—"very often I feel ashamed of Scotland."

More than a few contributors to *Akros* 50 and 51 refer to the defeat of the Devolution Referendum in 1979 while speaking of the sense of shame, guilt and inertia which they, like Crichton Smith, feel has overtaken the public life. "Since the debacle of the Devolution referendum," says Donald Campbell, "Scotland has been engulfed by a great tidal wave of provincialism," and Geddes Thomson writes that "our most recent failure to know ourselves . . . has added dimensions of despair and apathy to the unresolved social and political questions that hang like miasmata over Scottish cultural life." It is precisely this climate of feeling in which Iain Crichton

Smith's *Selected Poems* and verse autobiography, *A Life*, must find their way to a Scottish readership. And it is also *from* this climate of feeling that the books emerge.

The life in *A Life* can, in some respects, be seen as representative of a generation coming to maturity during World War II: a childhood and adolescence spent in a Gaelic-speaking community, four years at Aberdeen University, two years of National Service after the war, teaching school and observing both the human and the school-masterly species at Clydebank and Oban for thirty years, and then Taynuilt after 1983—"alone with my typewriter at last"—and a kind of homecoming. A pretty drab existence, except in the telling. The *Selected Poems* tells the same story in a more leisurely way and with greater formal variety, although never with any real Yeatsian gaiety or MacDiarmidesque audacity. (Perhaps those poets "Writing in English over in Ireland" had the right idea. At least they entered a dance, "another world . . . echoing with its own music.") But there is great and ultimately stoic integrity to this work of Crichton Smith's, and a clear refusal, as Geddes Thomson sees, to accept "The adamantine scorn for messy human considerations which MacDiarmid expresses in the hymns to Lenin." Crichton Smith also has his poem to Lenin where he finds it "Simple to condemn / the unsymmetrical, simple to condone / that which oneself is not." Instead of doing this—Devolution or no Devolution—one might understand that:

> . . . the true dialectic is to turn
> in the infinitely complex, like a chain
> we steadily burn through, steadily forge and burn
> not to be dismissed in any poem
> by admiration for the ruthless man
> nor for the saint but for the moving on
> into the endlessly various, real, human,
> world which is no new era, shining dawn.

In their various ways, this seems to me to be what the best Scottish poets are doing just now, whether in English or Scots. But none of them looks to be producing a contemporary equivalent for the display of virtuosity, energy and vision that was *A Drunk Man Looks at The Thistle*. For that, one must turn to the work of a remarkable novelist whose massive book, *Lanark*, is also called "A Life"— Alasdair Gray. In this fiction, and in other fictions by Gray, one may be seeing the emergence of a major figure as independent of groups, movements, twilights, renaissances, revivals, and the like as Joyce himself. Alternatively, once could turn to the apotheosis of concretism in the environmental work made and assembled by Ian Hamilton Finlay—MacDiarmid's nemesis and living contradiction—at Stonypath garden in Dunsyre, Lanarkshire. But both Alasdair Gray and Finlay would require a separate essay; and, besides, I should bring this survey to an end.

From *Another Chicago Magazine*, 1987

Inside History and Outside History: Seamus Heaney, Eavan Boland, and Contemporary Irish Poetry

Seamus Heaney, *The Redress of Poetry: An Inaugural Lecture delivered before the University of Oxford on 24 October 1989*, Oxford University Press; Seamus Heaney, *The Government of the Tongue: Selected Prose 1978–1987*, The Noonday Press; Seamus Heaney, *The Place of Writing*, Scholars Press; Eavan Boland, *A Kind of Scar*, Attic Press; Eavan Boland, *The Journey and Other Poems*, Carcanet Press; Eavan Boland, *Selected Poems*, Carcanet Press; Eavan Boland, *Outside History*, Carcanet Press and W. W. Norton and Co.

In 1989, Seamus Heaney was elected to succeed Peter Levi as Oxford Professor of Poetry. Before turning to his inaugural lecture—which he has called *The Redress of Poetry* (abridged in the *TLS* and now published entire by OUP)—along with some key moments in his two recent volumes of essays as a way to introduce a few issues in contemporary Irish poetry parallel to some I have discussed in recent columns on the Scottish and the Welsh, I think I should note that a minor prophecy ventured back in *ACM* 14 turned out to be accurate. I noted there, as Levi assumed his own professorship, that one of his more remarkable experiments had been a series of verse sermons in rhyming couplets first published in a volume called *Death is a Pulpit*, and asked: "Will the Oxford Professor turn to verse at some point in his series of lectures?" Well, indeed he did, although he waited until the very end of his five-year term before delivering his verse-lecture, *Goodbye to the Art of Poetry*. Because it has now been published (by Anvil Press), and because it anticipates in some ways what Heaney has to say in his inaugural lecture, I will quote some lines from near the beginning.

> What poetry and what greatness may be
> bothers all professors of poetry:
> there is something ridiculous I confess
> in sharp-eyed connoisseurship of greatness:
> better to seek for what is genuine:
> a world spacious enough to wander in,
> the truth live in the ear as truth of tone,
> a line that rings stone ringing on stone
> or a line like the sea heard in a shell,
> never again so clearly or so well
> as it was in the beginning, in childhood,
> when poetry was the untrodden wood.

After bothering himself, ridiculously or not, with a variety of definitions of what "poetry may be," Levi concludes that he thinks "Pasternak's is the most sublime: / 'eternity's hostage in the hands of time'." When Heaney expresses his pleasure with Levi's final lecture by saying he felt it helped confirm him in his new situation, I think he may be pondering, more than anything else, that Pasternak quote.

What he *says*, in fact, is that, as an Irish poet, he is glad that Levi had begun and ended his own tenure by exercising two ancient offices of the poet in Gaelic society: to lament the dead and to give praise to the living. His own aim, in his inaugural lecture, will be to examine how poetry "relates to our existence as citizens of society—how it is 'of present use.'" His focus, that is, has to do with what happens to poetry "in the hands of [our own] time" where it is constrained by a variety of political, moral, and ethical imperatives. In the end, however—as also in many of the essays appearing in *The Government of the Tongue* and *The Place of Writing*—his praise of the living turns out to be praise of the living word, eternity's hostage, and that domain of the genuine in poetry which Levi calls "a world spacious enough to wander in," a "truth live in the ear as truth of tone," and "a line like the sea heard in a shell . . . / as it was in the beginning." Present use—a notion that poetry's redress "comes from its being a revelation of potential that is denied or constantly threatened by circumstances" understood to be political or social—is in tension, sometimes fruitful and sometimes not, with the promptings of the auditory imagination, and "unless the redress of poetry is effected primarily by work that sets itself upright by virtue of free, uncensored impulse, its other aspiration to correct the world's imbalances will be seriously debilitated." Heaney believes that a sin against the ear is "the poetic equivalent of the sin against the Holy Spirit."

As Heaney's sense of "redress" points two ways, so also does his related notion of the tongue's "government." I don't know if the phrase "the government of the tongue" appeared first in his T. S. Eliot Memorial lecture of 1986 (which in turn gave him a title for the volume of selected prose) or in his sonnet sequence called "The Clearances," first published in that same year and later in *The Haw Lantern*, in which the noun becomes a finite verb and Heaney, in that other Gaelic office of lamenting the dead, writes in the fourth sonnet of the eight in memory of his mother that he "governed [his] tongue / in front of her" because "with more challenge than pride" she'd tell him that he knew things and could say things which she didn't know and couldn't or wouldn't say.

> I governed my tongue
> In front of her, a genuinely well-
> adjusted adequate betrayal
> Of what I knew better, I'd *naw* and *aye*
> And decently relapse into the wrong
> Grammar which kept us allied and at bay.

The social context of poetry sometimes makes for similar "well-adjusted adequate betrayals" from its poets which keep them also— poet and society, like Heaney and his mother—"allied and at bay." "The vitality and insouciance of lyric poetry," says Heaney in the title essay from *The Government of the Tongue*, "its relish of its own inventiveness, its pleasuring strain, always comes under threat when poetry remembers that its self-gratification must be perceived as a kind of affront to a world preoccupied with its own imperfections, pains and catastrophes." In such a context, poetry learns to govern its tongue. "All poets who get beyond the first excitement of being blessed by the achievement of poetic form confront, sooner or later, the question which Zbigniew Herbert confronts in 'A Knocker'," his poem about having only a piece of wood and a wooden stick for an instrument, not "the green bell of a tree" or "the blue bell of water," and how to respond when he strikes the board with his stick to its prompting for "the moralist's dry poem / yes-yes / no-no." But Heaney also believes "that poetry is its own reality and no matter how much a poet may concede to the corrective pressures of social, moral, political and historical reality, the ultimate fidelity must be to the demands and promise of the artistic event." The primal "excitement of being blessed by the achievement of poetic form" was indeed not only the initial, but also the authentic prompting. Poets who confront the question of Herbert's "A Knocker" end up, "if they are lucky . . . outstripping it rather than answering it directly." Herbert himself writes a poem persuading us that "we are against lyric poetry's culpable absorption in its own process by an entirely successful instance of that very process in action: here is a lyric about a knocker which claims that lyric is inadmissible."

The convolutions of all this ought to suggest that Heaney's search for a fundamental permission to write an unfettered and perhaps autonomous poetry has become nearly obsessional. While the poetry in *The Haw Lantern* has to some extent distanced itself from the immediate issues of contemporary history, the recent prose has, if anything, intensified Heaney's "argument with himself" characteristic of the verse from *North* to *Station Island*. Essay after essay grapples with the issue of political/aesthetic tensions in the work of East European, Russian, Irish, and sometimes English poets. Where social, psychological and artistic contradictions have been most extreme—in Czechoslovakia, Poland, and the Soviet Union before 1989—Heaney's attention to a poetry attempting to resolve them is most keen. And he tells us in his introduction to *The Government of the Tongue* that he keeps returning to the poets of the Eastern block "because there is something in their situation that makes them attractive to a reader whose formative experience has been largely Irish . . ." and who has "lived with the awful and demeaning facts of Northern Ireland's history over the last couple of decades." In the essays from that book which I have in mind, and in the inaugural Oxford lecture as well, the argument, although it meanders a bit and admits the voices of various "hecklers" along the way, turns out to have a similar form. All available evidence is marshalled which would warn the poet that he had best "govern his tongue" as Zbigniew Herbert does in "A Knocker" (Heaney's filial and domestic "naw-naw / aye-aye" finding its political analogue in the moral citizen's "yes-yes" / "no-no"). But then comes a turn—anticipated, called into question, but finally affirmed—where "the government of the tongue" is seen fundamentally in terms like these:

> When I thought of "the government of the tongue" as a general title for these lectures, what I had in mind was this aspect

of poetry as its own vindicating force. In this dispensation, the tongue (representing both a poet's personal gift of utterance and the common resources of language itself) has been granted the right to govern. The poetic art is credited with an authority of its own. . . . And just as the poem, in the process of its own genesis, exemplifies a congruence between impulse and right action, so in its repose the poem gives us a premonition of harmonies desired and not inexpensively achieved. In this way, the order of art becomes an achievement intimating a possible order beyond itself, although its relation to that further order remains promissory rather than obligatory. Art is not an inferior reflection of some ordained heavenly system but a rehearsal of it in earthly terms; art does not trace the given map of a better reality but improvises an inspired sketch of it.

Not Platonism, this, but closer to a paraphrase of Pasternak as quoted by Levi: "Eternity's hostage in the hands of time." Although these sentences come early in the essay, Heaney's final assent to what they claim for poetry is deferred until it can be tested by austerities such as Herbert's. In the Oxford lecture, there is merely an exchange of Herberts—the English George replacing the Polish Zbiginiew—but the test is essentially the same and the conclusions fully parallel.

In his observations about Dante in *The Government of the Tongue*, Heaney contrasts two poets, Eliot and Mandelstam, who turned to the *Comedia* "at a moment of mid-life crisis." Although Heaney's own negotiations with Dante go back many years, I think we find him in these essays in a crisis of his own—one brought on perhaps by fame, certainly by the protracted and unresolved years of troubles in the north of Ireland, possibly by the death of his mother. But for the same reason that he refuses to subordinate art and poetry to politics and ideology, his Dante is the Dante of Mandelstam and not the Dante of Eliot. Mandelstam's Dante is not a poet "whose tongue is governed by an orthodoxy or system." Mandelstam found in Dante "a vindication by language" and extolled in his remarkable *Conversations* "the power which poetic imagination wields" and an "idea of imagination as a shaping spirit which it is wrong to disobey." Indeed, it is more Mandelstam himself than Dante who is the exemplary presence in *The Government of the Tongue* and who leads Heaney in his introduction to the volume to propose such aesthetic absolutes as "timeless formal pleasure" in the "release" and "liberated moment" of the poem in which the poet "is intensified in his being and freed from his predicaments." Mandelstam is "a burning reminder of the way in which not only the words 'truth' and 'justice' may be salvaged from the catastrophe of history, but the word 'beauty' also: a reminder that humanity is served by the purely poetic fidelity of the poet to all words in their pristine being." And yet, again, the essays that follow this statement of faith are acknowledged to be "symptomatic of an anxiety that in arrogating to oneself the right to take refuge in form, one is somehow denying the claims of the beggar at the gate." Mandelstam's position—and Heaney's too—must be tested by such claims in the act of writing prose which helps "to allay this worry and to verify what I believe."

In the Oxford lecture—which treats chiefly poetry written in English and so avoids the issue of translation implicit in *The Government of the Tongue*—Heaney finds the conflicting awareness and double sense of "redress" (like the double sense of "government") manifested in the work of poets such as the white Australian Les A. Murray, the black Caribbean Derek Walcott, feminists like Adrienne Rich, and men from the northern English working class like Tony Harrison. Should the poem's redress mean an efficacious "instrumentality in adjusting and correcting the world's imbalances" or "the setting-upright of poetry . . . into a distinct eminence as itself," or somehow both together? When the question is extended to Irish poets in the second essay in *The Place of Writing* and the political issue is Irish nationalism, Heaney improvises a solution with the figure of a lever.

> To work is to move [as with a lever] a certain mass through a certain distance. In the case of poetry, the distance moved through is that which separates the historically and topographically situated place from the written place, the mass moved is one aspect of the writer's historical/biographical experience, and each becomes a factor of the other in the achieved work. The work of art, in other words, involves raising the historical record to a different power.

But the lever of the English language does the moving (for a Walcott or a Rich as much as for a Montague), and even if its fulcrum may be an ideology of one kind or another—Marxist, feminist, nationalist—which denies to English its patriarchal, racist or imperial sway, the poet must nonetheless embrace the handle as he moves the mass. And when the mass occupies its new place (the historical record raised to a different power), what does it become? Is it an imbalance corrected or a free-standing eminence set up? The old questions remain. And, indeed, may not the poet have so keenly worked the lever—kissed the rod, Heaney's willing to admit, of a language programmed with a consciousness perhaps politically subjecting him—that the handle stands erect beside an unmoved mass, and upon it, as upon a flagpole, we find the poet flying, hoisted with his own petard?

Well, I disfigure some of Heaney's figures here, mix and mangle his metaphors. But I cannot leave this business of levers and go on to the prose and verse of Eavan Boland without noticing one more thing. In his essay on recent Irish Poetry in *The Place of Writing*, Heaney talks about the "grave suspicion" among recent Irish poets "of any idiom that might possibly be construed as nationalistic" as a result of the renewed troubles in the north and the increasing difficulty of expressing "fidelity to the ideals of the Irish Literary Revival, which were essentially born of a healthy desire to redress the impositions of cultural imperialism, without seeming to become allied with a terrorist campaign that justified itself by self-righteous rhetoric against British imperialism of the original, historically rejected and politically repugnant sort." Still, in spite of a ban on "the visionary prophetic, the patriotic witness, [and] the national epical" among contemporaries and their eagerness to work exclusively in modes identified as "the ludic, the ironic, the parodic, the satiric, the pathetic, the domestic, the elegiac and the self-inculpatory," a lever of one kind or another still seems to be in their hands. It has just grown to be a very *long* lever, and it has been passed on by Louis MacNeice rather than by Yeats. "MacNeice is clearly an Irish poet who positioned his lever in England and from that position moved his Irish subject matter through a certain revealing distance." With his successors—Derek Mahon, Michael Longley, and Paul Muldoon—" we can begin to consider how important the length of the arm of the lever is when it comes to the actual business of moving a world" which may seem "intractable when wrestled with at close quarters." Indeed, Muldoon's lever on the Troubles "has never been less than the proverbial forty-foot pole, and yet paradoxically he has managed to relay the vehemence and squalor and helplessly self-validating energies which have characterized the history of the last twenty years."

If all this seems true of Muldoon and the others, one begins to wonder where Irish women stand. And I hope it is clear by now that there is something distinctly phallic in this business of lengthening levers. Although Heaney touches upon feminism in his

Oxford lecture and alludes to the poetry of Adrienne Rich, I'm not
aware of any essays by him which engage at length the poetry of
Irish women. Eavan Boland's recent verse and prose are therefore a
useful complement to Heaney's writing on his male contemporaries.
And it's fair to say that Boland wrestles with her world at close
quarters, however difficult that may turn out to be.

   In fact, if myth is a kind of lever, Boland would much rather
drop it in order to push and shove with her bare hands. In *A Kind of
Scar*, recently reprinted in *The American Poetry Review* as "Outside
History," she describes her dismay when, as a young woman, she
turned to the work of Irish male poets and discovered only mythic
and emblematic women in their poems, passive and simplified
women. These poets "moved easily, deftly, as if by right among images of women in which I did not believe and of which I could not
approve. . . . This was especially true where the woman and the
idea of the nation were mixed: where the nation became a woman
and the woman took on a national posture." Sick to death of the
"fictive queens" and "national sibyls"—the Dark Rosaleens and
Cathleen ni Houlihans who bodied forth in poetry the nation as
woman and the woman as nation—Boland was not, however, willing to resign her nationality. She would, indeed, claim her place as a
national poet on behalf of women tired of being the "subjects and
objects of Irish poems" and ready to become the authors of them.
On behalf of women such as herself, that is, but also on behalf of
those women "outside history" whose painful survival or humiliations or defeats had been displaced by the "hollow victories, the
passive images [and] rhyming queens" of a poetry continuing to
trade in distorting myths and exhausted fictions. Boland did not
blame the nationalists for what she had inherited, but rather poets.
"The irony was that few Irish poets were nationalists. By and large,
they had eschewed the fervour and crudity of that ideal. But long
after they had rejected the politics of Irish nationalism, they continued to deploy the emblems and enchantments of its culture. It was
the culture, not the politics, which informed Irish poetry: not the
harsh awakenings, but the old dreams."

   A Kind of Scar is a heady essay, a passionate statement in prose
of a position implicit in Boland's poetry for some time. Perhaps in
part because she lived away from Ireland in London and New York
during nine crucial years, Boland responds all the more intensely to
conventions which she finds mendacious in an Irish poetry from
which she feels she was exiled twice—once as the daughter of a diplomat who lived abroad, and once simply as a daughter. Humiliated

first by anti-Irish bigotry encountered in the London of the 1950s, she found herself eventually internalizing fictions telling her that the Irish nation to which she returned was not available to her in poetry. Her project, analogous to many undertaken by feminists in Britain and America, is made to seem all the more urgent given the obstinacy of at least two cultures.

The aim of Boland's poetry, then, is to repossess her nation on behalf of those, chiefly women, who have been dispossessed, both by history and by literature, as she herself inscribes her signature as part of a tradition which has cut her off from its archive and put her at a distance from its energy. She now sees the poems of resistance and the political songs which helped sustain her as a child in London as dangerous and deceptive in their crude posturing and in their angers, their glamorization of action and resistance. At its deepest level, she came to believe, the Irish experience was about defeat—especially in the lives of women whose particular stories, with their particular degradations and survivals, had not been told by male poets. Boland would be a witness to defeat. She would work at what she calls "the improbable intersection" where the truths of womanhood meet the defeats of a nation, finding in Anna Akhmatova, as Heaney finds in Mandelstam, a distant precedent and formidable example. "I had," she says, "the doubts of a writer who knows that a great deal of their literary tradition has been made up in ignorance of their very existence; that its momentum has been predicated on simplifications of their complexity. Yet I still wished to enter that tradition; although I knew my angle of entry must be oblique."

In the space remaining, I would like to quote, along with two more passages of supporting prose, as much of Boland's recent poetry as possible. It strikes me as work of a very high order, and a great advance on the poetry published in her early books. Most impressive of all is the title sequence of her new volume called, like the *APR* printing of her essay, *Outside History*. But certain poems that first appeared in *The Journey* and the Carcanet *Selected* anticipate that sequence in interesting ways and underline the arguments of her prose. For example, in the "Envoi" to *The Journey*, she writes: "My muse must be better than those of men / who made theirs in the image of their myth. . . . If she will not bless the ordinary, / if she will not sanctify the common, / . . . then I / am the most miserable of women." Instead of a nation "displaced / into old dactyls, / [and] oaths made / by the animal tallows of the candle" rejected in "Mise Eire," she affirms in a poem called "The Oral Tradition" a source of

the ordinary which she hopes her muse will bless. It is the overheard conversation of two women "standing in shadow" and speaking of another who had given birth to a son in an open meadow.
Their conversation, and the conversations of other women like
them, is a manifestation of the feminine oral tradition in which Boland seeks to root her poetry. But how can one transcribe those oral
sources in such a way that the felt life and human courage are communicated without the taint of the male poet's false-heroic, the old
dactyls and the oaths? I am not sure whether these stanzas are
meant to communicate the sense of a solution to this crux, or yet
another statement of the problem.

> It had started raining,
> the windows dripping, misted.
> One moment I was standing
> not seeing out,
> only half-listening
>
> staring at the night; the next
> without warning
> I was caught by it:
> the bruised summer light,
> the musical sub-text
>
> of mauve eaves on lilac
> and the laburnum past
> and shadow where the lime
> tree dropped its bracts
> in frills of contrast
>
> where she lay down
> in vetch and linen
> and lifted up her son
> to the archive
> they would shelter in:
>
> the oral song
> avid as superstition,
> layered like an amber in
> the wreck of language
> and the remnants of a nation.

The initial section of the *Outside History* sequence involves a
more direct encounter with a woman who has got a story to tell.

Boland remembers a week-end when, "raw from college," she stayed at Achill in a friend's cottage "with one suitcase and the set text / of the Court poets of the Silver Age." An old woman "came up the hill carrying water. / She wore a half-buttoned, wool cardigan, / a tea-towel round her waist. / She pushed the hair out of her eyes with / her free hand and put the bucket down." In the poem, we never learn what the old woman said, only that Boland didn't really listen. But in the essay, which also begins with this memory, Boland tells us, "She was the first person to talk to me about the famine."

> The first person, in fact, to speak to me with any force about the terrible parish of survival and death which the event had been in those regions. She kept repeating to me that they were great people, the people in the famine. Great people. I had never heard that before. She pointed out the beauties of the place. But they themselves, I see now, were a sub-text. On the eastern side of Keel, the cliffs of Menawn rose sheer out of the water. And here was Keel itself, with its blond strand and broken stone, where the villagers in the famine, she told me, had moved closer to the shore, the better to eat the seaweed. . . . I knew, without having words for it, that she came from a past which affected me. When she pointed out Keel to me that evening when the wind was brisk and cold and the light was going; when she gestured towards that shore which had stones as outlines and monuments of a desperate people, what was she pointing at? A history? A nation? Her memories or mine . . . ? "I have been amazed more than once" wrote Helen Cixous, "by a description a woman gave me of a world all her own, which she had been secretly haunting since early childhood."

In the poem, however, the story passes Boland by, the questions are not asked, the amazement at a secret haunting is not there, and . . .

> . . . nothing now can change the way I went
> indoors, chilled by the wind
> and made a fire
> and took down my book
> and opened it and failed to comprehend
>
> the harmonies of servitude,
> the grace music gives to flattery
> and language borrows from ambition. . . .

Instead of listening to the woman's witness, Boland read her Raleigh and her Wyatt, studied for exams. In the prose version, in fact, she says she "memorized" this poetry, and she calls it "the cadences of power and despair. . . . I turned my back on her in that cold twilight and went to commit to memory the songs and artifices of the very power systems which had made her own memory such an archive of loss." The rest of the sequence deals, directly or obliquely, with what it means to turn around and face the Achill woman, to put down Raleigh and to put down Wyatt, to memorize the subtext and text of Keel rather than the Court poets of the Silver Age or the Irish songs of fictive queens and sibyls and resistance. By the third section of *Outside History*, Boland internalizes the old woman's story and understands the need, literally, to make her body "an accurate inscription / of that agony: the failed harvests, / the fields rotting on the horizon." Thus incarnate, thus spoken, the stories, along with the survivals or defeats which they communicate, can enter history as the poet does herself in the anchor poem of the sequence.

> There are outsiders, always. These stars—
> these iron inklings of an Irish January,
> whose light happened
>
> thousands of years before
> our pain did. They are, they have always been
> outside history.
>
> They keep their distance. Under them remains
> a place where you found
> you were human, and
>
> a landscape in which you know you are mortal.
> And a time to choose between them.
> I have chosen.
>
> Out of myth into history I move to be
> part of that ordeal
> whose darkness is
>
> only now reaching me from those fields,
> those rivers, those roads clotted as
> firmaments with the dead.

But the poem and the cycle do not end there. Neither is optimistic, although both are deeply committed to the notion of redress in Seamus Heaney's primary, political sense. The poem and the cycle end like this:

> How slowly they die
> as we kneel beside them, whisper in their ear.
> And we are too late. We are always too late.

Too late, not heard, not seen. Or—not having looked, not having listened or remembered—not sufficiently alive in time to seize its moment and extend its offerings or intervene before its opportunities are suddenly cut off. "Always, I am moving towards her," Boland writes of a woman—who could well stand for all of the women in her poems—once seen weeping at a cafe table where "behind her, / outside the picture window, is / a stand of white pines."

> I raise one hand. I am pointing to
> those trees, I am showing her our need for these
> beautiful upstagings of
> what we suffer by
> what survives. And she never even sees me.

And yet Boland *is* always moving toward this woman, as she does also toward her daughter in her interrogation of the Ceres myth in the third section of her cycle from which I have already quoted two lines. Ceres, as she has it, "Went to hell / with no sense of time," seeing only "wheat at one height, / leaves of a single colour" rather than "the failed harvests" and "the fields rotting to the horizon." But Boland demands time—"my flesh and that history"— to make the same descent. It is, in the cycle as a whole, a descent into the past and present experience—human, mortal, and particular—of women who have suffered or are suffering, victims of history driven outside history without amanuensis, poet, historian, or comforter. Or, in this particular poem, the experience of a young girl, someone with a future, flesh and blood Persephone, who, with back turned on the poet and the world, waits. And what, if anything, *is* myth? It is "the wound we leave / in the time we have" . . .

> which in my case is this
> March evening
> at the foothills of the Dublin mountains,
> across which the lights have changed all day,

holding my hand
sickle-shaped, to my eyes
to pick out
my own daughter from
all the other children in the distance.

I doubt that Boland is "too late." Her daughter will turn, even as she herself turned toward the Achill woman. But what she is up against, described in her essay and engaged in her poems, has the weight of centuries behind it. If she has not yet resolved all the contradictions of her problematic and subversive discourse—her interrogation of myth is not fully deconstructive and creates some fairly abstract emblematic figures of its own—she has nonetheless written some excellent poems which are, I think, unparalleled in recent Irish poetry, and she has written an essay which should be required reading, not just for Irish poets and for women, but for all of us. As she says,

There is a recurring temptation for any nation, and for any writer who operates within its field of force, to make an ornament of the past; to turn the losses to victories and to restate humiliations as triumphs. In every age language holds out narcosis and amnesia for this purpose. But such triumphs in the end are unsustaining and may, in fact, be corrupt. If a poet does not tell the truth about time, his or her work will not survive it. Past or present, there is a human dimension to time, human voices within it and human griefs ordained by it. Our present will become the past of other men and women. We depend on them to remember it with the complexity with which it was suffered. As others, once, depended on us.

From *Another Chicago Magazine, 1991*

Part V

ॐ

After Auden:
Some Poets of the 1970s

Reviews from *Poetry:*
April 1974 to March 1977

Eleven books by British poets and five by Americans; by and large, the British are the more interesting. I shall therefore focus on them. But I might note, before getting under way, that with Auden's death the general situation in British poetry is different from what it was when he was alive and writing. There is now no living British poet acknowledged to be major by anything such as a critical consensus. Although the literary Mafia will require a successor to Auden and want to recruit a great poet from among the ranks of the good ones with no conspicuous loss of time, it might be just as well if we had none for a while, either real or imagined. There are many good poets writing now. That should be enough.

Michael Hamburger

Ownerless Earth: New and Selected Poems, E. P. Dutton & Co.

Michael Hamburger is certainly one of these and the publication of his new and selected poems is an important event. It is a fine volume ending with a truly distinguished long poem. Hamburger's qualities as a poet have been obscured for some time now by his reputation as a translator, critic, and editor. This book should change all of that and make it clear that he is a poet before he is anything else. It ranges from poems written as early as 1941 to those sections of "Travelling" which recently won him *Poetry's* Levinson Prize, from the closed stanzas and strict metres of his work from the early 1950s to the free and open forms of the previously uncollected poems.

297

298 **Reading Old Friends

This book is weighted heavily in favor of the recent work, and rightly so. There could be even fewer of the poems taken from the volumes before *Weather and Season* (1963), or none at all. The subjects of many are literary or trivial, and they frequently read like exercises (although sometimes quite brilliant exercises). Hamburger says in an author's note that he "may well have rejected poems . . . that are better made, more finished, than some of the later pieces I have included; but, if so, those more finished pieces don't interest me, and I have no use for them now." For me, the book really begins on page 65 with the section called "Observations and Ironies." It includes five of the poems from *Weather and Season* as well as the first eleven uncollected poems, which do not appear in strict chronological order but continue on from this point to overlap with poems first published in the three volumes previous to the present one.

If Hamburger's poems can be taken as manifestations of the moral consciousness of the modern European Jew—which they can and must be—it is necessary to add immediately that the poet's ancient, glittering eyes are gay. His work is not very often flawed by the puritanical and solemn earnestness characteristic, for example, of some of Jon Silkin's poetry. Here is Hamburger:

> The year opens with frozen pipes,
> Roads impassable, cars immovable,
> Letter delivery slow;
> But smallpox from Pakistan
> Carried fast from Yorkshire to Surrey,
> And no lack of news:
> In the Andes a landslide
> That burried a town;
> In Dalmatia, earthquakes;
> Bush fires around Melbourne,
> Cooking wallabies, koala bears.
> In Algeria, random murders on either side;
> Paris a playground for thugs.

This is the first section of a rather chilling poem about natural, political, and moral disintegration which can later ask quite seriously: "Amid such omens / How do we dare to live?" But there is a certain grim pleasure taken in the spread of the pox and a positive delight in the cooking of the wallabies and koala bears. In his introduction to his (just displaced) *Oxford Book of Modern Verse*, Yeats expressed enthusiasm for a story told of a soldier wound up in his entrails like one of Yeats's own Byzantine mummies in its mummy-cloth. He thought the *humour* of that story might be a proper approach to war and declined to anthologize any of the poems of Wilfred Owen. If Michael Hamburger writes with an outraged moral consciousness, and he often does, he is also a connoisseur of the chaos that outrages him and threatens to destroy his world.

In his excellent critical book, *The Truth of Poetry*, Hamburger distinguishes between the romantic/symbolist/magical impulse of a poet like Mallarmé or Rilke and the moral/political/revolutionary impulse of a poet like Brecht, observing that both impulses may be at work within the same poet. It seems to me that both impulses are very likely to be at work in a poet writing today—they certainly are in Hamburger. There are several possibilities, then. First, that the two impulses will neutralize one another and make for silence; second, that two quite different kinds of poetry will be written as one or another of the two impulses dominates at a particular time; and finally, that the struggle between the two impulses will generate the energy that produces a poem in which the tension is effectively resolved. Hamburger writes most of the poems which one might anticipate, given these possibilities. There are straight political poems, sometimes satirical or ironic, sometimes more or less didactic; there are poems that manage to transmute even the most recalcitrant (including political) materials into more or less purely formal structures; and there are poems in which the magician and moralist in Hamburger meet and fight it out. Throughout, there is a preoccupation with the possibility of falling into silence, and there are many poems about language, about words: "I can't do without them. / But I hate them as lovers hate them / When it's time for bodies to speak."

This question of language is very important, for Hamburger is not the kind of poet to take his language for granted (and it may be worth noting that he was born and lived in Germany, presumably speaking German, until the age of nine). There is something unnatural and suspicious, after all, about the practice of poetry.

> Because I was writing my poem on sticklebacks—
> Day in, day out, again and again
> Till I scrapped it, tore up all the drafts—
> I forgot to feed them. Mere babies, they gobbled up
> Every unarmoured, toothless and spikeless creature
> Left alive in the tank—
> Tinier still they'd picked off

The fry of fishes potentially four times their size—
To the last food grain competed for Lebensraum,
Then weakened and died.

That may well be funny—Hamburger and the reader both would
just as soon have the poem as the fish—but this, however, takes us
a thousand miles beyond a stylish demur somewhere between the
writing desk and the aquarium to a place where language becomes
homicidal, odious, and obscene, where, by repetition after repetition, we are made to gag at pronouncing, again and again, words.

Words cannot reach him in his prison of words
Whose words killed men because those men were words
Women and children who to him were numbers
And still are numbers though reiterated
Launched into air to circle out of hearing
And drop unseen, their metal shells not broken.
Words cannot reach him though I spend more words
On words reporting words reiterated
When in his cage of words he answered words
That told how with his words he murdered men
Women and children who were words and numbers
And he remembered or could not remember
The words and numbers they reiterated
To trap in words the man who killed with words.
Words cannot reach the children, women, men
Who were not words or numbers till they died
Because ice-packed in terror shrunk minds clung
To numbers words that did not sob or whimper
As children do when packed in trucks to die
That did not die two deaths as mothers do
Who see their children packed in trucks to die.

A horrific vision, yes; Eichmann in Jerusalem. And yet I'll warrant
there was a compensating excitement in writing it out. The tension I
spoke of earlier exists even here, perhaps especially in passages like
this. He did not, when his pen stopped moving, throw up in the
sink. He probably exulted in getting it all down so accurately.

There is something in every poet that wants to renounce poetry: Prospero whispers in one ear and Lenin in the other. But most
poets don't renounce it; nor does Michael Hamburger. Instead, he
continues to investigate the relationship between language and pos-

session of all kinds—and he travels. His book may seem at first to be a journey toward that point at which the Efficacious Word is finally found and uttered, a point—in space, in time, in mind—which becomes, by naming it, real and one's own. But it is in fact a journey well beyond that point (or delusion) through an ownerless earth indeed, an earth not to be possessed by language (or by any other human instrument), although it may be encountered in terms of language, travelled or experienced in terms of its strange agency. At the end of the final sequence, Hamburger's perspective is that of geological time, and his evolutionary vision is dialectical and complex.

> Slowly, detained by love,
> He went, but never
> Slowly enough for Earth
> In her long slow dream
> That has not finished yet
> With the gestation of man,
> The breaker of her dream,
> And has not finished
> Digesting the teeth and bones
> Of her dinosaurs.
> Making and breaking words,
> For slowness,
> He opened gaps, for a pulse
> Less awake, less impatient
> Than his, who longed
> To be dreamed again,
> Out of pulverized rock,
> Out of humus,
> Bones, anthropoid, saurian,
> And the plumage of orioles;
> Cleared a space, for the poems
> That Earth might compose
> "On the other side
> Of mankind"
> And our quick ears
> Could not hear.

This final sequence, "Travelling," is presumably known to readers of *Poetry*—or at least two sections of it are. It needs to be read in full, and many times. Achieving sometimes the serenity of parts of *Four*

Quartets (of which it only now and then seems derivative), it is (although it is other things as well) a uniquely successful love poem:

> Last of my needs, you
> I'll unlearn, relinquish
>
> If that was love. Too late,
> Let you go, return, stay
> And move on. Let you be,
> Nameless.
>
> Begin again, saying:
> Mountain. Lake. Light.
> Earth. Water. Air.
> You. Nothing More. No one's.

To cease from naming. To name again.

R. S. Thomas and Edwin Morgan

R. S. Thomas, *H'm*, St. Martin's Press; Edwin Morgan,
From Glasgow to Saturn, Carcanet Press.

R. S. Thomas is from Wales and Edwin Morgan from Scotland. There have been times in the recent past when the so-called Celtic fringe of Britain has looked far more like a center than a circumference as far as poetry is concerned. And, of course, in the not so recent past as well. The classic syllabus for Modern British Literature still turns out to be a largely Irish affair. While neither Thomas nor Morgan ought to be thought of merely as a regional poet, local experience, nevertheless, figures importantly in the work of each.

Of those two other Thomases—Edward and Dylan—R. S. Thomas is closer to the former, of whom he has written: "His is a minor voice for what that word is worth, but one of great integrity and individuality." The same might be said of his own work. I wish, however, that I had before me a substantial selection from his six previous books rather than the volume at hand. It is a rather slight affair. The problem with many of these poems is that they tend to depend too heavily on their last lines, ending with a surprise, a paradox, an irony, a didactic jab, a quip, or an epigrammatic twist of some sort. Add to this that they also begin very abruptly, and you find that you have poems that often work the way a joke does—the effect depending on an electric brevity and a punch line. Not that the poems are funny—far from it. Thomas is a preacher, and he does a good deal of preaching here—about nasty machines, sciences, and cities; about good old religion and the good old countryside. I think I share, in fact, most of his values. And as one long ago converted to Theism (if not to Christianity) by Christian poets, I certainly don't object to his writing *God* down on the page instead of searching out some occult surrogate. But sometimes these poems sound too much like the language of a fundamentalist tent meeting. Imagine Billy Sunday, after having terrified you with Hell-fire, turning on the charm, smiling warmly, and speaking these lines:

> It's a long way off but inside it
> There are quite different things going on:
> Festivals at which the poor man
> Is king and the consumptive is
> Healed; mirrors in which the blind look
> At themselves and love looks at them
> Back; and industry is for mending
> The bent bones and the minds fractured
> By life. It's a long way off, but to get
> There takes no time and admission
> Is free, if you will purge yourself
> Of desire, and present yourself with
> Your need only and the simple offering
> Of your faith, green as a leaf.

Now that's the worst poem in the book, so I'm not being fair. But here, once again, is the problem implicit: "Seeking the poem / In the pain, I have learned / Silence is best, paying for it / With my conscience. . . . One thing I have asked / Of the disposer of the issues / Of life: that truth should defer / To beauty. It was not granted." Prospero whispering, not Lenin. The poem I have quoted above is already more than half way to silence; much more of that and next there will be nothing at all.

Perhaps all of the short poems should be read as one long poem. Ten out of thirty-nine poems begin with the word *and,* while others begin with *but,* or with a fragment of a dialogue already underway, or with phrases like *as life improved.* Continuity is also suggested by poems touching key events in Biblical history. But because the individual units seem so often to be for one reading only, one is disinclined to work out a comprehensive scheme. If there is a single argument that runs through the book, this is it:

> The flesh is too heavy
> To wear you, God of light
> And fire. The machine replaces
> The hand that fastened you
> To the cross, but cannot absolve us.

Many of Edwin Morgan's poems are also for a single reading only, but they are intended to be. Some, in fact, are not really for the printed page at all, but for declamation. And I mean poems to be *declaimed*, not just read aloud. Morgan has recently translated Mayakovsky into Scots under the title *Wi The Haill Voice*. There's an energy in his own poems that certainly requires the haill voice too, and, luckily, this energy animates many of the pieces that can get along without a platform and performer. For example, "Columba's Song."

> Where's Brude? Where's Brude?
> So many souls to be saved!
> The bracken is thick, the wildcat is quick,
> the foxes dance in the moonlight,
> the salmon dance in the waters,
> the adders dance in the thick brown bracken.
> Where's Brude? Where's man?
> There's too much nature here,
> eagles and deer,
> but where's the mind and where's the soul?
> Show me your kings, your women, the man of the plough.
> And cry me to your cradles.
> It wasn't for a fox or an eagle I set sail!

But Morgan's range is wide. Wide enough, in fact, to touch both of the antagonistic poles of Scottish poetry—Ian Hamilton Finlay and Hugh MacDiarmid—and an amazingly large number of points along the way between them. The trouble with being versatile and working in many forms is that readers (and especially critics) will want one thing or another, this sort of poem or that. Even though the possibility exists that a book manifesting widely divergent techniques can achieve a shape and identity as its parts combine to form a whole, this is not very often admitted, and poets who don't stick pretty much to one mode are likely to be abused for not doing so. All the more reason why I should apologize for feeling that the book doesn't manage to cohere. Morgan's propensity for trying to pull off strange virtuoso pieces is partly responsible for this. These tend to be overcharged with his admirable energy; they fuse out or explode. And I'm not persuaded by the science fiction poems, the computer assisted poems, or the poems written partially or wholly in made-up words or noises. But the excitement of a poet delighting in language and willing to play with it, and to take risks, is engaging even in poems which are seriously flawed. The book ends with a series of monologues having to do with a particularly grisly abortion, and with ten well-made and moving sonnets about the Glasgow poor. There are probably five or six good poets in Edwin Morgan. But a fatal triple-headed muse—trivial, typographical, and trendy—has a few of them in thrall.

Elizabeth Daryush and Barbara Guest

Elizabeth Daryush, *Selected Poems*, Carcanet Press; Barbara Guest, *Moscow Mansions*, Viking Press.

No such muse has Mrs. Daryush in thrall. She must necessarily appear in this company looking rather like someone who has suddenly stepped out of the wrong century to find herself at the wrong party wearing the wrong clothes. There she stands in her brocades speaking her *o'ers* and *'twixts* and *'tweens* in her very proper accent. She must be somebody's ancient aunt or somebody's Granny. But the effect of her presence is curious. Suddenly, everyone's language sounds indecorous, full of improprieties and vulgarities. She is introduced by her companion as Robert Bridges' daughter. The companion's name is Yvor Winters and he says: "She is the best poet produced in England between T. Sturge Moore and Thom Gunn."

Even Winters, however, had his reservations about Daryush's poetry. First of all there is the question of syllabics. The debate, of course, has been going on from the time of Campion. Saintsbury found syllabics "hardly at any time a sufficient key, even in appearance, to English verse," and most apologies for the practice tend to sound somewhat disingenuous. Michael Hamburger speaks of "free verse with a bad conscience." But Daryush has written consistently in syllabics for years (though also in iambics) and provides an appendix for her book elucidating her position. Here is the gist of it. "The poems without line-capitals are those written in syllabic metres (by which I mean metres governed only by the number of syllables to the line, and in which the number and position of the stresses may be varied at will) and are so printed as a reminder to the reader to follow strictly the natural speech-rhythm, and not to look for stresses where none are intended." There follows a discussion of what constitutes a proper elision and what doesn't (implicitly critical of Bridges' system in *The Testament of Beauty*), and the statement concludes asking for "subtler and more freely-followed accentual patterns than can be obtained . . . by stress-verse proper." Here, then, is one of the syllabic poems.

> Faithless familiars,
>   summer friends untrue,
> once-dear beguilers
>   now wave ye adieu:
>
> swift warmth and beauty
>   who awhile had won
> my glad company
>   I watch you pass on.
>
> Now the still hearth-fire
>   intently gloweth,
> now weary desire
>   her dwelling knoweth,
>
> now a newly-lit
>   lamp after shall burn,
> the roving spirit
>   stay her, and return.

Well, it won't knock them out in Iowa City. The poem, in fact, is the one Yvor Winters quoted to generations of students in order to illustrate what might constitute (instead of the poems of Marianne Moore, for example) effective syllabic verse. His own appreciation of its rhythm in *Forms of Discovery* is articulated in uncharacteristically vague and not very Wintersian terms: "The rhythm is a verse rhythm, the poem moves and lives, and we can hear it." Which is pretty much the same as saying: "It's poetry, man, and you can just sort of like dig it." But never mind. I don't really dig it very much myself, but I can recognize it (from a certain distance) as an honorable poem. An unprejudiced reading will imprint it on one's memory.

Syllabics aside, Daryush treats most of the traditional themes of poetry in many of its traditional shorter forms. There are sonnets (quite a lot), quatrains, tercets, and couplets. There are poems about love, nature, the seasons, mutability, mortality, and so on. Abstractions like anger, enmity, patience, and frustration are personified; there is a lot of archaic diction and there are inversions, contractions, and clichés of all kinds. But there are also some good poems. Instead of thinking of Daryush as a contemporary of Barbara Guest, perhaps it would be useful to think of her as a contemporary of Landor or of Herrick or, to keep on going back, of the lutanists and madrigalists out of Fellowes. (That one does so think suggests her range. Also, one thinks of Emily Dickinson and even Hardy now and then.) But the problem is, on the other hand, that she is not a contemporary of Landor nor Herrick nor Dowland, and so may have to be content to be seen by most readers of modern poetry as a kind of quaint Pierre Menard. That would be a pity, really. Although this is a difficult book to get into, it can be read with no harm being done to anything but one's preconceptions about what poetry has to be in the twentieth century.

Barbara Guest counts syllables too, but more in the manner of Charles Olson than of Elizabeth Daryush. In a poem for John Coltrane she writes:

> Words
>   after all
> are syllables *just*
> and you put them
>   in their place . . .

Olson at his best was capable of unique and arresting jagged rhythms, lineation and syllabification that sound *just* indeed. Few of the poets of the New York School achieve anything like the rhythmical configurations which Olson and his closest early associates achieved in the course of their reinvention and reorientation of modernism in the 1950s and early 1960s. The blurb writers at Viking—unable quite to decide whether to stress Guest's affiliation with, or independence from, the New York School—talk about her involvement with painting. "I detest this pencil. I wish I had a 'crayon,'" she writes in one poem. I wish she had a better ear. Many of these poems, rich in imagery and ideas as they may be, are simply boring rhythmically. If they are long as well, like "Knight of the Swan," then they are deadly. As the man said, poetry ought to be at least as well written as prose:

> The swan with an abrupt gesture of its wings set him down
> in the forest (nearby) nearby was a lake from whence
> they had originated it was indeed nearby the knight
> began to relax and to breathe to suspire he cast
> aside those odious thoughts of his origin he began
> (with dreamy asides) to like wings there was obviously
> too much noise when a wave hit a concave stone. . . .

The element of play and parody here (and it goes on) does not justify the tediousness of the writing. When lines and syllables are functioning for Guest, she can give us poems like the first part of her interesting sequence called "Byron's Signatories":

> *His air of the underworld*
>
> His air of the underworld . . . the underleaf
> of the catalpa together with the ruddiness
> of his lisp.

Now that is small, but excellent and musical. I could even say that the rhythm is a verse rhythm, that the poem lives and moves, and that we can hear it. The sister art of poetry is music. If such a choice ever became necessary, it would be better for poets to move in a circle of musicians rather than in a circle of painters.

Jon Stallworthy

The Apple Barrel, Oxford University Press; *Hand in Hand*, Oxford University Press.

Jon Stallworthy is a poet who has written intelligently about Yeats and movingly about Owen; one who has collaborated on solid translations from the Russian and the Polish; and one who has recently edited an ambitious anthology of love poetry. *Root and Branch*, a volume of poems published in 1969, is presumably still in print. I mention it because it contains "The Almond Tree," which, for me, is Stallworthy's strongest poem. *The Apple Barrel* selects poems from *The Astronomy of Love* (1961) and *Out of Bounds* (1963) while *Hand in Hand* brings together the recent work. Early in *The Apple Barrel*, Stallworthy prints an apology for (at least) his early poems:

> You blame me that I do not write
> with the accent of the age;
> the eunuch voice of scholarship,

or the reformer's rage
(blurred by a fag-end in the twisted lip).
You blame me that I do not call
truculent nations to unite.
I answer that my poems all
are woven out of love's loose ends;
for myself and for my friends.

One wouldn't blame him at all except that the eunuch voice of scholarship (his libel, not mine) does, indeed, sound in these poems; and that Stallworthy's odd Tory nostalgias often make for a stridency less palatable than the reformer's. Yeats, Stallworthy's master, refused in a famous and pretty silly little piece to write a war poem, but out of "love's loose ends" (for himself and for his friends?) he produced not only love poems of great intensity, but also some of the finest public poetry of our time. And Yeats was not afraid of rant.

You blame me that I do not face
the banner-headline fact
of rape and death in bungalows,
cities and workmen sacked.
Tomorrow's time enough to rant of those,
when the whirlpool sucks us in.

"Turn away from the bitter farce," he concludes. Which is far too easy—for the poet or for anyone else. The posture of the poem is as stereotypical as that of its opposite—the fire-breathing protest poem—and almost every line contains its cliché. In its own way it is as much a pastiche as anything by an imitator of an imitator of Ferlinghetti or Corso or Patchen.

There is a related poem by Stallworthy that is more specific in its terms of reference and which has considerable currency given that it has a home in *The Norton Anthology of Modern Poetry*. Although the poem is from *Root and Branch*, and therefore doesn't appear in *The Apple Barrel*, I want to quote a few lines from "A Poem About Poems About Viet Nam" in order to make what seems to me an important point about Stallworthy's orientation as a poet.

Lord George Byron cared for Greece,
Auden and Cornford cared for Spain,
confronted bullets and disease
to make their poems' meaning plain;
but you—by what right did you wear

suffering like a service medal,
numbing the nerve that they laid bare,
when you were at the Albert Hall?

Evidently there was a poetry reading at the Royal Albert Hall
in 1965 and some poems were read against the war in Vietnam.
Whose? Ginsberg's? Bly's? And is their work somehow less honorable than Byron's or Auden's? (The life of John Cornford is another
matter.) Is "Witchita Vortex Sutra" rant and "Spain 1937" a dispatch
from the front? (". . . in love and war / dispatches from the front are
all.") Auden decided that "Spain 1937" was rant and cut it from the
canon of his work. And he didn't, the footnote in *The Norton Anthology* notwithstanding, drive an ambulance in the Spanish Civil War.
My point, though, is really that the poem in question is deceptive.
Appearances to the contrary, it exploits the suffering of the war for
its own ends every bit as much as any conceivable protest poem by a
noncombatant that it might be opposing. Its real subject is the poet's
own snobbery. It's O.K., mind you, to be a snob in a poem. But you
have to be a big enough snob to pull it off—like Yeats himself.

Then there are poems like "Here Comes Sir George" toward
the end of *The Apple Barrel*. Sir George passes "the boys" (at his
club? the setting isn't altogether clear) who mock him, call him
"Victoria's Uncle" and "The Rearguard of the Raj." Stallworthy answers that he ruled a province, in fact, not "as a Maharaja / prodigal
with silver and bayonet; / but with cool sense, authority and
charm. . . ." These still attend him . . .

crossing a room
with the *Odes of Horace* under his arm
and in his button-hole a fresh-cut bloom.

So he reads Horace. And if the rhyme had required "posy" or
"nosegay" we would have had it. The piece concludes:

Honour the rearguard, you half-men, for it
was, in retreat, the post of honour. He—
last of the titans—is worth your study.
You are not worth the unsheathing of his wit.

The last time I heard people derisively labeled "half-men" was
in the nastiest sonnet of Rupert Brook's *1914* sequence where he
talks about "half-men and their dirty songs and dreary, / And all

the little emptiness of love" and advises setting off for the Western Front "as swimmers into cleanness leaping." This echo jars oddly with Stallworthy's recasting of the conclusion of Wilfred Owen's "Apologia Pro Poemate Meo." "These men are worth your tears. / You are not worth their merriment." Not that one sympathises with "the boys"; nor that the nostalgic politics of the piece necessarily lowers its merit as a poem. Rather that it should have been better made—and has been by Ted Hughes in "The Retired Colonel."

In a prefatory note to *The Apple Barrel*, Stallworthy recalls Virginia Woolf's advice to a young poet to publish nothing before he was thirty. It is often hard to imagine that these poems are selected from a young man's books. In this context of nostalgic politics and over-cautious competence, one longs to see for a moment some chances taken, some passion, some irreverence, some of the rituals of youth. What we have instead is a too fastidious and sometimes very awkward restraint characterized by the wonderfully awful line: "Ritual is perhaps too large a word." What there is of youth in *The Apple Barrel* is the student's attempt to please his teachers. The title of one of these early books was *Out of Bounds*, but Stallworthy is always *in* bounds. He has gone to school on the poems of the English Renaissance and on the poems of Yeats and he has served a long and careful apprenticeship. But poems upon the Quincentenary of Oxford College X or Y, or Epithalamia spinning out complicated Renaissance conceits, or Donne-like Astronomies of Love are for the exercise book. In spite of my irritation with them, I prefer the poems treating memories or vestiges of British Imperial power in terms of Stallworthy's ambivalent fascination with historical processes which have "put down the mighty / from their family seats" to this kind of thing from the title poem of his first book:

> The astronomy of love is this:
> by night, when heaven glows
> pale between your arms, to kiss
> a constellation of ten toes.
>
> Then kiss the glimmering knees that point
> to larger planets in love's chart,
> and through the hips' wide orbit mount
> the milky way towards her heart.

The poems collected in *Hand in Hand* extend the charts of these particular heavens in several directions. Love poems are difficult to write, and God knows they are good for us if they are good. The blurb finds Stallworthy's to be delicate and lyrical and passionate and reminiscent of the Greek Anthology. Sometimes they are all of those things. But such poems are easily ruined by slips that would only flaw other kinds of poems and which make these suddenly ugly or awkward or coy or cute: "the children you wanted lie locked in my scrotum" . . . "the pen stirs under my thumb . . . and the words come" . . . "the kiss that seals my groin to yours" . . . "love is yeast" . . . "Let / them observe, love, our *enjambement*. / They shall be guests at the secret / wedding of form and content" . . . "Lying in late: / two croissants, warm / in each other's arms, / on a dazzling plate. . . ." It's enough to send one to pornography for some real fucking. The poems get better when the relationship disintegrates. "The Beginning of the End" and "Making an End" leave the poet, at the conclusion of the volume, holding the hand of his "light-headed son" and revisiting the Almond Tree. Anyone who reads "The Almond Tree Revisited" and "At Bedtime" (both of them strong poems) owes it to himself to look up "The Almond Tree" in *Root and Branch*. This, Stallworthy's best love poem, I would like to quote in full to qualify my criticism of his work by making clear that, at his best, when poetry seems to be demanded by the pressure of experience rather than just desired, Stallworthy can be very good indeed. But it is long and I have space enough only for these stanzas:

> On the darkening wind a pale
> face floated. Out of reach. Only when
> the buds, all the buds, were broken
> would the tree be in full sail.
>
> In labour the tree was becoming
> itself. I, too, rooted in earth
> and ringed by darkness, from the death
> of myself saw myself blossoming,
>
> wrenched from the caul of my thirty
> years' growing, fathered by my son,
> unkindly in a kind season
> by love shattered and set free.

Paris Leary

The Snake at Saffron Walden, Carcanet Press.

Paris Leary's range is much greater than Stallworthy's and his language is richer and more evocative in his formal pieces, more

idiomatic and colloquial in his less formal. In attitude, the two are
sometimes very close. Perhaps the difference is that what must
come across in Stallworthy in terms of Yeatsian denunciation comes
across in Leary by way of a parody of Auden:

> I sit in a roadside diner
> On Highway 23
> Come from hearing a minor
> Poet read at me
> And the breath of the hip bard
> Affects the flashy day
> And I respond to the cigarette
> And the tuna-salad plate
> And think of tooth-decay . . .

In fact, Leary seems to have responded by becoming a British subject. Given the recent immigration in this direction among British
poets anxious to put feathers in their hair, dance with the locals
around the ethnic bonfires, and make a fast buck, you've got to give
him credit for being so unfashionable as to go the way of James and
Eliot—although, on second thought, one recalls that writers as different from one another as Lowell, Burroughs, and Jonathan
Williams have chosen recently to live in England—so perhaps the
gyres are turning once again. In any case, I can't read this book
without recalling a few of the Leary poems that ought to be in it—
poems that I know from the anthology he edited with Robert Kelly
in 1965, *A Controversy of Poets*. The aim of that book was to establish
some kind of dialogue (still absolutely necessary, and still not likely
to happen) between the straight types chosen by Leary and the
more hip chosen by Kelly. Leary wrote the first of two postscripts
with a judicious wit and asked some real questions. Kelly, forgetting
the spirit of the occasion, clobbered him with a manifesto in the
second postscript. Kelly's men won the day and Leary went to
Leicester.

The Snake at Saffron Walden is an interesting book, and I would
fault the publisher for not making it a longer one. It seems to me
that the expense of printing another signature (given that this is essentially a Selected Poems) would have been solidly justified by
making room for more work and allowing the poet to build a structure for himself that would look less like a miscellany. This book,
like *Hand in Hand*, is only slightly over pamphlet length. But then
the times are hard and we should be grateful, I suppose, for what
we get.

In a poem responding playfully yet seriously to the question "What five books would you pick to be marooned with on a desert island," Leary describes his choices—all written by himself for "a desert island of the heart." First he writes "a kind of perpetual first novel, / tiresome about childhood" and next a committed, uneven political morality conceived with an awareness that "Compassion is a sort of expertise." In his third book "The urgent ecstasy of a generation / declines into [his] better travel-poems." In the fourth, he writes his "dullest book," his "holy scriptures, / journal, testimony, and confessions." His last collects his inadequate attempts to write of love. There is something of all five books in *The Snake at Saffron Walden*, and, in the best piece, "Welsh Poem (for a friend going blind)," three of the five kinds dovetail successfully together. After providing a kind of Braille landscape of song for his friend, after visiting the Vale of Ffestiniog, travelling from the River Dovey to the Long Mynd, from Cambria into Ludlow in his poem, Leary concludes:

> May those dark Welsh saints
> who were unpronounceable before canonization was new,
> who did strange Christian things
> we should not understand,
> give you the bright sleep
> that the young Merlin slept
> when the world was young and magic
> invocation, not forbidden knowledge.

At the end of a "travel poem," then, is the testimony and love that come with certain kinds of journeys.

Nearly all of the "travel poems" are strong. We have lines from Victoria Park Pavilion in Leicester, St. Mary's Church in Ashwell, Herts., St. Mary's Abbey in Haddington, Salle Church in Norfolk, the Suffolk Wash, Binsey Church, Stinsford Churchyard, and Lundy Island. To some extent the focus of these poems is predictable—like that of the visiting British poet's American poem which must contain, as Ken Smith says, a filling station—and there are a good number of churches, churchyards, and abbeys to think about. But the poems do reward one's close attention, and they are not just a matter of catching landscape tones. Leary knows what he ultimately travels towards. The title poem is written on hearing that a cobra was loose in Saffron Walden on the same day he had been exploring the town:

By The Bunch of Grapes
or the unfriendly stuffed fountain,
in the long chin of heat
the sheepskin-coat shop dimpled into,
in the danger darkness of the hotel lounge
the flat shape
could have hooded and against my feet
the pavement grown cold and numb
and the sky flattened that was tall and bent,
an icy tropic in my single limb.

While I feel that Leary is a far better poet in his more sober and less demotic moods, it is important to recognize the pretty obvious advantages accruing to a poet willing to work within a wide range of idiomatic possibilities and free himself from any restrictive inhibitions attendant upon a fastidiousness about such things as diction. The section, for example, called "Weary" from "Cousin Belle Prescott" reads in full:

She props her breasts up on Mamma's rosewood table
and with an elegant acerbity says, "Crap!"

Or there is the conclusion of "Downcount" spoken by a "grid black man in that / hoodoo world between eye / and eyelid":

But our carapaces, he says, will puncture
like spooked space-suits in a Sci-Fi do.

In context, the lines from both poems work to good effect. There are times, however, when Leary's less formal, more colloquial poems seem to be a little uneasy in their skins and, especially when spirits are high, a bit forced. This may or may not have something to do with his decision to live in England. At any rate, the best poems in the book do not make noises like these from "Cookham": "Yoo-hoo, you over there, / didn't I know you down at the Kings Head? / Coo-ee, kids, come back, / don't gape, it's your Grandad's sister, sil-lies . . ." Though the poem is mildly amusing, it is a pity that it couldn't have been dropped from the book to make room for one or another of these poems from *A Controversy of Poets*: "Summa Contra Gentiles" or "Manifesto."

Anne Stevenson

Correspondences, Wesleyan University Press.

Anne Stevenson's *Correspondences* is an epistolary family chronicle. It is an ambitious book and, I think, a good one. The mosaic of letters (along with the occasional newspaper clipping and journal entry) achieves its effect by appealing to what Stevenson can safely assume is a well-cultivated and characteristic midcentury taste in many readers for documentary method. In fact, the method may be mock-documentary. Feeling a little embarrassed, I picked up the phone to see if there really was a Chandler Family Archives in Clearfield, Vermont. There seems to be no Clearfield, Vermont. It was like phoning Mississippi and trying to get in touch with directory assistance for Yoknapatawpha County. Of course, this doesn't mean that there are no originals for the letters—however distant from their style and content the poems may have been driven by the logic and aesthetic of this very schematic book, and however strange the names might seem to the correspondents. It would be interesting to know. I have read one review that criticizes Stevenson for awkwardly made-up period pastiche, and another that congratulates her for transmuting into poetry such difficult and recalcitrant materials. She must be amused. John Willett has recently written about the "delicate balance of relationships between the factual (or found) and the imaginative in art," remarking that "the appearance of authenticity counts far more than any genuine correspondence between the work of art and the world." Given Stevenson's loaded title, I think that's a nice quote.

In a poem contrasting Thomas (the orthodox) with Edward (the Puritan) as theologians, Paris Leary writes: "Edward, minister among the rum-stricken redskins and the dollar Elect, / you said the very clouds excremented on you for the people's sins. / Thomas, you had the vision; Edward, you the shit." In *Correspondences* the Puritan shit begins to fly. The patriarch of the Chandler family is Adam Ezekiel (1772–1853) who writes condolences to his bereaved daughter after the death of her husband:

My wretched daughter,

I have studied your letter with exacting and impartial attention.
What shall I say?
Except that I suffer, as you, too, must suffer
increasingly from a sense of the justice of your bereavement.

What did you expect, Elizabeth,
from your childhood preferring, despite my prognostications,
the precarious apartments of the world
to the safer premises of the spirit.

This kind of thing becomes the family habit. The bereaved daughter, properly chastened by Daddy, writes a few years later to her brother Reuben on the occasion of his engagement that "the utter carelessness / of your happiness (and selfishness) / breaks through my aching wound like a vengeful worm . . ." while Rube, after his wife splits, writes her of "the causes of strife between us— / your selfishness, your vanity, your whims, wife, / your insistent and querulous disobedience". Like father, like son. Jacob Milton Chandler (who believes that "by doing good with his money a man, as it were, stamps the Image of God upon it and makes it pass current for the merchandise of heaven") reminds his daughter, Maura, that her parents' kisses were loans—"Loans upon interest these many long years! Now it is time to repay them, graciously, selflessly, with little acts of kindness and understanding." Things are particularly rough on the ladies. Maura, having decided to repay those kisses graciously and selflessly by marrying her cousin, Ethan Amos Boyd, writes in her Journal on January 1, 1900:

> Without false pride.
> Without true faith.
> With little hope
> and with no glad energy,
> but still, thank God,
> steeled firm in belief
> that there is a right way
> and a wrong
> through our human loneliness,
> I begin this New Year's
> Day of my life in marriage.

After Boyd goes bankrupt and bananas in 1929, the Chandler Home, rather like Howards End, slowly comes to be dominated and humanized by the women of the family, particularly by Ruth Arbiter, Boyd's daughter and old Adam Ezekiel's great-great-granddaughter. She writes poems, is capable of an affair with a rather schmaltzy English novelist, and composes a death-bed monologue in her journal which is one of the best things in the book.

Although the family ethos—which is also the American ethos—still drives Ruth's daughter Kathy to a mental asylum in 1954 to compose a letter to her mother sounding like an early poem by Anne Sexton, the dead hand of the past is slowly losing its strength and Kathy—out of hospital, divorced, writing in London under the name Kay Boyd—is able to resist her sister's invitation to come home after her mother's death and end the book by asking her father, as the figure of Kathy merges with Stevenson herself, "Can these pages make amends for what was not said? / Do justice to the living, to the dead?" The story, of course, is an old one, but Anne Stevenson's way of telling it is always interesting and often moving. Stylistically, the letters are in various modes (including prose), the most frequent and effective being a modified version of William Carlos Williams's triadic stanza.

> Dear Kay. So . . . a summer
> Four months since she died.
> And your decision not to return,
> wise, I wonder?
> Because of course you're missed.
> Poor father!
> He's in no mood for anger.
> Tries to live normally:
> office hours, meals, long walks.
> Sundays, his string quartet.

It's treated as a workhorse stanza and it usually does the job.

David Steingass

American Handbook, University of Pittsburgh Press.

Nick Arbiter, Kay Boyd's brother, speaks the penultimate poem of *Correspondences* on the road between Vermont and Wyoming. David Steingass is also on the road between East and West in *American Handbook*, and attempting to write one of those familiar state of the union messages which American poets like to send back from their travels incorporating letters about their own lives and times. Steingass's first book was called *Body Compass*. Here, as in that book, he travels according to the logic of his feelings and needs, according to the directions of a body compass. The section titles, as he moves from New England to Hawaii, are suggestive: "This Hard

Honor," "The Blue Dream," "Living Like Indians," "Realizing What Has Passed Is Gone," and "Fear of Home." The locus of values in the book is basically that of the naturalist or the Indian, although Steingass doesn't pretend to be either. The general territory is that which is still being charted, to take examples from three generations of American poets, by Kenneth Rexroth, Gary Snyder, and Robert Hass. And Steingass, like these others, understands that language, the word-map, will only take him so far, and will ultimately fail vision:

> This time I have jumped with you
> Into the fusion
> Of what appears, and what we feel
> We see, I want to say, but cannot.

Still, *so far* is a long way. At least as far as Hawaii.

The language of the second half of the book is more interesting and accurate than the language of the first. Many of Steingass's subjects demand a leaner, cleaner, and more austere treatment than they get. There is a certain tendency in the earlier (as sometimes in the later) poems for the writing to become cluttered, clogged, or clotted. He seems at times to be an absolutely compulsive maker of similes—just the sort of ornamentation that his kind of poetry ought to do without. Similes, as I say, and other kinds of artiness: "Dense asterisks of rolling hills," snow which "has colonized everything but this / Smooth wooden locomotive / of an island," rooms which "nest, distinct as so many / One-act plays," fields that wait "like old friends / Stand in line," curtains which hang "listless as carp out the kitchen window," a swing like a metronome and a house like a pendulum (not to mention a pair of scaled shins which *tick* like pendulums) and a soul which is "like an oppossum in adversity." Better that the poems should be stripped, muscled, and lithe.

> Plowshares turn Mankato's full belly
> inside out. (it is a fight:
> > knot the rein tips
> > loop your neck
> > > under one armpit
> > lean back on the knot between shoulder blades
> > dig your heels against earth
> > > plow
> > > > team.

                    never loop both arms:
                            team spooks
                            single trees snap
                            you're up over the plow)
                listless with heat and boredom
        arrowheads come
        birdpoints: dull puff-eyed
        obsidian ticks

The "Hard Honor" of the first section of the book is New England's—and the hard honor of physical work—scything the lawn, wedging, chipping ice from a cabin door, rowing at dawn with a lobsterman. And the hard honor of animals. From the second sections's "The American Porch" the travelling begins—from an American porch to whose maternal and elegiac swing "You / Never return . . . The anchor half of the century / Flowers to atomic proportions." Alert to details of both sympathetic and alien life styles, overhearing and recording the speech of people around him, painting both a ravaged and a still vibrant, sometimes almost virgin American landscape, living with friends and living quite alone, dreaming and remembering, Steingass works his way west and through a series of poems culminating in the sequence "Lotusbound." From about midway I found myself enjoying the book enormously. The final sequence in particular—with "Fear of Home" as its coda—gives immediate and lasting pleasure. I quote the coda in full.

        Windfall woods. A leaning pine
        Stretched into fur, reared and stared
        And slowly blinked. I stood, pissing,
        Eye to eye with a black bear. My heart
        Jackhammered into my knees. We backed away
        As slowly as growth, the way limbs
        Slip into twilight. Shadows
        Filled our space.

        I have died to be living here
        Where trees grow for keeps,
        Gaunt and passionate as statues, and finally
        Split up, into dreams.
        These sweet canyons are the heaven of bears.

The sky opens like the century to them.
I am covering ground thinking of home.

And wondering where. Moss grows lopsided
Over there. Trails vanish
Into the swamp like rows of stitching
On a prickly scalp. Fireflies
Or foxfire sputters downhill
Toward the last hollow tree.

A good poem—except for the similes.

William Hunt and William Everson

William Hunt, *Of the Map That Changes*, Swallow Press;
William Everson, *Man-Fate*, New Directions.

It was Thomas Mann, I believe, who once said that Karl Marx needed to read Friedrich Hölderlin. William Hunt is a Friedrich Hölderlin who has read Karl Marx. Or a Thomas Traherne who has read Thomas Hobbes, a Hermes Trismegistus who has read Aristotle. In his marvelous and original poems, mystical phenomena explode in a world of brute contemporary fact—the burning bush grows through the concrete and asphalt of Clark Street, Chicago. Although I don't intend to say a lot about *Of the Map That Changes*, don't be deceived by the brevity: of the several books under review, this is the one to read first. I offer no criticism of these poems. I find them to be remarkable as they manipulate, as in some kind of gigantic endless sestina, their constantly repeating words and images— rain, stars, roads, maps, ghosts, wheels, trees, songs, glass, foliage, night, windows, snow, cold—and as they appear and disappear behind their strange, problematic, insistent, didactic, transparent opaque titles: *How It Might Be, The Ladder You Offer, So that Women Will Talk to Trees, What You Can Get From the Body, This Is a Way, Of What Is To Come, Your Life After Death, What Remains, How It Got Too Cold, How It Stopped*. If as a critic I can't find the language to describe the best and most characteristic of these poems, as a poet I am keen to enter into dialogue with them. David Lenfest has memorably remarked that the obsessive theme of this obsessive book has to do with "the politics of the dead in the lives of the living." So it has. But one might stress *in the lives of the living* and add that, for the transmigration of every soul, there is a transgressing murmur of a half-buried empirical epistemologist.

These words separate us into sound;
the panels of light on your arms, and your arms also,
hold us together:
these systems, these choices:
the child, the woods (the wife, the storm)
exclude what I would have said otherwise of the stars.

Half-buried and transgressing. Only a murmur. Hunt's main business is to persuade us that he sees what he sees. "Her lament was more foreign than we could feel," he writes in one poem. Hunt's lament is not—although it is foreign. I am as persuaded of certain experiences of the spirit in these poems as I am of those in the poems of John of the Cross.

Even if we are one, or two, interchanged,
or the same, with a signal of breath to recognize
the other after life, or after this series of lives
in a drift (which you will get) of stars, tonight
there are no stars. But there are those lights
that cross the veils of rain or snowfall, fan-like
with the trouble of dreams. We try to escape to each
other and are not ourselves. Before turning off the light
I lifted the stove's lid and saw the red eyes
of the mouse. He crouched full of another life.

Hunt has waited a long time—he is forty—and has made a fine first book from years of hard work. We probably profit from the delay and from much rewriting. One has a sense of certain poems here growing richer and more dense over an extended period of composition. Hunt's work has none of the casual spirit of much of Steingass. It is highly intellectual, sometimes very difficult. But it can also go straight for the heart. Everyone should read it.

Everyone, presumably, *has* read Brother Antoninus at one time or another. He is back to being William Everson these days, and the center piece in *Man-Fate*, "Tendril in the Mesh," is the transitional poem. After the first public reading of the poem, Everson tells us in the preface, he "stripped off his religious habit and fled the platform." "Tendril in the Mesh" is a poem about sexual love, and therefore about a subject only slightly less difficult to deal with in language than the mystical experience that Everson, in modes more familiar than William Hunt's, has treated before. The tradition, of course, is to express the latter experience by writing metaphorically of the former and, as Brother Antoninus, Everson has published poems of erotic mysticism in *The Crooked Lines of God* and *The Hazards of Holiness*. Although there are residues of that kind of writing in "Tendril in the Mesh" (and one pure example of it in the epilogue), "The Swan Song of Brother Antoninus," as Everson calls the poem, is in large measure naturalistic in its treatment of sexual experience. I am afraid it is hopelessly over-written. The worst blunders of Jon Stallworthy's erotic poems (which, after all, are basically reticent and fastidious) are here carried to rhetorical extremes which are surely destined for comic footnotes in some future feminist memorandum. I forbear quotations. Happily, there are some shorter poems that follow "Tendril" which are more successful. They work out, Everson explains, the implications of his break with his order. But the best passages have more to do with the sea at Stinson Beach and the nearby hills than with love, God, or Dominicans. Meanwhile, for love poems, as for mysticism, read William Hunt. As he says:

> We have been a conversation
> but soon we shall be song.

John Fuller

Poems and Epistles, David R. Godine.

"Fifty coolies / Pierre Boulez"; "go all goosey / Claude Debussy"; "something terser / vice versa"; "off their hinges / Celtic fringes"; "Coed-y-Brenin / jobless men in"; "Smith to Yale / Texas gaol"; "one excuse is / gastric juices"; "purely mental rapes / Apollonian sour grapes"; "liar's quinsy / Dr. Kinsey"; "etcetera / blah blah blah." Those are John Fuller rhymes. The knockabout idiom developed in Fuller's epistles via the Burns stanza has its immediate source in W. H. Auden's *Letter to Lord Byron*, one of the few successfully sustained comic poems between *Don Juan* and the early work of Kenneth Koch. The enduring influence of Auden, in fact, can also be seen, with and without anxiety, in the Peter Porter and Elizabeth Jennings volumes which I shall be discussing. All three poets share with Auden a commitment to an anti-Romantic, anti-Modernist poetics; Ms. Jennings writes him an elegy, complete with the carpet slippers and the "leather skin," and Porter borrows the syllabic organization of "Spain," the approach to a cultural occasion of "Metalogue to the Magic Flute," the *paysage moralisé*, the ironic political song in trimeter quatrains (rhyming "Fanon" with "sine qua non," "Brechtwerk gay" with "Ethnic Shadowplay"), and other characteristic procedures. But it is Fuller, who has published a discerning *Reader's Guide to W. H. Auden*, who writes a book approaching something like a systematic dialogue with that fussy shade which, if not appropriate to the heaven of Blake and Bloom, is just right for that part of Soho where Ian Hamilton edits the *New Review*.

> If *Ian Hamiltons* galore
> (Offhand, I can distinguish four
> Or five. I hope there are no more)
>   Think it's addressed
> To them, too bad. You're tooth and claw
>   Above the rest.

Tooth and claw, indeed! But what is the American reader, uninformed about or uninterested in the London literary-political scene, to make of it? There was a time when Ian Hamilton *was* the rest. For the eyes of the recipient, then, and for those in-the-know or on-the-make, the epistle continues:

> The Fat Men quivered at your glance,
> Careers destroyed by your advance.
> Still you are wooed at every chance
>   Like an heiress,
> And lead the dunces quite a dance
>   From *Westbourne Terrace*.
>
> At least ten years ago there were no
> Worse than those who, sipping *Pernod*,
> In Lallans ruined the *Inferno*
>   With tips from *Pound*.
> Now we've *(facilis descensus Averno)*
>   The *Underground*.
>
> Ten years have witnessed a gigantic
> Increase in the transatlantic
> Subterranean mode, each antic
>   Sillier than the last,
> Most a mere throwback to a frantic
>   *Dadaist* past.
>
> Sexual boasting, prayer mats,
> Ampersands, athletic chats

On breathing or the evil that's
 Instinct in iambs,
Tall stories, empty as the flats
 Of *Harry Hyams.*

Oh those Primitivist Panzers
Steamrolling *Newcastle* or *Kansas*
With misspelt lower-case bonanzas
 Of pot and *Zen*
In which mistrust of things like stanzas
 Shows they are men

And fit to blast an epic trail
Though with a certain mannered, frail
Excess that rises to a wail
 When they're ignored,
Ripe as the scrawlings in a gaol
 Or a locked ward

Where mania's nurtured by the nurses
Eager with poultices and curses:
For unread poets get free purses
 From an *Arts Council*
As interested in their verse as
 In kinds of groundsel.

You haven't stopped all this, but still
You've drawn attention to the ill.
Though to the Bank of Time he will
 Remain a debtor,
The patient's choking on your pill
 And may get better.

Hilarious, of course. It's quite impossible not to like this, and I
do like it, and yet one must run the risk of being thought a bore and
say straight out that several of the very things mocked in the passage constitute the chief strengths of modern British poetry, such as
it is, and *guess* that even John Fuller himself, not to mention Ian
Hamilton, may suspect this from time to time. But who, as I say,
could possibly dislike it? And who, pills/bills/frills, would not be
pleased to learn—unless he should be someone so insensitive as to
value experiment and to want to see it supported—that much of the
patient's share of the Arts Council coffers has been paid in doctor's

fees, some of it, one hopes, to cover malpractice insurance. In an *Epistle* to James Fenton—who is also the recipient of some *Baroque Quatrains* in Porter's book (it's a small world, folks)—we are invited to read Colin Falck (whose name Fuller has the decency to rhyme with "body talk") instead of all the "foul-mouthed transatlantic spivs / Wooing *Trigram*"; further—winding up for the pitch with *flecker, trekker, mecca, verum pulchrum*—"I'm glad, of course, that you're with *Secker* / And not with *Fulcrum*." That was written in 1972. While we're busy laughing at it, the sad thing is that Fulcrum is now inactive, that Trigram is hopelessly overburdened, that Cape-Goliard has closed down, that *Agenda* has lost much of its original energy and purpose, that many of the most innovative English poets have had to go to America for publication or employment or both. Leaving the world to darkness and to thee, Colin Falck. English poetry threatens to return to the tedious sterilities of the 1950s.

But I mustn't get solemn; one is meant to be having a good time here. Indeed, one *does* have a good time here. Too good, perhaps, to keep one's values wholly intact. Along with Hamilton and Fenton, the letters are addressed to Angus Macintyre, an Oxford colleague of Fuller's (who gets at unpronounceable *Achaglachgach* a letter from unpronounceable *Llanaelhaiarn*); Bryan Kelly, the composer with whom Fuller has often collaborated; and David Caute, the novelist and historian. All of the epistles are full of the characteristic throwaway rhymes, and edgy with an equally characteristic throwaway wisdom. They are funny, flippant, nervous, awkward, nervy, elegant, couth and kulchured, irreverent, irrelevant, opinionated, learned, allusive, longhaired, longhorned, smug, smutty, philistine, mock-philistine, bored, lively, livid, friendly, fierce and fighting, fat-assed, worried, wearied, committed, timely, public, private, pubic, political, antipolitical, stimulating, irritating, antiacademic, donnish, dapper, dotty, and so on by turns. My personal favorite is the long and wonderfully prejudiced piece on music addressed to Kelly which takes, as it happens, as in nearly all of the other letters too, opinions quite contrary to my own on nearly all conceivable issues related to the subject. This has its own strange pleasures, as any reader of good polemic knows. If the spiritual home of the epistles is at the gossipy center of literary London, their actual place of composition was far-away Wales, where Fuller was on leave from his university. Both the distance and the leisure put him in a position quite like Auden's in Iceland when he wrote *Letter to Lord Byron*. He can comment on even the most horrendous events—during a year, as he says in his note, of hijackings, IRA bombs, and the tragic Munich Olympics—without quite taking them seriously. For the most part, anyway. When the tone does suddenly change, it can be very moving. In the letter to Macintyre he has been writing about respectable middle-class (specifically, middle-class academic) compromise, escapism, and complicity in political and social injustice—another favorite, if not *the* favorite, theme of the early Auden. It ends like this:

> We need some vision to achieve,
> A heart to wear upon our sleeve,
> We need a holy spell to weave
> Some sacred wood
> Where we can teach what we believe
> Will do us good.
>
> I see you smile. All right, it's late.
> But, Angus: though it lies in wait
> With terrible reproaches, fate
> May yet forgive
> Our scared retreats, both small and great,
> And let us live.

To David Caute (who plays Fuller's Isherwood), he writes: "Your novels are at least committed . . . You show what forces pull the triggers / While still creating live figures. . . . You are the man we want to read, / The kind of writer that we need." And, in conclusion to Fenton:

> Some day I'll join you in the street
> Where suffering and truth must meet:
> It isn't easy not to feel effete
> This side of anguish,
> When those who can't choose what to eat
> Don't speak our language.
>
> Meanwhile we have to try to bring
> Some order to that circus ring
> Where people think and feel and sing,
> For at its centre
> There's no escape from anything,
> And we must enter.

All of these emotions are appropriate enough to a time in which Fuller finds, reversing Auden's "ironic points of light" of

"September 1, 1939," "Random flares of evil" in the "massive darkness." The range of tone in the epistles is more considerable than a first and inevitably rapid reading suggests. Still, one should read them chiefly because they are funny. Taken together, they constitute a rare tour de force, a small comic masterpiece. The competition, in case anyone is interested, comes from another poet and critic and jack-of-all-trades associated with *The New Review*, Clive James. His letters, including one to Fuller, go these one better by pulling off a series of seven, each in a different rhyme scheme; and his *Felicity Fark*, an endless bit of topical versing in couplets with antecedents again the same as Fuller's—in Auden, in Byron, in Pope—is reported to have sold ten thousand copies in England within a year. But we must move on now from Fuller's epistles to his poems, and we should do it with a grin or a giggle:

> The toughs are measuring their phalluses
> And most of them upon analysis
> Prove to have general paralysis
> Of the insane.
> *Wallace* (I don't want to be callous) is
> Upright again.
>
> *Howard Hughes* has lost his, *Nixon*
> Proves to have one that only sticks on,
> *Agnew's* is as real as Dixon
> Of *Dock Green*,
> *General Westmoreland's* glows and clicks on
> Like a machine.

If you want the news on Norman Mailer's, Cassius Clay's, Andy Warhol's, Hugh Heffner's, and Bobby Fisher's, you must send David R. Godine your $7.95 and help to pay for Fuller's defense in the libel suit.

The poems which make up the other half of Fuller's volume are various and, for the most part, successful and interesting. There are a few failures here, like the stridently unfunny and predictable "God Bless America" (Adrian Mitchell's sort of thing), and an antiacademic academic sequence—Audenesque again with its "antagonist with whom / We ever contrive grandmaster draws"—which strikes one, as Sean Golden has said of something similar, as being more a part of the problem than a part of the solution. But the level of formal achievement is usually high in this part of the book, and often enough the effects are stunning. There is an impressive sonnet sequence, "The Labours of Hercules"; there is a longish poem in tetrameter couplets, "The Art of Love," which has the muscle and wit of the best parts of Auden's overlong tetrameter epistle of 1940 and which might also be profitably compared with Kenneth Koch's recent poem of the same title; there are poems in terza rima, in quatrains, in a wide range of other stanzas and meters; there are the songs set by Bryan Kelly, a riddle, a monologue, a footnote, and a poem in what I think is an invented form combining certain characteristics of the villanelle and the sestina. The intelligent, conscious, and effective use of Audenesque resources is consistent. This is exactly the kind of song which Auden would have written had he been, like Fuller, the father of daughters.

> Dear girl, your bud unfolded
> And brought you to this peace,
> But my drab heart is still patrolled
> By its corrupt police. . . .
>
> My body's single, and my love
> A melancholy roar.
> The children hide their faces when
> I stand outside the door.

In "Ghost Village," the Audenesque theme of exile and quest tosses up some equally Audenesque allegorical figures moving through the landscape. "Did Squire Tribute, coming from beyond the ridge / Where the harnessed pismire superb in its plumes of dust / Pretended to be a horse on a careless errand, / Judge?" Most interesting of all, perhaps, is Fuller's attempt to extend the possibilities of those early Auden poems in short lines, themselves deriving in part from Laura Riding, such as "This Loved One," "Never Stronger," "Easy Knowledge," "Too Dear, Too Vague," and "On Sunday Walks." The title of the poem in question is "The Wreck," and it seems to me to be one of the most suggestive and actually useful poems to have been written after a close reading of Auden since Ashbery's "Rivers and Mountains." It repays careful study (as does a shorter poem in the same idiom, "Annotations of Giant's Town"). At three hundred or so lines, it manages to sustain effects that Auden himself inevitably restricted to a context of between fifteen and forty lines. Partly parodic, it also looks sideways (with a little affection?) at a modernist alternative to Fuller's characteristic brand of neo-classical formalism. Here is a snippet:

> In the end
> There is no land.

> We speak from systems
> Respecting customs,
> With good throw
> And follow-through
> Relax on green,
> Or shocked at pain
> In warm wicker
> On half-acre.
> When tilting plank
> Suggests we sink,
> To cry stop
> Is out of step.
> Fledglings shrivel
> On dusty gravel
> Where high bird
> Cries hard
> All day, all night,
> Too late, too late.

I can't move on from *Poems and Epistles* without remarking that no one ought to be taken for granted or thought to be entirely predictable. Nestling in these woods there is a poem which might have come in an unguarded moment when doing research on some of those "transatlantic spivs" for the Epistles, or at least after hearing a reading by Robert Bly.

> Air darkens, air cools
> And the first rain is heard in the great elms
> A drop for each leaf, before it reaches the ground.
> I am still alive.

Actually, that conclusion is the famous unwritten last line of James Wright's "Lying in a Hammock at William Duffy's Farm in Pine Island, Minnesota."

Elizabeth Jennings and Peter Porter

Elizabeth Jennings, *Growing Points*, Carcanet Press; Peter Porter, *Living in a Calm Country*, Oxford University Press.

While John Fuller does more than his share of literary politicking in his Epistles, he is just young enough at thirty-eight to have missed the literary politicking in the 1950s of the Movement and The Group. Elizabeth Jennings is an ex-Movementeer and Peter Porter is an ex-Groupie. They have been around. Jennings published a *Collected Poems* in 1967, and was, with Lawrence Durrell and R. S. Thomas, first in line when Penguin inaugurated its useful but uneven series of *Modern Poets* in 1962. Porter, one of the trio in *Penguin Modern Poets 2*, is a native Australian who has published seven volumes of verse. Both have done a good deal of journalism, criticism, translating, editing, and broadcasting. Characteristically, while Jennings has chosen to translate Michaelangelo and edit Christina Rossetti, Porter is drawn to translate Martial and edit Pope. When Jennings is writing badly she is labored, abstract, and sentimental; when Porter is writing badly he is brittle and superficially witty. But Porter is not bad very often; he is a far more interesting poet than Jennings. What they share in these volumes is an obsession with the pains (and sometimes the pleasures) of middle age, the anticipation of death, a concern for the place and plight of the artist, and a respect for craftsmanship. Both poets are well into that period of their work paralleling—and influenced by—Auden's when, as Prospero, he dismissed Ariel (and poetry-as-magic), saying: "I am glad I have freed you / So at last I can really believe I shall die." But what a difference between the two. While Jennings can write a good poem about Rembrandt's late self-portraits, Porter can paint with great courage and power something approximating their verbal equivalents—complete with a mirror in which he sees only "the face of an old man / With a big nose."

Growing Points is a longish book of shortish poems. They are reasonably enough organized into groups—of sonnets, religious poems, poems about art and artists, and so on—with the opening piece setting an autumnal mood and the closing piece, "Gained," declaring that "The day is not impoverished any more." Throughout, poems in Jennings's familiar meters and stanzas alternate with largely unsuccessful attempts to find substitutes for the largely unsuccessful experiments with prose poetry and free verse of earlier volumes in experiments with long lines, irritatingly printed in ugly run-ons.

My guess is that Jennings writes too much and probably publishes all of it. There are some very good poems and passages here, all right, but you need to do a lot of weeding. What is particularly upsetting is to find, say, a truly exceptional quatrain—and there are several of these—in a poem that is otherwise uninteresting, or a distinguished and original line sandwiched between banalities. It's too bad. My objections, in general, are to clichés of diction and imagery which appear with some regularity, from the autumn leaves of the first poem to the sunrise and sunset of the last; to the habitual and unoriginal use of literary stereotypes; to breathless questions at the conclusions of poems ("Where does the river lead?", "Hope is still hunted. Who will find?") or, alternatively, barren unresonant statement ("I / Am amazed still at the authority of your perception, your gentleness."); to awkward hyphenating ("Strewn-with-siesta square"); to gushiness of all kinds ("Is this the onset / Of that long-travelling, / Never answered / Question, 'Who am I?' / It could be."); to the abstractions, sentimentality, and laboriousness which I mentioned earlier; to the frequent lack of energy ("I am obsessed with energy / I never touch."). There are a lot of bad moments in poems about artists and thinkers—from Thomas Aquinas "making cogitations," to Freud and Adler "leaping down our / Apparently never-before-discovered minds," to Hopkins surviving "the no-understanding of others." And there are things that "ring true," gardens which inevitably become "a metaphor for Eden," "pangs" upon seeing, "breath-taking" beginnings and "breath-regaining" pauses, "worn-out thoughts," "scars of doubt," and even poems which should never have been seriously considered, like the monologue spoken by Christ on the cross.

The extraordinary thing is that Jennings can turn two-thirds of these faults into virtues. It is, in a way, a matter of taking risks. Had she not been willing to risk writing the unresonant statement "I / Am amazed still at the authority of your perception, your gentleness," she might well not have written elsewhere the equally abstract but very resonant "Self-portraits understand, / And old age can divest, / With truthful changes, us of fear of death" (with, in context, its effectively delayed pronoun, recalling the syntax of Berryman's *Dream Songs*). Had she not risked ending a poem by asking "Where does the river lead?" she might not have ended another "Waiting for, O, what men, what histories?" and still another: "Can you suggest a safe place for the being / Harassed just here, alive, alert, laid open?" Had she not risked being gushy, she would not have written "But I in the middle of it was mute / Begging within myself for one, / Yes just one day and a different sky." Without the "cogitations" of Aquinas, we might not have had a poet and philosopher "writing / In the reign of Charlemagne, paring simplicities to a peace no Emperor was ever enticed by or even dreamed of." If she had not been willing to think abstractly about "the artist"—the painter, the composer, the poet—she would not have written the fine conclusion of "Wonder."

Prophets may preside and they will choose
Clouds for a throne. The background to their speech
Will be those fiery peaks a painter gives
As a composer shares an interval,
As poet pauses, holding sound away
From wood, as worshippers draw back from gods.

And without being willing to risk the monologue of Christ on the cross, she might not have written:

The moon is assured. The sun has put its back
against the wood, the trees
Carry their rotten fruit like a swollen sack.
Stand among all of these
And learn from desertion and luxurious lack
Why some fall on their knees.

Significantly, the title of the poem from which this stanza is taken is "Not Abstract," and, in many of the best poems in *Growing-Points*, Jennings is very particular, very specific indeed. "And justice, mercy were bereft / Of all abstractions," she writes in "After A Play." "So were we, / Talking so low yet passionately." One often finds the precision, the sensuousness, and the exactness of observation which she admires in Christina Rossetti's work. She is on record these days as aiming chiefly at clarity and simplicity. Perhaps these are the most difficult things of all to achieve in poetry, for, as Peter Porter has said, "if you just say what you mean, what you mean may be so banal there's no point in saying it. Maybe you should say something a bit more interesting than what you mean." Abstraction as such is not, finally, the issue, as Yvor Winters would remind us—although ineptly conceived, awkward, and inaccurate abstractions are *an* issue in the book. Clarity and simplicity can be achieved by using, among other tools, abstract language skillfully. In "Rhetoric," "Bright symbols bubbled" for the poet, who nonetheless "searched the night for some simplicity." In "Losing and Finding," there is "something elegiac" in an event "Simply because this whole thing was direct." Jennings is not the kind of poet who is likely to find it acceptable to "say something a bit more interesting" than what she means. And that will indeed limit her range, her development, and her appeal. But perhaps it will also yield poems and passages—in *Growing-Points* there are only passages—that achieve something like what Yvor Winters was asking for when he wrote of "the ability to imbue a simple expository statement of a complex theme with a rich association of feeling, yet with an utterly pure and unmannered style." She achieves this, I think, in certain lines of several poems in *Growing-Points*, notably, for example, in the conclusion of "Rembrandt's Late Self-Portraits."

> To paint's to breathe,
> And all the darknesses are dared. You chose
> What each must reckon with.

Peter Porter, as I mentioned earlier, dares such darknesses in *Living in a Calm Country*. The old Porter *sprezzatura* is at work in the book, sometimes even in its deepest reaches; but much of the writing here is very grim stuff indeed. The satirist's scalpel, so frequently effective before in poems on social themes, goes to work here on the face he sees in the mirror. He will allow no delusions, no self-deception. While many of the poems have settings in Italy, Australia, or England, the "calm country" of Porter's title is really the human body, which, as Auden said in *The Age of Anxiety*, is the only landscape in whose symbolic terms we may imagine and seek out a "state of prehistoric happiness." Porter's seeking in this landscape produces something more like a combination of historic disappointment and prehistoric dread. "Millenia / stop short at three score years and ten / and the only thing on earth that will never / wither away is the state," he writes in "The Storm."

> Captains of industry smile on white terraces,
> the regatta sails like drops of blood
> fleck the blue estuary—
> Back in the Nursing Home
> a change on a chart is recorded, the angels
> are tossed in its turbulence.
> Why write poems?
> Why, for that matter, march on Moscow
> or ask your daughter if she loves you?

There is the Auden touch again—the captains of industry, the Nursing Home—but followed by the terrible Porter questions. And just as we are about to say that these things are very different, that you should *not* march on Moscow and *not* ask your daughter if she loves you, but that you definitely *should* write poems because, if well done, they can instruct or delight, Porter concludes.

The calm. While it lasts, there is man,
and suppose him a creature it's worth
making God for. In that calm, as at Babel,
mercurial masons are singing the truth,
serene diapasons of business and profit,
university judgements, priceless preferments,
courage and cowardice. Perhaps it did happen,
the Renaissance, when even the maggots
had Humanist leanings.
                    The storm will return
but before it claps down on the foreshore
and harbour, put out the lights, the nightlights
and phosphorous and turn the sea upwards
inverting the stars—the long winking banks
are like Mozart or Nature, carrion-joy
that the dumb in the fields pay the price of
and grieve for; a central unfairness
which looks good to the living, loving
on bones of the dead with basset-horns
maundering, and flushed by their faces,
happy as stopwatches, unlectured
by sick-beds or dreams, awaiting
the tempest, the null epicentre.

That, it seems to me, is a strange and remarkable passage; furthermore, it is a passage typical of the poems in this book. Here are two
others:

Never to be what I say as never to know,
For instance, if the ferryman will be the same
Across the river, or whether a voice reading
COSMO MEDICI MAGNO ETRURIA DUCI
Is my old headmaster or the floating oracle
They promised me when I renounced my love
To become a good resentful husband.

*

Tiptoe through the granaries and old lead workings—
This is the bridgework of a Protestant Book of Beauty,
    The flowers Luther leered at, types of
    Forgiveness for aunts and abbatoirs.

Being translated into pretty Music Programme vowels,
A morning canto for Anglo-Saxon reasonableness—
The thundering of bells overhead,
The rendering of praise overheard.

Porter is also immensely quotable and memorable in single
lines and pairs of lines: "I won't die young to make my language
work"; "The gods are dead, I meet their proud originals"; "Discovering the mystery too late, / *It is not fulfilled, it is only done*"; "Even
our rulers eat themselves to death"; "After a lifetime of blood let-
ting, we deserve / a vegetable future"; "my daughter has dark /
Celtic skin which shrivelled in the sun of death / When my mother
wore it"; and, of a bird, "We may / take his eggs and measurements, / but we cannot levitate."

In a poem on middle age, Porter asks in conclusion: "how shall
we get through the afternoon?" The answer is clearly, for him, "by
writing poems." But "Why write poems? / Why, for that matter,
march on Moscow?" To get through the afternoon, of course. Anglo-
Saxon reasonableness aside, it just works out that way. That bird
whose eggs and measurements were taken had overheard some
"pointless / poignant words: *I am a child of the / Enlightenment, I expect to be happy.*" If Porter is a child of the Enlightenment, he certainly does not expect to be happy. Nor should we.

A marvellous mustiness surrounds me;
The Book of Useless Knowledge in my hand,
I salute the thousand green horrors, the self. . . .

I might have been born in Galicia,
in the poet-killing provinces:
the olives look to me outside Cortona.

Instead, my vote went to verandahs.
What has this to do with the land
of disappointment? A style, or lack of style.

There is not, mind you, any more self-pity in any of this than
there is delusion or self-deception. Nor do I think that Porter, any
more than Elizabeth Jennings, tries to say "something a bit more
interesting" than what he means—although he usually means
something more interesting than does Jennings. Although Porter
has agreed with Auden that "the man who really tells the truth is
the man who goes to elaborate lengths to conceal it from himself—
like Boswell"; and although he writes in a poem on Hesiod that he

seeks "The permanently upright city where / Speech is nature and plants conceive in pots . . . The opposite of a sunburned truth-teller's / World," he is certainly a truth-teller—without the sunburn, maybe, but not concealing anything from either himself or his reader. On three occasions in this book, there is some ironic and self-deprecating talk about a "masterpiece" that Porter might produce: "You have a cruel masterpiece / crying to get out"; "I, too, am licensed to produce a masterpiece"; "I'm in retirement till I make / my violent masterpiece." While he is clearly capable of producing it—and perhaps thereby of saying something more interesting than what he means?—the last joke about not being able or willing to do so in "Cat's Fugue" is beautifully achieved. It is vintage Porter, funny and sad. The style, the wit, and the land of disappointment are surely one.

> It's about a cat
> bigger than Bulgakov's, east
> of Jeoffry in the night sky of the Lord;
> it stalks like plague along the grass
> fathering history on the post-diluvial age—
> named Jesus at the whole Jerusalem,
> the Day of Modernism dawns; professors touched
> by wings fly purring to the moon.
> These are its juvenilia and in Horatian
> retrospect I see the cat
> restored to its domestic stalking one salt
> Iberian morning in the light
> when genius saddened at the cold keyboard
> is jacked with white and black—
> again our dainty-footed man's companion
> strikes a balance with the dust
> and props the world against its weary gravity.

John Cotton and D. M. Thomas

John Cotton, *Kilroy Was Here*, Chatto and Windus, Ltd. and The Hogarth Press; D. M. Thomas, *Love and Other Deaths*, Elek Books, Ltd.

The books by John Cotton and D. M. Thomas are less ambitious then those I have discussed so far. Cotton's is considerably less ambitious. It is a longish pamphlet, really, of more or less acceptable short poems, too many of them on subjects suggested by photo-graphs. Cotton's writing is clean and unpretentious, cautious and careful. Too cautious and too careful, I should guess, if he is to de-velop as a poet. The best three poems in the volume are the title piece, "Kilroy Was Here," a poem taking off from a quote from a travelogue about St. Dominica; and the last one, which is also the longest, on the Raj. Caviling perhaps about "punctuated" and "par-amours," one can admire these lines from "Raj."

> In the city the white caps of Congress
> punctuated the crowds
> on betel mottled pavements
> near somebody else's
> Gateway to India,
> While sculptured millennial lovers
> continued to fondle
> their moon-breasted paramours,
> and holy bathers
> courted cholera and immortality
> in that order.

There are always plenty of paramours in D. M. Thomas's work, and one must respect, if even at a certain hesitant distance, his nervous, experimental, and erotic muse. I myself, in fact, re-spected it enough a few years ago to attempt a rescue of one of its offspring. He had produced a kinetic-concretist affair called the *Lov-er's Horoscope*, which, when you spun certain dials on the wheel, told you, according to the best information available to astrologers, what to stick in which orifice and, as I recall, for how long and at what time of the day or night. I had one in my bedroom until I rented my house to some theology students a couple of years ago when I was away from home for a while. What became of it I never learned. The rest were, presumably, burned. One of our great uni-versities had agreed to establish an experimental publishing outfit under the direction of a friend of mine. However, when this turned out to be the first experimental item on the experimental line-up, they reneged on the plan—and on my friend's contract as well—and censored the *Horoscope*. I drove to Chicago, where they were being produced, and saved a station wagon full from the flames, giving them away to friends and saving one for myself. The rest were shipped to the university in question. Perhaps, in fact, they weren't burned at all, but distributed among the members of the board of trustees; it is impossible to know. Anyway, Thomas is at it again, what with three erotic sequences here, one based on the *I Ching;* another on the figure of Eve's apocryphal rival, Lilith; and the third on what he calls "a central contemporary myth: the kidnapping of a diplomat by extremists." I'm afraid I'm not very enthusiastic about any of them. It sometimes looks, especially in the case of poor Lil, as if Crazy Jane had been knocked up by Hughes's Crow, the unlikely issue having been midwifed by Nathaniel Tarn's Bride of God and Brother Antoninus working together. But perhaps I was soured on such things and prematurely aged by my brush with the law over the *Horoscope.* Peter Porter has said, apropos of something else, "Nothing is worse than the man who pretends to be a ferocious Savonarola when really underneath he's just a fun-loving monk." Although we know there *is* something worse—namely, the Savonarola who pretends to be a fun-loving monk—any confusion of the two is distracting, and there is something of both in Thomas when he writes these erotic poems. Still, the first half of *Love and Other Deaths* has to do, not with the traditional erotic pun, but with the other deaths, and one can admire poems like "Cecie," "The Journey," "Rubble," and "Dream" while not much liking some of the poems which follow. In general, I think Thomas is at his best both in this book and in his previous volume, *Logan Stone,* when he writes poems deriving from his family experience and his search for roots in Cornwall. In "Rubble," for example, there is no more attempt to disguise real emotions or find a pleasant substitute for them than there is in Porter's work. Thomas sits in his ailing mother's room, longing to leave, wanting to "heat / her milk and water, kettle / for her bottle, pull out the commode, / compel myself to kiss her, and go." But that is by no means all there is to it. Along with the painful candor, the concluding lines communicate the burdens both of love and mystery.

> It is as though the black hole
> drawing her into itself
> is conditioning my love
> to require absence. She knows
>
> it. She is content. There is
> a queer radiance in the space
> between us which my eyes
> avoid occupying: the radium
> Madame Curie found, when desolate
> she returned at night to the empty table.

Notes

Places and Poems: A Self-Reading and a Reading of the Self in the Romantic Context from Wordsworth to Parkman

1. Morris Dickstein, "'The Very Culture of the Feelings': Wordsworth and Solitude" in *The Age of William Wordsworth: Critical Essays on the Romantic Tradition*, eds. Kenneth R. Johnston and Gene W. Ruoff (New Brunswick and London: Rutgers University Press, 1987), 317.

2. Ibid., 316, 317.

3. John Stuart Mill, *Autobiography*, Chapter 5, in *English Prose of the Victorian Era*, eds. Charles Frederick Harold and Willard D. Templeman (New York: Oxford University Press, 1962), 709. Citations from Wordsworth's *Prelude* are from *William Wordsworth: The Prelude 1799, 1805, 1850*, eds. Jonathan Wordsworth, M. H. Abrams, and Stephen Gill (New York: Norton, 1979).

4. In light of his subsequent career, it is worth noting that the friend was Peter Michelson.

5. The first three capitalized references are of course to the interpretations of Wordsworth in M. H. Abrams, *Natural Supernaturalism: Tradition and Revolution in Romantic Literature* (New York: W. W. Norton, 1971); Geoffrey Hartman, *Wordsworth's Poetry, 1787–1814* (New Haven: Yale University Press, 1964); and James K. Chandler, *Wordsworth's Second Nature: A Study of the Poetry and Politics* (Chicago: University of Chicago Press, 1984). As for the Established Church, W. H. Auden wrote in *New Year Letter* at the end of the 1930s:

> Thus Wordsworth fell into temptation
> In France during a long vacation,
> Saw in the fall of the Bastille
> The Parousia of liberty. . . .

A liberal fellow-traveler ran
With Sans-culotte and Jacobin,
Nor guessed what circles he was in,
But ended as the Devil knew
An earnest Englishman would do,
Left by Napoleon in the lurch
Supporting the Established Church.

6. Perhaps the angriest recent case against Wordsworth as a poet of place is made by Wendell Berry in his essay "Poetry and Place" in *Standing by Words* (San Francisco: North Point Press, 1983). Working almost entirely with the Prospectus to *The Recluse*, Berry argues that Wordsworth:

> affirms the existence both of individual conscience and of a supreme intelligence, but has affirmed no earthly thing between them that can correct his understanding of either or bring the two into harmony. . . . What fills [Wordsworth] with fear and awe is to enter "the Mind of Man." That sets him praying— and well it ought to, considering the arrogance of that mind as represented here. . . . It is hard to tell which is greater, Wordsworth's spiritual presumptuousness or his poetic impudence. . . . This mind, moreover, has no problems with "the external world." It is simply "exquisitely . . . fitted" to it. When the two are "blended," Paradise will be renewed. . . . [This] has behind it all in human arrogance and ambition that speaks in Milton's Satan's determination that "The mind is its own place. . . ." Ahead of it, it has all the propaganda and the works of the scientific romanticism that accompanied the industrial revolution. For if the poetic individual mind can pass unalarmed the heaven of heavens and the whole spiritual order of the universe, why cannot the scientific individual mind do so as well? (174–175)

Given the terminology of Karl Kroeber which I borrow later in this essay, one might say that it is no surprise that a farmer-poet like Berry might be outraged by a predator-poet like Wordsworth.

7. John Matthias, "The Mihail Lermontov Poems," *Crossing* (Athens, Ohio, and London: Swallow Press, 1979), 117. Three sections from this cycle are reprinted in *Northern Summer* (Athens, Ohio, and London: Swallow Press, 1984), 158–168.

8. Karl Kroeber, *Romantic Landscape Vision* (Madison: University of Wisconsin Press, 1975), 25.

9. Ibid., 111.

10. Ibid.

11. Berry, *Standing by Words*, 92.

12. Ibid., 192–193.

13. Kroeber, *Romantic Landscape*, 119.

14. Ibid., 119.

15. Ibid., 119–120.

16. Michael Ignatieff, "An Interview with Bruce Chatwin." *Granta* 21 (Spring 1987), 30–31. Chatwin's book is *The Songlines* (New York: Viking Press, 1987).

17. Kroeber, *Romantic Landscape*, 124.

18. Ibid., 125.

19. Hartman, *Wordsworth's Poetry*, 172 ff.

20. Jeremy Hooker, *Master of the Leaping Figures* (Petersfield: Enitharmon, 1987), 76.

21. Matthias, "Epilogue from a New Home." *Turns* (Chicago and London: Swallow Press, 1975), 104–105. Reprinted in *Northern Summer*, 73–76.

22. Matthias, "Epilogue," 105–106.

23. Chandler, *Wordsworth's Second Nature*, 173–175.

24. Kroeber, *Romantic Narrative Art* (Madison: University of Wisconsin Press, 1966), 88.

25. The books are Julian Tennyson's *Suffolk Scene* (London: Blackie and Son, 1939); and Edward Thomas's *The Icknield Way* (1913; reprinted London: Constable, 1980). These, along with Norman Scarfe's *The Suffolk Landscape* (London: Hodder and Stoughton, 1972) and Ronald Blythe's *Akenfield* (New York: Pantheon, 1969), were useful in very specific as well as more general ways. Some poems in *Crossing*—"Brandon, Breckland: The Flint Knappers," for example—derive directly from Tennyson. And as I note in my text, Edward Thomas on the Icknield Way is himself a human presence, though not quite a character, in "An East Anglian Diptych: Ley Lines, Rivers."

26. Matthias, "Poem for Cynouai." *Crossing*, 27; reprinted in *Northern Summer*, 108–116.

27. Cf. Michael G. Cooke on pleasure and play in Wordsworth, "Romanticism: Pleasure and Play," in *The Age of William Wordsworth*, especially 74–83. Cooke's contrast between Huizinga's apsychoanalytic notion of play and Schiller's concept of "play-drive" in *On the Aesthetic Education of Man* is particularly instructive.

28. Citations here are from two poems in *Turns*: "Double Derivation, Association, and Cliché: from *The Great Tournament Roll of Westminster*," 78–84; and "Clarifications for Robert Jacoby: 'Double Derivation, . . .' part iv.,

lines 1–10; part vii, lines 1–15, 22–28," 85–89. The poems are reprinted in sequence in *Northern Summer,* 58–67.

29. Hooker, "Crossings and Turns: The Poetry of John Matthias," *The Presence of the Past* (Bridgend, Midglamorgan: Poetry Wales Press, 1987), 103.

30. Hooker, "Poem and Place," *The Poetry of Place: Essays* (Manchester: Carcanet Press, 1982), 181.

31. Ibid., 183.

32. Ibid., 184.

33. Ibid., 186.

34. Part of the problem, of course, is inherent in the act of writing (or, analogously, of painting). John Barrell writes in *The Dark Side of Landscape* (New York: Cambridge University Press, 1980) that the "opposition . . . between a desired closeness and a necessary distance, everywhere apparent in [Constable's] earlier pictures, becomes impossible to conceal in the pictures painted at the end of Constable's life—those in which, as Conal Shields and Leslie Varris have written, the objects are 'glimpsed *through* [my italics] a maelstrom of paint.' The paint neither imitates now, nor creates—it obscures, or as we say it comes between the painter, and the image he is trying to paint, of a social landscape. There is an analogy here, too, with the problems Wordsworth found, in trying to use the language of poetry, purified certainly of poeticisms, to describe a harmonious relationship of man and nature: that the language, however simple, seems to be an unnatural medium which must exclude the articulate poet from the inarticulate community of nature" (159). Cf. James A. W. Heffernan, *The Re-Creation of Landscape* (Hanover, N.H.: University Press of New England, 1984):

> On one level, Wordsworth's account of what he saw and felt at Snowdon can be read as the poet's apotheosis of nature. . . . But Wordsworth's lines on the spectacle at Snowdon are not simply a tribute to the transforming powers of nature or God: they are also a demonstration of what can be done by the language of transformation in poetry—in short, by words. . . . For all his determination to make poetry speak "the real language of men" and to keep an eye upon natural objects in the act of describing them, Wordsworth here fully exploits the transforming powers inherent in language itself. . . . We do well to ponder the passage with which he concludes book 5 of *the Prelude.* . . . Wordsworth seems at first to derive the power of language from the power of nature—from "the motions of the winds." But essentially he represents the power of language as independently transformative, and he reveals this power in the very language with which he describes it. (158–159)

35. Matthias, "Poetry of Place: From the Kentucky River to the Solent Shore." *The Southern Review* 21:1 (Winter 1985), 183–184.

36. Matthias, "An East Anglian Diptych: Ley Lines, Rivers." *Another Chicago Magazine*, 15:54. Also published, along with "Facts from an Apocryphal Midwest," in *A Gathering of Ways* (Athens, Ohio: Swallow Press, 1991).

37. As it is impossible to account for everything here, I omit any reference to an attempt between 1980 and 1982 to integrate myself with the landscape and history of Wemyss Castle Estate in Fife, Scotland, where my mother-in-law moved after she was obliged to sell the house in Suffolk. The title poem of *Northern Summer* deals with this ultimately alienating experience.

38. Poets seem to respond to Parkman, even English poets. One cycle which anticipates my own is Donald Davie's "A Sequence for Francis Parkman," *Collected Poems: 1950–1970* (London: Routledge and Kegan Paul, 1972), 119–129. In "A Letter to Francis Bradford," Davie writes, and relevantly indeed to my own situation, "American, / You met with spirits. Neither white nor red / The melancholy, disinherited / Spirit of mid-America, but this, / The manifested copiousness, the bounties."

39. Parkman's romantic credentials, which I have no space to rehearse, have been amply established by many critics, perhaps most impressively by David Levin, *History as Romantic Art* (Stanford: Stanford University Press, 1959).

40. Charles Haight Farnham, *A Life of Francis Parkman*, 3d ed. (1900, 1901: reprinted New York: Greenwood Press, 1969), 196.

41. Ibid., 265–266.

42. For example, Howard Doughty, *Francis Parkman* (New York: Macmillan, 1962), cites this passage from *Pioneers of France in the New World:* "Day dawned. The east glowed with tranquil fire, that pierced with eyes of flame the fir-trees whose jagged tops stood drawn in black against the burning heaven. Beneath, the glossy river slept in shadow, or spread far and wide in sheets of burnished bronze; and the white moon, paling in the face of day, hung like a disk of silver in the western sky. Now a fervid light touched the dead top of the hemlock, and creeping downward bathed the mossy beard of the patriarchal cedar, unstirred in the breathless air; now a fiercer spark beamed from the east; and now, half risen on the sight, a dome of crimson fire, the sun blazed with floods of radiance across the awakened wilderness" (243). There is, admittedly, one Constable-like tree— that "patriarchal cedar"—awash in the Turneresque light.

43. Farnham, *A Life of Francis Parkman*, 214.

44. Ibid., 196.

45. Doughty, *Francis Parkman*, suggests the El Greco connection (256).

46. Doughty makes the Shakespearian, Miltonic, and Melvillian comparisons in his brilliant chapter on La Salle, 262–283; Otis A. Pease, *Parkman's History* (New Haven: Yale University Press, 1953), 31–33, ranges for comparisons from Homer through Scott, Byron, and Cooper. Levin, stresses the Byronic element (64 ff.).

47. Doughty, *Francis Parkman*, 224.

48. Matthias, "Facts from an Apocryphal Midwest." *Another Chicago Magazine*, 17:71–77, and *A Gathering of Ways*, 25–49. The final prose paragraph of "The Boat-Maker's Tale," like the end of my essay, leans heavily on Doughty's compelling interpretation of *La Salle and the Discovery of the Great West* and draws upon his terminology to indicate the psychological similarities between La Salle and Parkman. It was inevitable that I, too, should focus on Parkman's narration of the St. Joseph-Kankakee portage which Doughty treats in *Francis Parkman*, 275–276. I thank him for what I have borrowed here, especially passages from the original French of La Salle's *Relations* and the account of the portage written by Father Charlevoix.

Robert Duncan and David Jones: Some Affinities

1. See especially Duncan's *The Truth and Life of Myth* and David Jones's "Art and Sacrament" in *Epoch and Artist*.

2. For this reason, Duncan finds Jungian psychology uncongenial. "I don't disbelieve in the existence of archetypes, but I wouldn't posit their importance in the way Jung does. Where I don't join Eastern philosophy at all, is that I think that everything we see is posited in the material world. So that an archetype doesn't get a chance to be very *arche*. Instead of looking at an archetype, we'd better look at a tree or a particular individual" (*TNAP*, 72).

3. Cf. Charles Altieri on Duncan's "traditional myth of the world as a book." "If the earth is a book, its author can no longer be a transcendental self-contained God but one involved in natural process, speaking through the codes science has taught man to read, and recognizing that nature is itself being created in and through the acts of those trying to read and imagine the Book." Altieri sees Duncan's God as "a force seeking to realize itself in evolution" (*ET*, 152).

4. David Jones's version of Christ's rebuke to those who felt Mary Magdalene's act of pouring out the precious ointments to be reprehensible goes like this: "Let her be. I tell you straight that wherever in the whole world is sung the *chanson* of my deeds this shall be told for an *anamnesis* of her." Hague comments that Jones uses *anamnesis* to make it plain that he has in mind "a re-calling, re-creation, re-presenting of what has already been

done: so that the art-work, in this case the *chanson*, brings into being again what had happened in the house of Simon the leper." Interestingly, he also tells us that the word used in Mark 14.9 is not *anamnesis*, but *mnemosyne*. He calls the change "a good example of deliberate mythologizing" (*Ag*, 44).

5. When Duncan and Jones evolve a comprehensive myth for the form of their work, it is, finally, to the figure of Christ himself that they turn. Duncan's statement that "we play in art" is only one aspect of the analogy drawn in *The Truth and Life of Myth* with Christ's incarnation and passion. Carry Nelson summarizes the full argument of Duncan's concluding pages in his book *Our Last First Poets*. "In form, eternity becomes mortal. 'In every true poet's voice . . . you will hear a counterpart of the Son's sorrow and pain of utter undergoing . . . the poet understands the truth of the anguish of Christ's passion as a truth of poetic form.' Amidst the melodies and con-catenations of the language, the poet speaks and the potentiality of utter-ance is momentarily specified. Like the creator, the poet oversees 'the figure of the Son given up into the terrible guarantee of the poem.' As a poet assumes a single mask, his projected inwardness becomes other, inacces-sible: 'The Son's cry to the Father might be too the cry of the artist to the form he obeys'" (*LFP*, 105–6). David Jones's *Anathemata* is simultaneously a sequence of associations "apt to stir in [his] mind 'in the time of the Mass'" and a journey through time beginning in the "fore-time" of prehistory which anticipates the human history to be redeemed by the "true myth" of the sacrifice and its anamnesis which is the poem's beginning and its end. Assimilated at key moments to a series of sea voyages, the poet's journey— and the form of the poem's enactment—is seen to be analogous to "what is pleaded in the Mass": "Precisely the argosy or voyage of the Redeemer, consisting of his entire sufferings and his death, his conquest of Hades, his resurrection and his return in triumph to heaven" (*A*, 106). Perhaps Jones here reverses Duncan. Instead of "The figure of the Son being given up to the terrible guarantee of the poem," the figure of the poem is given up to the terrible guarantee of the Son.

6. Duncan has, in fact, said in the first Ekbert Faas interview that "a good deal of *The Structure of Rime*, of course, is presumed to be autistic."

7. They also, of course, refer to themselves and to each other.

8. Cf. especially "Art and Sacrament" in *Epoch and Artist*, 170; and "Abstract Art," 265–266.

9. Kathleen Raine calls David Jones's own small quarters in Harrow "a magical room." She writes in her autobiography that she remembers someone saying of him perceptively, "He still lives in a dug-out" (*The Lion's Mouth*, 98).

10. And this, I think, may well involve an abandoning of the God-desses for the Gods, as perhaps Duncan anticipates having to do in "Occult Matters" from *The H. D. Book* when he concludes: "But in my life dream, I

have not seen the Maiden, for I stand in her place or in her way" (I:5, 19). Similarly, precisely because Duncan was her son, he was never able to see his mother; the mother becomes the son as Brigid, the Goddess of the Brigantes, may have become a version of Baal, the sun at its most powerful (fire itself) in that part of Britain not far from where David Jones stood painting at the home of Helen Sutherland. Cf. the conclusion of *Towards an Open Universe:* "If the sea is first mother of the living, the sun is first father, and fire is his element. Here too death and life, the heat of our blood and the light of our mind, in one reality. That I have seen in poems as the fire upon the hearth, the genius of the household, as if the secret of our warmth and companionship were hidden in a wrathful flame" (*PNAP*, 221).

11. Altieri also observes that "as Heidegger points out, the obedient word honors the Christian idea of Logos—the idea of the word as God's form-giving command. The poet's word in this Christian framework is incarnational: the poet repeats Christ's redemptive death into nature in order to be reborn with the power to authorize a new law or set of symbolic relationships revaluing a purely empirical order." The Greek Logos (before Plato) requires of its poets, he says, "the willingness to sustain a continual struggle with the Strife that Heraclitus envisions at the heart of all things. What the Greek word lacks is a form of teleology; without the Christian model of a world moving toward God, the effort to gather and unify strife must be an end in itself and doomed to eventual failure" (*ET*, 159).